INDIA IN GREECE;

OR,

TRUTH IN MYTHOLOGY

INDIA IN GREECE;

OR,

TRUTH IN MYTHOLOGY:

CONTAINING

THE SOURCES OF THE HELLENIC RACE, THE COLONISATION OF EGYPT AND PALESTINE, THE WARS OF THE GRAND LAMA, AND THE BUD'HISTIC PROPAGANDA IN GREECE.

BY E. POCOCKE, ESQ.

GYAN

Published by

Gyan Publishing House
5, Ansari Road
Daryaganj, New Delhi-110002
Phone: 011-47034999, 9811692060
E-mail: books@gyanbooks.com

Distribution Network
gyanbooks.com
India, USA, Canada, UK, Australia

ISBN: 978-93-6208-033-2 (PB)
First Published, 1852

2nd Impression 2024

Printed at: Gyan Press, Delhi.

INDIA IN GREECE; OR, TRUTH IN MYTHOLOGY:
Author: E. POCOCKE

INDIA IN GREECE.

INDIA IN GREECE;

OR,

TRUTH IN MYTHOLOGY:

CONTAINING

SOURCES OF THE HELLENIC RACE, THE COLONISATION OF EGYPT AND PALESTINE, THE WARS OF THE GRAND LAMA, AND THE BUD'HISTIC PROPAGANDA IN GREECE.

BY E. POCOCKE, ESQ.

ILLUSTRATED BY

MAPS OF THE PUNJAB, CASHMIR, AND NORTHERN GREECE.

LONDON:
PUBLISHED BY JOHN J. GRIFFIN AND CO.,
53, BAKER STREET, PORTMAN SQUARE;
AND RICHARD GRIFFIN AND CO., GLASGOW.
1852.

TO

H. H. WILSON, M.A., F.R.S.,

ETC. ETC.,

BODEN PROFESSOR OF SANSCRIT IN THE UNIVERSITY OF OXFORD.

SIR,

The pledge made by a stranger, at a casual interview, characterised on your part by much urbanity, of distinctly tracing to their true sources the "Pilgrim Fathers" of the Hellenic Race, is thus far redeemed. To you, Sir, as the honoured TRI-CALA of Oriental Literature, this Historical Sketch of the fortunes of the Western Pandions of Athens, the Hellenes or Chiefs of the Hela in Greece, the Cashmirians of Bœotia, and of the Thessalian Himalayas, is humbly inscribed by the Author,

E. POCOCKE.

PREFACE.

Nothing but a thorough conviction of the importance of testing the stream of History at its very source, would have induced that process of investigation with whose partial results the reader is here presented.

A gigántic mass of absurdities now lies exposed, for a sifting examination. It remains for the patient sagacity of European scholarship, working upon both Occidental and Oriental materials, to re-build, I trust, upon no unstable foundation, that Temple of History which national vanity has destroyed, and whose ruins national Bud'hism has obscured.

A thorough persuasion that no nation, as a body of men, would or could, gratuitously, through a series of ages, invent a series of tales, in themselves *fabulous*, in their results *historical*,—determined me in the resolution to enter upon a process which should test the doctrine of invention, or non-invention, and thus gain some criterion for an impartial and a final decision. That problem is now solved. A plain, practical, and positive appeal to the very language of the first Hellenic settlers, will give a correct answer to the patient inquirer after truth. Those primitive colonists have been traced with a precision that nothing but the singular cohesion of the constituent parts of that ancient form of society called "a tribe," could have secured. This is a species of argument that will be duly appreciated by the contemplative mind.

The evidence thus gained, is evidence drawn from no partial source—it is evidence *drawn forth* from nations whose impress is of the highest antiquity.

Amid the ruins of empires, or the transient memory of the mightiest conquerors, Time has very generally respected both the form and the name of the grand features of nature. Cities and Polities may have been swept from the earth; Dynasties of unrivalled splendour may have passed away, leaving scanty memorials,—possibly none—to record their renown; but it is not so with the history ineffaceably written on the venerable forms of mountains, seas, and rivers. These compose a language so vast and so enduring, that compared with them, the Pyramids, must be considered as dwarfed toys of agglutinated sand which must crumble to atoms before the structure of this language shall be destroyed.

One of the most valuable points, in connection with the results here wrought out, is this geographical basis. It has interpreted correctly, and it will continue to interpret correctly, those singular tales, in early Greek history, which have generally passed current with the literary world, under the name of "Myths." They are now proved to be fables, just in proportion as we *misunderstand* them; truths, in proportion as they were once *understood.*

Our ignorance it is which has made a myth of history; and our ignorance is an Hellenic inheritance, much of it the result of Hellenic vanity.

The Sanscrit scholar will find a few irregularities in that process which I have developed. They are such as belong to a form compounded of the old Pehlvi and the Sanscrit; the latter serving as the basis, and the former the inflective power. A superficial glance over this branch of my investigation, will convey some idea to the philologist of two interesting facts. First.—The primitive dialects, whence sprang the Greek of Homer. Secondly. The exact way in which the Greek consonantal and vocalic combinations were pronounced by Herodotean and Thucydidæan Greeks.

The apparent irregularities of orthography occurring in connection with the same word, will be found to be more imaginary than real. It will be well for the reader to accustom himself to such variations of form, but not of power, nor of signification. He will thus consider Lakedaimon, Lacedæmon; Cabul, Cabool, Kabul, Kabool; Tibet, Thibet; Cashmir, Cashmire, Casmir, Kashmire, Cashmere; Ladakh, Ladak, Ladac; Attock, Attac, Atac, Uttuck; Goclapes, Gooklopes, Guclopes, Cuclopes, Cyclopes; Panjab, Punjab, Punjaub, Panchab; Phenicia, Phœnicia, Phœnikia, Phainikia; as identical. And so with geographical nomenclature generally. When, however, such varieties appear in this work, they will, with few exceptions, be found to arise from the necessity of running parallel with the irregular meanderings of the

Hellenic or Oriental streams. A notable example of the singular variety of these forms, will be found under the name Budha.

It is evident that two classes of literature must now be studied in connection with ancient Greece. First,—The *Mythology* of Greece, showing what Greeks thought and wrote in connection with their divinities, and the immense mass of legend in juxtaposition with them. Secondly,—The *History,* which at present lies buried beneath this mythology; which, as forming the very earliest records of Hellas, must be studied like any other portion of established history.

Henceforward, let us not, succumbing to an easy indolence, deny on *theoretical grounds* the existence of those truths which *Geography* has restored to *History.*

E. P.

London, Dec., 1851.

CONTENTS.

INDIA IN GREECE.

INTRODUCTION.

Were an Englishman to sit down, purposing to write the history of his native country previous to the Norman conquest—to sketch the outlines of the Anglo-Saxon constitution, laws, and customs; were he to speak confidently of the old Saxon kings; their attendants, military and civil; to unfold the origin of their people, the structure of their language, and their primitive settlements; it would not be too much to expect that he should have some knowledge of the Saxon tongue.

And yet, what must be said of the confidence of the antiquarians of Greece, who, though themselves Hellenes, have, with a profound ignorance of the early language of Pelasgian Hellas, turned twilight into darkness, by absurd attempts to derive the words and customs of remote antiquity from the Greek language—a language at that period not in existence? But this vain-glorious confidence is not the only thing for which they are answerable. They have thereby unwittingly originated a gigantic system of absurdities and a tissue of tales, the opprobrium of history, and the torment of the inquiring mind. We feel that all this mass of error has a foundation in positive fact; we feel that agency, the most vital, the most energetic, the most constant, is at work; mighty actors come and go upon the scene, and mighty changes take place. And yet we are called upon by Theorisers to renounce the instincts of our nature; to class the siege of Troy, the Argonautic expedition, the history of Heracles, the history of Theseus—nay, the whole busy, crowded scene of early Hellas, with the product of mythopœic propensities, and secretions from the fancy. Alas! for this dream! I shall prove incontrovertibly, not only that *such* things were distorted *facts*, but I shall demonstrate that the Centaurs were not mythical[1]—that the Athenian claim to the symbol of the Grasshopper was not mythical—that the Autochthons were not mythical—that the serpent Pytho was not mythical—that Cadmus and the dragon's teeth were not mythical—that Zeus was not mythical—that Apollo was not mythical—that the Pierian Muses were not mythical—that Cecrops was neither legendary nor mythical; but as historical as King Harold. And this I purpose to effect, not by any rationalising process, but by the very unpoetical evidences of latitude and longitude, which will certainly not be deemed of a legendary nature.

I would here repeat a remark made on another occasion[2] on the historical basis of mythology. Perhaps within the whole compass of mythology there is no system altogether more plausible than the Grecian. Its coherence betrays art in arrangement, but weakness in the main incidents. A basis, however, it undoubtedly possessed, which was neither of an inventive nor fictitious character. What that basis was, is certainly not to be eliminated from either poet or logographer, or historian, independent of extraneous aids. Such aids are presented to the inquiring mind in those two most durable records of a nation,—its language and its monuments. These adjuncts, though of foreign origin, are,

[1] I use this term here, as synonymous with "invention, having no historical basis."

[2] See my "Greek Mythology," in vol. i. of the "History of Greece," in the "Encyclopædia Metropolitana," 1851.

fortunately, available for the elucidation of Greek mythology. There is nothing more calculated to blunt the keenness of investigation than any theoretic maxim which lays down some general position to meet general difficulties. Here, acquiescence must be the rule, and research the exception. Nothing can be more tempting to indolence. To assume individual or national *feeling* as the exponent of *fact*, and fact too possibly foreign to that individual or nation, must be a perilous mode of rescuing from error or re-establishing truth. The theory of "The Myth," as laid down by some distinguished German writers, and adopted by certain authors in this country, is, at best, only capable of sound application where a people has had *no connection with another nation, either by commerce, war, religion,* or other inter-communication,—a category, in fact, which *history* scarcely supposes. There is, says this theory, a tendency in the human mind, when excited by any particular feeling, to body forth that feeling in some imaginary fact, scene, or circumstance, in the contemplation of which it may find relief. And we are gravely told that whatever thought arose in a man's mind, whatever sensation varied his consciousness, could be expressed by him only in one way, namely, *by dragging forth the concrete images, fictions, or inventions that he felt arise contemporaneously with it.* But this is a complete Petitio Principii. The great mythi of antiquity are *not feelings bodied forth to relieve the mind;* still less are they concrete images, fictions, and inventions. Whenever an important mythus has existed, an important fact has been its basis. Great principles do not arise from idealities; a *national myth* cannot be generated without a *national cause,* and a national cause implies *agency,* not *invention;* but a theory based upon the evidences of *feeling,* is as mythological as a myth itself.

In this investigation, the corruptions of language to be

encountered (and they must be honestly encountered and fairly vanquished) include positively nothing less than the whole circle of early Greek history. When I use the term "early," I allude to all the genealogies, local histories, and heroic agencies of what is called "Mythical and Legendary Greece"—a phraseology, however, most unfortunate, and totally wide of the fact; for to him who reads these chronicles in their plain, original sense, no nation will appear less connected with mythology than the Pelasgic or Hellenic.

The wrecks of noble institutions—of a mighty people, far advanced in civilisation, highly religious, skilful in the arts, skilful in political science—everywhere strike the gaze and excite the pity of him who truly reads the old annals of Greece;—annals, not such, indeed, as are left us by Homer; for in his time the glory had well nigh passed away, and the Avatar of a new incarnation, which was scarcely more godlike than the last, was again about to descend upon Hellas. History, then, the most interesting —the most eventful—the most indubitable, is hers. But it is not the history of the gods of Homer—the gods of Hesiod; nor is it history drawn from the etymologies of Plato, the etymologies of the logographers, or the antiquarians of Greece; men who knew nothing of the ancient language of their own country. It is not such a system that can become a correct guide to the student of history. He will, in all cases where it is possible, go to the fountain head; he will throw from him the corrupt text and the corrupt commentaries of centuries—his inheritance of ignorance; and, calling in the testimony of a dialect coeval with the first Pelasgian and the first Hellenic settlements, will appeal to truth, and the decisions of judgment unclouded by prejudice.

He who would master the Protean struggles of language, as it roams from east to west, assuming every variety of complexion and every form—though beneath that everlasting change there is an everlasting stedfastness—will bring to the effort, not only a keen vision, but will possess a power of discerning, beneath disguises ever-varying, the strongest likeness; beneath dissimilar nationality, a unity of parentage. To command success, he will exercise a jealous vigilance over his discoveries; he will bring to the test of experience his choicest theories; but if he have not this test of verification, he will still look upon them as theories, but not facts.

I shall not here enlarge upon philology in connection with the Pelasgian settlements, polity, and religion. He who may desire ample evidences of the affiliation, the structure, and the relative rank of the great families of language, and of the precision with which they may be classified, will find an excellent manual in the masterly work of Professor Bopp.

On Indo-Classical affinities, we have had many admirable works, written by men of the highest talent, Sir W. Jones leading the way. But it is this very idea of their being *affinities*, and *affinities only*, that has effectually barred the path to decisive results. A vowel, a stray consonant, a consonant too much, a vowel too little—the merest non-coidentity of forms: these were once sufficient to draw down the wrath of the philological guardians of the treasure-house of time, with a warning to the rash scrutiniser of its contents, that nothing is to be found within.

Yet there is much gold there.

I beg to impress upon the mind of the reader, that I do not deal in affinities; that I do not deal in etymologies: with the latter, particularly, I have no manner of concern. I am not writing a book of antiquarian amusement. That which I am writing is History—history, as marvellously as it is correctly preserved. As I am now about to speak of the first settlers in the land of Hellas, it would be well for the reader to discard totally, if possible—if not, as much as possible—all preconceived notions of the immigrants into this remarkable land; and I trust I shall not incur the charge of presumption, if I counsel him, in the usual forensic strain, "to dismiss from his mind all previous reports, and to be guided solely by the evidence that will be brought before him." And, lest I should be imagined to be indulging in easy self-confidence, it will be proper to remark that *the evidence is already taken;* that it is *in a foreign language;* and that I merely perform the office of an interpreter,—with what degree of fidelity it will not be difficult for the reader to decide.

It was not enough for us to have inherited a mass of disfigured documents,—but, alas! our work was to be made more difficult, by the superscription of new tales over the old parchment! Fortunately for us, no erasures have been made. Our only method now is to restore the text of the old history. But how are we to begin? Our way seems effectually barred by the dictum of those theorists who virtually define "ancient history" as "invention." I deeply regret this spirit of theorising; it has been gaining ground of late years in Germany; and, but recently, its most able exponent in this country has carried this principle into the regions of hypercriticism.[1] "The real question at issue," says an able writer in the Edinburgh Review, "is not so much whether there ever was a basis of historical truth for the poetical legend; whether any such events as the siege of Thebes, or the expedition against Troy, actually occurred; as whether we are now able to extricate this kernel of truth from the mass of fable with which it is overgrown, and to exhibit the naked skeleton of historical fact, stripped of all its coverings of poetical

[1] See "The History of Greece," by G. Grote, Esq., London, 1849.

embellishment." When we find the same nation who were the colonists of Greece, composing not only history but mathematical treatises in a poetic form, this poetical form will produce, in our minds, no solid objection against the statements contained therein. When we discover that a nation holds a belief in tutelary divinities, active in the defence of their prime heroes or most pious worshippers,—the statement of such interference, founded on such a belief, will not in the slightest degree invalidate any matter of fact recorded in such a document—or rather, any records consistent with common sense. If the Centaurs, the Muses, Poseidon, Erectheus, the Autocthons, the Tettiges or Grasshopper symbols of the Athenians, be proved geographically, by latitude and longitude, to repose upon an historical basis—perfectly rational, perfectly harmonious with the first colonisation of Greece—I believe it will be readily granted, that, after this, such subjects as the siege of Thebes and the siege of Troy will present no difficulties.

Speaking of these primitive histories, Mr. Grote has observed: "I describe the earlier times by themselves, as conceived by the faith and feeling of the first Greeks, and known only through their legends; without presuming to measure how much or how little of historical matter these legends may contain. If the reader blame me for not assisting to determine this,—if he ask me, why I do not withdraw the curtain and disclose the picture, I reply, in the words of the painter Zeuxis, when the same question was addressed to him, on exhibiting his masterpiece of imitative art: 'The curtain is the picture.' What we now read as poetry, and legend, was once accredited history, and the only genuine history which the first Greeks could conceive or relish of their past time. The curtain conceals nothing behind, and cannot by any ingenuity be withdrawn. I undertake to show it only as it stands; not to efface it—still less to repaint it."[1]

To say that "the curtain is the picture," is, fortunately for history, a mythical saying; and to affirm that "the curtain contains nothing behind, and cannot by any ingenuity be withdrawn," rests on that feeling which, thirty years since, would have classed the railway locomotive, and its glowing eye of night, with the eye of the Cyclops. The case may be stated as follows:—The PICTURE is INDIAN—the CURTAIN is GRECIAN; and that Curtain *is now* WITHDRAWN.

[1] "Hist. Greece," vol. i. Pref. p. xiii.

I.

THE EVIDENCES OF INDIAN COLONISATION.

" Munera præterea, Iliacis erepta ruinis
Ferre jubet, pallam signis auroque rigentem,
Et circumtextum croceo velamen acantho:
Ornatus argivæ Helenæ: quos illa Mycenis,
Pergama cum peteret, inconcessosque Hymenæos,
Extulerat: matris Ledæ mirabile donum.
Præterea sceptrum, Ilione quod gesserat olim
Maxima natarum Priami, colloque monile
Baccatum, et duplicem gemmis auroque coronam.
Æn. I. 651—659.

AMONG the strongest peculiarities of the so-called heroic period of Greece, appear the perfection of the Arts and the abundance of gold; the profusion of golden vessels; their varied yet elegant workmanship; the beauty of embroidered shawls; the tasteful, the ample produce of the loom; the numerous ornaments of ivory; the staining and working of that material; the gift of necklaces as a valuable present — sometimes, too, from the *Gods;* the brazen tripods and the cauldrons; the social refinement and comfort; the magnificent palaces of Alcinous and Menelaus; and, finally, in the great contest of Troy, the constant use of the *war-chariot both by Greeks* and *Asiatics.* "But the most magnificent example of the art of metallurgy," observes Mr. Ottley,[1] "was the famous shield of Achilles. In the centre were the waves of ocean, rolling round the extremities; then followed, in a beautiful series, scenes of

[1] "Social Condition of the Greeks," By the Rev. J. B. Ottley, M.A., late Fellow of Oriel College, Oxford. See Hist. of Greece, p. 368. "Encyclopædia Metropolitana," vol. xv., 1851.

pastoral life, tillage, the harvest, and the vintage; there, too, was the siege, the ambuscade, and the battle; judicial inquiry, and political deliberation; the musical festivities of a marriage, and the evolutions of a national dance. The grouping of these scenes, respectively,—their number, variety, and contrast, attest the skill of the artist, or of the poet, or of both. How the difference of colour was produced is uncertain; it might have been by paint, since ivory was stained to adorn the bits of horses; or, perhaps, by the effect of fire, for the art of fusing metals was known. Indeed, casting, gilding, and carving, both in wood and metal, were practised at a much earlier time by those who are described in Exodus, as 'devising cunning works' to work in gold, and in silver, and in brass, and in cutting of stones to set them, and in carving timber, to work in all manner of workmanship. That temple, which the piety of Solomon dedicated, and which his opulence enriched, owed the beauty and the delicacy of the sculptured decorations to the skill of a Tyrian artificer. The descriptions of it, recorded in the national archives of Judea, may vindicate Homer from unduly exaggerating either the abundance of the precious metals, or the progress of the ornamental arts. Nor was the warrior altogether unindebted to the labours of the needle and the loom; wild animals were embroidered on his belt—the trophies of his dexterity in the chase, and the decoration of his person in the fight. More ample robes were either received as the pledge of courteous hospitality, or won as the prize of valour. Such occupations suited the secluded life and intellectual habits of Oriental females; they are mentioned early, with an emphasis of description, which seems to mark their costliness and value. 'Have they not sped? Have they not divided the prey?—to Sisera a prey of divers colours; a prey of divers colours of needlework on both sides, meet for the necks of them that take the spoil.' Such garments were stored in the treasury of Priam. Sidonian artists were most expert in their fabrication: but the high-born ladies of the court were, apparently, no mean proficients. Helen weaves a representation of a battle between the Greeks and the Trojans; Andromache copies flowers in a veil; the web of Penelope is proverbially known—that funeral offering for Laertes from the hand of filial affection; while another, which she presents to an unknown guest, is thus beautifully described:—

In ample mode,
A robe of military purple flow'd
O'er all his frame: illustrious on his breast,
The double-clasping gold the king confest.
In the rich woof a hound, mosaic drawn,
Bore on full stretch, and seiz'd a dappled fawn;
Deep in the neck his fangs indent their hold;
They pant and struggle in the moving gold:
Fine as a filmy web beneath it shone
A vest, that dazzled like a cloudless sun:
The female train, who round him throng'd to gaze,
In silent wonder sigh'd unwilling praise.

POPE'S *Hom.*, *Od.* xix. 261.

"It was natural that the goldsmith and the jeweller should be put in requisition, when the materials of their trade were abundant. We trace them in female dress, and in the implements of the toilet; in both there is, together with the magnificence of real wealth, much of the simplicity of real taste. There were necklaces of gold and of amber; there were ear-rings, whose pendant drops imitated either the form or the brilliancy of the human eye; the hair was curled or braided, and covered with a veil; the robe was fastened over the bosom with golden clasps; a fringe surrounded the waist, and completed the full-dress costume of a lady of the Homeric age. The appointments of her palace were as costly as the decorations of her person; its walls glittered with silver, tin, ivory, brass, and amber; her tripod has four handles, graced by eight golden doves; her lyre has a silver frame, her basket is silver,[1] and her distaff gold; the ewers and basins which are served at the banquet, and even the bath which alleviates fatigue, are of the like precious materials."

But what, I would ask, has become in the *historical* times of these arts, of these luxuries, and more particularly of the equestrian hero, his faithful equerry, and his car? The war-car, after a long banishment from Greece, once more makes a prominent figure on the distant field of Cunaxa; but for Greece, it has been for ages a neglected arm of her military service. Now, the whole of this state of society, civil and military, must strike every one as being eminently Asiatic; much of it specifically Indian. Such it undoubtedly is; and I shall demonstrate that these evidences were but the attendant tokens of an Indian colonisation, with its corresponding religion and language. I shall exhibit dynasties disappearing from Western India, to appear again in Greece: clans, whose martial fame is still recorded in the faithful chronicles of North-Western India, as the gallant bands who fought upon the plains of Troy; and, in fact, the whole of Greece, from the era of the supposed god-ships of Poseidon and Zeus, down to the close of the Trojan war, as being *Indian* in language, sentiment, and religion, and in the arts of peace and war. Much I shall, I doubt not, incontestably establish; much must be left to a future period. Yet that which is granted to be fairly wrought out, may stand as an earnest of the correctness of the principle by which these results have been produced.

It was no futile imagination that led Evémerus[2] to

[1] Od. iv. 131. Some ancient jewellery found in Ithaca in a tomb amidst ruins which tradition designates as the residence of Odysseus, are as exquisite in their workmanship as any of those ornaments which Homer describes. Their date is unknown. See Hughes's Greece, vol. i. p. 160.

[2] Evémerus or Euhémerus (Εὐήμερος) a Sicilian author at the time of Alexander the Great and his immediate successors. Most writers call him

assert that men, once existing as the conquerors, kings and benefactors of mankind, subsequently re-appeared as deified beings. If I do not establish this throughout the whole range of the so-called Greek Mythology, it is not for want of ample proof, but for lack of time sufficient to remove the disguise from the host of masqueraders that figure in the band of grotesque Greece. I have, however, unmasked not a few of the most intractable of these beings, such as the Centaurs, the Athenian grasshoppers, the Autochthons, &c., &c., who now, stripped of their disguise, at length assume the appearance of the ordinary representatives of Eastern society. Let it be observed, that this is not a process similar to the rationalism of modern German theologians, nor is it the exegetical system of Palæphatus. It does not treat of what *might have been;* it speaks of what *was;* a result obtained from the superiority of *translation* over plausible conjecture, applied to the solution of knotty difficulties. The learned Jacob Bryant exercised his vast erudition on a theory rendered impracticable solely by the medium of its adaptation. Seeking in multifarious dialects for that information which was to be found in one alone, he left out of sight the grand principle of the *origin* of the nation whose history he was investigating. Guided by the manifest light of a mighty emigration,

a native of Messene, in Sicily. His mind was trained in the philosophical school of the Cyrenaics, who had before his time become notorious for their scepticism in matters connected with the popular religion; and one of whom, Theodosius, is frequently called an atheist by the ancients. Evémerus is said to have sailed down the Red Sea, and round the southern coasts of Asia, to a very great distance, until he came to an island called Panchaea. After his return from this voyage, he wrote a work, entitled Ιερα 'Αναγραφή, which consisted of at least nine books. The work contained accounts of the several gods, whom Evémerus represented as having originally been men who had distinguished themselves, either as warriors, kings, inventors, or benefactors of man, and who, after their death, were worshipped as gods by the grateful people."—SMITH'S *Greek and Roman Biog.*, vol. ii., p. 83.

I have been led as much as possible by the *language* of that emigration. I have examined that early society, and the phases of that society, on the same broad principle that directs the researches of the modern historian when he treats of European colonies; and though many blemishes may obscure, many imperfections mar, the unity of the picture, I trust that sufficient will have been accomplished not only to prove the correctness of the principle on which this investigation proceeds, but likewise to subserve the cause of truth. The student of early Indian history will be pleased to find established by this record of *primitive Greece*, the fact of the wonderfully early existence of the Jaina doctrines,—a matter of keen dispute among some of the most distinguished Orientalists, but one which I doubt not will now take its place among historical facts.

I would here make a few observations upon the work of Palæphatus, who was, according to Suidas, an Egyptian or Athenian, supposed to have lived subsequently to the time of Alexander the Great. Of this author, Mr. Grote observes,[1] "Another author who seems to have conceived clearly and applied consistently the semi-historical theory of the Grecian myths, is Palæphatus. In the short preface of his treatise concerning incredible tales, he remarks, that 'some men, from want of instruction, believe all the current narratives, while others, more searching and cautious, disbelieve them altogether.' Each of these extremes he is anxious to avoid. On the one hand, he thinks that no narrative could ever have acquired credence unless it had been founded on truth; on the other, it is impossible for him to accept so much of the existing narratives as conflicts with the analogies of present natural phenomena. If such things ever had been, they would still continue to be,—but they never have so occurred; and the extra-

[1] Hist. Greece, vol. i., p. 557.

analogical features of the stories are to be ascribed to the license of the poets." Again,[1]—"Palæphatus handles the myths consistently, according to the semi-historical theory, and his results exhibit the maximum which that theory can ever present. By aid of conjecture we get out of the impossible and arrive at matter intrinsically plausible, but totally uncertified. Beyond this point we cannot penetrate, without the light of extrinsic evidence, since there is no intrinsic mark to distinguish truth from plausible fiction."

With the concluding remarks of Mr. Grote, I entirely agree. The system of Palæphatus is essentially semi-historical, inasmuch as it is by the aid of *conjecture*, and conjecture alone, that he arrives at matters intrinsically plausible, yet totally uncertified. But with the certainty that Sanscrit was the language of Pelasgic and Hellenic Greece, we have exactly that "intrinsic mark" which is the test of truth and fiction; and, what is scarcely less valuable, that which will enable us to divide historical fact from etymological fiction. Both logographers and poets, from the most ancient date, not excepting Homer and Hesiod, manifest a profound ignorance, or a profound contempt, for the primitive state of their native land. The divinities of Homer totally misled subsequent poets and logographers; while the autochthonous parentage of the people of Erectheus, as sung by Hesiod, and the Attic symbol of the grasshopper, will demonstrate how very early both the old language and the old religious duties of Greece were merged in a new order of things. The mysteries of Hellas, once the public and undisputed worship of the whole land, were henceforward the only asylum for a religion whose adherents, the Helots, were crushed by foreign conquest. We shall, therefore, be cautious in taking for our guide, in matters of Pelasgic, or mythologic,

[1] Hist. Greece, vol. i., p. 561.

or heroic history, either Homer or Hesiod, logographer or poet, save when their accounts are conformable to Sanscrit sources. While Hesiod has taken for Greek, or adopted as Greek, the Harpies, the Cyclopes, Poseidon, Here, Erectheus, the Centaurs, the Gorgons, Typhœus, and a host of agencies, who at once become monsters under his transforming hand, it will be the business of the historical student, whenever such terms have been misunderstood, or mistranslated by that author, to restore them to their original and consequently correct signification. A positive and clear history will thus be found to arise simultaneously with the true nomenclature. The same effect will be produced by the same process with the logographers. In many cases these authorities have so metamorphosed the original names of men, cities, and religious rites, that nothing but a specific course of study, founded on the principles here laid down, and wrought out by the light of persevering sagacity, brought to bear at once upon the twofold literature of the East and West, can restore these corrupt or mistaken travesties to their true form. This, then, (and let us not be ashamed to confess it) is a branch of study of which we have been hitherto entirely ignorant. But our prejudices and our taste equally revolt against a scrutiny that tends to destroy that atmosphere of poetic vitality with which our heroes were invested; the idea of which is so strongly intertwined with our very nature, so interwoven with all that is graceful in art and beautiful in poetry, that the strongest thirst for truth can scarcely persuade us to abandon the enchanting spot, where the united glories of mind and art detain us in a dazzling trance.

II.

THE SOURCES OF HELLENIC HISTORY.

"Still, if our course be consecrated to philology, we will not therefore banish the study of facts and ideas. We will not close our eyes upon the most brilliant light that has come from the East; and we will endeavour to comprehend the grand spectacle presented to us. We will study India with its philosophy and its myths, its literature, and its laws, *in its language*. Nay, it is more than India, it is a page of the origin of the world that we will attempt to decipher.

"We are deeply convinced, that in the same proportion as the study of words (if it be possible), without that of ideas, is frivolous and worthless, that of words, considered as the visible symbols of thought, is solid and fruitful. There can be no genuine philology without philosophy."—Professor Bournouf, *Discourse on the Sanscrit and its Literature*, pronounced at the College of France.

If all that we are destined ever to learn of primitive Hellas is to be gained from the books of her historians alone, then the amount of our knowledge will be scanty indeed, and a hope of any addition to the mysterious volumes which contain the records of her early life, will be for ever precluded. All the evidences arising from Hellenic sources have been sifted, combined, and classified, with a sagacity the most profound; and the early history of Greece, as eliminated from her own writers, has reached the *"ultima Thule"* of fact or of positive infidelity. The ardent enquirer after truth, repulsed at the mysterious gates of this city of the dead, burns to effect an entrance within its silent gloom. In his restless zeal, he tries every avenue of hope. His courage rises with the difficulties of his enterprise, and if, like the great explorer of the tombs of Egypt, he is for a time deserted by light, he summons fresh courage to meet the emergency. Into how narrow a compass does all our knowledge shrink, of that first, that strange people the Pelasgi! It is on the very threshold of the temple of history that we are doomed to encounter this mockery of life. I shall hopefully grapple with the phantom. But

c 2

first arises the thought: What means have I for varying the method of my investigation, since the progress hitherto attempted has resulted in disappointment? Can I depend upon the usual guides to historical truth?—to what kind of errors are they liable? What is the source, and what the extent, of their information? These guides are discordant in their accounts, and varying in their antiquity; so far they are to be looked upon with a cautious eye; but I shall not, on account of any external imperfection, rashly refuse to receive the information they convey, and account them wholly fabulous because I cannot comprehend the poetic machinery by which they are introduced to my notice. On the contrary, it is not improbable that they may present valuable truths, under a garb which they themselves do not suspect to be a disguise. Let us examine this. It is readily granted, that the language of a nation, is one of its most durable monuments. Its buildings may have crumbled into dust, its people may have become extinct, and all but this evidence of its existence may have passed away. The English language *illustrates* and the Greek *confirms* this assertion. Amidst the numerous dialects which compose the former, the Saxon has left by far the strongest impression upon our native tongue. The simple deduction independent of history, is clear;—that people once speaking the Saxon language lived in this island; it is then equally clear, that these were *Saxons*. Apply this to Greece: what is it that strikes the literary student so forcibly as this identity of structure, of vocables, and inflective power, in the Greek and Sanscrit languages? Every day adds fresh conviction—produces fresh demonstration, of this undeniable fact. The Greek language is a derivation from the Sanscrit; therefore, Sanscrit-speaking people—*i. e.*, Indians, must have dwelt in Greece, and this dwelling must have preceded the settlement of those tribes which helped to produce the corruption of the old language; or, in other words, the people who spoke that language—*i. e.*, the Indians, must have been the primitive settlers; or, at least, they must have colonised the country so early, and dwelt there so long, as to have effaced all dialectic traces of any other inhabitants: just as the Saxons displaced the feeble remains of the dialect of the ancient Britons, in this island, and imparted a thoroughly Saxon stamp to the genius of the English language. But, if the evidences of Saxon colonisation in this island—(I speak independently of Anglo-Saxon history)—are strong both from language and political institutions, the evidences are still more decisive in the parallel case of an Indian colonisation of Greece,—not only her Language, but her Philosophy, her Religion, her Rivers, her Mountains, and her Tribes; her subtle turn of intellect, her political institutes, and above all the Mysteries of that noble land,—irresistibly prove her colonisation from India. I purpose to bring forward such evidences as will effectually demonstrate the causes of an immigration that dates from so venerable an antiquity; the identical class of religionists, that spread the blessings of civilisation on her shores and islands; the parent institutes and parent philosophy of Hellas, and the causes which have hitherto thrown an impenetrable gloom over her early history. I propose to show the identical localities, whence this confluence of the Oriental tribes flowed like a mighty tide towards the West and South, enriching the lands with its current of civilisation. The countries through which these early colonists moved, will, I trust, be as distinctly exhibited; thus forming a complete chain of evidence from land to land. The consideration of the philosophy, poetry, history, and religion of the Pelasgian colonists—(too often gratuitously set down as barbarians, or as "savages feeding upon leaves and acorns,") will remove many difficulties that prevent a just comprehension of the first chronicles of Greece. I trust that the same evidences which have carried conviction to my mind

—the same interest that has attended me in my researches into the origin of this ancient people, may accompany the reader in the perusal of these pages.

Who then were these Pelasgi?—who, as if to puzzle us still more, are sometimes called Pelargoi. Let us see what evidences we can obtain from the language of Greece, and if we have any, how far they are valid? Perhaps, even, this language may furnish us with no information at all? It will not. This may appear strange, but a simple course of demonstration will establish this to be the fact.

Before, however, I proceed to this point, it will be well to present an abstract of the varying effects of this investigation, produced, through the medium of Greek etymology, in the absence of Greek history. The want of positive and practical result in an inquiry conducted by the learned with much sagacity, and continued with much persevering erudition, would of itself prove the inefficiency of the process employed. One of the most ordinary derivations of the name Pelasgi, is drawn from the term "Pelagos," the sea, intimating that they were a people who came into Greece by sea. Another etymologist finds the explanation in "Pelargoi," storks, either from the linen dress of these ancient people, or from their wandering habits. We are referred by others to "Peleg" for the source of this mysterious name. Both Müller and Wachsmuth, preferring Pelargos as the original form of the word, derived the term from "Pelo," to till, and "Agros," the field. Another writer considers they were called Pelasgi from the verb *pelazo;* and a third thinks they were called Pelargoi from their barbarous language. We have, from these and other sources, the maximum of what can be effected by the aid of Greek mythology; but what is the practical result? Is there anything tangible or precise in any definitions hitherto given? Do we ascertain thereby the exact spot whence these people set out? the countries through which they passed? their ability to civilise the people with whom they mingled? their peculiar characteristics, political or religious? If we have not gained some such information, the practical results of our investigations are perfectly valueless, save for that wholesome mental exercise which they encourage.

We must, then, candidly conclude, that any Greek process of etymology for eliminating positive results, is here at fault. "Profound night," observes Mannert, "rests on this portion of history: a single gleam of light alone pierces the darkness which envelopes it. On one side of the Pelasgi, many tribes of the Illyrians practised navigation, as, for example, the Phæacians of the island Scheria, afterwards Corcyra. At the head of the Adriatic, existed long-established commercial cities, and artificial canals were seen at an early period. Everything seems to intimate that, at a period of remote antiquity, the shores of the Adriatic were inhabited by civilised communities." These are just conclusions; but they are conclusions not resulting from any vague system of etymological interpretation. There is one author, to whose valuable speculations, founded on a rare and well-directed sagacity, I bear a willing testimony.[1] The evidences through which I have gone, based upon authorities totally different from those of the learned writer, have yet produced an aggregate, amply confirming his conjectural conclusions. It is my object, however, to form that chain of evidence by which alone the rational mind can lay hold of truth; and in lieu of generalities and vague suggestions, to present such corroborative proof as will amount to historical fact. But before we take another step in this inquiry, it will be of advantage first to probe the extent of our own ignorance, then to apply a remedy. The former I shall endeavour to effect by a few plain propositions; the latter will be found in the process adopted throughout this work.

[1] Ritter, "Die Vorhalle der Europäischer Völke."

POSTULATES.

1. Let it be granted that the names given to mountains, rivers, and towns, have some *meaning*.
2. Let it be granted that the language of the Name-givers *expressed* that meaning.
3. Let it be granted that the language of the Name-givers will *explain* that meaning.

THEN,

The Greeks dwelt in a land called Greece.

1. They named mountains, rivers, towns; which names had a *meaning*.
2. Their language *expressed* that meaning.
3. Their language will *explain* that meaning.

If their language will *not explain* that meaning, then they, the Greeks, *did not* give those names; but some other nation, speaking some other language, and that other language will tell who that other nation was.

NOW,

The Names given are Geographical.
The Name-givers are Historical.

HENCE,

The geography and history of a country must be sought either in the language of the Name-givers of that country, or in a translation of the language of the Name-givers of that country.

Let us apply this to Grecian Geography.

As a Greek, let me translate Stympha,—I cannot. Dodona,—I cannot. Cambunii Montes,—I cannot. Hellopes,—I cannot. Aithices, Bodon,—I cannot. Chaonia,

Crossæa, Ithaca,—I cannot. Phocis, Locri, Magnesia, Thesprotia,—I cannot. Corinthos, Ossa, Acarnania,—I cannot. Arcadia, Achaia, Bœotia, Elis, Larissa,— I cannot.

The terminations *iotis* and *tis* (occurring four times in the province of Thessaly only), I cannot. Mount Tymphe, Othrys, Pharsalus, I cannot.—What then can I do? If it be said that certain of these people, or certain of these places were named from men, called Chaonus, Ithacus, Magnes, Thesprotus, Corinthus, Acarnan, Pharsalus, Bœotus, then, what is the meaning of *these* names?

Surely an Englishman can tell the meaning of Smith, Brown, Wood, John's-son, Green, Black, &c., and though Good, Shepherd, Wiseman, Lamb, may have no particle of the qualities which once gave these titles; the fact cannot be done away with, that the names are *English*, and they may be explained in English. A similar process will deal with foreign names found in this country—they must of course be sought for in a foreign language. We are, then, ignorant, let us not deny it, of the simple meaning of the name of nearly every place in Greece; and yet we flatter ourselves that we are writing what we call Classical Geographies and Grecian Histories. But now mark the perilous position to which this admission will reduce us. If we, through either the vanity or the ignorance of Greeks, are unacquainted with the original import of the Geographical nomenclature of Greece, then are we equally ignorant of the History of that period, if our Grecian informants have not, with historical facts, given us the full value of *historical names*.

What I have now to show is, that they have given us those names; but as those names have no *signification* attached; they are *historically*, as the earliest map of Greece is *geographically*, worthless; nay more, they have led, and still lead us, astray. They have told us of

Pelasgoi and Pelargoi, and forthwith our literati expend their energies upon problems impossible of solution, with the feeble means at their disposal. They attempt to draw from the Greek language, a language not in existence at the Pelasgian settlement of Hellas,—a history of the origin of the Pelasgians,—a process similar to an investigation of the origin of the Saxons, by the sole aid of the English language.

What then, having confessed our ignorance of men and things in the olden times of Greece, that is, in the time of the Pelasgian race,—what then is the remedy? Simply to refer to the *Pelasgian,* instead of the *Greek* language, for solid information in lieu of fabulous commentary. Is that language still in existence?—It is. It is the Sanscrit, both pure, and in the Pali dialect: sometimes partaking of the form and substance of the Cashmirean, and very often of the structure and vocables of the old Persian.[1] But what, it will be asked, is your proof of this? My proof is one of the most practical that can be imagined; a proof geographical and historical; establishing identity of nomenclature in the old and new country of the Greek settlers, and acquiring the power, by this language, of restoring to plain common sense the absurdities of the whole circle of Greek literature, from Hesiod and the Logographers downwards. Of these, ample evidences will be given as I proceed. These are large claims; but not inconsistent with the facts of the case. I shall proceed to illustrate these propositions by geographical evidence, beginning with an account of the positive source of the Pelasgi.

[1] The Thibetan likewise will be found a valuable aid.

III.

THE EMIGRANTS.

نگه کن برین گنبد زرنگار — که سقفش بود بي ستون استوار
سرا پردهٔ چرخ گردنده بين — در و شمع هاي فروزنده بين

Behold yon azure dome, the sapphire sky,
Rear in unpillared might its canopy;
That vast pavilion, gemmed with worlds of light,
Whose circling glories boast a boundless flight;
And as they roll, survey man's chequered state
And scan the destinies of mortal fate!

"*On Providence.*" From the Pandnameh of Sadi

He who would have a correct view of society as it existed in the highest antiquity—it matters not in what countries—will, for his truest source of information, refer to those principles which are unaffected by climate or by lineage. Before this, as an impartial tribunal, he will arraign the records of history; and, weighing their evidences by this authority, he will be guided to an impartial decision.

Among those dispensations of unerring Providence, by which good has been brought out of evil, we cannot sufficiently admire the directing hand of the Great Ruler of the world, in turning to the purposes of civilisation, and the refinements of social comfort, the struggles of the oppressed, and the cruelty of the oppressor. These instances are not rare. They form so many links in the chain of time, to strengthen our conviction of an Overruling Power. The persecution of the Albigenses—the expulsion of the Moors from Spain—the tyranny of that monarchy in Holland—the revocation of the edict of

Nantes—the atrocious massacre of St. Bartholomew, and its still more atrocious approval by him who claimed to be the Vicar of Christ upon earth—the tyranny of James the Second in this country—all these, and other enormities, eventuated in results most beneficial to the interests of humanity. But, perhaps, in no similar instance have events occurred fraught with consequences of such magnitude, as those flowing from the great religious war which, for a long series of years, raged throughout the length and breadth of India. That contest ended by the expulsion of vast bodies of men; many of them skilled in the arts of early civilisation, and still greater numbers, warriors by profession. Driven beyond the Himalayan Mountains in the north, and to Ceylon, their last stronghold in the south, swept across the valley of the Indus on the west, this persecuted people carried with them the germs of the European arts and sciences. The mighty human tide that passed the barrier of the Punjab, rolled onward towards its destined channel in Europe and in Asia, to fulfil its beneficent office in the moral fertilisation of the world. The Brahminical and Bud'histic sects, who to this day hold divided sway over the greater part of Asia, were the two great champions in this long contest. The former was victorious. The chiefs of the Bud'histic faith were driven to take refuge beyond the reach of their oppressors, carrying with them into Bactria, Persia, Asia Minor, Greece, Phœnicia, and Great Britain, the devotion of their early sages, and an astonishing degree of commercial energy, attended by singular skill in the sciences of astronomy and mechanics. The virulence of religious feud had run high, and the poets of the Brahminical sect sang of their vanquished opponents with a contempt and ferocity so unnatural, as to give their compositions the air of the wildest fiction; their language, like their exultation, was extravagant; but the reality of their victory is not less certain than the gigantic expulsion of the Bud'hist worshippers. It was the issue of this struggle that thenceforward was for centuries to give its devotional complexion to the world throughout northern Asia, and with no unfrequent intervals, from the western bank of the Indus to the Pillars of Hercules. In the Greek language alone —or, rather, the Sanscrit, which we receive as Greek— there are evidences the most convincing, to substantiate this statement. One doctrine and one language were the guard and the missionary of the Bud'hist faith. That language was a modified Sanscrit; and, disfigured as it is by a second-hand reception from the Greeks, it offers abundant evidences of the truth of my position, by the readiness with which the names of tribes, rivers, and mountains, are still to be perceived, and faithfully translated, even through this corrupt medium. Those who are not familiar with the transmutations and disguises of language, may not readily comprehend both the certainty and the ease with which such changes may be detected: of these the ordinary dialectic varieties of the Greek will convey a very imperfect idea. As this mighty emigration from India, though intimately connected with the early settlements of Greece, acts only a subordinate part in that complete and united movement, which, as it were, with one effort, gave a population to Hellas, I purpose giving a general view of its results, reserving, for a more connected examination, the original seat, the actual progression, and the final settlement, of the true Hellenic population. For the present, I shall take a rapid view of the Pelasgi.

There is, perhaps, nothing more mysterious in the wide circle of antiquity, than the character, wanderings, and original seat of the Pelasgi; a people whose history has effectually baffled the inquiries of the well-informed Greeks of antiquity and the ingenuity of modern research. And now, that I am about to solve this vexed problem, it will doubtless be a subject of astonishment that the same result was not obtained earlier. Still, the distance of the migratory movement was so vast, the disguise of names so complete, and Grecian information so calculated to mislead, that nothing short of a total disregard of theoretic principles, and the resolution of independent research, gave the slightest chance of a successful elucidation. And, though I claim no peculiar merit for the result of this investigation, I cannot but feel happy that I have been permitted to add my testimony to the cause of Truth.

PELASA, the ancient name for the province of Bahar, is so denominated from the *Pelasa* or *Butea Frondosa*.[1] Pelaska is a derivative form of Pelasa, whence the Greek "Pelasgos."

This country was the very stronghold of the Bud'histic faith,—a religion detested by the Brahmins, because it denied the doctrine of Castes, as well as the necessity of a mediatorial Priesthood. The fierce but protracted conflict between these rival sects, as already noticed, ended in the expulsion of a vast population.

The "MAGHĔDĀN" (whence the form "MAKEDONIA") are the people of Maghĕd'ha, another name of the province of Pelasa or Bahar. It is so called from the numerous families descended from the sage Magha, in the sacred books of India proudly styled "the offspring of the sun." The Maghadas came into India at the time of Crishna,

[1] "The Butea is rather a large tree, not very common in the lowlands, but much more so up among the mountains. It casts its leaves during the cold season: they come out again, with the flowers, about the months of March and April, and the seed is ripe in June or July. The leaves which are alternate and spreading, are from eight to sixteen inches long. Its flowers are papilionaceous and pendulous, and their ground of a beautiful deep red, shaded with orange and silver-coloured down, which gives them a most elegant appearance."—DR. ROXBURGH'S *Description of the Pelasa Tree*. *Asiatic Researches*, vol. iii., p. 469.

and settled in this region,[1] then called Cicada,[2] the still older name of this Bud'histic province. That there is nothing mythological in this account of Crishna, will be distinctly seen; for Crishna, the son of Dēvāki, is actually named in the "Chandogya Upanishad," towards the close of the third chapter, as having received theological instruction from Ghora, a descendant of Angiras.[3]

In process of time, the kings of Bahar so extended their territories by conquest, that the name of Magadha was applied to countries lying along the course of the Ganges,[4] and even to the whole of India. We have, then, the nomenclature of this Indian province, in quadruple sequence, Pelasa, Cicada, Maghadha, and Bahar or Bihar. The latter name it derived from the numerous *biharas*[5] or monastic establishments of the Jainas, a sect which the orientalist will be surprised to hear, existed in the most ancient Grecian society. Although the province of Pelasa or Bahar sent forth a body of emigrants so powerful as to give a general name to the great Oriental movement which helped to people the mainland and islands of Greece, yet the numbers from this province alone, give no adequate idea of the population that exchanged the sunny land of India for the more temperate latitudes of Persia, Asia Minor, and Hellas. The mountains of Ghoorka; Delhi, Oude, Agra, Lahore, Moultan, Cashmir, the Indus, and the provinces of Rajpootana; sent forth their additional thousands to feed the living tide that flowed towards the lands of Europe and of Asia. With these warlike pilgrims on their journey to the far West,—bands as enterprising as the race of

[1] Wilford, As. Res. [2] Wilson, Sansc. Lex. "Cicada."

[3] Colebrooke, "Asiatic Researches," vol. vii., p. 293.

[4] Properly "Anu Gangam." See Col. Wilford's "Ancient Geog. of Ind.;" Asiat. Researches, vol. ix.

[5] Vihara, or Bihara, a Jaina monastery. The name of this province has also been derived by some, from the aboriginal tribe of Bahrs.

Anglo-Saxons, the descendants, in fact, of some of those very Sacas of Northern India,—like them, too, filling the solitudes, or facing the perils of the West,— there marched a force of native warriors, sufficiently powerful to take possession of the richest of the soil that lay before them.

Though unsuccessful in the great struggle that terminated in the expulsion of themselves and their religious teachers, their practised hardihood left them nothing to fear from the desultory attacks of any tribes who might be bold enough to obstruct their march.

That their movement, however, toward the land of their adoption was not uniform, though possessing singular harmony in their Grecian colonisation, and that not a few intermediate settlements were effected,—some of them of a durable character,—is evident from the names of tribes, rivers, mountains, and religious sects, which lie scattered in profusion between the north-western frontier of India, and the north-eastern boundary of Greece.

I would here pause awhile, to impress upon the reader the vast extent of this Pelasgic emigration, and its historical value. The primitive history of Greece is the primitive history of India. This may appear a startling theory: it is not the less a simple fact. It is the history of much of India, in its language, in its religion, in its sects, in its princes and bravest clans; and he who shall attempt to decypher those venerable manuscripts, miscalled "*Greek Mythology*," and "*Greek Heroic-Legends*," without bringing these combined lights to bear in one focus upon their time-worn surface, will still continue a stranger to the true history of primitive Hellas. To the reader, unless thoroughly convinced of the source, direction, and vast extent of this emigration, many of my future observations may appear the result of a romantic, or, at least, a too enthusiastic temperament.

And here I would introduce the authority of one[1] whose sagacity and profound learning enabled him to grasp, and to classify, and to store up, every particle of solid information to be derived from purely classical sources. "I will here," he observes, "close my account of these researches; for I feel that *the greater extent they assign to the Pelasgians, the more scruples will they raise.* I am now standing at the goal from which a survey may be taken of the circle, where I have ascertaiued the existence of Pelasgian tribes; not as vagrant gipsies, but firmly settled as powerful nations, *at a period for the most part prior to our historical knowledge of Greece.* It is not as a mere hypothesis, *but with a full historical conviction* that I assert there was a time when the Pelasgians, then perhaps *more widely spread than any other people of Europe,* extended from the Po and the Arno, almost to the Bosphorus. The line of their possessions, however, was broken in Thrace; so that the chain between the Tyrrhenians of Asia, and the Pelasgians of Argos, was only kept up by the isles in the north of the Ægæan.

"But in the days of the genealogists and of Hellanicus, all that was left of this immense race, were solitary, detached, widely-scattered remnants, such as those of the Celtic tribes in Spain; like mountain-peaks that tower as islands, where floods have turned the plains into a sea. Like those Celts, they were conceived to be, not fragments of a great people, but settlements formed by colonising or emigration, in the same manner as those of the Greeks, which lay similarly dispersed."

These remarks of the illustrious Niebuhr, are amply confirmed, by the sifting process to which I have subjected the Greek geographical accounts, in their broadest and most practical form. Those geographical terms, whether of mountains, tribes, rivers, or cities, they heard

[1] Niebuhr, Hist. Rome, vol. i., p. 52.

with the ears of Greeks, they wrote down in the fashion of Greeks, and the result was, a medley of names, uniform only in their corrupt orthography. The actual extent of the Pelasgic race, (which, in fact, became a synonym for the general population of India, when transplanted to Europe and Asia,) far exceeded the idea of Niebuhr. So vast were their settlements, and so firmly rooted were the very names of kingdoms, the nomenclature of tribes—nay, the religious systems of the oldest forms of society—that I do not scruple to assert that the successive maps of Spain, Italy, Greece, Asia Minor, Persia, and India, may be read like the chart of an emigrant.

As such, I shall peruse them; the information they give will neither be deceptive, nor, I trust, will it be unfaithfully rendered. To the perfect coherence and practical result of this branch of my investigation, I fearlessly appeal; nor will any casual error of interpretation invalidate the correctness of the principle.

IV.

SOURCES OF GREEK ERROR.

"No pleasure is comparable to the standing upon the vantage-ground of Truth (a hill not to be commanded, and where the air is always clear and serene), and to see the errors and wanderings and mists and tempests in the vale below: so always that this prospect be with pity, and not with swelling or pride."

Lord Bacon. "*Essay on Truth.*"

But if the very basis of our geographical knowledge, as derived from the Greeks, is totally unsound in its nomenclature, not less deceptive is the history in connection with it. Thus, Strabo, one of the most judicious writers upon Greek geography, in presenting us with the antiquarian origin of the Abantes, very gravely tells us that, having settled in Phocis, and built the city of Abæ, they afterwards removed thence to Eubœa, and in consequence were called "Abantes."[1] The geographer, however, does not state whence they derived the original appellation "Abæ." Yet these are the clans that distinguished themselves pre-eminently on the plains of Troy, as daring and hardy warriors. Justice shall be done to their birth-place. Homer has nobly sung their fame, and I feel proud, as the *historical* exponent of a bard,[2] too often gratuitously set down as non-historical, to declare the lineage of these magnificent chieftains of an ancient race. The Abantes, were the splendid Rajpoot tribes of Abanti,[3] or Ougein, in the province of Malwa.

[1] Strab. 444.

[2] See Col. Tod's Account of the Rajpoot Bardai, in his "Rajast'han."

[3] Written "Avanti," the "v" and "b" are pronounced indifferently in India, according to provincial use.

Again: Asius, one of the early poets of Greece, about B.C. 700, makes King Pelasgus, the ancestor of the Pelasgi, spring from the black earth.

> "Godlike Pelasgus, on the mountain chase,
> The sable EARTH gave forth—her mortal race.[1]

Now here is a statement in perfect keeping with what, first tradition, and next, the splendid heresy of the Greek language, made perfectly consistent with the national vaunt of an autochthonous origin. But how stands the plain historical fact in connection with this? Do we desire truth, and not theory? Then, it will be understood that it was GAYĀ, a sacred city of Pelasa, that brought forth King Pelasgus, and not GAIA the earth. This is history in Sanscrit; but fable in Greek. Again: Æschylus makes King Pelasgus the son of Palæcthon;[2] and this he undoubtedly was; yet was he not the son of PALÆ-CTHON, or "Old Land"[3] of the Greeks. Pelasgus was a son of the PALI-CTHON, or "the land of Pali;" so called from Pali, the language of Palasa, Magadha, or Behar.[4] It is not a

[1] Ἀντίθεον δὲ Πελασγὸν ἐν ὑψικόμοισιν ὄρεσιν
Γαῖα μέλαιν' ἀνέδωκεν, ἵνα θνητῶν γένος εἴη.
ASIUS. (Ap. Paus. viii. 1, 4.)

[2] Supp. v. 248.

[3] Niebuhr has very naturally fallen into this error of Æschylus. Æschylus heard and wrote as a Greek, not as a Pelasgian. (See Niebuhr's Rome, vol. i., p. 29, note.)

[4] "In Ceylon, according to Captain Mahony, and in Ava, according to Mr. Buchanan, the appellations of Pali or Bali, and Magadhi, are considered as synonymous, at least when applied to their sacred language; which I consider from that circumstance, to be the old dialect of Magadha, which is called also, the kingdom of Pali by the Chinese. In India, the name for Magadha is unknown, but its origin may be traced through the Puranas."—COL. WILFORD'S *Ind. Geog.*, *As. Res.*, vol. ix., p. 33.

Since the above was written, most valuable and authentic works connected with the Pali-Bud'histic literature, have been brought to light and translated. See particularly the "Mahawanso," translated by the Hon. G. Turnour.

little ludicrous to mark the Hellenic explanation of names, even the most historical, of which the Greeks have made a mythology as ridiculous as that to whose origin, mythopœic propensities and invention are attributed. And yet, while the genealogies of the gods and the tale of the Centaurs are received as fabulous and legendary, the Greek tales of the origin of their tribes are read as historical truth. Still, neither are the former *inventions*, nor the latter *facts*, but both equally rest upon a disguised historical basis; a truth to be amply demonstated in the course of this work. Thus, we are told[1] that the Locrians derived the name "Ozolœ," from the fetid springs (*Ozō*, to smell), near the hill of Taphius on the coast, beneath which it was reported that the Centaur Nessus had been entombed. A different version of this term was given to the Ozolœ who inhabited the eastern part of Œtolia. They were so named from the ill-odour (*ozee*) of their bodies and clothing; the latter, the raw hides of wild beasts. Another effort was made to amend this ethnological title. The inhabitants of this country, it appears, were not called Ozolœ from *Ozō*, but from a certain *Ozos* (branch or sprout,) which was miraculously produced, miraculously planted, and miraculously grew up into an immense vine. As, however, there was an indelicacy connected with the origin of this vine-stock, the inhabitants became highly displeased with the appellation, and changed their names to Œtolians! When the reader distinctly sees, as he will, in the geographical division of this work, that these Oz-olœ were Ooksh-walœ, or "Oxus people," he will understand the amount of credit to which Greek antiquarians are entitled. And this process of endeavouring to account for difficulties found in Greek authors,—themselves the mistaken interpreters of Sanscrit words by homogeneous Greek sounds,—this very process, introduced

[1] Strabo, 426.

by the Greeks, do the literati of Europe still continue! What marvel that the darkness is of such a nature as to tempt the flight of the mythopœic theory. I would here introduce the sound observations of a writer,[1] who has shown himself to be possessed of just views relative to the philology of the Greeks, and their application of that science to practical purposes. "The study of foreign tongues," he observes, "never, either as an object of curiosity, or as an *aid to historical investigation,* formed with them a distinct class of pursuit. This is a peculiarity of Greek literary history, which will be required to be noticed more in detail hereafter. The Pelasgians were considered by the ancients as standing to the Hellenes somewhat in the same relation as the Anglo-Saxons to ourselves. The Anglo-Saxon is a dead language, and a knowledge of it, consequently, is of little practical utility in the present day. Yet its study continues to be zealously prosecuted as well on account of its philological as its antiquarian interest. With the Greeks, the case was different. The allusions in the extant classics to the Pelasgian dialects, spoken or extinct, are so scanty or so vague, as to prove that their affinities had never suggested matter for serious scrutiny." Now, bearing in mind the analogy of the Anglo-Saxon and the Pelasgian,—the English and the Greek,—an exact analogy,—what would be thought of the sanity or competence of that Englishman who should gravely derive, from the English language, the Anglo-Saxon names of rivers, towns, and mountains in this island? I name these things, with a feeling of regret that etymological trifling should be a substitute for historical truth, and with an earnest hope that a brighter dawn is yet in store for the earliest history of Hellas.

The same ignorance of primitive Grecian society, which marked Greek writers, from Homer downwards, is shown

[1] Col. Mure, Hist. of Greek Literature, vol. i., p. 50.

in the treatment and etymological manufacture of the Cyclops; a being for whom the flexible language and lively genius of the Greeks soon had a fitting tale prepared. How satisfactorily did the "circular-eye" of this strange being take its place in the middle of his huge forehead! The amplification of the monster, and his wondrous story, then became easy. In Homer,[1] indeed, the Cyclopean race is spoken of in a more natural and simple manner than in subsequent writers, yet still in such a way as to demonstrate at once the total loss of the old signification of the term, and to give to the actual era of the Homeric writings the most recent date that can be attributed to them. But if it be entertaining to view the process by which the Greeks first misunderstood a Pelasgic term, then fitted out a tale upon their own translation of what they imagined to be Greek, it may not be less instructive to contemplate the results of the rationalising process of the modern school; results, however, far more acceptable to the inquiring mind, than a total negation of any historical foundation for what is termed mythology and legend. In the one instance, valuable results are often obtained; in the other, a total hybernation of the intellect is fostered. A celebrated German writer informs us that the Cyclopes have reference to the circular buildings of the Pelasgi, which terminated in a point like a bee-hive, where there was a *circular aperture;* from the circular form of these buildings (κύκλος), and the round opening at the top resembling an eye (ὤψ), this race of men may be considered to have derived their names.[2] By another ingenious author,[3] we are told that the early Greek pictured to himself the Olympian god in the act of hurling his bolts; that the image thus presented to his mind was that of the god closing one of his eyes for the

[1] Odyssey, vi. 5; ix. 106, 240.

[2] Kruse's Hellas, i. 440. [3] Ast. Grund. der Phil.

purpose of taking a more effectual aim; and hence the fable. On the same principle, was the name given to the Scythian nation, the Arimaspi—"*one-eyed;*" excellent archers, who obtained this epithet from closing one eye in directing their arrows. From a third,[1] we learn that the Cyclopes were a caste of miners; that when they entered the bowels of the earth, the lamp which they carried with them to light them on their way, was regarded as their only eye; and hence the *single eye* of the Cyclopes. This is further supported by a passage of Agatharchides, preserved in Photius, descriptive of the manner in which blocks of marble were obtained from the quarries of Egypt, where the workmen carried a lamp on their foreheads, to light them in their mining operations.[2] Now these, and other accounts of this strange race, are sufficiently plausible, though here we have, unfortunately, three different results. First, they are Builders; secondly, they are Archers; thirdly, they are Miners. What then is to be said of a system by which various results, in an indefinite series, may be produced? We cannot but suspect that the formula for calculation is incorrect. And such it proves to be; not only so, it is still further an impossible one. Let us examine this. Homer knows the Cyclopes only as a race of shepherds—lawless, stern, and gigantic. Agriculture they neglect; they have no political institutions; but, living with their families in mountain caves, they exercise a savage sway over their dependants; they scruple not even to gorge their ferocious appetites with human flesh.[3] Polyphemus is, with Homer, the only representative of the genuine one-eyed Cyclopic race.[4] Apollodorus, and others subsequently, vary this account. They describe them as skilful architects—as a Thracian tribe. From Thrace, they repair to Crete; they build the mighty walls of

[1] Hirt. Geschich der Bauer., i. 198.

[2] Schol. i. 8.

[3] Homer, Od. vi. 5; ix. 106.

[4] Od. i. 69.

Argos, Mycenæ, and Tiryns.[1] "Such walls," Dr. Schmitz has judiciously observed, "commonly known by the name of Cyclopean walls, still exist in various parts of ancient Greece and Italy, and consist of unhewn polygons, which are sometimes twenty or thirty feet in breadth. The story of the Cyclopes having built them, seems to be a mere invention, and admits neither of an historical nor of a geographical explanation. Homer, for instance, knows nothing of Cyclopean walls, and he calls Tiryns a *πόλη τειχιόεσσα*.[2] The Cyclopean walls were probably constructed by an ancient race of men,—perhaps the Pelasgians,—who occupied the countries in which they occur before the nations of whom we have historical records, and later generations being struck with their grandeur, as much as ourselves, ascribed their building to a fabulous race of Cyclopes. According to the explanation of Plato,[3] the Cyclopes were beings typical of the original condition of uncivilised men; but this explanation is not satisfactory, and the cosmogonic Cyclopes, at least, must be regarded as personifications of certain powers manifested in nature, which is sufficiently indicated by their names."[4] The Platonic definition cannot be accepted, for the simple reason, that it is a Greek theory applied to a term which is not Greek. Certain it is, however, that these walls, of which we have been speaking, were built by the Pelasgians, and, for the same reason, it is equally probable that they were built by the Cyclopes; and for this I appeal to the Pelasgian language. I must then, in the first place, beg the reader to observe, that when these walls were built, *the Greek of Homer was not in existence,*—the language of Pelāsa was still the principal medium of oral communication in Greece. In short, the term "Cuclopes"[5] is a corrupt

[1] Strab. viii. p. 373. App. ii. 1.
[2] Il. ii. 559.
[3] Ap. Strab. 6, xiii. p. 592.
[4] Smith's Dict. Antiq. i. 909.
[5] Κύκλοπες.—See Append., Rule 5.

form of GOĆLOPĔS; the GOĆLA CHIEFS,[1] that is, the chiefs who lived in the Goćla country, a district lying along the banks of the Jumna; the "Goćla-pĕs" being so called from their pastoral habits in tending the Goćlas or herds of cattle. The Goćla district was the residence of Nanda and of Krishna during his youth,[2] and the scene of that prince's triumph amongst the Gopis, or Pastoral Nymphs; and so far Homer is correct, in giving to his Cyclops "Polyphemus" the character of a shepherd.

That part of Greece which was colonised by these Guc'lapes of the Jumna, was the GUC'LA-DES, by the Greeks written CUCLA-DES, by us CYCLADES,[3] that is, "the land of the Guc'las." Thus, on simple geographical and Pelasgic evidence, by independent reference to the language and original country of these early Hellenic settlers, the first outlines of their history are at once restored, and rescued from the mythological category; in which category the historical derivation of the Cyclades must now take its place.[4] Here, then, the Homeric description of the savage Cyclopes of the cave, and the record of the Cyclopic settlement in Greece, are in exact keeping with the real signification of that Pelasgian term which descended to the time of Homer. Thus is the Pelasgian language brought in connection with that people by whom these walls were said to have been built.

[1] From Gokoola, and Pa, a prince or chief.—See Rule.

[2] Wilson's Sansc. Lex. *s. v.*

[3] The Sanscrit *des* signifies a "land or country."

[4] Derived from *κύκλας δος*, "round or circular."

V.

ORIENTAL RESEARCH.

"As long as the study of Indian antiquities confines itself to the illustration of Indian history, it must be confessed that it possesses little attraction for the general student, who is apt to regard the labour expended on the disentanglement of perplexing and contradictory mazes of fiction as leading only to the substitution of vague and dry probabilities, for poetical, albeit extravagant fable. But the moment any name or event turns up in the course of such speculation, offering a point of connection between the legends of India and the rational histories of Greece and Rome—a collision between an Eastern and a Western hero—forthwith a speedy and a spreading interest is excited, which cannot be satisfied until the subject is thoroughly sifted by an examination of all the ancient works, Western and Eastern, that can throw concurrent light on the matter at issue. Such was the engrossing interest which attended the identification of Sandracottus with Chandragupta in the days of Sir William Jones—such the ardour with which the Sanscrit was studied, and is still studied, by philologists at home, after it was discovered to bear an intimate relation to the classical language of ancient Europe. Such more recently has been the curiosity excited on Mr. Turnour's throwing open the hitherto concealed page of Buddhistic historians, to the development of Indian monuments and Pauranic records."—*James Prinsep, Esq., late Sec. As. Soc.*

Thus wrote the talented and deeply-lamented scholar, whose ardent zeal in the cause of Oriental research shortened an existence which was an ornament to the society in which he moved, and the cynosure of the literary world. It is not without a feeling of melancholy interest that I look back upon the honoured record of those names which have shed a ray of splendour on the annals of our Eastern empire. They have passed away without being cognisant of the inestimable value of their own labours, and of the noble harvest of renown which, through their instrumentality, is yet to be reaped by their country. The warrior-scholarship of India, too, that realisation of the most splendid theory of intellectual and physical power, has consecrated its rare endowments to the cause of historical research. Both the warrior and the peaceful student have left the scene of their mighty energies, unconscious of that empire of intellectual wealth which they have won for Christendom at large. Often repelled in their bold enterprise of uniting and consolidating the historical empire of the East and West, of establishing for both a community of religion, policy, and origin, they returned again and again to the charge, instinctively conscious of the fact, and undeterred by derision and defeat. The names of Wilford and Tod are an honour to this class of men; and while the noble candour of the former in confessing the literary imposition of which he had been the victim, is only equalled by his daring enterprise to penetrate the mysteries of the ancient world; the steady convictions of the latter, firmly urged and ably supported, will be found amply established by the practical geographical evidences here laid before the reader.

I am now standing at the fountain-head of civilisation,—the very source of the most ancient and the most mighty monarchies. The vision is distinct, for I hold the vantage-ground of the high table-land of Western Asia. The warlike pilgrims of the Oxus are moving towards the east, the west, and the south; they are the patriarch bands of India, Europe, and Egypt. At the mouths of the Indus, dwell a sea-faring people, active, ingenious, and enterprising, as when, ages subsequent to this great movement, they themselves, with the warlike denizens of the Punjab, were driven from their native land, to seek the far distant climes of Greece. The commercial people dwelling along the coast that stretches from the mouth of the Indus to the Coree, are embarking on that emigration whose magnificent results to civilisation, and whose gigantic monuments of art, fill the mind with mingled emotions of admiration and awe. These people coast along the shores of Mekran, traverse the mouth of the Persian Gulf and again adhering to the sea-board of Oman, Hadramaut, and Yemen (the Eastern Arabia), they sail up the Red Sea; and again ascending the mighty stream that fertilises a land of wonders, found the kingdoms of Egypt, Nubia, and Abyssinia. These are the same stock that, centuries subsequently to this colonisation, spread the blessings of civilisation over Hellas and her islands. The connection, therefore, which is so constantly represented by Greek historians as subsisting between Egypt and Athens, as well as Bœotia, and other parts of Greece, is perfectly natural, and in fact is just what we should anticipate from a people, who so highly honoured and deeply venerated their parent state as to receive from its hands their sacred fire, and their ministers of religion.

Of the triple connection that links Egypt, Greece, and the lands of the Indus, there will remain no longer the shadow of a doubt, as the reader accompanies me in the geographical development of the colonisation of Greece, in which the ingenious people of the Abu Sin (the Abussinians[1] of Africa) founded the mercantile and thriving community of Corinthus. This is past controversy; for the Abusin, a classical name for the Indus, is reproduced in Greece as the Cor'-Indus (Corinthus), that is, the people of the Cori Indus.[2] As I shall cautiously avoid all dependence upon mere similarity of names, or philological deductions, unless amply supported by collateral evidence, I beg the reader to observe that what I have now advanced rests upon a geographical basis, of whose solidity, when he comes to survey the breadth and the depth, he will feel ample assurance. As these evidences will be found to appeal to the practical sense of every individual, I shall offer no apology for neglecting to support them by classical or modern authorities. The remarks of Colonel Tod,

[1] Abyssinians.

[2] The Corī is a mouth of the Indus.

however, on this point are so full of sound judgment, and so much to the purpose, that I cannot avoid introducing them in this place. "Whether Rameses found his way from the Nile to the Ganges, or whether Rameses found his Lanca on the shores of the Red Sea, we can but conjecture. The Hindoo scorns the idea that the rock of Ceylon was the abode of Rama's enemy. The distance of the Nile from the Indian shore forms no objection to the surmise: *the sail that spread for Ceylon could waft for the Red Sea,* which the fleets of Tyre, of Solomon, and of Hiram covered about this time. That the Hindoos navigated the ocean from the earliest ages, the traces of their religion in the isles of the Archipelago sufficiently attest."[1] That the people of the country of the Indus ranked as navigators, in the most venerable antiquity, is perfectly clear, from the ancient Institutes of Menu, where "merchants who traffic beyond sea, and bring presents to the king," are expressly mentioned.

In the Ramayuna,[2] the practise of bottomry is distinctly noticed.[3] "In fact," as Heeren remarks,[4] "no law had ever forbidden this species of commerce; on the contrary, the Institutes of Menu contain several regulations which tacitly allow it in giving the force of law to all commercial contracts relative to dangers incurred by sea or land." These institutes of Menu, running up to the vast antiquity of B.C. 1400, give an idea of the early commercial energies of India; which all my subsequent observations will fully carry out.[5]

[1] Tod's Rajasthan, vol. i., p. 113.

[2] Ramayuna, iii., 237, written B. C. 1300. [3] Menu iii., 158; viii., 157.

[4] Heeren's Indians, p. 124.

[5] The translator of Heeren observes, "That ships belonging to Hindoos went to sea, and that a proportional interest for the hazard of the sea was to be paid on money borrowed, must be perfectly true." He does not, however, consider this fact as necessarily proving that the seamen were Hindoos. Positions such as the mouth of the Corī or the Indus, Corinth in Greece, Portsmouth in England, or Havre in France, furnish a practical comment upon such a doubt.

But to return to the primeval movements of mankind. I have glanced at the Indian settlements in Egypt, which will again be noticed; and I would now resume my observations from the lofty frontier which is the true boundary of the European and Indian races. The PARASOOS, the people of Parasoo-Rama, those warriors of the Axe,[1] have penetrated into and given a name to PERSIA; they are the people of Bharata;[2] and to the principal stream that pours its waters into the Persian Gulf, they have given the name of EU-BH'RAT-ES (EU-PH'RAT-ES) THE BH'RAT-CHIEF.

Near the embouchure of the "Great Bharata," or "Euphrates," are a people called the ELUMÆI; they are a powerful tribe from the Y'ELUM, or "Hydaspes" of the Greeks; who, unfortunately for history, were content to give foreign names without a translation, and to write these names very incorrectly. The Elumæi were a race of Rajpoot equestrian warriors, on the "HYD-ASP-ES," *i.e.*, "the River of the Horse-chiefs,"[3] who dwelt in the vicinity of the ACE-SIN-ES, the chiefs of the waters of the Indus.[4] As usual, we find these Kshetriyas, or warriors, in juxtaposition with the Brahminical caste, who are styled Chal-Dæans,[5] that is, the tribe of Devas, or Brahmins, whose original starting-point is distinctly shown to have been "Shin-ar,"[6] the country of "The people of the Indus."

But that an emigration also took place from Indian districts still more easterly is evident; for the "Bopalan," or "people of Bopal,"[7] built the vast city, which the

[1] Parasoo, the Axe. [2] Bharata, the name of India.

[3] Hud-asp-es (*Ood*, water; *asp*, a horse; *es*, a chief).

[4] *Aca*, water; *Sin*, the Indus; *es*, a chief.

[5] Chal-Dæa (*Cul*, tribe, and *Deva*, a god or Brahmin).—See Append., Rule 6, 7.

[6] Properly *Sin-war*.

[7] Bhoopalan, people of Bhoopal in Malwa; Bopaul forms the exact

Greeks strangely called "Babulon,"[1] while it is equally clear that a settlement—I will not enter into its date, though even that I believe might be satisfactorily established—was made in the country by the people of Bhagulpoor and its neighbourhood. These colonists may be seen grouped along the southern banks of the Euphrates, they are called singularly enough "ANCO-BAR-I-TIS," that is, "ANGA-POOR-I-DES," the country of Anga-poor. "Anga" is that district which, in classical Hindoo writings, includes Bengal proper and Bhagulpoor.[2] To the south of Anco-bar-i-tis, the reader will observe the city of PERISA-BORA, a singular euphonic Greek commutation for PARASOO-POOR, the city of Parasoo. Nor does that grand emporium, Benares, remain unrepresented in the land of the Parasoos; its inhabitants are distinctly seen near the banks of the Tigris, as "COSSÆI," that is the people of CASI, the classical name for Benares.[3]

boundary of the old Hindoo province of Malwa, lat. 23° 77′, long. 77° 30′ E., 100 miles from Ougein.

1 "And it came to pass as they journeyed from the east that they found a plain in the land of Shinar, and they dwelt there."—*Gen.* xi. 2.

2 Wilson, Sansc. Lex. "*Anga*," "Bhagulpoor" (Boglipoor) is a district in the province of Bahar, situated between the 24th and 26th degrees of north latitude, occupying the south-eastern corner of that province, together with a small section from Bengal."—HAMILTON'S *E. Ind. Gazette*.

3 Benares (Sansc. *Varanashi*, from the two streams, Vara and Nashi) stands on the convex side of the curve which the Ganges here forms, in lat. 25° 30′ N., long. 83° 1′ E. It is one of the holy cities of India, and was anciently named Casi, or the splendid, which appellation it still retains. The country for ten miles round is considered sacred by the Hindoos. The Brahmins assert that Benares is no part of the terrestrial globe, but that it stands upon the points of Siva's trident; as a proof of which they affirm that no earthquake is ever felt within its holy limits. This is a grand point of pilgrimage to the Hindoo population, and, as Hamilton observes, "Some learned Hindoos relax so far as to admit the possible salvation of Englishmen, if they become firm believers in the Ganges, or die at Juggernauth; and they even name an Englishman who went straight to heaven from Benares. But it appears that he had also left money for the construction of a temple."—*Hamilton, E. I. Gazette*, vol. i., p. 170.

The ancient map of Persia, Colchis, and Armenia, is absolutely full of the most distinct and startling evidences of Indian colonisation, and, what is more astonishing, practically evinces, in the most powerful manner, the truth of several main points in the two great Indian poems, the Ramayuna and Mahabaratha. The whole map is positively nothing less than a journal of emigration on the most gigantic scale. But, alas! unhappily for history, the Greeks of antiquity, like the French of the present day, so completely made their own language the language of the civilised world, and by their graceful and insinuating manner so confirmed this advantage, that they had few or no inducements to become philologists, not even to trace the origin of their own language or to acquire that of another nation. Perhaps the only exception to this failing is contained in the record of the Homerid of Chios, in his hymn on the festivities of Delos, in which the Ionians are represented as expert linguists. The attempts of Plato in his Cratylus, those of Varro in his essay on the etymological sources of the Roman language, are replete with the most singular puerilities.

It is now proper to revert to the primitive colonisation of Hellas; and to point out the exact localities which furnished the race whence sprang her warriors and her statesmen, her poets and her religion; for until this be accomplished, that which may be the basis of individual conviction, can never be the foundation for the confidence of another. I therefore address myself with pleasure to this duty, thankful that I have been permitted to pass the gloomy barriers of the mighty past, and to bring back with me records that I doubt not will carry conviction to the minds of the dispassionate.

VI.

THE HELLENES.

"Ἕλληνος δ ἐγένοντο θεμιστόπολοι βασιλῆες
Δῶρός τε, Ξοῦθός τε, κᾶι Αἴολος ἱππιοχάρμης."
Hes. Frag. p. 278. *Marktsch.*

CHIEFS of the WAR-CAR, guards of holy Right,
Dorus and Æolus, and Zuthus' might
From HELLEN sprang.

THE land of HELLAS, a name so dear to civilisation and the arts, was so called from the magnificent range of heights situated in Beloochistan, styled the "HELA" mountains. "Their lofty range," observes Thornton,[1] "stretches from north to south generally, between the meridians 67° 68°. They are connected with the elevated region of Afghanistan by the Toba mountains, of which they may be considered a prolongation, and which rise in the two summits of Tukatoo, in lat. 30° 18′, long. 67°, to a height estimated at between 11,000 and 12,000 feet. If we consider this mountain as the northern limit of the Hela range, it will be found to extend from north to south, a distance of about four hundred miles, and to terminate at Cape Monze, projecting into the Arabian Sea, in lat. 24° 48′. About lat. 29° 30′, a large offset extends eastward, forming the mountains held by the Muree tribe of Kalum, and joining the Suliman range about Hurrund and Dagel. Southward of this the Hela range becomes rapidly depressed towards the east, descending with considerable steepness in that direction to the low level

[1] Thornton's Gazetteer of the Punjab, vi., p. 221.

tract Cutch Gundava; viewed from which, these mountains present the appearance of a triple range, each rising in succession as they recede westward." Such, on the excellent authority above quoted, are the Hela mountains, which sent forth the first progenitors of Greece.

The chiefs of this country were called "Hēlāines,"[1] or the "Chiefs of the Hela." I have not the slightest doubt, however, that both the name of this mountain, and that of the chiefs of the country, was of a secondary form, viz., "Heli," "the sun," demonstrating that they were of the genuine race of Rajpoots, who were all worshippers of that luminary. In this case the formation of the term HELĒNES in Sanscrit, would be identical with the Greek. Of this fact there can be no reasonable doubt, from the following considerations. Hel-en (the Sun King)[2] is said to have left his kingdom to Aiolus, his eldest son, while he sent forth Dorus and Zuthus to make conquests in foreign lands.[3] Haya is the title of a renowned tribe of Rajpoot warriors, the most extensive of the north-western worshippers of Bál, or the sun. They were also called "Asii," or "Aswa," and their chiefs were denominated "Aswa-pas," or the "Aswa Chiefs," and, to use the words of Conon, as quoted by Bishop Thirlwall,[4] "The patrimony of AIOLUS (the HAIYULAS) is described as bounded by the river Asopus (Aswapas)[5] and the Enipeus." Such then was the Asopus, the settlement of the Haya tribe, the Aswa chiefs, the sun worshippers, the children of the "Sun King," or Helēn,[6]

[1] From *Hela*, and *Ina* a king; Hela-ina, by the rules of Sandhi, or combination, making Helaīnes, "The Chiefs of Hela."

[2] *Heli*, sun; *Ina*, king.

[3] Apollod., 1731. Thirlwall, Hist. Greece, vol. i., p. 101.

[4] Hist. Greece, vol. i., p. 101.

[5] Aswa-pos (*As-opos*), "Aswa chiefs" (*Aswa*, a horse, and *pos*, a chief).

[6] The misunderstanding of the familiar use of the term "Sons" in the earliest historians of Hellas—who, in plain terms, are the *Indian* writers of early Greece—has led to a total negation of its historical value, and the

whose land was called in Greek, HELLA-DOS, in Sanscrit, HELA-DES (*Hela*, Hela; *des*, land). Of Achilles, sprung from a splendid Rajpoot stock, I shall briefly speak when developing the parent geography of the Dolopes; but as that magnificent race, and the Abantes, who were likewise worshippers of the sun, play such a distinguished part in the *history*—not *mythology* of Hellas, I cannot better illustrate their position in the most venerable annals of Greece than by presenting the reader with the brilliant yet faithful picture of the noble tribes of the Aswas, drawn from Colonel Tod's "Annals of Rajast'han." Meanwhile, I would remark that these were the clans, who, descending from the Amoo, or Oxus—in fact the "Ox-ud-racæ,"[1] or "Rajas of the Oxus," boldly encountered the Macedonian hero. These were the chiefs who founded a kingdom around, and gave an enduring name to, the Euxine Sea. They were the chiefs of the Oxus, and their kingdom was that of the OOX-INA (EUX-INE), or kings of the Oxus, a compound derived from *Ooxus*, and *ina*, a king. Of this the Greeks made Euxinos. The old tale ran, that this sea was first called AXEINOS, or *the inhospitable*; that it was then changed to EU-XEINOS, or the *hospitable*. We have thus a most fortunate preservation of the old term; *ooxa* with *ina*, will, by the rules of Sandhi, exactly make good the old name Ookshainŏs (Αξεινος). Thus, the Greek *Myth* is "Αξεινος, "the inhospitable" (sea);

substitution of the theory of mythological invention, which has no guarantee from the plain facts of the case. The ancient chieftains of Afghanistan, like the Scots, their immediate descendants (of whose ancient power, position, and rule in the north of this island, I hold the most interesting and undeniable proofs), used the term in the ordinary phraseology, of the clan, as "Hector of the Mist," "Sons of the Mist," "Sons of the Douglas," "Sons of Mac Ivor." The same misapprehension of the nomenclature of the Sacha tribes, other Hellenic settlers, has still further propped up the feeble claims of mythology. "The Serpent," "The Eagle," "The Sun," are, simply and ordinarily, the "Serpent-tribe," "Eagle-tribe," "Sun-tribe."

[1] *Oxus* (*Ud*, water; *Raja*, a king).

the Sanscrit *History*—Ookshāinos, "the chiefs of the Oxus."[1]

These were the mighty tribes, who by their numbers and their prowess, gave, from their appellation "Asii," its enduring name to the continent of "Asia."

"The Aswas," observes Colonel Tod, "were chiefly of the Hindoo race; yet a branch of the Suryas[2] also bore this designation. It appears to indicate their celebrity as horsemen.[3] All of them worshipped the horse, which they sacrificed to the sun. This grand rite, the Aswamedha,[4] on the festival of the winter solstice, would alone go far to exemplify their common Scythic origin with the Getic Sacæ, authorising the inference of Pinkerton, that 'a grand Scythic nation extended from the Caspian to the Ganges.'

"The Aswamedha was practised on the Ganges and Sarjoo[5] by the Solar Princes, twelve hundred years before Christ, as by the Getes in the time of Cyrus; 'deeming it right,' says Herodotus, 'to offer the swiftest of created, to the chief of uncreated beings:' and this worship and sacrifice of the horse, has been handed down to the Rajpoot of the present day. The milk-white steed was supposed to be the organ of the gods, from whose neighing they calculated future events: notions possessed also by the Aswa, sons of Boodha,[6] on the Yamuna and Ganges, when the rocks of Scandinavia, and the shores of the

[1] The Greek "Oxus" should be properly "Ooksha," so called from *Ooksha*, an ox; which, as the reader will perceive, is at once very fair English and Sanscrit.

[2] "Suryas," the Sun-tribes (from *Surya*, the sun).

[3] *Aswa* and *Hya* are synonymous Sanscrit terms for "Horse"—*Asp* in Persian; and as applied by the prophet Ezekiel to the Getic invasion of Scythia, B.C. 600, "the sons of Togarma, riding on horses"—described by Diodorus; the period the same as the Tacshak invasion of India.

[4] *Aswa*, a horse, and *Medha*, a sacrifice.

[5] The Gogra or Gharghara River.

[6] Woden. The "b" is interchanged with "v," and this again with the "w"—Bodhan, Vodhan, Woden.

Baltic, were yet untrod by man. The steed of the Scandinavian god of battle was kept in the temple of Upsala, and always 'found foaming and sweating after battle.' Similarity of religious manners affords stronger proofs of original identity than language. Language is eternally changing—so are manners; but an exploded custom or rite, traced to its source, and maintained in opposition to climate, is a testimony not to be rejected. When Tacitus informs us that the first act of a German on rising was ablution, it will be conceded, that this habit was not acquired in the cold climate of Germany, but must have been of Eastern origin; as were the loose flowing robe, the long and braided hair, tied in a knot at the top of the head."[1] And here I would pause to direct the attention of the reader to the well-known passage of Thucydides, so forcible an evidence of the Scythic origin of the Athenians, and so amply confirmed by the geographical evidences I shall bring forward. "It is not long since," observes that sagacious writer, "that the more elderly among the rich Athenians, ceased to wear linen tunics, and to wreathe their hair in a knot, which they clasped by the insertion of a golden grasshopper. Hence, also, this fashion was, on a principle of national affinity, extensively prevalent among the more ancient Ionians."[2] The original land of the people of Attica, practically shown, with the powerful aid of latitude and longitude, and exhibiting that people as dwelling among the Ionians of the parent-stock, will amply account both for their linen dress and the style of arranging their hair.

"The Rajpoot," continues Colonel Tod,[3] "worships his horse, his sword, and the sun, and attends more to the martial song of the bard than to the litany of the Brahmin. In the martial mythology, and warlike poetry of the Scandinavians, a wide field exists for assimilation; and a

[1] Rajast., vol. i., p. 65. [2] Thucyd. i., c. 6. [3] Rajast., vol. i., p. 68.

comparison of the poetic remains of the Asii of the East and West, would alone suffice to suggest a common origin."

As an evidence of the soundness of this opinion, it is sufficient to observe, that the European, "Scandinavian," and the Indian, "Kshetrya," or "warrior caste," are identical; the former term being a Sanscrit equivalent for the latter. "Scanda-Nabhi" (Scandi-Navi) signifying "Scanda chiefs;"[1] so that both language and practice prove the Indian origin of this race.

I add other extracts from Colonel Tod, for the advantage of the sceptics of the Trojan war,—not as a proof of that event, for that I shall elsewhere amply demonstrate—but to remind them how thoroughly Indian was Hellas at the period of that mighty struggle.

"The war-chariot is peculiar to the Indo-Scythic nations, from Desaratha,[2] and the heroes of the Mahabharat, to the conquest of Hindust'han, when it was laid aside. On the plains of Coorukhéta, Crishna became charioteer to his friend Arjoona; and the Getic hordes of the Jaxartes, when they aided Xerxes in Greece, and Darius on the plains of Arbela, had their chief strength in the war-chariot."[3]

[1] Scanda is the name of Kartikeya, the Hindoo god of war.

[2] This title of the father of Rama denotes a "charioteer." (From *Das* ten, and *Rhatha* a car. "Whose car bore him to the ten quarters of the universe."—WILSON, *Sansc. Lex.*, s. v.)

[3] "The Indian satrapy of Darius," says Herodotus, "was the richest of all the Persian provinces, and yielded six hundred talents of gold." Arrian informs us that his Indo-Scythic subjects, in his wars with Alexander, were the *élite* of his army. Beside the Sacasenæ, we find tribes in name similar to those included in the thirty-six Rajcula (Raja-tribes). The Indo-Scythic contingent was two hundred war-chariots and fifteen elephants. By this disposition, they were opposed to the cohort commanded by Alexander in person. The chariots commenced the action, and prevented a manœuvre of Alexander to turn the left flank of the Persians. Of their horse, also the most honourable mention is made: they penetrated into the division where Parmenio commanded, to whom Alexander was compelled to send reinforcements. The Grecian historian dwells with pleasure on Indo-

I here take the opportunity of observing, that one of the heroes just noticed will be found to be not only an Indian chieftain, but one of the Grecian gods.

Speaking of the worship of arms by the military race, Colonel Tod observes, "The devotion of the Rajpoot is still paid to his arms and to his horse. He swears 'by the steel,' and prostrates himself before his defensive buckler, his lance, his sword, or his dagger. The worship of the sword in the Acropolis of Athens by the Getic Attila, with all the accompaniments of pomp and place, forms an admirable episode in the history of the decline and fall of Rome; and had Gibbon witnessed the worship of the double-edged sword,[1] by the Prince of Méwar, and all his chivalry, the historian might even have embellished his animated account of the adoration of the scymitar, the symbol of Mars."

Such were the warlike tribes, "the Children of the Sun," that first peopled the land of Hellas. If the reader will now refer to the double map of the old and the new settlements of the sons of Hellen, he will distinctly see a system of colonisation corresponding to the various provinces in the parent country of the emigrants. Bordering on the Eubœan sea, he will discern the "LOCRI." These are the inhabitants of LOGURH, a district of considerable extent in Affghanistan, south of the city of Cabool. It extends up the northern slope of the high land of Ghuznee; and, as its elevation in all parts exceeds six thousand feet, the climate is very severe in winter. The Logurh River, with its various feeders, intersects and drains this district, which, being well watered, fertile, and cultivated with much care, is one of the most productive parts of the country.[2] Adjoining the small

Scythic valour: "There were no equestrian feats, no distant fighting with darts, but each fought as if victory depended on his sole arm." They fought the Greeks hand to hand."—Rajast., vol. i. p. 69.

[1] Khanda.

[2] Lat. 34° 20′, long. 69°.

Grecian province of Locri, of which the Ozolian Locrians (whom I shall shortly notice) are a section—are the Bœotians, lying immediately to the north-west of Attica, embosomed in the mountains of Helicon, Parnassus, and Cithæron.

The soil of this country was famed for its fertility, and its inhabitants for their vigour and military hardihood; and often did they bear off the prize of the gymnastic contest at the Olympic games. Their square-built figure, and the massive mould of their martial form, pointed out this race as essentially adapted to deeds of warlike emprise. Nor is this to be wondered at; they were the Kshetriyas, or great warrior-caste of north-western India; the "BAIHOOTIANS," a people who came from the fertile banks of the Behoot, or Jailum,[1] the most westerly of the five great rivers of the Punjab, which intersect that region east of the Indus. This mighty river rises in Cashmir, the whole valley of which it drains, making its way to the Punjab, through the pass of Bramula, in the lofty range of Pir Panjal. The regular derivative form of Behuti is Baihooti, signifying the "people of the Behut." The term Bahoot, however, is more especially connected with the "Bahoo," or "Arm" of Brahma, whence the warrior caste of India was, by a poetical Hindoo fiction, supposed to have sprung. Immediately flanking the province of Bœotia to the east is the large island of EU-BOIA; so called from its having been colonised by the warlike clans of the EU-BAHOOYAS. And now observe the extraordinary antiquity of the Hindoo mythologic system. These warriors are Bahooja,[2] *i.e.*, "Born from the arm (of Brahma.") Not only so, they are *Eu*-bahooyas, *i.e.*, *The*

[1] Called also Jelum, Jilum, Veshau, and Veynt.

[2] *Bahoo*, the arm; *Bahoo-ja*, Arm-born. The letter "j" often assumes the soft sound of the "y," a Sanscrit letter equivalent to the Greek "i." The Greek "Eu" is the corresponding form to the Sanscrit "Su," "well," in every case. *See* Appendix, Rule 9.

Bahooyas or warriors *par éminence*. Hence their settlement was "Eubœa," or the land of "the Great Kshetriyas." Thus it is clear, that this part of the mythology of India is coeval with the settlement of the island.

The principal feeder of the Jailum is the Veshau, which so far exceeds the upper feeders of the Jailum, that its fountain-head should be regarded as properly the source of that great river. "The Veshau flows by a subterraneous passage from Kosah Nag, a small but deep lake, situated near the top of the Pir Punjal mountain, and at an elevation of about 12,000 feet above the level of the sea. 'Here,' Vigne states,[1] 'its full strong current is suddenly seen gushing out from the foot of the last and lofty eminence that forms the dam on the western end of the lake, whose waters thus find an outlet, not over, but through, the rocky barrier, with which it is surrounded.'[2] The stream, thus produced and reinforced, subsequently receives numerous small feeders; passes through the City Lake, the Manasa Lake, and the Wulur, or Great Lake, and sweeps through the country, confined by embankments, which prevent it from overflowing the lower part of the valley. The whole course of the Jailum through the valley, before it finds an outlet through the pass of Baramula into the lower ground of the Punjab, is about one hundred and twenty miles, for seventy of which it is navigable. It is the opinion of Vigne, that the river made its way gradually through this pass, and thus drained the lake, which, according to tradition, formerly occupied the site of the valley. The Jailum was unquestionably the Hydaspes of the Greeks. It is still known to the Hindoos of the vicinity by the name of *Betusta*, corrupted by the Greeks, according to their usage, with respect to foreign names. The scene of

[1] Kashmir, iv., 144, quoted by Thornton.

[2] This remarkable spot is in lat. 33° 25′, long. 74° 45′.

the battle, between Porus and Alexander, is generally placed at Julalpoor."[1]

It is impossible not to be struck with the singular similarity of the tract of country both old and new; the land which these martial emigrants left and that on which they entered. Both richly watered with numerous streams, and both extremely fruitful. The Wulur, or the "Great Lake," in the parent country, the Lake Copias in the land of Hellas, the Kshetriya or warrior caste, in either region of the world, complete the harmonious landscape of antiquity; and this singular identity of taste, as well as of locality, I shall again have occasion to notice. As in the lands of the far-off Sinde, so in their new settlements, the ingenious and lively people of Attica are found close neighbours to the Bœotians. What a vivid picture does this fact convey of the steadiness of the progress, and compactness of the array which brought these martial bands of the HELAS to their final settlement in Greece, the land of their adoption! How truly did they exchange one land of mountain and of flood, for another almost its exact counterpart! How powerful and resistless must have been their progress, that they should arrive at their destined home, in such unbroken order!

[1] Thornton, Punj., vol. i., p. 290.

VII.

ATTICA.

. . . . pars ducere muros,
Molirique arcem, et manibus subvolvere saxa;
Pars optare locum tecto, et concludere sulco.
Jura, magistratusque legunt, sanctumque senatum.
Hic portus alii effodiunt: hic alta theatris
Fundamenta locant alii, immanesque columnas
Rupibus excidunt, scenis decora alta futuris."—*Æn.* i. 427—433.

WHO could have imagined that from the present barbarous land of Afghanistan, the elegant, the refined, and the witty Athenian should have set out!—yet so it was. The northern course of the Indus was his first home. The ATTAC indeed, gave a name to the far-famed province of ATTICA! The Attac is at present a fort and small town on the east bank of the Indus, 942 miles from the sea, and close below the place where it receives the waters of the Cabul river, and first becomes navigable. "The name," writes Thornton, "signifying '*obstacle*,' is supposed to have been given to it under the presumption that no scrupulous Hindoo would proceed westward of it. But this strict principle, like many others of similar nature, is little acted on. The banks of the river are very high, so that the enormous accession which the volume of water receives during inundation, scarcely affects the breadth, but merely increases the depth. The rock forming the banks is of dark coloured slate, polished by the force of the stream, so as to shine like black marble. Between these 'one clear blue stream shot past.' The depth of the Indus here is thirty feet in the lowest state, and between sixty and seventy in the highest, running at the rate of six miles an hour. There is a ford at some distance above the confluence of the river of Cabool, but the extreme coldness and rapidity of the water render it at all times very dangerous, and on the slightest inundation, quite impracticable. On the right bank, opposite Attac, is Khyrabad, a fort, built according to some by Nadir Shah. The locality is important in a military and commercial point of view, as the Indus is here crossed by the great route which, proceeding from Cabool eastward, through the Khyber Pass into the Punjab, forms the main line of communication between Afghanistan and Northern India. The river was here repeatedly crossed by the British armies, during the military operations in Afghanistan; and here, according to the general opinion, Alexander, subsequently Timour the Jagatayan conqueror, and, still later Nadir Shah, crossed."[1]

If the energetic people of the Attac had their "barrier" at this point of the far-famed river of the Sindh, the triangular peninsula, which they afterwards inhabited in the land of Hellas, bounded on the north by Bœotia and the Euripus, and on its southern and eastern shores by the waters of the Saronic gulf and the Ægæan, proved a more effectual "Attac," or barrier, than they had ever before possessed; and while the barrenness of her soil protected the classic land of Attica from an overwhelming population, it taught her to turn her attention to the development of the arts of industry, in which she so much excelled, and the completion of a marine that enhanced the glory of her more peaceful activity. "The sterility of Attica," says an eloquent author,[2] "drove its inhabitants from their own country.

[1] Thornt., Punj. vol. i., p. 61. [2] Wordsworth's Pictorial Greece.

It carried them abroad. It filled them with a spirit of activity, which loved to grapple with difficulty and to face danger; it did for them what the wise poet says was done for the early inhabitants of the world by its Supreme Ruler, who, in his figurative language, first agitated the sea with storms, and hid fire, and checked the streams of wine which first flowed abroad in the golden age, and shook the honey from the bough, in order that men might learn the arts in the stern school of necessity. It arose from the barrenness of her soil, as her greatest historian observes, that Attica had always been exempt from the revolutions which in early times agitated the other countries of Greece, which poured over their frontiers the changeful floods of migratory populations, which disturbed the foundations of their national history, and confounded the civil institutions of the former occupants of the soil. Attica, secure in her sterility, boasted that *her* land had never been inundated by these tides of immigration. She had enjoyed a perpetual calm, she had experienced no such change; the race of her inhabitants had been ever the same; nor could she tell whence they had sprung; no foreign land had sent them; they had not forced their way within her confines by violent irruption. She traced the stream of her population in a backward course, through many generations, till at last it hid itself, like one of her own brooks, in the temporary recesses of her own soil."

As a practical comment upon this graceful summary of national belief, I would observe that the geographical evidences I have brought forward of the ancient birth-place of the splendid race of Attica, will now be amply confirmed by the same course of demonstration, a demonstration that will prove harmonious and complete in all its proportions; for it is based upon truth. One simple but ingenious Attic boast gives at once the key to the Autochthonous origin of the Athenians. They were, then, not AUTO-CHTHŌNS, "sprung from the same earth," but ATTAC-THĀNS, *i.e.* the people of "THE ATTAC-LAND."[1] Thus fades mythology, and the doctrine of mythopœic propensities, and the negation of an *historical basis* for fable, before the light of a positive geographical and historical fact! Again,—"The belief that her people was *indigenous*, she expressed in different ways. She intimated it in the figure which she assigned to Cecrops, the heroic prince and progenitor of her primæval inhabitants. She represented him as combining in his person a double character; while the higher parts of his body were those of a man and king, the serpentine folds in which it was terminated, declared his extraction from the earth. The cicada of gold which she braided in her hair, were intended to denote the same thing; they signified that the natives of Attica sprang from the soil upon which they sang, and which was believed to feed them with its deer. The attachment of the inhabitants of this country to their own land was cherished and strengthened by this creed; they gloried in being natives of the hills and plains which no one had ever occupied but themselves, and in which they had dwelt from a period of the remotest antiquity. Such, then, were some of the circumstances which gave to this small province the dignity and importance which it enjoyed amongst the nations of the world."[2]

The source of the *grasshopper* symbol of the children of Attica, is by the plain and very unpoetical aid of geography, as clearly developed, as that of their *autochthonous* origin. This ingenious people who compared themselves to TETTĪGES, or GRASSHOPPERS, could they have referred to the original cradle of their race, would have discovered that while the

[1] Solution:—

Greek	AUTO - CHTHŌN.		Sanscrit	ATTAC - THĀN.	
	THE SAME	LAND.		THE ATTAC	LAND.

[2] Wordsworth's Pict. Greece; "Attica."

northern section of their tribe dwelt on the ATTAC, adjoining the magnificent valley of Cashmir, with whose princes their tribe was connected by policy and domestic alliances, and whose lineage long ruled over the brilliant Athenians,[1] by far the greater part of that primitive community whose descendants raised the glory of the Attic flag above all the maritime powers of Hellas, dwelt in a position eminently befitting their subsequent naval renown. They were the "PEOPLE OF TATTA," or "TETTAIKES."[2]

Now, hold we the clue to the happy choice of their new settlements made by these sons of "HELA-DES," or the "LAND OF HELA."

Practised mariners, expert traders, with the mercantile resources of the sea-board line of Sinde, and Mekran on the west, the magnificent Indus by which they could ascend to the northern Attica, a position which would serve as a noble depot for overland traders, whose merchandise was again easily conveyed down the Indus to the seafaring Tettāikes, or people of Tatta—these energetic sons of commerce enjoyed all the advantages of the vast traffic resulting from the coasting voyages, towards the Persian gulf. To the east, the brilliant commercial establishments on the gulfs of Cutch and Cambay;[3] to the south, an almost interminable line of coast, dotted with the lucrative settlements of a thriving trade.

It is easy to perceive, that a voyage down this immense extent of coast was merely a subject of time—that Ceylon

[1] This I shall distinctly demonstrate in the sequel.

[2] Τεττῑγες, "Tattaikes," derivative form from "Tatta," signifying "The people of Tatta." In the sequel, I shall demonstrate the true origin of the term "Tatta," which ranges far beyond the foundation of this city, though it was of an antiquity so truly venerable.

[3] The Institutes of Menu, the Ramayuna, and the Mosaic accounts of the early magnificence of Egypt, all demonstrate the early splendour of this commercial people; for Egypt and India were of one race.

with this immaterial drawback, was as accessible as the Gulf of Cambay, and that even to double Cape Comorin, and ascend the eastern shores of India to the mouths of the Ganges, where a rich store of commercial imports again awaited their traffic, was simply a prolongation of their voyage.

Ample and easy means of obtaining supplies were everywhere presented along the Indian coasts; nor can we for a moment doubt that the intermediate traffic from town to town, was of the most lucrative nature. In fact, these people of the eastern coasts of India, as well as those of Poonah on the west, will be distinctly shown on that early chart of their wanderings, called "the Classical Atlas," on which the names of the varied Indian races and Scythic tribes are recorded, in characters as indelible as the rock inscriptions of Girnar.

But to return to the Tettaikes, or People of Tatta. "This city of Sinde," observes Thornton,[1] "is situated about three miles west of the right or western bank of the Indus, and four miles above the point where the western and eastern branches of the river separate. Its site is consequently close to *the vertex of the Delta of the Indus*. The town appears to have been formerly insulated by the water of the Indus, and it is still nearly so during the season of inundation. Dr. Burnes states that it was once thirty miles in circuit; judging, no doubt, from the vast space in the vicinity overspread by tombs and ruins. These extensive ruins are scattered from Peer Puttah, about ten miles south of Tatta, to Sami-Nuggur, three miles north-west of it. The ruins of the great fortress of Kulancote show it to have been constructed with much labour and skill, in a massive style of building. 'The vast cemetery of six square miles,' observes Kennedy, 'may not contain less than a million of tombs—a rude guess—

[1] Gaz. of Punjab, vol. ii., p. 266.

but the area would admit of four millions.' In these ruins, the masonry and carving, both in brick and stone, display great taste, skill, and industry. The bricks, especially are of the finest sort, nearly equalling porcelain. Kennedy observes, 'The finest chiselled stone could not surpass the sharpness of edge and angle, and accuracy of form.' What wonder, when they came from the hands of the men of ATTIC RACE! 'Tatta[1] viewed at some distance from the outside, presents a very striking and picturesque appearance, as its lofty houses rise over the numerous acacias and other trees everywhere interspersed, and which,' says Kennedy, 'formed altogether as fine a picture of city scenery as I remember to have seen in India.' Who in this picture does not call to mind the groves of Academus and the architectural magnificence of Hellenic Attica! I cannot refrain from quoting the beautiful language of Dr. Wordsworth, so singularly just, and so singularly the mirror of the parent city of Attica:—"Not at Athens alone," he observes, "are we to look for Athens. The epitaph,—*Here is the heart: the spirit is everywhere,*—may be applied to it. From the gates of its Acropolis, as from a mother city, issued intellectual colonies into every region of the world. These buildings, ruined as they are at present, have served for two thousand years as models for the most admired fabrics in every civilised country of the world. They live in them as their legitimate offspring. Thus the genius which conceived and executed these magnificent works, while the materials on which it laboured are dissolved, has itself proved immortal."[2] The classical

[1] Alexander Hamilton, who visited Tatta in 1699, calls it a very large and rich city, about three miles long, and one-and-a-half broad; and states that 80,000 persons had, within a short time previously, died of the plague, and that one half of the city was uninhabited. This would lead us to the conclusion, that previously to that calamity, the population was above

[2] Greece, Pictorial and Descriptive, p. 131.

scholar will now be enabled to test the value of that philology which derives the name of Attica from "Acte," the shore. The same test also he will be enabled to apply to the derivations of "Thessalos" and "Epirus," both of which will be found to rest upon a foundation equally insecure.

And here I would remove another classical prejudice which has stood undisturbed and unsuspected for very many centuries, occupying apparently the strong ground of the Historical *Olympiads*, which position, alas! is no guarantee for truth. Having displaced the Autochthons of Attica from their mythological position by the aid of Geography, I would throw the same searching light upon "Philippos" of Macedon. We must understand, then, that he was no PHIL-IPPOS, or "Lover of Horses," but the BHILI-POS, or BHIL-PRINCE. His son, Alexander, claimed descent from Hammon: he was correct; for, if the reader will examine the map of Afghanistan, he will find as practical a proof of the fact as he could desire, in "HAMMON" between lat. 30° 42′ and 31° 54′; and long. 61° 8′ and 62° 10′. And these same Bhils, that is, the Bhil-Brahmins planted this same Oracle of HAMMON in the deserts of Africa, whither I have already shown that they had sailed; where they founded "PHILAI," *i.e.*, BHILAI, the city of "THE BHILS," in lat. 24° north, long. 33° east.

Again: I greatly doubt, if now, after a search of two thousand five hundred years, the exact locality, residence, and lineage of that strange being, the Centaur, should be discovered, all classical students would not, with me, deeply regret the discovery, as destroying one of the most innocent and delightful amusements of the speculative mind. But

150,000. Tatta has been supposed to be the Pattala of the ancients. Pottinger states that the earliest mention he has found of it, is in the ninety-second year of the Hegira. Burnes says, "The antiquity of Tatta is unquestioned."—*Thornton, Gaz. Punjab,* vol. ii., p. 267.

the old adage of the might and prevalence of truth must be vindicated. Adjoining the Tettaikes, or the ATTICANS, both of Greece and India, is the small province of MEGARIS, which now figures near Currachee as MAGAR Talao, or the Alligators' Pool.[1] "Magar Talao, in Sinde, is a collection of hot springs, nine miles north-east of Kurrachee, and swarming with alligators. De la Hoste states that there are two hundred of these animals in a small space, not exceeding one hundred and twenty yards in diameter. Some of them are very large, and their appearance, basking in the sun, is not unlike a dry date tree. These thermal springs are situated amidst rocky and very barren hills; and spring out of the bottom of a small fertile valley, thickly wooded with date trees and acacias, over which the white dome of the shrine is visible.[2] The principal spring issues from the rock upon which the shrine is built, and has a temperature of about 98°, the water being perfectly clear, and of a sulphureous smell. Another spring about half-a-mile distant has a temperature of 130°."[3]

Again, the astonishing compactness of this primitive emigration is forcibly apparent. I think it can scarcely be doubted, that these combined maritime tribes of Sinde, and their north-western tribes of the Attac, embarked simultaneously in one of the most powerful fleets that ever was seen in those early days. Their course would be similar to that of their predecessors from the same point—and I would venture to suggest that possibly one of the same emigration might have colonised both Egypt and Greece, especially as the Dodanim are spoken of by Moses, as classed with other people of vast antiquity.[4] I will not, however, press this point; for the Dodas themselves, in their original settlements, were situated so far to

1 *Magar*, an alligator, and *Talao*, a pool (Sansc. form, "*Makar*").
2 The shrine of Magar Peer, or, "The Alligators' Saint."
3 Thornton, vol. ii., p. 31. 4 Genesis, x. 4.

the north, and so many of their cognate tribes and clans are to be seen hovering over Greece in high latitudes, that it is not improbable that this northerly section of Afghanistan may have sent forth its martial colonists over land—by which route, in fact, they could have encountered no opposition sufficient to break down their warlike force, nor to disturb their steady advance towards the west. The reader will now begin to comprehend, with increasing clearness, the meaning of that constant communication between Egypt and Attica and Bœotia—those frequent missions dispatched from the former country—particularly the religious propaganda (I know not how to choose a more appropriate term,—for such it undeniably was)—which unhappily sowed the dragon's teeth in Bœotia.[1] The reasons for sending an apparently Egyptian—but in reality an ATTIC, Prince to rule over Attica, in the person of Cecrops, will now be evident to the dispassionate inquirer after truth. These, and many more histories, have been vainly charged on Greek writers as the result of mythopœic propensities,—by men who, while they have shunned the means necessary for the recovery of history, have not scrupled to propound theories, that are absolutely as mythological as the mythologies they have condemned.

After the very astonishing manner in which the Sindian emigration has hitherto maintained its united form, a glance at the map of Greece would tell us where to look for the *original* settlements of the Corinthians—nor are we disappointed—for, immediately adjoining Magar Talao (the Megaris of Greece), we find the people of the COR'-INDUS (CORINTHUS), that is, that tract of coast stretching from the River Cori to the Indus, embracing the immediate vicinity of either river. The Cori, flowing into the south-eastern

[1] These causes and results—of vast moment in the ancient world—I shall, without any rationalising process, place in the category of history, when treating of the foundation of Thebes.

extremity of the sea-coast of Sinde, is an arm of the sea, supposed to have been formerly the estuary of the most eastern branch of the Indus, and still receiving part of its waters during high inundations. At Cotsair, twenty miles from the open sea, it is seven miles wide.[1] The sources of the Indus, the mighty artery of North-Western India, have been always difficult of access, from the vigilant jealousy of the Chinese, who rule Thibet, and who, as Thornton observes, have succeeded in excluding Europeans from that country. The inquiries of Moorcroft, Trebeck, and Gerard have established, beyond any reasonable ground of doubt, that the source of the longest and principal stream of the Indus is at the north of the KAILAS Mountain, which gave the term "KOILON," heaven, to the Greeks, and CŒLUM to the Romans; one of the practical influences of mythology which extended to the Saxons. Mount Kailas is regarded in the Hindoo mythology as the mansion of the gods and Siva's paradise, and is probably the highest mountain in the world, being estimated by Gerard to have a height of 30,000 feet.[2]

Hail, mountain of delight!
Palace of glory, blessed by Glory's king!
With prospering shade embower me, while I sing
Thy wonders, yet unreach'd by mortal flight!
Sky-piercing mountain! in thy bowers of love
No tears are seen, save where medicinal stalks
Weep drops balsamic o'er the silvered walks![3]

Such is a graceful illustration, of plain practical fact—of a geographical feature of stupendous magnitude, which gave rise to a mythologic fable, or to the appropriation of one already made. The basis is not only historical, but geographical; and yet, notwithstanding these facts, a

[1] The Corī mouth is in lat. 23° 30′, long. 68° 25′.

[2] Thornton, Gaz., vol. i., p. 264.

[3] Hymn to Indra, translated by Sir W. Jones.

mythologic superstructure of the most elaborate nature has been reared thereon; and while the towering Kylas, with its rivers and rocks, has by the Hindoo been generally unverified as a great physical fact, his imagination and his poetry have created an efficient substitute for the satisfaction of his faith. And thus it was with the native of Indus and of the rocky heights of the Hela, when he became a settler in the Hellas; and thus it was with his polished descendant in Athens, who, though called a Greek, was yet as thoroughly Sindian in his tastes, religion, and literature as any of his forefathers. And yet, who that considers the masculine vigour of the Hellenic mind,[1] and its political energies, would imagine that so constituted, it could place faith in untested fables—that the subtle genius of Themistocles, and the intellectual majesty of Pericles, would placidly hail traditions discarded by the historic mind as transparent fictions? Yet so it was! The same judgment that so profoundly harmonised with the severe grandeur of the Olympian Jove, enthroned by Pheidias amid the marshalled columns of the national temple, bowed to the legend of Aphrodite, the foam-born Queen of Love, and the genesis of monsters, endowed with godlike powers, but debased by monstrous passions. Strange as this anomaly may appear, it is reconcileable with the noble sincerity of the Hellenic attributes. Endowed with the most active sensibilities, the Greek sought to satisfy the ardent aspirations of his devotional yet warlike spirit; he yearned to be enrolled among the band of heroes whom their valour had exalted to the dazzling halls of Olympus. How deeply the grand reality of this reward was impressed upon the most powerful intellect, is shown by the awful apostrophe of Demosthenes to the heroes who fell at

[1] See my "Preliminary View of the Influence of Mythology over the Early Greeks," in the "Hist. of Greece," vol. xv. of Encyclopæd. Metropolit. 1851.

Marathon, and the breathless attention which then absorbed the very soul of the Athenian. There existed, however,—and let us beware of any crude theories to the contrary—there existed an *historical basis* for a *national mythology*[1]—but that mythology never arose from pure *invention*. It has ever been the Indo-Hellenic practice to disguise that historical basis—I do not say intentionally—by poetic imagery—by Bud'histic and Lamiac miracles;[2] miracles as wonderful as those claimed to be wrought by the Lamaism of the West—miracles, of which the history of "The Chief of the Clan Heri"[3] (who is Bud'ha) furnishes a complete series—whose best Commentary is to be found in the Mahawanso.[4] Be it our duty to decipher that which the Hellenes have obscured. We now hold the key. We know the starting point of their first emigration. We know the legends of their original country; those legends will yet be proved to be plain and direct histories, by the contrasted records of Greece, India, and Egypt; and, I may add, Persia and Assyria also; for these are of kindred race. By the adjusted accounts and by the monuments left by the three first, and by the interwoven histories of the two former, we may hope to evolve a statement of events more authentic than that connected with the first two centuries after the Olympiads, and I scruple not to say far more interesting—for these ancient annals contain the germs of the arts and the civilisation with which we are now everywhere surrounded.

Mount Kylas, the Paradise of the Hindoo, and the source

[1] Of this fact, I have incontrovertible evidence based upon a *substantial geography*.

[2] See more especially this history in connexion with Apollo.

[3] { Heri-cul-es.
{ Heri-tribes-chief.

[4] *Vide* Mahawanso, with an introductory essay on Pali Bud'histical Literature, by the Hon. George Turnour, Ceylon Civil Service. Ceylon, 1837.

of the chief stream of the Indus, is described by Moorcroft, who viewed it from a table land between 17,000 and 18,000 feet high, as a stupendous mountain, whose sides as well as craggy summits, are, apparently, thickly covered with snow.[1] "The Indus, near its source, bears the name of Sin-kha-bab, or Lion's mouth, from a superstitious belief that it flows from one. Within eight or ten miles of its source, it was found, at the end of July, to be two and a half feet deep, and eighty yards wide. The country through which the lofty feeders of the Indus flow, varies in elevation, from 15,000 to 18,000 feet. It is one of the most dreary regions in existence; the surface being for the most part formed by the disintegration of the adjacent mountains. It is swept over by the most furious winds, generally blowing from the north. These are at once piercingly cold, and parchingly dry, and no vegetation is visible but a few stunted shrubs, and some scanty and frost-withered herbage. It is, however, the proper soil for the production of shawl-wool, which is obtained from the yak, the goat, the sheep, certain animals of the deer kind, and even, it is said, from the horse and dog. Close above Attac, the Indus receives on the western side, the great river of Cabool, which drains the extensive basin of Cabool, the northern declivity of Sufeid Kob, the southern declivity of Hindoo Koosh, and Chitral, and the other extensive valleys which furrow this last great range on the south.

"The Cabool river appears to have nearly as much water as the Indus, and in one respect has an advantage over it, being navigable above forty miles above the confluence, while the upward navigation of the Indus is rendered impracticable by a very violent rapid, immediately above the junction. Both rivers have gold in their sands, in the

[1] The exact locality of the source of the Indus may be stated with much probability to be in lat. 31° 20′, long. 81° 15′.

vicinity of Attac."[1] It is CABOOL, at that time "GOPALA," of which the sacred historian speaks, under the form "Havilah, where there is gold," the river Pi-son, "Ba-sin" ("Aba-sin"), or the Indus "being that which compasseth the whole land of Havilah."[2] Nothing can be a more distinct narrative of the primitive cities and races of mankind, nor can anything be in greater harmony with the north-western dynasties of Asia, and the first settlements of Greece, than the account given by the venerable historian of the Jewish dispensation. Nothing can bear a higher testimony to the sacred writer than the extreme accuracy, as well as immense value to primitive history, of his inspired record, when duly read; and to this I shall have occasion to refer at a future period of my investigation.

"For about ten miles below the Attac, the Indus, though in general rolling between the high cliffs of slate rock, has a calm, deep, and rapid current; but for above a hundred miles farther down to Kala Bagh, it becomes an enormous torrent, whirling and rolling away huge boulders and ledges of rock, and between precipices, rising nearly perpendicularly several hundred feet from the water's edge. The water here is a dark lead colour, and hence the name Nilab, or blue river, given as well to the Indus as to a town on its banks, about twelve miles below Attock."[3]

We have already seen the Aboa-sin giving its name to Abu-sinia, in Africa, and we now observe the NIL-AB (that is the blue water), bestowing an appellation on the far-famed "NILE" of Egypt. Ample and overpowering evidences, however, as we progress in this investigation, will arise to prove the colonisation of Egypt from the coast of Sinde. Ward observes, "that the population of the banks of the Indus are almost amphibious. The boatmen of lower Scinde, for example, live like the Chinese in their boats.

[1] Thornton, Gaz. Punj., vol. i., p. 269. [2] Genes. ii. 2.
[3] Thornton, Gaz. Punj., "Indus."

The leisure time of every description of persons is spent on the water, or floating on it. Such familiarity with the water, naturally inclines the population to regard it as the great medium of commercial intercourse. In proceeding up the stream when the wind is unfavourable, as is generally the case during the half-year between the autumnal and vernal equinoxes, way must be made exclusively by tracking. During the other half-year, southerly winds prevail, and the boats run up under sail before it, except where the use of sails becomes dangerous from peculiar circumstances. The length of the navigable part of the river, from the sea to Attock, has been ascertained by measurement to be nine hundred and forty-two miles; that of the upper part is about seven hundred miles; making a total length, in round numbers, of one thousand, six hundred and fifty miles."[1]

Such is a description of the great river of the Indus and its border inhabitants at this day; and such, no doubt, judging by the steadfastness of the oriental type, both in language and custom, were the inhabitants on the banks of this celebrated stream from the most remote periods. Can we now, after surveying the primæval settlements of the Cor-Indi, and those people of the sea-board Attac, the Tattaikes, wonder at the happy choice of locality made by both these great mercantile people! We see that both came to their new country fraught with all the appetences and qualifications of a great commercial people; both made a most brilliant as well as judicious choice of their respective coasts and harbours, and both ran a noble career in the civilisation of their species. The early abundance of gold—the graceful fabrics of the loom, and the arts of embroidery—these and a host of similar peculiarities distinctive of oriental life, all are now satisfactorily accounted for, by the simple geographical evidence

[1] Thornton, Gaz. Punjab, vol. i., p. 282.

of the exact origin and locality of the classical Athenian and Corinthian. What can be more thoroughly Indian than Homer's description of the venerable Nestor's cup :—

> "Next, her white hand an antique goblet brings,
> A goblet sacred to the Pylean kings
> From oldest time; embossed with studs of gold,
> Two feet support it, and four handles hold:
> On each bright handle bending o'er the brink
> In sculptured gold, two turtles seem to drink."

The early civilisation then—the early arts—the indubitably early literature of India, are equally the civilisation, the arts and the literature of Egypt and of Greece—for geographical evidences, conjoined to historical fact, and religious practices, now prove beyond all dispute, that the two latter countries are the colonies of the former.[1]

The same tendencies which induced the maritime Athenian, Corinthian, and Megarian to select in Hellas positions so favourable to commerce, influenced the movements of the LES-POI (LES-BOI), or CHIEFS of LES, a province lying along the coast, a little to the north-west of the Gulf of Currachie. These sea-faring people took up their abode in the isle of LES-BOS.

To the south of Megaris and Corinth, the "SAR'WANICAS," or "People of Sarawan,"[2] had at one time formed an important settlement, as is evident from their name left as a legacy to the "SARONIC Gulf."

Sarawan is bounded on the north and west by Afghan-

[1] It is not a little amusing to test Greek history by Indian geography. Saron, we are told, was a king of Trœzene, unusually fond of hunting; he was drowned in the sea, where he had swum for some miles in pursuit of a stag: the part of the sea where he was drowned, was called the "Saronic Gulf!"

[2] Sarawan. The full form is "Sarawanica," derived from Sarawan. The short "a" is often merged (see Appendix, Rule i.), and the Sanscrit "w" or "v" is rendered by the Greek "ω" or "o" (*vide* Append. Rule xvi.).

istan; on the east by Afghanistan and Cutch Gundava; and on the south by Jhalawan, Kelat, and Mekran.[1] Sarawan is about two hundred and fifty miles in length from north-east to south-west, eighty miles in its greatest breadth, and has a surface of about 15,000 square miles. It is in general a very mountainous, elevated, and rugged tract. On the west is the lofty range, called the Sarawanee Mountains. There are, however, some level and productive tracts. The valley of Shawl "in the north is fertile, well watered, well cultivated, and has a fine climate, though rather sharp in winter. It produces in abundance grain, pulse, madder, tobacco, and excellent fruits."[2] To the north of Sarawan and Shawl, lies the river ARGHASAN, which gave its name to the province of ARGOS. The Arghasan rises in the western declivity of the Amran Mountains, and flows westward to its confluence with the Turnak.[3] "It is a rapid transient torrent, seldom retaining any depth of water for more than two or three days, and leaving its bed dry for the greater part of the year. It was found totally devoid of water when the British army marched across it, in 1839."[4] I cannot think but that either this district was once far more important than at present, or that the river now called Agund-ab formerly bore the name of Arghas. Be this as it may, certain it is that those who lived in the district of Arghas[5] were called ARGH-WALAS (ARG-OLIS),[6] or inhabitants of Arghas. And here I would casually remark, that the observant orientalist will, as this investigation proceeds, derive, through the sound basis of geography, as mirrored forth both from

[1] Between lat. 27° 53′ and 30° 20′, long. 64° and 67° 40′.

[2] Thornton, Gaz. Punjab, vol. ii. p. 160.

[3] Lat. 31° 31′, long. 65° 30′.

[4] Thornton, vol. i. p. 58.

[5] Arghasan is evidently the Persian plural of Arghas.

[6] *Wala* (in composition), a keeper, inhabitant, man, &c.; as *Doodh-wala*, milk-man; *Naw-wala*, boat-man; *Dilli-wala*, inhabitant of Dilli.

the Classical and Oriental side, facts most interesting to the philological student of the earliest dialects of India; nor, I trust, will this unfolding of a primitive phonetic system be without its advantages to the scholar in his attempts to decipher the ancient inscriptions of India and her earlier colonies. Certain it is, that he will be not a little surprised to find the Sanscrit of Western India, after its collocation in Egypt, through the Sindian settlers, still copiously existing in Herodotus in the names of persons and places, as well as in the offices, and the graduated ranks of Egyptian society. The singularly sharp and clipping style in which Sanscrit terms were reproduced in Greek, has effectually barred all suspicion of their real origin—and they require a course of systematic re-adjustment as methodical as an hieroglyphic investigation. In this respect, the Latin language is a much more faithful record of the names of oriental tribes, rivers, and countries, than the Greek of Herodotus, or his predecessors.

To the north of the Argh-walas (Argolis) will be found the now comparatively insignificant village of Akkehu, the record of a tribe and distinct race of far more importance than at the present day. The proper derivative form to express "the people of AKKEHU" is "AKKAIHU." There is no difficulty in finding them on the Corinthian Gulf as "ACHAIA."[1] A tribe of the Logurhs (whose district lies somewhat to the south-west of Akkehu, and whom we have already described,) settled down in Greece in a distinct and separate body. Their new habitation was on the Crissæan Bay, and the land bounded by the north-eastern shores of the Corinthian Gulf. They offer a striking proof of the durability of the habits and practices of Eastern tribes. These "LOCRI OZOLŒ" are

[1] Akkehu, a village in the north of Afghanistan, lat. 36° 50′, long. 66° 7′.

"LOGURHI OOKSH-WALŒ," *i.e.*, "The Logurh settlers on the Oxus." This is an exemplification of what has frequently occurred in the history of a people of tribes. Some violent disruption among the leading members of the clan;—some confused union with another sept, and the best friends have become the most inveterate foes;—and this was as often the case with the Afghan settlers in Scotland, and with their descendants down to a comparatively recent period.[1]

[1] The Scotch Clans — their original localities and their chiefs in Afghanistan and Scotland, are subjects of the deepest interest. How little did the Scotch officers who perished in the Afghan campaign think that they were opposed by the same tribes from whom they themselves sprang! A work on this subject is in progress.

VIII.

THE NORTHERN TRIBES.

"Je sais bien qu'il existe toujours contre cette histoire une motive de défiance, parce qu'elle ne possède aucune garantie de sa véracité fournie par nos écrivains d'occident. Étrange condition de l'Inde! Tout indique qu'elle a été riche, et par conséquent civilisée, de bonne heure. De temps immémorials, les sages, les marchands, et les conquérants ont dirigés leurs pas vers cette contrée qui remuait tant de passions diverses, ils en ont rapportés, les uns des systèmes de philosophie, les autres de riches trésors, et les derniers quelques lauriers, achetés chèrement. Aucun d'eux n'est deigné nous transmettre des détails authentiques sur un pays dont ils convoitaient la sagesse, et l'opulence."

LANGLOIS, *Pref. to Harivansa.*

WE have now seen in the Indian tribes of the LOGURH, the ATTAC, the BAIHOOT, MAGAR, COR-INDUS, ARGHWALAS, SARAWAN, LES-POI, AKKAIHU, LOGURH-OOKSH-WALŒ—the parent states of the LOCRI, ATTICA, BŒOTIA, MEGARIS, CORINTHUS, ARGOLIS, settlers on the SARONIC, LESBOI, ACHAIANS, and LOCRI-OZOLŒ. I shall now proceed to fill up in some slight degree this general outline of a great historico-geographic fact. At the same time, it must be borne in mind as a principle, that we by no means get the true original orthography of the names of places which occur at this day in Afghanistan; for disguised under modern forms, the old Hindoo names in many cases, still subsist, as I shall shortly show, and this principle applies both to Greece and Persia; still, they are not unfrequently so distinctly noted, as to present to the acute observer, historical facts of great importance.

TAULANTII, BULLINI, CHAONIA.

With this group situated in North Western Epirus, I propose to continue the examination of the political element which constituted primitive Hellas. The convictions arising from these, and other apparently detached members of the Grecian aggregate, will be found even more powerful than those produced by the larger masses whom we have accompanied to the second land of the HELAS.

"BULLINI"[1] is the Greek form of writing "BOLANI," or "The People of the BOLAN." The Bolan pass is situated in Beloochistan, on the great route from Northern Sinde, by Shikarpoor and Dadur, to Kandahar and Ghuznee. "It is not so much a pass over a lofty range, as a continuous succession of ravines and gorges, commencing near Dadur, and first winding among the subordinate ridges, stretching eastward from the Hala chain of mountains, the brow of which it finally cross-cuts, and thus gives access from the vast plains of Hindostan, to the elevated and uneven tract, extending from the Hindoo Koosh to the vicinity of the Indian Ocean. Its commencement on the eastern side, from the plain of Cutch Gundava, is about five miles north-west of Dadur;[2] the elevation of the entrance being about eight hundred feet above the level of the sea. The valley through which the road runs, is here about half a mile wide; the enclosing hills, five hundred or six hundred feet high, consist of coarse conglomerate. The road ascends along the course of a river, called among the mountains the Bolan, or Kouhee. The river in this part of the pass, varies in depth from a few inches to about two feet, and in the first five miles of the road is crossed eight times. At Kundye, or as it is sometimes called, Kondilan, six miles from the entrance, the pass again

[1] See Append. Rule xviii.

[2] Lat. 29° 30′, long. 67° 40.

expands into a small oval valley, six hundred yards by four hundred, with a hard surface of stones and pebbles. This, in time of heavy rains, becomes a lake, and then, as Outram observes, the steepness of the enclosing hills would preclude the possibility of escape, to an army caught in the torrent. At Beebee Nanee, a road strikes off due west, to Rod Bahar and Kelat, while the principal road continues its north-westerly course, towards Shawl and Kandahar. Here the serious difficulties of the pass commence, from the increased roughness and acclivity of the ground, and from its being commanded from various parts of the impending cliffs. From Siri-Bolan to the top of the pass, the route takes a westerly course, and for a distance of ten miles, is totally without water. The last three miles of this distance, is the most dangerous part of the pass, the road varying from forty to sixty feet, and flanked on each side by high perpendicular hills, which can only be ascended at either end. The elevation of the crest of the pass, is 5793 feet. The total length is between fifty-four and fifty-five miles; the average ascent ninety feet in the mile. The Bengal column, in 1839, spent six days in marching through the pass, entering it on the sixteenth, and leaving it on the twenty-first of March. Its artillery, including eight-inch mortars, twenty-four pounder howitzers, and eighteen pounder guns, were conveyed without any serious difficulty. The Bolan Pass, though very important in a military point of view, as forming the great communication between Scinde and Khorasan, is inferior in commercial interest to the Gomul, farther north."[1] They were the chiefs of this rugged ground that took up their abode in a district in Greece, very similar to the country just described.

[1] Thornton, Punjab, vol. i. p. 112. The western extremity and highest point of the Bolan Pass, is in lat. 29° 52′, long. 67° 4′.

The TALAN, or people of Tal,[1] as the reader will observe, lie a little to the north-west of the Bullini; they are the inhabitants of the TALĀN-DES.[2]

Tal, or Tull, is a "small town in Afghanistan in the desert of Sewestan, on the route from Dera Ghazee Khan to Dadur."[3] The modern district of Sewestan is a corrupt form of Siva-Stan, or Land of Siva; still more clearly proved by the adjoining Pisheen, another corruption for Bheeshan ("Siva"). The rugged land of CHAONIA, in Greece, had its representative in Afghanistan as "KAHUN." Kahun lies a little to the south-west of the Bolan Pass. We have then, singularly enough, the two groups, TAULANTII, (TALAN) BOOLUNI, (BOLAN) KHAONIA (KAHUN)—in both Greece and Afghanistan, relatively situated. It would seem from this, that the ties of mountain clanship, and mountain neighbourhood were of unusual strength. "Kahun in Afghanistan is a fort and town among the mountains, inhabited by the Murrees Beloochees, and extending from the southern extremity of the Suliman Range to that of the Hala. It is situate in an extensive valley or rather plain, fifteen miles long and six broad. The air is very pure, and the heat less than in the plains of Sewestan or Sinde."[4] If the Taulantii, the Bullini and Chaónia, in Greece, are the reflections of the Talan, Bolani, and Cahun in Afghanistan, not the less singular is the transfer of the mountains of "KHERAN," the "KERAUN"-ii Montes of Chaonia. These the classical reader will recollect, were those unfortunate mountains, that, being so often smitten with "Keraunos," or "Thunder," were hence, we are told, called the "Keraunii

[1] Generally spelt Tull.

[2] Written by the Greeks, TAULAN-TOS, and TAULAN-TII.

[3] Tull is in lat. 30° 5′, long. 69° 4′. Thornton, vol. ii. p. 276.

[4] Thornton, Gaz. Punjab, vol. i. p. 328.

Montes," or Thunder Mountains!! Kheran, or Kharan, is the "capital of a small district of the same name, bounded on the east by Jhalawan, on the west by Punjgoor. It is in general arid and barren, yielding a little wheat and barley, but not sufficient for the support of the inhabitants."[1] Kharan, the capital is situated close to that range of mountains now called Wushuttee, which forms, as it were, the very counterpart of the Keraunian hills, and which are essentially the mountains of Kheraun, or the "Keraunii Montes."

To the east of Chaonia, or the people of Cahŏn, lay tribes who had not sprung from the Sindian provinces; they are the ATINTANES, the Greek mode of writing "A-SINDANĔS," *i.e.* Non-Sindians.

I would now direct the reader's attention to the most salient feature in the land of Hellas. The mountain chain of PINDUS, traversing a considerable portion of Greece, about midway between the Ægæan and Ionian Seas, and forming the boundary between Thessaly and Epirus, takes its name from the PIND.[2] Pind Dadun, situated a short distance south of that mountain chain, which rising boldly from the right bank of the Jailum, stretches far into Afghanistan, seems, from the distinct manner in which its connecting features are reproduced in Hellas, to have given its original name to the present "Salt Range," whence the "Pind," or "Salt Range" of Afghanistan was naturally transferred to a corresponding remarkable feature in Greece. It is not a little remarkable that, in the latter country, the true Pindus, where, about the thirty-ninth degree of latitude, it sends forth the lateral chain of mountain, Othrys, forming the southern boundary of Thessaly,—should give nearly the corresponding length

[1] Thornton, Gaz. Punjab, vol. i. pp. 379, 380.

[2] The present name is Pind Dadun Khan.

of the Pind in Afghanistan, viz., a distance of about sixty miles. The Pind, now the Salt Range, is an "extensive group of mountains, stretching generally in lat. 32° 30′—33° 30′, in a direction from east to west, from the eastern base of the Suliman mountains in Afghanistan to the river Jailum, in the Punjab.

This range is, in different parts, known to the natives under various denominations; but it is by Europeans comprehended under the general term, "Salt Range," in consequence of the great extent and thickness of the beds of common salt, which it contains in many places. The general direction of the range is from north-west to south-east. The salt is granular, the concretions being very large and compact; so that platters and other utensils are made out of it, and take a high polish. Most of the torrents of the Salt Range carry down gold dust in their sands, which are washed in search of the precious deposit, in numerous places, throughout the greater part of the year. Dr. Jamieson expatiates, with the earnestness of sanguine excitement, on the mineral wealth of the Salt Range, concluding in these terms:—"Such is a rapid account of the riches of this district, and there are few, if any districts in the world, where iron, gold, sulphur, salt, gypsum, limestone, and saltpetre are met with in such quantity."[1] Along a range of heights, to the west of the Pindus, and for the greater distance running parallel with it, dwelt the people called the "Athamanes," a very ancient race, whose habits in many respects seem to have approximated to the North American tribes, (who, in fact, are of the same stock with the ancient Hellenes,) particularly in assigning to their females the active labours of husbandry.[2] These were the people of the Afghan district,

[1] Thornton, Gaz. Punjab, vol. ii. p. 168.

[2] Heracl. Pont. Frag., Cramer's Greece, vol. ii. p. 95.

called "The Daman," or "The Border," and so called because it stretches between the Suliman mountains and the Indus. "The DAMAN," of which the Greeks, with their ordinary euphonic affix, made A'Daman,[1] and the country Adamania, (Athamania) thus exactly corresponds, by its mountain range of Acanthius, to the people of the "Daman," who are situated between the Suffeid Koh—corresponding to the Acanthius, and the Indus corresponding to the Achelous—both DAMANIA in Afghanistan, and ATHAMANIA in Greece running nearly north and south.[2] The people of "TALLAR," in the "Daman," have kept close company with their original neighbours; for, grouped along the western slopes of Mount Pindus, in the immediate neighbourhood of the Damanians (Athamanians), they are to be seen under the name of the "TALARES."

The "AC-HELOUS,"[3] or HELA'S-WATER, the largest river in Greece, and so named from the Hela mountains in Sinde, traverses the whole country from north to south, like the Indus in the Punjaub. To the east of the Ac-Helous, the Hela's-water, or the Hellenic Indus, is another considerable river, the ARAC-THUS, *i. e.*, the "River of the ARAC-LAND."[4] The Arac is a pass on the most north-easterly of the four routes which, diverging from

[1] *Vide* Append., Rule xvii., xviii.

[2] The Daman, where not under the influence of irrigation, in general presents the appearance of a plain of smooth hard clay, bare of grass, but sprinkled with dwarfish bushes, tamarisks, and occasionally trees of a larger size, but seldom exceeding the height of twenty feet, either the soil or the climate being unfavourable to their further growth. The Daman is two hundred and twenty miles long from the "Kala," or the Salt Range, on the north, to the confines of Scinde on the south, and has an average breadth of about sixty miles. Lat. 30° 33′, long. 70° 71′.

[3] *Aca*, water; *Helavas*, the people of the Hela mountains. The form "Helavas" becomes Helawas—Helous. (*See* Append., Rule xvi.)

[4] *Arac-* and *des*, land; "thus, tus, tis, dus," are the Greek forms for *des*. (*Vide* Appendix, Rule xxii.)

the valley of Siah Sung, debouch into that of Bamian.[1] Our geographical evidences are now rapidly strengthening every step we take. There is a remarkable point in Greece, where four mountain ranges converge. The Cambunian, Pindus, Tympha, and Lacmon. The latter glows like a gem, throwing its light on the noble bosom of Hellas. Behold in Mount LACMON, the LUGHMAN[2] of Afghanistan! To this central point run the Pindus and the Athamanian mountains in Greece, the Pind and the Daman mountains in Afghanistan—now blending with Lacmon, Mount KERKETIUS runs nearly north and south, while advancing north to Lughman, Mount KERKETCHA rivets this powerful geographical evidence. The Kerketcha range connects the Hindoo-Koosh with the Suffeid Koh, and separates the valley of Cabool from the plain of Jelalabad. At its highest point, it has an elevation of eight thousand feet. It is, in general, very rugged and rocky, but where there is any soil, it is covered with large and flourishing timber.

Mount Kerketius, in Hellas, the representative of the Kerketcha range in Afghanistan recals to the heart of an Englishman recollections as melancholy as the memory

[1] These passes are the lines of communication between the valley of Cabool and Cunduz, and lie over that range which connects the south-western extremity of Hindoo-Koosh with the Koh-i Baba mountain further south. It is the highest of the four passes, and has an altitude above the sea of 12,909 feet. Lat. 34° 40′, long. 68° 5′.—THORNTON'S *Punjab*, vol. ii. p. 180.

[2] "Lughman in Afghanistan, a district north of Jelalabad, and bounded on the north by Hindoo-Koosh, on the east by the river of Kama, on the south by the river of Kabool, and on the west by the river Alishang. It forms part of the province of Jelalabad, and thither the ruthless Mahomed Akbar Khan conveyed the British prisoners reserved from the massacre of Khoord Kabool. It is forty miles long, thirty miles broad, and, though having a rugged surface, is fertile, well watered and populous. It lies between lat. 34° 25′—35°, long. 70°—70° 40′."—THORNTON'S *Punjab*, vol. ii. p. 26.

of Napier and the banks of the Sind are glorious. It was in the Kerketcha range, in the route from Tezeen to Jugduluk, that the treacherous slaughter of the whole British force, amounting to 3,909 regular troops, was effected by the subtle craft of a barbarous foe, aided by the unexampled rigours of the severest winter. Alas! how different from the military splendour and the ardent valour of the host that won the battlements of Ghuznee !

> "When they were young and proud,
> Banners on high, and battles passed below,
> But they who fought are in a bloody shroud,
> And those who warred are shroudless dust ere now,
> And the bleak battlements shall bear no future blow."
>
> CHILDE HAROLD.

The province of Thessaly, as being the mirror of a portion of Afghanistan and the Punjab, gives rise to feelings of the most chequered interest, forming, as it does, the record of our greatest triumphs and our greatest disasters. It was the Macedonian hero who invaded and vanquished the land of his forefathers unwittingly. It was a Napier, who, leading on the small, but mighty army of civilised Britain, drove into headlong flight the hosts of those warlike clans from whose parent stock himself and not a few of his troops were the direct descendants. Thus, twice has the army of civilisation signalised in Afghanistan and the Punjab its victory over the army of barbarism.

Mount Lacmon—the Lughman of Afghanistan, gave its name to that great river which disembogues itself into the Thermaic Gulf; it is called "HA-LIACMON,"[1] *i.e.* "the Lacmon," which pervades the eastern section of the "ELUMIOTIS,"[2] or the new "LAND OF THE y ELUM." Another stream also rising in Mount Titarus, to the east of Mount Kerketius, receives its name from that remark-

[1] *Ho Lughman*, "the Lacmon."
[2] *Elumyo*, Elumean; *des*, land.

able Pass called "the Tatara," which, leaving the route through the Khyber Pass, a little east of Jamrood, takes a circuit to the north and rejoins it at Duka, its western termination.[1]

We have then, ranging both in Greece and Afghanistan, from east to west, the following salient corresponding features:—The DAMAN and ATHAMAN chain, blending into LACMON and LUGHMAN; the PINDUS and PIND, running towards the same point; then the KERKETIUS and KERKETCHA; and still more towards the east, the TITARUS and the TATARA, while the Cama mountain Sierra, ranging to the north west from the neighbourhood of LUGHMAN or LACMON gave its name, "the CAMA-LAND, or CAM-BUNI" [2] to the CAMBUNIAN mountains. One more point of identity I would add, namely, that the HESTIŎ-TIS, or the LAND OF THE EIGHT CITIES, and the HESHT[3] NUGGUR, or EIGHT CITIES, are both respectively situated in the neighbourhood of Lughman and Lacmon, and complete the strong, connected and irrefragable chain of evidence of the Singetic colonisation, and the more minute our examination of these early settlements, the more harmoniously do we find the component arrangement of the whole. This truth is clear, that while the torrent of invasion has swept over the

[1] The Tatara Pass, in Afghanistan, through the Khyber mountains, between Jelalabad, is north of the Khyber Pass. It is very difficult, being scarcely practicable for cavalry, yet of great importance, as, if left undefended, it affords a means of turning the Khyber Pass. The Tatara Pass is in lat. 30° 10′, long. 71° 20′.

[2] The *Cama* and *Būma* (properly *Bhumi*) the earth, land, or region. The Persian derivative form is *Būm,* a country or region. The letters "m" and "n" constantly interchange. The Cama River takes its name from the district through which it passes; it rises in the valley of Chitral, in the Hindoo-Koosh, and flowing south-west, traverses Kaffiristan, whence it proceeds in a south-westerly direction into Lughman, a province of Afghanistan, and falls into the Cabool River at its northern side, in lat. 34° 24′ N., long. 70° 35′ E.—THORNTON'S *Punjab,* Kama.

[3] *Hesht,* eight; *des,* land.

plains and pastures of the world, carrying with it the men, the cities, and the names; the mountain homes of our race throughout the habitable globe have virtually not only preserved that mountain race itself, but its name and its lineage. As though gifted by nature with a chartered and imperishable title, it still holds forth to the sagacious mind a true and venerable document for historical training. Egypt, Palestine, and Greece, in triple harmony proclaim this truth.

HAZARA[1] is a commercial town in the Punjab, which is situate on the route from Lahore to Attock.

It is comparatively in the vicinity of LUGHMAN and KERKETCHA, and still nearer to the TATARA Pass. The reader will now observe the emigrants from that city settled upon a branch of the river TITARES-ius. Their city bears the Greek form "AZOROS;"—the same mountain tribes founded "HAZOR," in Palestine; and there their cities, their lineage, and their worship are still more distinct than in Hellas. I shall endeavour to include them in my sketch, for such it must necessarily be; seeing that the geography, antiquities, and authorities are trebled on each point of investigation. It has been already remarked that the existing nomenclature of Afghanistan, although wonderfully preserved, like that of Hellas, is still the subject of the same corrupt orthography, which early affected the true record of Greece. Thus we have seen "Sivastan" figure as "Sewestan," and "Bhishan" as "Pisheen"—for which the Afghans of the present day, like the Greeks of old, would be ready to render a plausible derivation,—in fact, nothing can be a stronger case in point, or afford a stricter analogy of thought and form of expression, than the origin they give of the name "Afghan." It is identical with the frivolous style of derivation that characterised their Hellenic descendants.

[1] Lat. 33° 50′, long. 72° 45′.

This will be noticed in its proper place, when the true explanation will be found to yield an historical fact of great value, and an etymological truth of much interest to the Orientalist.

I come now to one of the strongest evidences of mythology—mythology first Indian, then Greek. That evidence carries up both mythology and its historical basis to an extraordinary antiquity, being coeval with the naming of the very mountains of Hellas, and with its first towns. Both Kerketius, in Greece, and Kerketcha, in Afghanistan, Lughman in Afghanistan, and Lacmon in Greece; —and Gonoussa, Gomphi, and Perrhæbia in the former are evidences of this; and the Orientalist will, perhaps, be somewhat surprised to find the god-ships of the East fixed at an antiquity so great. On the chain of Pindus, nearly central, and in "LINGUS[1]-MONS," he will read the "LANCAS," the same as the LUNCES-TIS of the North."[2] Not far off, a little to the east is seen in KARKETIUS, Siva's son, KARTIKEYU,[3]—an euphonic change with which the Greek is very familiar. That my translation is correct will shortly be corroborated. The Vahan or Vehicle of Kartikeyu is the "Peacock," or "BERHI;" hence this, the Hindoo god of war, and leader of the celestial armies, is called "Berhinabahan," or "the Peacock-mounted," being painted as riding upon that bird—his name is also "Ganga," as born from the Ganges. The regular derivative form of Berhi is "BERHAI;" and "BERHAIPÆ" is the "PEACOCK-CHIEFS," and Berhaipia (PERRHAIBIA),

[1] I have taken the crude form, as being identical with the Greek mountain.

[2] It is quite time to lay bare the foundation of the Greek temple of thought, when we find Greek Lexica of undoubted merit, following implicitly the etymologists of Greece. To these, however, there are some admirable exceptions. (*See* the excellent New Cratylus of the Rev. J. W. Donaldson.)

[3] Generally Kartikiya; sometimes Kartika.

the "land of the WAR PEACOCKS." Hence, the warrior title of Perhaibia and Perhaibiæ Saltus in the neighbourhood of Mount Kerketius, as also on Mount Pindus. The prince of these "Perrhaibians," Müller observes,[1] "was called Guneus."

The Greek term GUNEUS,—the title of this military chieftain of the Thessalians, is a corruption of the Sanscrit name "GANGYUS," the designation of the Hindoo god of war. GONNUS was likewise a Perrhaibæan town, so called from Gongyus, and signifying Gonga's town. We have thus the appropriate name of the Hindoo god of war, given to a Hindoo military chief, and to a town, the residence of a Hindoo military clan. On the derivation of "Gomphoï," Müller remarks,—"It is indeed probable that the name Gomphoi (Γόμφοι) expresses the *wedge-shaped* form of these rocks." Now here is precisely an instance of the peril incurred by attempting to account for an *Indian* name by a *Greek* vocable; for when these warriors of the Peacock, or war tribe of India, gave this name, their language was not Greek, but a modified Sanscrit. How stands the case then? We have seen that "Gonnus" and "Guneus," are "Gongus" and "Gangyus," "Gonga's-chief" and "Gonga-ton." GOMPHOI, is "GONG-BHAI,"[2] or the "Gonga clan, or war-clan."[3]

A singular and most perfect relique of ancient days proves the truth of the foregoing observations. If the reader will direct his glance towards the southern base of Mount Titarus, on the map of Greece, he will see at the junction of the two northern sources of the river Titarus, the city of

[1] Müller's Dor., vol. i. p. 29.

[2] *Bhai*, properly "a brother," is a term used among the warlike Rajpoots to denote the *Bhayaud*, or "brotherhood," the military clans which hold their respective villages by a purely feudal tenure.

[3] The "ng" in "Gangus" was easily nasalised by the Greeks as "Gān-us" or "Gonnus."

"PERRHAIBIA OR OLOOSON." He will bear in mind that "Titarus," both river and mountain in *Greece*, take a name from the "Tatarus" mountain pass of *Afghanistan*—"There the name OOLOOS," observes Elphinstone,[1] "is applied to a whole tribe, or to an independent branch. The word seems to mean a clannish commonwealth. An Ooloos is divided into several branches, each under its own chief, who is subordinate to the chief of the Ooloos. During civil wars in the nation, the unsuccessful candidate for the command of an Ooloos joins the pretender to the throne, and is brought into power on the success of his party." This, then, is the Olooson (Ooloosān)[2]—the Perrhaibæan clan of warriors. Perrhaibæans, at once mythological and historical, Trojan and ante-Trojan, Greek[3] and Afghan.

"The peacock," observes Colonel Tod, "was a favourite armorial emblem of the Rajpoot warrior; it is the bird sacred to their Mars (Kumara), as it was to Juno his mother, in the west. The feather of the peacock decorates the turban of the Rajpoot, and the warrior of the Crusade, adopted from the Hindu through the Saraceu."[4] Then with a noble burst of feeling, he goes on to say, "Let us recollect who are the guardians of these fanes of Bál, his peepul[5] and sacred bird (the peacock); the children of Soorya and Chandra,[6] and the descendants of sages of yore; they who fill the ranks of our army, and are attentive, though silent observers of all our actions; the most

[1] Account of the Kingdom of Cabul, vol. i. p. 211.

[2] Persian plural of Ooloos.

[3] Ὄρθην, Ἠλώνην τε, πόλιν τ᾽ Ὀλοοσσόνα λευκήν.—HOM. *Il.* ii. 736.

[4] "Le Paon a toujours été l'emblême de la noblesse. Plusieurs chevaliers ornaient leurs casques des plumes de cet oiseau; un grand nombre de familles nobles le portaient dans leurs blazons ou sur leurs cimiers; quelques-uns n'en portaient que la queue."—*Art.* "*Armoire*," *Dict. de l'Ancien Régime.*

[5] Ficus Religiosa.

[6] The Sun and Moon (tribes).

attached, the most faithful, and the most obedient of mankind.

"The martial Rajpoots are not strangers to armorial bearings, now so indiscriminately used in Europe. The great banner of Méwar exhibits a golden sun on a crimson field, those of the chiefs bear a dagger. Ambér displays the *Panchranga*, or five-coloured flag. The lion rampant on an argent field, is extinct with the state of Chanderi. In Europe, these customs were not introduced till the period of the Crusades, and were copied from the Saracens, while the use of them among the Rajpoot tribes can be traced to a period anterior to the war of Troy. Every royal house has its palladium, which is frequently borne to battle at the saddle-bow of the prince. The late celebrated Kheechee leader, Jey Sing, never took the field without the god before him. 'Victory to Bujrung,' was his signal for the charge, so dreaded by the Mahratta, and often has the deity been sprinkled with his blood and that of the foe. Their ancestors, who opposed Alexander, did the same, and carried the image of Hercules (Baldeva,) at the head of their array."[1] Such, too, were the Berrhaibians, or "chiefs of the Peacock war-clans" of the Helas, the Perrhæbians of the Greeks. Again, both Lacmon and Lughman are corrupt forms of Lacshman. Lacshman was the half brother and faithful companion of Ramachandra,[2] and the settlement of the tribe that takes its name from his son is distinctly seen in the mountains CANA-LOVII, "GANA[3]-LŎVA," or the "TRIBE OF LŎVA;" they settled in "LUNCESTIS," LANCA'S LAND.[4]

[1] Tod's Rajasth., vol. i. p. 138.

[2] Wilson's Sans. Lex., *s. v.*

[3] *Gana*, a tribe.

[4] *Lances-des*, Lanca's land. Lanca is commonly translated "Ceylon," but there is no doubt that Lanca is the proper name for that north-western country of India, immediately in the vicinity of Cashmir, as I shall demonstrate in my "History of Rome."

With the north-western part of Macedonia we fall in with Tartarian latitudes, and a Tartarian people; they are the Bottiæans and the Briges; properly the "Boutias and the Birgoos," both lying to the east of Cashmir; while the Emathian range is the representative of a part of "Emadus," or "Himalaya." The "Birgoo" of the present day is situated close to the south-eastern frontiers of the province of Spiti.[1] As a proof of the connection between the Birgoos (Briges) and the "Gana Lova" (Cana Lovii), "tribe of Lova," both political, dynastic, and geographical, I would quote the excellent authority of Colonel Tod, who, speaking of the Birgoo-jeer, (the Birgoo,) one of the royal Rajpoot tribes, observes, that the "Race was Sooryavansi, and the *only one*, with the exception of the Gehtote, which claims from *Lova*, the elder son of *Rama*; and, for the presence of fourteen tribes of Rama,[2] the great sovereign of Oude, whose family clan is in full force in Greece, I refer the reader to a most singular specimen of Greek orthography, inscribed on Mount Oita, or 'the mountains of Oude;'[3] viz., 'CALL-ID-ROMOS,' which being interpreted first into Sanscrit, and next into English, will stand thus, 'CUL-AIT-RAMAS,' 'TRIBE OF OUDE RAMAS.'" I should here remark, that the Ramas were Sooryavansi, or of the Sun tribes; their mythology, history, language, and worship, with one arm reached to Rome, with the other to Peru.

I must now return to the consideration of the province of "THES-SALIA," a Greek euphonism for DES-SHALIA, or the "LAND OF SHAL," Shāl, for the convenience of pronunciation spelt Shawl. This is an elevated valley or table land, bounded on the east by the Kurklekkee mountains

[1] About lat. 32° N., long. 78° 40′ E.

[2] See the fourteen tribes of the Oitæ (people of Oude), in Müller's "Map of Greece."

[3] "Oita" is the common Greek geographical form of "Oude," *passim*.

overhanging the Bolan Pass, and on the west by the heights connected with Chehel Tan. "The soil is generally fertile, being a rich black loam, yielding wheat, barley, rice, lucerne, and similar vegetation suited for fodder, besides madder, tobacco, and esculent vegetables. The wildest parts of the enclosing mountains are the haunts of wild sheep and goats; the more aceessible tracts yield ample pastures to the herds and flocks of the mountains. Orchards are numerous, and produce in great perfection and abundance, apples, pears, plums, peaches, apricots, grapes, mulberries, pomegranates, quinces, and figs."[1] It is thus apparent, that the same fertility that characterised the Hellenic Thes-Salia, was the boast of its predecessor in Afghanistan. The chief town of this rich province of Greece, so famed for its cavalry, was the "CITY OF SĀL," "PUR[2]-SAL," strangely written by the Greeks PHAR-SAL-OS. I have little doubt but that the proper name both for the Afghan and Greek province now noticed, was "Shali;" and that it was so named from "shali," rice in general, but especially of two classes, the one like white rice growing in deep water, and the other a red sort, requiring only a moist soil;[3] this is amply descriptive of the capabilities of the well-watered "Land of Shali,"[4] or Thes-Salia.

The great artery which waters this rich country finds an egress through a single chasm, celebrated for its romantic beauty, called the DEMBHĚ[5] or "CLEFT." "The entrance of the Peneus," says Dr. Wordsworth, "through

[1] Thornton, Punj., vol. ii. p. 189.

[2] From *Pur*, a city; and *Sal*, city of Sal. *See* Rule for change of "ū" or "oo," to "ā" or "ă." (*See* Rule vi. Appendix.)

[3] Wilson's Sans. Lex. *i. v. Sali.*

[4] Shali is thus pronounced with the "h," but spelt Sali; the "s" partaking of the sound of "sh" in the word "shall:" when written in the English character it is marked "ṡ" to distinguish it from the clear-sounding "s."

[5] Of which the Greeks made "Tempe."

the narrow defile of Tempé, between the mountains of Olympus and Ossa, a few miles before its entrance into the sea, suggested to Xerxes the reflection, that Thessaly might easily be flooded by damming up this only outlet of the stream, and the opinion that Thessaly was actually covered by the sea in more ancient times, appears not only probable in itself, from a consideration of its physical formation (and it may be suggested from its very name,) but is confirmed by the ancient traditions which have assumed the form of mythological legends with respect to that country. Neptune, in these accounts, strikes the rock with his trident, and opens a passage for the imprisoned water, by the fissure."[1] The reader will not fail to recollect that the same achievement was performed in the draining of Cashmir, by Casyapa, a celebrated Bud'histic saint; and he will shortly understand the value of the term Poseidon, when he will duly appreciate that primæval industry and piety were once united in one individual. As we gradually unravel the primitive geography of the Indo-Hellenic settlements, we shall, just in that proportion, be prepared to comprehend the first history of those colonists, for, if we are foiled in the just view of the earliest geography of the land, most assuredly we shall not obtain any correct view of its *history*, as they are inextricably bound up with each other.

[1] Dr. Wordsworth's Greece, Pictorial and Descriptive.

IX.

THE HIMALAYANS.

Πόλιες ΜΕΡΟ-ΠΩΝ[1] ΑΝΘΡΩΠΩΝ.

"The Cities of the Mountain Chiefs."—Hom.

There are three distinct features in which north-western Asia is reproduced in Greece. These demonstrate, in the most comprehensive form, three separate groups of original colonists. How the settlements founded by these respective bands may have been subsequently modified, cannot be decided without an attentive examination of the geography and history of India and Northern Greece. The Ac-Helous, or Helas-water, is properly the representative of the Indus. The Pene-i-os (Paen-i-Os, "The chiefs of the Ookshus" or Oxus,) and the Sperchīus (river Sverga) of the Ganges. All the evidences bearing upon this subject go to establish these facts indisputably. It is evident, however, that Western Thessaly was the stronghold of those powerful Aswas or Horse tribes, that gave such a distinctive name to the Ionians; one of these great clans, the Catti, will be shortly noticed.

The Ionians, (a Greek form of expressing "Hiyanians[2] and Yavanians, *i.e.* "The Horse tribes,") after their emigration into Greece, formed on the western

[1] *Mer* and *Merŏ,* a mountain; and *pŏs,* a chief. The application of "articulating men" (μέροψ) is a fiction of the antiquarians of Greece of old standing, grafted on the true Sanscrit term, which afterwards passed into poetical use.

[2] *Hiyan,* plural of *Hiya,* a horse—*Hiyanios* (Ionios) is a derivative form. *Yavan* signifies "a swift horse," a title identical with Hiyan. The

banks of the Pindus, and in fact in the whole of Western Greece, settlements of a nature so durable, as to give their abiding designations both to land and sea; their original seats will be seen on the northern Indus. From this great branch of the human family noticed by the Hebrew legislator as "Javan," was named the HIYĀNIAN (IONIAN) Sea, and HIPAIRUS[1] (EPIRUS). These great tribes, —the Yavanas,—are by Sanscrit writers designated as widely as their actual extent, viz., from Bactria (*i.e.* Bhooctria, or land of the "Great-war-caste") to the shores of Greece. Hence, the apparent looseness of the term, so often noticed by Orientalists.[2] The most south-westerly confluent of the Hellenic Oxus, is the PAMISUS, a name derived from the same source as the Paro-PAMISUS of the Greeks, *i.e.* the Hindoo-Koosh mountains in the immediate vicinity of the Oxus. The Paropamisus of the Greeks is the Pahar-oop'-Bamis, or the Mountain near Bami, or Bamian.[3]

Such a stream, in fact, exactly corresponding to the Pamisus of Thessaly, which flows into the Peneus, or Oxus of Greece, will the reader find rising near Bamisus (Bamian), and flowing into the Oxus of Asia. Nor will these Bamian people in Greece be found very far from their new Pamisus, they are the Bomi-enses (Bamian

ordinary resolution of the Sanscrit "v" into the Greek "o," and the "y" into its corresponding form "i," absorbs the two short vowels, and gives the form "I, o, n," and the derivative "Ionios." (*See* Appendix, Rules vi—xx.)

[1] From *Hi*, a horse; *pa*, a chief; and *ira*, the earth.

[2] The well-known identification of Ionia and Yavana by Prinsep, in the inscription of Asoka, the Buddhist emperor of India, is as satisfactory to the philologist, as to the historian.

[3] *Bamian* is evidently the plural form of *Bami*, the people of Bami. "*Pahar Bami*, the mountain of Bami,—commonly called Bamian; in Sanscrit, *Vami-nagari* or *Vami-gram*, emphatically called *Budha Bamian*. Bamian is represented in the books of the Buddhists as the source of holiness and purity."—*Wilford, As. Res.*, vol. vi. p. 463.

tribes) situated about twenty miles to the south of the source of the Pamisus.[1]

Ranged across the western flank of the great southern barrier of Thessaly, that extends from the Pindus to the Pagasæan bay, is a powerful body of Bud'histic adherents. We are now surrounded by the inhabitants of a northerly latitude; they have come from the extreme north-westerly boundaries of the Punjab, and the frontiers of Thibet. With them, as in the case of all emigrants, especially from mountainous lands, they have brought the names of the blue hills they loved so well:—

> Mirror'd by faithful hearts, the torrent's rush,
> The peaceful lake,—the hill's eternal snow,—
> Thou canst not banish from the soul; that gush
> Of mountain melody, and memory's flow.[2]

The lofty chain of heights which I have just noticed, replaces in Greece the vast north-western "Himalayas" of India. And here mythology and history are but one, and carry up the Hindoo system to a vast antiquity. The great Thessalian sierras of Mount OTHRYS are the ODRYS[3] of India. "ODRYS" is the Sanscrit name of the HIMALAYA, as KING OF THE MOUNTAINS. The name "Othrys" will be found much better preserved in its original form in a more northerly latitude than the Othrys of Thessaly; namely, in that range of heights called "ADRI-us Mons," flanking Dalmatia on the east. These

[1] *Bami* and *v'ensa*, a tribe; "v" lost by the ordinary Greek practice of Digamma. (*See* Appendix, Rule vii.)

[2] From MS. Poem.

[3] Properly "Adrīs." The forms Ădrīs, Ŭdrīs, or Ŏdrīs, represent but one sound. The Sanscrit short vowel "ă" sounds as the "u" in "but;" the same obscure sound with the "e" of "le, me, te, se" of the French, and the "o" in "Dumbarton." Adris is composed of *Adri*, a mountain, and *īs*, a king; by the rules of combination, *Adrīs*. The combination "th" is the Greek "Δ." (*See* Appendix, Rule xvii. "dh, th.")

Adrian or Himalayan people gave their name both to sea and land. The former, the ADRI-atic; the latter, the "ADRI-us Mons;" their fellow-emigrants were the people of "SKARDO," in Little Thibet; they are seen grouped by their side in Mons SKARDUS. Corroborative evidences, such as these, I could produce tenfold, but the immense field which lies before me, forbids anything but the merest notice of the various localities harmonising with the subject under investigation. We shall now be in possession of two clear historical records of the highest importance connected with a supposed mythological era of Greece. 1st. The high antiquity of both the Bud'histic and Brahminical sects in Greece. 2dly. The decisive existence of the Lamaic system in that country at a period equally ancient. The secession of the Bud'hists, those great dissenters of antiquity, from the Brahminical party, I shall distinctly carry up to an antiquity far superior to what has been called the legendary era of the Dryopes. These emigrants who have given the name of the Odrys, or Himalaya to the great southern range of Thessalian Hellas, are the inhabitants of BH (*u*) DHYŎ-DES, PH ( ) THIŎ-TIS, or "THE BUD'HA'S LAND;" and these Bud'has, to this day, stationed in the north-eastern frontier of Cashmir, are called BOD-pas, that is Chiefs of Budh.

The Bud'has have brought with them into Thessaly the far-famed *mythological,* but equally *historical* name of "Cailas," the fabulous residence of Cuvera, the god of Wealth, and the favourite haunt of Siva, placed by the Hindoos among the Himalayan mountains, and applied to one of the loftiest peaks lying on the north of the Manasa Lake.[1] Practically the Cailas,[2] a ridge of high mountains, is situated about 31° of north lat., slanting to

[1] Wilson's Sans. Lex., *v.* *Kailása.*

[2] Hamilton's E. Ind. Gaz., vol. i. p. 314.

the north-west and south-east, and almost parallel to the Himalaya, which those Hindoos called "Cailas," and which the Greeks very fairly preserved in "Caila" (Cœla) immediately to the north of the "Xunias Lake" (Xynias) or lake of Cashmir. While the Pamisus, or the "River of Bamian," takes its rise on the western verge of Othrys, the Greek Himalaya, the "Ap-i-danus," the great feeder of the Peneus or Thessalian Oxus, rises on a spur of the western Othrys. Ap-i-danus is connected with the history of the illustrious chief of Cashmir—a history involved in Indian mythology, which, like the mythology of Greece, is but history distorted. DANU was the daughter of Daksha, wife of Casyapa, and mother of the Daityas of Hindoo mythology. These beings will, in the course of our investigation, be found as historical as the Autochthons, or the *late* Athenian Grasshoppers. The AP-I-DANUS is DANUS RIVER, or DANUS-WATER,[1] and the reader will observe that it takes its rise immediately contiguous to the lake of the Greek Cashmir (Xynias), thus connecting CASYAPA the founder of Cashmir, his wife DANU, and his people the "DANA-oi," the DANAVAS of the Sanscrit! Both the "DANA-oi," and the ACHÆI of Homer are ranged close to the Greek Himalayan. The historical value of this geographical evidence will soon be apparent.

Among the Bud'hists, to the south of Othrys, or HIMALAYA NOVA, and settled along the sea-board, were the LAMIENSES,[2] or "Lama tribes," whose chief city was LAMIA, or "Lama's town." To the mountain promontory, which terminates the district of the MAG-NE-TES,[3] "the Land of the Magha, or MOGUL tribes"—these high northern settlers gave the name of one of the great

[1] *Ap-i*, water of—Danu. So in English, "Ullas-water."

[2] From *Lama* and *Vensa*, a tribe; "v" lost. (*See* Rule vii, Appendix.)

[3] *Magha-gane-des—Gane*, a tribe, and *des*, a land. The land of the Magha, Mog, Mogul tribe, who were of the same Buddhistic religion as the Mogs of Aracan, the Maghas of Maghada, and the Moguls of Tartary.

Bud'has of remote antiquity, a fact which goes far to strengthen our confidence in those Bud'histic writings which are allowed to be genuine. TISSAIOS, the Greek adjectival form of the name of the great Bud'hist-pontiff "TISSO," boasts an antiquity preceding, and in all probability long preceding, this settlement in Hellas; for the name "Tisso" is as much a transfer from the neighbourhood of the Himalaya as "Cailas" and "Othrys." The reader has only to turn his eyes towards the very focus which first darted the rays of this Bud'histic emigration into Greece, to be convinced of this,—for to the north of Cashmir, adjoining these Bhutias,—adjoining these Himalayas, he will still read the venerated name of "Tisso;"[1] hence the transfer to the lofty Greek promontory.[2] But our evidences pause not here, they are positively becoming cumulative. Immediately to the south of Lamia, "the Lama's town," is the river "Duras,"[3] disemboguing itself into the Lamiac Gulf. The river Duras, Dras, or Draus of Thibet—for it is thus variously written—flows through a valley of that name in Ladakh at a short distance north of the northern frontier of Cashmir. Rising on the "Bultul" or "Kantal Pass," it flows northward to the Indus, which it joins opposite to the valley of the Morul. Closely bordering on the Lamas' people, extending into the valley of the Spercheius eastward as far as Thermopylæ, were the Dryopes,[4] who had, it must be confessed, a name of a surprisingly mythological sound. These singular beings were said to be so named from "Drus," "an oak," and "Ops" "the voice;" the

[1] The Mahawanso,—whose authentic records were noted, first memorially B.C. 500, then in written documents,—gives a distinct notice of Tisso among the ancient Budhas. (*See* Ch. i. p. 1, "Mahawanso," by the Hon. G. F. Turnour.)

[2] Tisso in Northern Bultistan, lat. 35° 38′, long. 75° 20′.

[3] Lat. 34° 44′, long. 67° 9′. Duras is 9000 feet above the level of the sea, and in lat. 34° 22′, long. 75° 30′.

[4] Müller's Dorians, vol. i. p. 45.

Greeks thus insinuating that they spoke from the oak. Alas! their days of mystery are numbered. The reader will understand, then, that these people are no mythological beings, but DRUO-PES,[1] or "CHIEFS OF THE DRAUS," and that their southern settlement is in Doris, on the river CHARA-DRAS (KĪRA-DRAS), or the "Cashmir Dras,"[2] where they again appear as Dryopes; he will also see them again among the Cassopæi, or Çashmirians, at the sources of the Chara-dras ("Kira-Dras") in Epirus. So much for truth and so much for fable. The truth is the Sanscrit version, the fable is the Greek; yet both fable and truth repose upon an historical and geographical basis.

But I cannot be content with a passing notice of the people of the Dras; for, as a nation, we are deeply interested in their early history. Not only so, we have been closely connected with them; and, farther still, long did they dwell in our island, and by the interesting records and traditions concerning them that have descended to our own times, they have provoked our unabated and lively curiosity. Why should I conceal the fact? These DRUO-PES are our own ancient DRUI-DES or DRUIDS![3]

> Hark! 'twas the voice of harps, that poured along
> The hollow vale the floating tide of song.
> I see the glittering train, in long array,
> Gleam through the shades, and snowy splendours play;
> I see them now with measured steps and slow,
> 'Mid arching groves the white-robed sages go.

---

[1] "Dryopes" is the English form of "Druopes," (*see* Rule xiii.) from *Draus* and *Pĕ*, "a chief."

[2] *Kīra*, Cashmir,—Dras,—"the river Dras of Cashmir."

[3] *Druo-pĕs*, Chiefs of the Draus; *Dru-i-des*, the people of,—"the land of the Dras." This the Romans received as the appellative of the tribe. I hold the most interesting and authentic evidences of the early settlement of these and other neighbouring communities, which I shall shortly lay before the public.

The oaken wreath with braided fillet drest—
The Crescent beaming on the holy breast—
The silver hair which waves above the lyre,
And shrouds the strings, proclaim the Druid's quire.
They halt and all is hushed.[1]

These venerated sages, chiefs of the tribes of the Draus, were of the INDU VANSA or LUNAR RACE. Hence the symbol of the CRESCENT worn by these Druids; they too, like most of their race, were Bud'hists, and they shall tell their own history. Their chief settlement here, was "the E-BUDES," *i.e.* "the HI-BUD'H-DES,"[2] and their last refuge in Britain from the oppression of the Romans, the descendants from their own stock, was the "Isle of Saints" or "Mona."[3] This is indeed the Druid Bard—this, the minstrel of the Cymry—this, the Bhaut[4] of the ancient Rajpoot—this, the harper of Homeric song—this, the Demodocus of Homeric feasts—this, the glorious minstrel, who, in the guise of a divinity, draws homage from his fellows—this, in truth, the Delphic god—this, the founder of the wealthy shrine, the oracular response—this, the subject of the glowing lay, the living faith of the Homerid of Chios. This is the god, who, from his lofty watch-tower, spies the tall bark of Crete as it ploughs its way towards the Peloponnesus; he it is, whom the Bud'hist poet glorifies with the ascription of saintly power over the elements of nature.

The settlement of the people of the Draus in this island, the northern part of which was essentially that of the HI-BUDH-DES (E-BUDH-DES,) or the land of the Hiya Bud'has,

[1] Wordsworth's Druids. Cambridge Prize Poem, 1827.

[2] The Bud'has of the Hi or Hya tribe; *Hi-Budh-des,* the land of the Hya Bud'has.

[3] "Mona," properly "Mooni." "A holy sage, a pious and learned person, endowed with more or less of a divine nature, or having attained it, by rigid abstraction and mortification."—*Wilson's Sans. Lex., i.v.*

[4] The term Bardus is the disguised form of Bhaut with the Latin termination.

at once accounts most satisfactorily for the amazing mechanical skill displayed in the structure of Stone Henge, and harmonises with the industrious and enterprising character of the Buddhists throughout the old world; for these are the same people who drained the valley of Cashmir, and in all probability the plains of Thessaly.

Observe now this same race of Bud'hists in Thessaly, in that district which was written by the Greeks PH ( ) THIO-TIS, but by the first settlers B (*u*) DHYŎ-DES, or "BUDDHAS LAND." They are situated near the DURAS[1] or DRAS-River; and again, we see the town of HY-BUD'HA (HY-PATA),[2] near Othrys, the Himalayas of Greece. I would here remark on the singular transfer of mythology to history. It is from the HIMALA Mountains of the SACAS that the "SACA-SOONO," those sons of the Saca ("Saxons or SAC-SONS," for the words are at once Sanscrit, Saxon, and English)[3] derived their HIMMEL or "Heaven." Thus did the Indian Heaven become that of the German. Neither have the emigrants from Cashmir forgotten their beautiful lake, nor the saintly founder of their state. Both CASOO-LAKE and CASOO-TOWN, the grateful record of CASOO-PA,[4] the "Chasa-chief," the founder of Cashmir, occupy an intermediate position between Mount Othrys, the Hellenic, the Himalaya, and Mount Cailas; they appear respectively in Greek writings as X'OO-NIAS Lake and X'oo-niæ,[5] while nothing can be more prominent than the new position chosen for the people of "BURGO-PUR," that is BURGO-TOWN. They have taken up their abode close to the sources of their old

[1] Latinised as Dyras river.

[2] The Hi-Bud'has, identical with the E-Budes of Great Britain.

[3] *Soono*, a son.

[4] Casoopa, the founder of Cashmir.

[5] The Latin form is Xynias Palus, and Xyniæ. (*See* Append. Rule x. and xiii.) The Greek Xoo-neia is the *Casoo-naya*, Casoo-town.

river "Duras;" their settlement is on a mountain, which bears the modernised Greek form of "PHRUGIA-PURA."[1] Nor have the Brahmins forgotten the Ganges and its mountain sources, while the Lamas are found principally grouped around the northern shores of the Lamaic Bay, and at the embouchure of the great river, which there disembogues itself, a party of the AINEANES[2] or BRAHMINS, have taken up their abode at the sources of SBERGĪUS (SPERCHĪUS,) "the river of Paradise," and their chief town is SBERGIUM or PARADISE, while on the celestial river Spercheius[3] is built the city of Brahma (Ainia.)[4] This city does not bear the title of AINŒA *generally*, but *specifically*, for these emigrants have brought with them the name of their old dwelling-place, the town of OIN. "Oin" in the Punjab is a small town near the base of the mountains, enclosing Cashmir on the south. It is situated on the river Jailum, the navigation of which here again becomes practicable, after its interruption between Baramula and this place.[5]

Dodona again accompanies the Druopes, the Chara-Dras,[6] and the Cassopæi, or Cashmirians in Epirus. The Sbergīus (Sperchīus, or river of Paradise), which I have just noticed, is the Greek representative of the SBERGA-

[1] The Latin form is Phrygia Pura, and is of the same form as Naya-pala or Nepaul; similar combinations in Indian names are of common occurrence. The "y" Sanscrit takes the place of the "i" in Greek. (*See* Append. Rule xx.)

[2] Vena, Brahma. Vaina and Vainyanes, derivative forms of Vena, signify the descendants or people of Brahma; the "v" digammated, is lost. (*See* Rule vii. Appendix.)

[3] Sverga is the Hindoo Paradise. As the letters "v" and "b" are commutable, I have used that form which gave rise to the Greek "Spercheius." (*See* Rule xii. Appendix.)

[4] See Note 2.

[5] Thornt. Gaz. Punjab, vol. ii. p. 84. Oin is in lat. 33° 40′, long. 73° 50′.

[6] Properly *Cira-Dras*, that is, the "Dras of Cashmir."

APAGA[1]—the GANGES;[2] Spergāpaga, literally "Heaven's river," being the exact reflection of the adjectival form "Sbergīus," the heavenly river, that is, the Ganges. The Greek Sperchius, like its Indian namesake, takes its rise in the Thessalian Othrys, King of Mountains, the Himalayas of Greece. The Oitœi, or the people of Oude, are settled to the south. Again the pliant element of Greek etymology is at work; now to amuse, formerly to mislead us. Sperchein, "to hasten," was the philological representative of the river Sperchīus.

The small province of "DORIS," in Greece, derived its population from the river DOR, immediately adjoining the western frontiers of Cashmir. The river "Dor," in Cashmir, "Doda," and the great mountain "MER," transplanted into Greece as TO-MAR-OS,[3] are all in the same northerly direction.

Add to this that the "Dor" is one of the aboriginal war-clans of Goorkha, and we have a powerful series of facts, tending to fix these warriors in a high northerly latitude, immediately contiguous to the Himalaya mountains, or "Odrys," where we again find them in the Othrys of Greece. The military prowess of the Dorians, therefore, is not to be wondered at.[4]

[1] *Sberga*, heaven, and *apaga*, a river. By combination Sbergāpaga.

[2] *Ganga* or *Ganges*, "*the* River," by way of eminence.

[3] *See* Rule xiv. Appendix.

[4] "The records of this period (A.D. 812 to 836)," writes Colonel Tod, "are too scanty to admit of our passing over in silence, even a barren catalogue of names, which, as text with aid of collateral information, may prove of some benefit to the future antiquarian and historian."

Then follows this transcript of the annals of the country:—

"From Gajuni came the Gehlote; the Ták from Asér; from Nadolaye, the Chohan; the Chalook from Rahirgurh; from Sét Bunder, the Jirkéra; from Mundore, the Khairàvi; from Mangrole, the Macwahana; from Jeitgurh, the Joria; from Taragurh, the Réwur; the Cutchwaha from Nirwur; from Sanchore, the Kalum; from Joengurh, the Dassanoh; from Ajmér, the Gor; from Lohadurgurh, the Chundano; from Kasundi, the Dor; from

And now, if the future historian of Pelasgian Hellas will pause for a short time, and ask himself, honestly, how far he is acquainted with the people of the Hellenic Himalayas—how much he knows of their general writings, habits, original country, sacred books, and sacred rites; how far he is acquainted with the Brahminical, the Budhistic, and the Lamaic systems; how far acquainted with the history, written and traditional, of the Surya and Indo-Vansa tribes—a conscientious answer will give him his true position as an Hellenic historian for that vast period which, beginning with the great Budhistic mission of Cadmus, traverses the wars of the kindred tribes at Troy, and ends with the subjugation of those early religionists of Greece, the ELOOTHS[1] (HELOTS), clad in their Tartar sheepskin, who like the COKAUNES (CAUCONES), or inhabitants of COCAUN,[2] were some of the first Tartar tribes that formed the primitive population of Hellas.

It is vain to expect the emancipation of Grecian history from the disguises which overlay its beauties, unless the Budhistic miracles with which it abounds be placed on their just footing, and the full historical value given to every genealogy which is conformable to geographical evidence.

Delhi, the Túar; from Patun, the Chawura, preserver of royalty (Rijdhur); from Jhalore, the Sonigurra; from Sirohi, the Deora; from Gagrown, the Kechie; the Jadoo from Joonagurh; the J'hala from Patri; from Kanouge, the Rhatore; from Chotiala, the Balla; from Perungurh, the Gohil; from Jesulgurh, the B'hatti; the Bhoosa from Lahore; the Sankla from Ronéja; the Sehut from Kherligurh; from Mandelgurh, the Nacoompa; the Birgoojur from Rajore; from Kurrunghur, the Chundail; from Sikur, the Sikurwal; from Omergurh, the Jaitwah; from Palli, the Birgota; from Khunturgurh, the Jaréja: from Jirgah, the Kherwur; from Cashmér, the Purihara."—TOD'S *Rajastha*, vol. i. p. 248.

[1] Eluths is the common form in ordinary use. The many singular attempts made by the ancient and modern Greek antiquarians to arrive at the origin of these Helots, through the medium of the Greek language, will be duly noticed.

[2] Written also Kokhan and Kokhand.

I shall not then despair of seeing a trustworthy and a most interesting history of the first centuries of the Hellenic nation. But this history must be evolved on authorities totally independent of any Grecian writer, except as an outline or a clue to the truth.'

X.

THE CENTAURS.

Κάρτιστοι μὲν ἔσαν, καὶ καρτίστοις ἐμάχοντο,
φηρσὶν ὀρεσκῴοισιν, καὶ ἐπάγλως ἀπόλεσσαν·

Those Sons of Might, with hideous slaughter, drave
The mountain chiefs, the Bravest of the Brave.

Hom. Il., i. 267—8.

As a test of our progress we will now consider the history of the Lapithæ and Centaurs, and examine their mythological or non-mythological weight by the just scales of geographical science, aided by the language of the first settlers.

The CENTAUROI, according to the earliest accounts, a race of men who inhabited the mountains and forests of Thessaly, "are described as leading a rude and savage life, occasionally carrying off the women of their neighbours, as covered with hair, and ranging over the mountains like animals, yet they were not altogether unacquainted with the useful arts, as in the case of Cheiron;[1] in which passages they are called φῆρες (Phēeres), that is θηρες (Theeres).[2] Now in these earliest accounts, the Centaurs appear merely as a sort of gigantic, savage, animal-like beings; whereas, in later writers, they are described as monsters (hippo-centaurs), whose bodies were partly human and partly those of horses. The Centaurs are particularly celebrated in ancient story for the feast of Peirithous, the subject of which was extensively used by ancient poets

[1] Homer's Il., i. 268; ii. 743. [2] Wild beasts.

and artists."[1] Cheiron, the wisest and most just of all the Centaurs,[2] was the instructor of Achilles, whose father Peleus, was a friend and relative of Cheiron. He lived on Mount Pelion, from which he, like the other Centaurs, was expelled by the Lapithæ. His descendants in Magnesia, "the Cheironida," were distinguished for their knowledge of medicine. All the most distinguished heroes of Grecian story, are, like Achilles, described as the pupils of Cheiron, in hunting, medicine, music, gymnastics, and the art of prophecy.[3] It is not a little provoking to observe the unhappy tendency produced by Greek etymology. So completely, on this point, has it biassed, nay paralysed, mental energy, that the Greek Centaur, too bulky and too nondescript to be admitted within the portals of the temple of history, has not only been refused entrance, but his form reacting on the classical infidel, has given rise to a theory, in which the negation of existence forms the very life of history. The name of these Centaurs, is of course derived "ἄπο τοῦ κεντεῖν ταύρους," from goading bulls; that is, these Centaurs were, as we should say, "Prickers,"—they went on horseback after strayed bulls, or they hunted wild bulls. One was seen by Periander, tyrant of Corinth.[4] Pliny was particularly fortunate; he saw one embalmed in honey, this was an Egyptian Centaur, brought all the way to Rome. But it must have been also an *historical* Centaur; for this occurrence dates after the *Olympiads,*—nay, even so late as the reign of Claudius.[5] "The most inquisitive and judicious of the ancient antiquarians," observes Mitford, "appear to have been at a loss what to think of the Centaurs." Strabo calls them, "ἄγριον τι φῦλον," a mode of expression implying uncertainty about them, while he gives them an epithet,

[1] Smith's Myth. Lex., vol. i. p. 666.
[2] Homer's Il., xi. 831.
[3] Smith's Myth. Lex., vol. i. p. 692.
[4] Plut. Symp.
[5] Pliny, vii. 3.

for which no reason appears. Pindar[1] describes the Centaur Cheiron as a most paradoxical being, which he has described in two words, "φὴρ θειος," "godlike wild beast." For the perfect comprehension of the Centaurs, Cheiron, the Lapithæ, and the "φὴρ θειος" of Pindar, it will be necessary to understand the settlements of eastern Thessaly. They are settlements founded by people of very different countries, and of different habits; this alone would be sufficient to account for the frequent wars between the Lapithæ and the Centaurs. The mountain land of Olympus was, in common with the greater part of the eastern coast, peopled by the nations of the Punjab. They were emigrants from the banks of the river Ravée, not far from its junction with the Chenab. To the south, the mountain OSSA, though a colony from the OOKSHA or OXUS, was occupied by the people of OOCHA or OOCH.[2] The reader cannot but be struck with the singular harmony subsisting between the old and the new settlements of the Thessalians, as shown by the maps accompanying this book; which mirror forth at once both "Western Hellas" and the Singetic provinces in the original country. While the Pagasæ, "the people of PAK,"[3] have settled at PAGASÆ—the head of the Persian Gulf—the TEBHAI, people of Tebhee, their immediate neighbours to the south, have occupied the same relative positions in their new city of "THEBÆ." The MALI-PAI,[4] or "Chiefs of Mooltan," have taken up their abode at

[1] Pyth. iv.

[2] Ooch (Ossa), lat. 29° 13′, long. 71° 6′.

[3] Pak, lat. 30° 20′, long. 73° 13′. From *Pak-vasi*, "dwellers in Pak." The sound of the digammated "v" lost. (*See* Rule vii. Appendix.)

[4] The Malli of the Greek historians: from *Mali* and *Pa*, a chief. The following is the Greek system of corruption. The name of the town was Moola, Greek plural Mooloi, written by them Malloi. (*See* Rule vi. Appendix.) The present name is identical, the *tan* being merely the addition of *t'han* "land;" as *Mool-tan*, Mool-land,—so Pole land (Poland). It is not impossible that the Mooloi may have been settlers from the Moola Pass.

MALI-BAIA, "THE TOWN OF THE MALLI CHIEFS," adjoining whom are the emigrants from BEEBOO,[1] who have fixed their new settlement on the Lake BÆBOIS.

The BHOOTIAS appear to have gained a firm footing in north-western Thessaly, in the immediate vicinity of their old neighbours, the BIRGOOS. Both these appear respectively as "BOTTIŒI" and "BRIGES." In the time of Achilles, however, a portion of this Tartar tribe was running a victorious career. At this period, they occupied the plain on either side of the Peneus, having descended from their old settlements in Macedonia (amongst the Magas or Moguls). That the Bottiœi made these southern settlements is clear; for their name, which has fortunately been preserved in their native language, is precise upon this point. That name is in the language of Thibet— L'HOPATAI, the "LAPITHAI," or the people of BOUTAN.[2] The further progress southwards of this martial race was opposed by a band of warriors as daring and as resolute as themselves. Both their equestrian fame, the whole scope of their habits and history, and the people by whom they are surrounded, mark these warriors decisively. They, whom the Greeks wrote down as "KENTAUR-OI,"[3]

[1] Beeboo Triggur, lat. 30° 28′, long. 71° 40′. Baiboo, Lat. *Bœboo*,' derivative form from *Beeboo*.

[2] "In Hindustani, Tubet is called Bhotant, and a Tubetan, Bhootia. This country (Boutan) is but a part of the vast territory of Tubet. In Tubetan, the Boutan of the English is called L'hopato, and in Hindoostanee, Laltopivala."—*Asiat. Journ.*, vol. xv. 294. "Account of Tibet," Klaproth.—De Billy.—(The Mongols write Tubet.) Again:—"The term Bhote is applied by the Hindoos not only to the country named Bootan by Europeans, but also to the tract extending along, and immediately adjoining, both sides of the Himalaya; in which sense it is a very extensive region, occupying the whole mountainous space from Cashmir to China." —*Hamil. E. Ind. Gaz.*, vol. i. p. 270. (*See* Rule xix. Appendix.)

[3] At this stage of our history it may not be uninstructive to remark the darkness with which the Greeks have succeeded in beclouding one of the shrewdedst intellects of modern Europe. I allude to Buttman. "It

had come into Greece from a far more southern latitude than their opponents; and their language then was, and is to this day, widely different from that of the L'hopatai. These KENTAURS then, were KANDHAURS, or emigrants from KANDAHAR.[1] Sāl, the contiguous province to Candahar, takes its place on the map of Greece as "PUR-SALUS" (PHAR-SALUS), or the "CITY OF SAL."[2] There are two points of view in which the term, Kandahar, may be used as referring to these Kentaurs. The neighbourhoods of Kandahar, Punjab, and Thessaly are strictly "Cand-dhāra," or the "country of streams;" and the evidences I am about to bring forward will derive these "Centaurs," whatever their previous settlements may have been,—more immediately from the vicinity of the confluence of the streams of the Indus, where their position and the name of their tribe will be distinctly seen. In Greece, however, one important indication of their fixed settlement is distinct, though different intimations of their erratic life are to be met with in abundance exactly corresponding to their

is the opinion of Buttman," observes Keightley, (Mythology, vol. ii. p. 22,) "that the Centaurs and the Lapithæ are two *purely poetic names*, used to designate two opposite races of men; the former, the rude, horse-riding tribes, which tradition records to have been spread over the north of Greece; the latter, the more civilised race, which founded towns, and gradually drove their wild neighbours back to the mountains. He therefore thinks the exposition of Centaurs or *Air-piercers* (from *kentein teen auran*) not an improbable one; for that very idea is suggested by the figure of a Cossack leaning forward with his protruded lance, as he gallops along. But he regards the idea of the Centaurs, having been in its original, simply Kentor, as much more probable. Lapiths may," he thinks, "have signified *Stone-Persuaders* (from *Laas peithein*), a poetic appellation for the 'builders of towns.' Such is the etymological inheritance bequeathed to Europe by the Greeks!"

[1] Kandahar, pronounced Kandahaūr (Kentaūr).

[2] The letter "s," in this word, has the thick sound of "sh," and the "ā" the broad sound of "au;" hence it is written "Shawl," to give an idea of its pronunciation, not its orthography. (*See* Rule vi. Appendix.)

wandering habits described by the Greek logographers. But there is yet another point of view in which these Kentauroi may be considered, immediately and powerfully illustrating their history. "Har," or "HARO," (whence the Greek HĒRŌS, "a Hero,") signifies "war," and "the god of war," and is a well known Rajpoot appellation of that deity; KAND-HAR, therefore, is "The country of Har," or the "Haro" tribe, just as we have seen the Perrhibæans use the title of the warlike Cartikeya.

To the classical student, the term Haro is of as great an interest as to the Englishman. The term "Hērōs" occurs in Homer about one hundred and ten times,[1] and is applied not only to the prime chiefs but to inferior warriors. The classical scholar will now see the propriety of this general, as well as specific application. It is in no spirit of etymological trifling that I assure the reader, that the far-famed "Hurrah," of his native country, is the war-cry of his forefather, the Rajpoot of Britain, for he was long the denizen of this island. His shout was "HARO! HARO!" (HURRAH! HURRAH!) Hark to the spirit-stirring strains of Wordsworth, so descriptive of this Oriental warrior. It is the Druid who speaks—

> "Then seize the spear, and mount *the scythed wheel*,
> Lash the proud steed, and whirl the flaming steel—
> Sweep through the thickest host and scorn to fly,
> Arise! arise! for this it is to die.
> Thus 'neath his *vaulted cave* the Druid sire
> Lit the rapt soul, and fed the martial fire."[2]

I believe these Cand-Haroi, from every surrounding evidence in Eastern Thessaly, to have been the great Rajpoot tribe of the Catti, or Cathei, one of the Thirty-six Royal tribes of Rajasthan; every circumstance connected with the history of the Lapithæ and Centaurs goes to

[1] *See* Phil. Mus., vol. i. p. 72.

[2] Wordsworth's Druids. Cambridge Prize Poem, 1827.

prove this. I believe the Cand-'Hars[1] to have been settlers (from near the modern Candahar) upon the confluence of the great streams of the Punjab; and I speak of this tribe as synonymous with the Catti. Colonel Tod observes, writing of the Catti,[2] "all the genealogists, both of Rajast'han and Saurashtra, concur in assigning it a place among the royal races of India. It is one of the most important tribes of Western India, and one which has effected the change of the name from Surashta to Cattiwar. Of all its inhabitants, the Catti retains most originality: his religion, his manners, and his looks, all are decidedly Scythic. He occupied in the time of Alexander that nook of the Punjab, near the confluent five streams. It was against these that Alexander marched in person, when he nearly lost his life, and where he left such a signal memorial of his vengeance. The Catti can be traced from these scenes to his present haunts. He still adores the sun; scorns the peaceful arts, and is much less contented with the tranquil subsistence of industry than the precarious earnings of his former predatory pursuits. A character possessed of more energy than the Catti does not exist. His size is considerably larger than common, often exceeding six feet. He is sometimes seen with light hair and blue coloured eyes. His frame is athletic and bony, and particularly adapted to his mode of life."[3] The reader will bear in mind the numerous settlements already pointed out in Eastern Thessaly; by far the greater proportion from the very neighbourhood where the Catti were found in the time of Alexander's invasion.

To the settlements from Mooltan, Beeboo, Tebbee, Pāk, Ooch, respectively Meliboœa, Bœbeis, Thebœ, Pegasœ, and Ossa, I would add one more—namely,

[1] *Cand*, a country or region: properly Khand.

[2] Rajasthan, vol. i. p. 111.

[3] Rajasthan, vol i. p. 112.

"PHERÆ," situated near the southern shore of Lake Bœbeis. These, and many more cities, which I see before me, are all in the vicinity of the Catti. Here, then, is the explanation of the "PHEERES" of Homer—translated "wild beasts." But its application is still more distinct. "Peer,"[1] the old settlement in the Punjab,[2] is as much amongst its fellow-towns of that region as Pheeræ is among its Thessalian cities. In fact, both these towns, the "Phēræ" of Thessaly, and the Peer of the Punjab, were so denominated from an old Persian word signifying a "venerable elder or saint;"[3] and not a few towns of the Punjab are so named to this day. Among these, Peer-æ, or "Saints," were many well grounded in the useful arts and sciences. These Peer-æ were teachers of medicine, astronomy, music, and other accomplishments, which they communicated to young Rajpoots, such as Achilles, whose "DOLO-PES," or "Chiefs of Dola,"[4] lived both in Thessaly and the Punjab, in the immediate neighbourhood of the towns just noticed. The town of Dola, however, is a mere fragmentary exponent of the still older and original settlement of these Dolopians, or Chiefs of the Dola Mountains, in the Himalaya range, which have been already noticed. Cheiron was the most accomplished divine and leech of his time. He was truly called a "Peer" (Pheer-Theios), or "godlike Saint."[5] Like many divines of the present day, he was much in request as a superior tutor, though, like Bishop Beck in the days of the first Edward, he appears to have been equally well skilled in the martial arts.

"CHEIRON," so called from being one of the "KAIRAN,"[6]

[1] Now called "Peer Buksh." [2] Lat. 29° 21′, long. 70° 35′.

[3] The application of Peer to Mahomedan saints is of comparative antiquity; the original application to the saints of the Northern India runs up to a distant age. [4] *See* Dola, lat. 31°, long. 73° 10′.

[5] This is the unfortunate paradox of Φηρ Θεῖος, "a godlike beast."

[6] *Kīra*, Cashmirians. *Kīran*, Persian plural, derivative from *Kāïran*.

a "people of Cashmir," a province situated in the immediate neighbourhood of the Bhutias on the north (Phthiotis), and the Dola (Dolopes) on the south, was one of that class, called at the present day in Rajpootana, a "Charon."[1] The connection, therefore, between the Catti of Rajpootana and the Charon, and thus between Cheiron and the Centaurs, which latter I shall further identify with the Catti—will become apparent. And here again, I would remark, in no invidious spirit, on the effect of Greek etymology upon the best compendium of Hellenic mythology that has appeared. The author, Mr. Keightley, in speaking of this race, says:—"The most celebrated of the Centaurs was Cheiron, the son of Kronos, by the nymph Philyra. He is called by Homer 'the most upright of the Centaurs.' He reared Jason, his son Mideios, Heracles, Asclepius, and Achilles, and was famous for his skill in surgery, which he taught the two last heroes." He then observes, in a note, "the name of Cheiron plainly comes from 'Cheir,' the hand." This is certainly one of the best explanations of the term that can possibly be given, upon merely Greek etymological principles; but, like those vocabula imagined to be Greek, though in reality Sanscrit, that I have already pointed out, will be found to be as wide of the mark as the "Hekaton Cheires" of Hesiod, who when he was penning the term, imagined it to be very good Greek; and such it undoubtedly was, though at the expense of the sound sense contained in the Sanscrit words of homogeneous sound.[2] I make these remarks in no captious

[1] "The Charon, (*ch* as in *chief*,) is a term used to signify a panegyrist of the gods, a herald or bard; derived from the verb '*chăr*,' to diffuse (fame.)" —Wilson's *Sans. Lex.* On general phonetic principles the *k* and *ch* are frequently commutable; as *carus, chère.* Sans. *chira kira* a parrot.—*See* Bopp on this principle.

[2] The history of the Hekatoncheires will be duly noticed.

spirit; far otherwise; for the excellent manual above noticed will always deservedly maintain its high position, as the exponent of what Greeks thought, and wrote upon, and believed in. The true history, however, lying beneath these ingenious reveries of the Hellenic world, will, however, most assuredly no longer be concealed. But, to return to the Catti, as described by Col. Tod, "The arms of the Catti consist of a sword, shield, and spear." And now for the origin of the partially equine figure of the Centaur. "They are all horsemen, and are wonderfully particular in the breed of that animal. Mares are usually preferred. A Catti's mare is one of his family; she lives under the same roof, by which means she is familiarised, and is obedient to his voice in all situations. A Catti is seldom seen *but walking and galloping his beast.* He is so averse to walk on foot, that he rides *to the field* where he means to labour, and is prepared either to join a plundering party, or resist attack. The Cattis originally inhabited the country on the borders of the river Indus, and their migration thence can be traced, by tradition, with tolerable accuracy. They acknowledged no law but the sword; and no employment so honourable as a life of plunder. A Catti could collect, in the short period of three days, seven or eight hundred cavalry of his own caste, capable of undertaking the most hazardous and fatiguing expeditions; and their attachment to a roving life and habits of plunder was such, that no danger, however great, could overcome what might be considered as inherent in their disposition."[1] Now, observe the singular harmony of the Catti and Centaur customs of carrying off the women of their respective neighbourhoods. "A Catti to become a husband must become a ravisher: *he must attack, with his friends and followers, the village where his betrothed resides, and carry her off by force.* In

[1] Coleman's Hind. Myth. p. 280.

ancient times this was no less a trial of strength than of courage: stones and clubs were used, without reserve, both to force and repel; and the disappointed lover was not unfrequently compelled to retire, covered with bruises, and wait for a more favourable occasion." Remark, again, the position and mirror-like reflection in the name and characteristics of Cheiron and Charon. "*A Catti will do nothing without consulting* his wife, and a *Charon*, and he is in general guided by their advice. The most barbarous Coolies, Cattis or Rajpoots, hold sacred the persons of the *Charons*. The *Bhats* are the *Bards*[1] of the Rajpoot and Catti: they keep the genealogical table, or '*Vunah Wallah*' of the family, and repeat their praises. Their duty is hereditary, for which they have gifts of lands, and other privileges. The *Bhats* are more immediately with the Rajpoots, and *the Charons with the Cattis*."[2] Such was the position of Cheiron, with respect to Achilles, the "Dolapos," or "Chief of Dola."[3] The same sacred regard for the person and the presence of the Charon was shown in the case of Cheiron. The reader will recollect that the Centaurs when defeated by Heri-cul-es,[4] fled *for safety to Cheiron*, hoping that the hero would desist in his presence. Such then was the influence and sacred character of the "PEER THEIOS," (φηρ θειος), or "Holy Saint"—such the barbarous marriage customs of the CENTAUROI and CAND-HAROI, and such continued the equestrian fame of the Cattis of the Punjab, and of Thessaly. Hence sprang the noble stock of that splendid cavalry that earned such brilliant renown in the campaigns of Epaminondas. I will now show the actual presence of the Catti in Hellas. He is to be found in a position

1 *Bardus*, the Latin form, is merely a corruption for *Bhāt-us*.

2 Coleman's Myth. 283.

3 *Vide* the position of Dola in the Punjab and in Eastern Thessaly.

4 "Heracles," the Greek form, is a singularly clipping style; as usual the short "oo" is cut out. The Roman forms are generally purer.

which will indicate the correctness of my previous remarks. The reader is already aware of the transfer of the people of the Behoot, *i. e.* "Baihooti," in the Punjab, to Bœotia, "Boiotia," in Hellas. Let him remember that the former country of streams, was the very cradle of these Catti, of whom we have been speaking. Now will he see them again in Bœotia—they are the CATHÆ-RAN,[1] or CATHI-CHIEFS of MT. CITHÆ-RON. There is also another important settlement of this people, in Thessaly, contiguous to the scene of their respective conflicts: it is Su-Catt-'vusa[2] (S 'Catt' 'usa), written by the Greeks, "S 'COT-USSA," "Great Catti' town." In Hesiod's "History of Greece,"[3] this tribe will be found to play an important part, under the politic management of the great Jaina, pontiff of Olympus. One more settlement I shall point out, in the vicinity of "Xynias Lake," or "Cashmir Lake," a little to the north of the "Othrys,"—it is that of the "CATTI-MEN,"[4] appearing as "C'TI-MENA" on the map of Greece. The Catti are thus again brought into connection with the Dolopians, or Dola-Chiefs, and the Othrys or Himalayans, and the Xynians or Cashmirians. Again is Teebhee (Thebæ), one of their prime towns: the chief river bears the name of these Aswa-Chiefs, or Aso-pos (Aswapŏs)[5]—and they are settled in the immediate neighbourhood of Mount Parnes, *i. e.* the PARNES OF

[1] *Ran,* plural of Rao, a king or chief. (*See* Rule xv. Appendix). Catti, written also Cathei, Cathai, (the Lat. Cathæ,) is the regular derivative from Cathi. Arrian has the name Cathir. The Persian plural will be "Cathirān."

[2] *Su* (εὖ), well, or "High Caste," *Catti* and *Vusi,* "a dwelling." See rule for ethclipsis of the Sanscrit "oo" or "u." (Rule i. Appendix.)

[3] See chapter so named.

[4] *Manu* and *Menu* is as plain in English as in Sanscrit, being the comprehensive term for man. Man-u was the great legislator and saint, the son of Brahma, and thus the ancestor and prænomen of "MAN."

[5] *Aswa,* a horse; and *Pŏs,* a chief. The short vowels ă ĕ ŏ ŭ have but one power, and the visargah of the Sanscrit is the terminative "s" of the Greek and Latin.

Attica, or the Attac-Bar'nes. The Attac to this day retains the ancient name of Attac Baranes, showing its ancient connection with the holy city of Benares. Hence the "Mount Parnes," in Attica, as a boundary between that province and Bœotia.[1] Of this the reader will be satisfied, by a reference to the old settlements of Attica and Bœotia, in the Punjab.

[1] Attac and Behoot.

XI.

DODONA AND THE HYPERBOREANS.

"And the Sons of JAVAN; ELISHAH, and Tarshish, Kittim, and DODANIM."
Genesis, x. 4.

PLACED in a position nearly to intersect the Canalovian Mountains at right angles, are the tribes of the River Yelum, or Hydaspes—Y'ELUMYŎ-DES (ELUMIO-TIS)[1]; immediately in the neighbourhood of which country is to be found the celebrated oracle of DODONA. I trust that I shall be enabled to make the history of this far-famed shrine perfectly distinct; and that having already reached the fountain head of the primitive Indo-European emigrations, this mysterious oracle will no longer resist rational research, based upon a sound geographical foundation. I must beg the reader to bear in mind the distinct assertion which I have already made, of the NATIONAL UNITY of Egyptian, Greek, and Indian. This fact distinctly recognised, and surveyed without prejudice, even so far as to accept Hellenic authorities, when speaking of the colonisations from Egypt and Phœnicia, will prepare the mind for the reception of much valuable, but often rejected history. It is not by passing an arbitrary sentence upon the correctness either of logographer, poet, or historian, that truth is to be elicited. It is not by a balancing of possibilities, or by the assumptive theory of Greek invention, that a true knowledge of the past is

[1] *Yelumyu-des*, the land of the Yelum.

to be obtained. Caution is a commendable virtue; but extreme distrust is far more perilous to history than extreme facility of belief. The possessor of the latter quality may, among much fable, receive some history; while the sceptic as easily *invents* an *invention* for a nation as for an author. "It is universally allowed," observes Dr. Cramer, "that this celebrated temple owed its origin to the Pelasgi, at a period much anterior to the Trojan war; since many writers represent it as existing in the time of Deucalion, and even of Inachus.[1] Herodotus distinctly states that it was the most ancient oracle of Greece, and represents the Pelasgi as consulting it on various occasions. Hence the title of Pelasgic, assigned to Jupiter, to whom the temple was dedicated.

> "Then fixing for a space
> His eyes on Heaven, his feet upon the place
> Of sacrifice, the purple draught he poured
> Forth in the midst: and thus the god implored:—
> 'Oh, thou Supreme! enthroned all height above,[2]
> Oh great PELASGIC, DODONEAN, Jove!
> Who 'midst surrounding frosts, and vapours chill,
> Presid'st on bleak Dodona's vocal hill,
> Whose groves the SELLI, race austere! surround,
> Their feet unwashed, their slumbers on the ground,
> Who bear from rustling oaks thy dark decrees,
> And catch the fates, low-whispered in the breeze."[3]

"Of the existence of another oracle in Thessaly of the same name, no doubt, I imagine, can be entertained, and to this, the prayer of Achilles probably had reference. Setting aside the fables which Herodotus has transmitted to us respecting Dodona and its doves, to which he evidently attached no belief, his report of the *affinity which existed between the service of this temple and that of Thebes in Egypt, is deserving of our attention:* as it

[1] Æsch. Prom. Vinct., v. 679. Dion. Hal. Ant. Rome, i. p. 14.

[2] Ζεῦ ἄνα, Δωδωναῖε, Πελασγικὲ, τηλόθι ναίων.—κ. τ. λ.

[3] Pope's Homer, Il., xvi. 233.

confirms what we learn from other sources, that many of the superstitions of the Pelasgi were derived from the Egyptians, either directly, or through the medium of the Phœnicians. Strabo asserts that the duties of the temple were originally allotted to men, from the circumstance of Homer's mention of the Selli as being attendant upon the god: the term Selli was considered by many ancient writers to refer to a people of Pelasgic origin, whom they identified with the Helli; and also with the Tomari. The origin of the word Dodona seems not to have been ascertained . . . . Nor are we better informed as to the nature and construction of the temple, during the early age of Grecian history. Dodona was the first station in Greece to which the offerings of the Hyperboreans were despatched, according to Herodotus. All accounts seem to agree that it stood either on the declivity or at the foot of an elevated mountain called Tomarus.[1] Hence the term Tomuri, supposed to be a contraction for Tomaruri, or guardians of Tomarus, which was given to the priests of the temple."[2] If the reader will now refer to the map of the Punjab, he will at once rescue Dodona from the mythologic category; nothing, certainly, can be less mythological than latitude and longitude; to that test I appeal. Doda[3] is "a town in the Northern Punjab, amidst the mountains south of Cashmir, situate on the north-west bank of the Chenāb, nearly opposite its confluence with the river of Budrawar."[4] The tribe Dodo, or Dor, is, perhaps, the most ancient of the thirty-six Rajpoot tribes of the Hiya or Aswa Sachas. Colonel Tod observes, speaking of this tribe, "Though occupying a place in all the genealogies, time has destroyed all knowledge of the past history of a tribe, to gain a

[1] Strabo, vii. 328. [2] Cram. Geog. Greece, vol. i. p. 118.

[3] Dodān, plural of the tribe Doda. The Dodan-im of Moses.

[4] Thornt. Punjab, vol. i. p. 168—9.

victory over whom, was deemed by Pert'hwirajá, worthy of a tablet."[1] The dignified and powerful state of this great clan, which ranks, in the Mosaic account of the primitive genealogies of our race, on a par with Elisha (Ellas), and Javan, "Yavana," or the "Ionians," is still farther proved by their people being the central pivot of Soo-Meroo, the far-famed mountain of glory—the Olympus of the Hindoo deities. Soo-Meroo, however, both in Greece and in the Punjab, is as geographical a position as Snowdon; and "THE DODO" as much a fact as "THE DOUGLAS."

"Mér" is the well known term in North-Western Asia to express "a mountain"—"Soo[2]-MÉR,"[3] is "*the* mountain," par éminence—"the great mountain"—"the glorious mountain;" the Greek way of writing which was "TO-MAR-OS,"[4] as I have before noticed.

Doda, situate amidst the mountains south of Cashmir, is in lat. 33° 2′, long. 75° 18′; it is almost as near to the magnificent "Mér"—"the Soo-mer" of the Punjab, as the Dodon of Greece is to its To-már-os (Soo-Méru.) The residence of Clan Doda was about sixty miles from their grand mountain "Mér." "Mér and Sér, in the north of the Punjab, are two mountain summits, which rise to a great height and with sublime effect, fifty or sixty miles east of the eastern boundary of Cashmir. In their regular conical form, they as closely resemble each other as though they had been cast in the same mould, but they differ in hue, one being *completely white*, and the other as *uniformly black*. No explanation appears to have been given of the singular fact that, being of the same height,

[1] Tod's Rajastha, vol. i. p. 116.

[2] *Su*, or *Soo*, "well," is the Greek εὖ, *passim*.

[3] Pronounced like Mère of the French.

[4] The commutation of the letters "s" and "t," is of great extent throughout the Greek and Sanscrit languages. See Append. Rule 23.

and situate in the same latitude, one is covered with perpetual snow, the other is quite bare. They are probably, with the exception of the mountains in Rupshu, the highest mountains between the Sutlej and the Indus. Hügel clearly viewed them at Vizerabad, in the plain of the Punjab, overtopping the Panjals of Cashmir, and many other intervening mountains, though the distance is not less than one hundred and forty miles."[1] DODO and Mér then, or "Soo-Mer-os," are, in the Cashmirian "y'ELUMYŎ-des,"[2] almost as contiguous as Dodon and To-mar-os in the Macedonian ELUM-IO-TIS; and, still more pointedly to mark the identity of both, we have in a nearly equidistant and central position between Doda and Mér, the town of PAMBU-R. "Pambur" is again transferred to the Grecian Dodona; it now gives a name to the lake on which Dodona is situate. That lake is "PAMBO-'TIS," "PAMBOR-DES," "the LAND OF PAMBUR." Pambur, as the reader will observe, is situate to the north east of the Punjab: it lies on the route from Kishtewar to Cashmir, and is on the "Muru Wurdwun" River, forty miles above its confluence with the Chenaub.[3] Those ancient people, who are grouped along the western heights of the Grecian Tomaros, from north to south, are the Hellopes. These are the mysterious beings who have for centuries provoked the curiosity and the despair of the classical student. They are the "HELO-PES,"[4] or "CHIEFS OF THE HELA," and their land is called HELLOPIA—the land of the Hela Chiefs; their country "HELLA-DOS,"[5] or the

[1] "Mér and Sér may be considered situate about lat. 34°, long. 76°."—THORNTON'S *Gaz. Punjab; vide* Mér and Sér—Doda, &c.

[2] Land of the Yelum, or *Elumio-tis.*

[3] Lat. 33° 38′, long. 75° 40′. Thornt. vol. ii. p. 92.

[4] From Hela, the Mountain Hela, and *Pĕ,* a chief, a king.

[5] Properly Hela-des; *Hela* and *des,* a land. The genitive case is here given as showing the true source of "Hellas."

"LAND OF HELA, their tribe THE DODA,"[1] and their priests are named SELLI or BRAHMINS.[2] While the sacred tribe of Dodo, or the Dodān, fixed their oracle towards the northerly line of the "Hellopes," in Thessaly, the immediate neighbours of the Hyperboreans took up their abode towards the south of the holy mountain of To-Maros or Soo-Meroo. These were the PASHWARĀN,[3] or the emigrants from PESHAWER, who appear in the Greek guise of "PASS-ARON." We now readily see the connection between the settlements of the Dodān (Dodonian Oracle), Passaron (Peshawer people), and the offerings of the HYPERBOREANS, or the men of "KHYBER-POOR," who retained this appellation wherever they subsequently settled. The people of the Khyber and of Peshawer (Hyper-boreans and Pass-aron), are placed in immediate contiguity to each other in the maps of Afghanistan.

It was not without just reason that the memory of the Hyperboreans was so hallowed in the affections of the pious and the wise, among the nations of antiquity, as to induce a grateful record of their virtues in poetry and song. "In Cashmir," writes Müller, "plants, and animals, and men, exist in the greatest physical perfection." Bailly refers the origin of the arts and sciences, astronomy, and the old lunar zodiac, and the discovery of the planets, to the most northerly tract of Asia. In the Scriptures, the second origin of mankind is referred to a mountainous region eastward of Shinar; and the ancient books of the Hindus fix the cradle of our race in the same quarter. The Hindu

[1] Plural Dodān.

[2] SĔLOS, BRAHMA. (Rule ii.) See the Homeric description quoted page 123, also that of Cramer.

[3] Pashwar is a less common form than Pesh-war. Both *Pesh* and *Pash* (before), are in general use in Persia. Pesh-war, or Pash-war, is properly a frontier town; the Persian plural of which is Pash-warān; and the digammated "w" or "v" being dropped, gives Pass-'aron to the Greek language. (Rule vii. Appendix.)

Paradise is on MOUNT MERU, on the confines of Cashmir and Thibet.[1]

"The Hyperboreans," observes Diodorus,[2] "worship Apollo more zealously than any other people; they are all priests of Apollo; one town in their country is sacred to Apollo, and its inhabitants are for the most part players on the lyre."

> There the sacred virgin quire,—
> The breathing flute,
> The full-voiced lute,
> Thrill the soul with hallowed fire:
> While as they feast with joy o'erflowing,
> Laurelled, with golden light is glowing
> Each bright enwreathed tress.
> Nor age, nor sickness, 'mid your Saintly Band bears sway,
> Nor toils, nor war distract your day,
> Ye Lords of Righteousness.[3]

Such is the testimony borne to these Hyperboreans by the magnificent lyrist, Pindar, whose style I have endeavoured to clothe in an English dress. There is throughout the whole of this author a strong Bud'histic bias, while many of his doctrines are the exact counterpart of the chief Jaina tenets, one great source of which is to be traced to the Cashmirian philosophy and religion, introduced by the founders of CHAIRONÆA, or "the people

[1] Müller, Univ. Hist., iv., 19.

[2] Schmitz, Smith's Dictionary of Gr. and Rom. Biog.

[3] . . . . *παντᾶ δὲ χοροὶ παρθένων*
λυρᾶν τε βοαὶ καναχαί τ' αὐλῶν δονέονται·
δάφνᾳ τε χρυσέᾳ κόμας ἀναδήσαντες εἰλαπινάζοισιν εὐφρόνως.
νόσοι δ' οὔτε γῆρας οὐλόμενον κέκραται
ἱερᾷ γενεᾷ· πόνων δὲ καὶ μαχᾶν ἄτερ
οἰκέοισι φυγόντες
ὑπέρδικην Νέμεσιν.—PIND. *Pyth.* x. 38—44.

Vide Welcker's correct remark on the religious allusion of Pindar to this Θεοδαίσια or Εἰλαπίνη.

of CASHMIR."[1] Other powerful religious influences also will be noticed in their proper place, as especially acting upon Bœotia.

About five miles to the north of Dodon, was a remarkable town of these priests—its name given at a correlative time with that of the oracle Bodăn (Bodŏn), *i.e.* "the BOODHISTS;"[2] hence, it is clear, that "Dodon"[3] once represented the Brahminical, and Bodon the Boodhistic sect. This town appearing in Greek as "DAMASTIUM," is "Dham," "asti," (Saint's Town), or "All Saints." It was to Dodon and to these "Dhammos"[4] that the HYPER-BOREANS sent their offerings. What wonder, when they were of the same stock, and were of old the fellow inhabitants of the same land, these HYPER-BOREANS being, as I have already shown, the "KHYBER-POOREANS," or "people of KHYBER-POOR," *i.e.* the city and district of the Khyber.[5] One of the Khyber settlements will be seen in Thessaly, on the eastern branch of the Phœnix river. Its name is tolerably preserved as "KYPHARA" and "KYPHÆRA."

[1] Kīra, Cashmir. *Kaira*, the descendants or people of Cashmir (also Kīrā); *Kairo-naya*, Cashmir town or province; as Naya-pala, Ne-pal from *Naya*, polity, government.

[2] Persian plural form of Boodha. See Append. Rule 7.

[3] I have not the slightest doubt that the Dodan of Cashmir, and consequently the Dodan of Epirus, were a Brahminical tribe. *Deva-deva*, God of gods, is the name of Brahma. Its euphonic changes will be Deodeo, then Do-do. I have traced to great extent the common substitution of "ŏ" for "v" Sanscrit. The general principle is noticed in Bopp.

[4] *Dhammo*, righteousness, is the Pali form of *Dherma*; Dhammo is a favourite prefix to the names of Bud'hist Theros, or Priests. As in the case of Dhammásókó, the great Bud'hist emperor of India. *See* Mahawanso, *passim*.

[5] Between lat. 33° 30′, 34° 20′; long. 71° 10′, 71° 30′.

XII.

THE CASHMIRIANS.

La communication entre Kachemir et Ceylan, n'a pas eu lieu seulement par les entreprises guerrières que je viens de rappeler, mais aussi par une commerce paisible. C'est de cette île que venaient des artistes, qu'on appelaient Rakshasas, à cause du merveilleux de leur art, et qui exécutaient des ouvrages pour l'utilité et pour l'ornement d'un pays montagneux, et sujet aux inondations.

TROYER, *Raja Tarangini.*

THE simple, but undeniable facts, which I have brought forward, resting upon a substantial geographical basis, will now commend themselves to the judgment of the dispassionate enquirer after truth, when he discovers, that not only the ATTAC, the LOGURH, the BEYHOOT, the ARGHOSAN, the LOGHURI-OOKSHWALÆ (LOCRI-OZOLÆ), MAGARI, SARAWAN, COR-INDUS, the LESPOI, ARGHWALAS (ARGOLIS), and AKKEHA, are represented with astonishing faithfulness in HELA-DES, or HELLA-DOS,—but that the province of Cashmir and its neighbourhood, and its tribes, and its Maha-bharatian history, are transported to this Hella Nova, with almost the faithfulness of a lithographic transfer from one material to another.

About thirty miles to the south of the Greek To-Maros, are situated the important people of the Cassiopæi; they too have come from the y' Elumyo-tis, or "the land of the river Yelum," which encircles their western and northwestern frontier; they are the tribes of CASHMIR—the

CASYA-pas.[1] And now behold an historical and geographical base, for a supposed mythological tale; for here we are fortunately brought into juxtaposition with the most important point in all India for an historical foundation. The most authentic document which north-western India possesses—(and north-western India is now made synonymous with Greece, more especially with northern Greece,)—is the Rajatarangini.[1] The Rajatarangini, written at Cashmir, the identical point whence the Cassiopæi, or "people of Casyapa," set out on their emigration into north-western Greece, is a dynastic record of the princes of that far-famed valley, whose chronicles ascend to the venerable antiquity of B.C. 2448.[2] The claim to an antiquity so vast will not, *per se*, form the slightest objection to the reception of a chronicle to whose astonishing age the Assyrian monuments, lately discovered, form a fitting pendant. The art of writing, so far from being an invention of moderate antiquity, will be found to range up to a period bordering upon the most venerable antiquity. The most ancient of the Vedas, which could never have been handed down by tradition—for there is nothing like *narrative* to promote memorial record—takes the date of B.C. 1500.[3] Now, as primitive Greece has practically

[1] Casio-pæi, Greek form.

[2] The "Raja Tarangini" is not one entire composition, but a series of compositions written by different authors at different periods; a circumstance, as Professor Wilson observes, that gives a greater value to its contents; as, with the exception of the early periods of the history, the several authors may be regarded almost as the chroniclers of their own times. The first series is by Calhana Pundit, who treats copiously of the earliest history of Cashmir. (See the admirable notices and very copious and very learned treatise of Professor Wilson on the Hindoo History of Cashmir, *Asiatic Researches*, vol. XV.)

[3] "La chronologie de Cashmir donne depuis l'année 2448 ans avant J. C. une série de périodes dynastiques et de rois; contre laquelle, ainsi que je crois l'avoir démontré, il ne peut s'élever aucune objection sérieuse."—CAPT. TROYER, *Raja Tarangini*, vol ii., p. 452.

become primitive India, and as the people of the latter country were, even from the most ancient times, most careful in genealogical records, it is impossible, knowing, as we do, that the Egyptians are the same people—acknowledging, as we do, the amazing antiquity of the art of writing amongst them, supported, too, by the authority of Moses,—it is impossible, on rational grounds, to deny the same art to the Greek—*i. e.* the Indian of primitive Hellas. I cannot in this place avoid introducing the remarks of the learned translators of the "Dabistan:"[1]—"So much at least may be considered as established. 1st. That the limits of history are to be removed farther back than those before fixed. That in the earliest times, primitive nations, related by language to each other, had their origin in the common elevated country of Central Asia, and that the Iranians and Indians were once united before their emigration into Iran and India. This great fact presents itself, as it were, upon the border of a vast abyss of unknown times."[2] These are just reflections; borne out both by the sacred historian, and by sound ethnological principles. But we must now return to the singular transcript of Cashmir and its neighbourhood, presented by Central and south-western Epirus.

Casyapur, or the "city of Casyapa," is not without its clear and distinct notice in the earliest Greek historian, Herodotus, who, in the usual style of Greek orthography, wrote the name of the city as "Caspa-tur-os," a corrupt form of "Caspa-dwar"-os,[3] the Sanscrit *v* being as usual replaced by the Greek *u*; Pakta-war, the neighbouring

[1] "The Dabistan," by Shea and Troyer, Orient. Transl. Fund.

[2] Preliminary Discourse, p. 76.

[3] *Dwar*, literally "a door," is a common affix to Indian towns; as *Ram-dwar*, &c., so that the simple element Basyapa remains.

province to the north, he calls Paktua-ka, a very fair derivative of the same word "Pakta,"[1] the ancient province of Casya-pur, or Cashmir.

"Kashmir is an elevated tract north of the Punjab, enclosed by very lofty mountains, having in the middle a level and alluvial soil watered by the river Jailum, and in all other parts, a very uneven surface, formed by numerous ridges and gorges, extending from the plain to the culminating line of the surrounding range. The etymology of the name of this celebrated region has singularly perplexed antiquarians. Wilford[2] derives the name from the Chasas, a very ancient and powerful tribe, who inhabited the Himalaya and Hindoo Coosh, from the eastern limits of India to the confines of Persia. They are mentioned in the Institutes of Menu, and other sacred books of the Hindoos, and still hold large tracts in northern Hindoostan. Humboldt states[3] 'that its primæval name was CASYAPAMAR, signifying the habitation of Casyapa, a mythological personage, by whose agency the valley was drained.' Casyapa, according to the Hindoo authorities, was the grandson of Brahma, and lived as an ascetic, on the mountain contiguous to the lake which originally occupied the valley. The city founded in the country thus drained, was called after the saint Casyapur, or 'Town of Casyapa,' converted in ordinary pronunciation into Cashappur, and passing ultimately into Cashmir. Abul Fazel, in his abridgment of the Raja Tarangini, merely states, that Kushup, an ascetic, first brought the Brahmins to inhabit the country, after the water had subsided."[4] I would here suggest that there may possibly be no difficulty in

[1] Forms from Pakta; Pactyus, a, um, and Pactyukus, a, um, the Πακτυακα of Herodotus.

[2] Caucusus.—*Asiatic Researches*, vol. vi., 455, 456.

[3] Asie Centrale, i., 102.

[4] Thornton, Cashmir.

reconciling these apparent variations. The matter may perhaps be thus stated :—

The Chasas . . .	The great tribe.
Casya Pa	The Chasa chief.
Coh Chasas (Cau-casas)	The mountains of the Chasas.
Chas-păyŭs (Cas-pius) .	The sea of the Chasa chiefs.
Chas-mīr (Cash-mīr) .	The lake of the Chasas.[1]
Casopas (*Casso-pœi*)	The people of Casyapa, or the Chasa chief, or The Cashmirians.

Cashmir has on the north, Bulti, or LittleThibet; east, the mountainous tracts of Zanska, Kishtewar; south, Jamu, Chumba, Rajawur, and some other small hilly districts occupying the southern declivity in the mountains inclosing the valley in that direction, and sloping to the plain of the Punjab; on the west is the wild unexplored country held by the Dardas, and the remnant of that once powerful race,—the Guikkers. If the limits be considered as determined by the culminating ridge of the tortuous range of mountains which on every side enclose it, Cashmir will be found to be one hundred and twenty miles long, from the snowy Panjal on the south-east, to the Durawur ridge in the north, and seventy miles broad, from the Futi Panjal on the south, to Shesha Nag at the north-east. The shape of the outline is irregular, but has a remote resemblance to an oval. Hügel estimates the plain forming the bottom of the valley, to be seventy-five

[1] *Mir*, properly "the ocean." (*Vide* Wilson's Sans. Lex., lib. v.) But I am inclined to think it is not only the Latin "mare" but the "meers" of England, as Winder-meer; nor must we forget that these Cashmirians once lived in this isle.

miles long, and forty miles broad.[1] The general aspect of Cashmir is simple and easily comprehended; it being a basin bounded on every side by lofty mountains, in the enclosing range of which are several depressions, called popularly passes, as they afford means of communication between the valley and the adjacent countries. The Panjals, or mountains forming the range which encloses Cashmir, appear, with little exception, to be of igneous origin, and basaltic, their usual formation being a beautiful amygdaloydal trap. In June, 1828, the city of Cashmir was shaken by an earthquake, which destroyed about twelve hundred houses and one thousand persons. Besides the low alluvial tract extending along the banks of the Jailum, and forming the greater part of the cultivable soil of the valley, there are several extensive table lands of slight elevation, stretching from the mountains various distances into the plains.

These Karywas, as they are called by the natives, are described by Vigne as composed of the finest alluvial soil, usually free from shingle. Their surface is verdant, and generally smooth as a bowling-green, but they are divided and deeply furrowed by mountain streams. He considers the appearance they present a strong proof of the tradition that the whole valley was once occupied by a lake. The grandeur and splendour of Cashmirian scenery result from the sublimity of the huge enclosing mountains, the picturesque beauty of the various gorges extending from the level alluvial plain, to the passes over the crest of the enclosing range; the numerous lakes and fine streams rendered often more striking by cataracts; the luxuriance and variety of forest trees, and the rich and multiform vegetation of the lower grounds. Vigne is untiring in

[1] The tract thus defined lies between lat. 33° 15′, 34° 30′; long. 73° 40′ 75° 30′.

its praise, calling to his aid the mellifluous eloquence of Milton :—

> Sweet interchange
> Of hill and valley, rivers, woods, and plains ;
> Now land, now lake, and shores with forest crowned,
> Rocks, dens, and caves.[1]

The Cashmirians probably excel all other branches of the great Indian nation, in physical qualities. Vigne describes the men as of broad Herculean build, and of manly features: Moorcroft regards the aboriginal race as in general tall, and of symmetrical proportions, and adds, that amongst the peasantry are to be found figures of robust and muscular make, such as might have served for models of the Farnesian Hercules. Elphinston and Foster, also, bear evidence to their athletic and finely proportioned formation. How little did these eminent travellers imagine that this was the very race, this identical people of Cashmir, and its immediate neighbourhood, that helped to form from their splendid stock, the manly vigour of Hellas, and the exquisite beauty of her daughters. Both CHÆRONEIA and PLATÆIA are settlements from this district; CAIRONAYA[2] being the people of Cashmir, and PLATÆIA being BALTÆIA those of BALTI.[3] From such a distance did that northern vigour emanate, which gave at once to Hellas her warriors and her poets.

"The language of Cashmir is a dialect of Sanscrit, and is written in the Devanagri character. It contains a large admixture of Persian, in which the records and correspondence of the government are written. Cashmir abounds in monuments of a peculiar style, *generally indicating very remote antiquity*, and clearly referable to a period previous to the Mahomedan invasion."[4] Of these,

[1] Par. Lost, ix. 115.

[2] *Cairān*, the Cashmirians.

[3] From Balti is the derivative Baltai (Baltaia). Greek form is Blataia (Plataia, Lat. *Platæa*), "b," "p," and "v," as usual, commutable.

[4] Thornton, vol. i. pp. 339—372.—"The early history of Cashmir, which

the temple of Cooroo Pandoo has already been noticed. Such are the people of *Casyapa*, or the *Cassopæi*,[1] of Hellas, as described by undoubted authority—authority that gives an overpowering weight to the geographical evidences already, and about to be, brought forward. Now hold we a sufficient clue to the splendid shawls—the pepla of both goddesses and princesses. In the ruby mines and mineral wealth of the neighbouring regions we see the magnificent necklace of Harmonia, presented by the "DEVAS,"[2] or Devi, or θέοι, or priests, at her nuptials, and the explanation of that abundance of gold once existing throughout Greece, in articles of regal luxury and of private wealth; now is explained the frequent use of *ivory*, and its artistic adaptations; now are explained the graceful forms of the so-called Grecian, but, in reality, the Cashmirian beauties; now do we distinctly discern the sources—the everliving models of those magnificent and manly forms that have been eternized by the skill of Pheidias. It is thus incontrovertible, that, while the Attac, Tatta, the Kori, and the Indus and Magar gave at once to Greece her practised seamen, and her commercial bias, in the communities of

lies rather within the province of the Oriental antiquarian than the limits of the present work, has been drawn from darkness and methodized, by the varied learning and cultivated judgment of Professor Wilson."—See his "History of Cashmir," As. Res., vol. xv. pp. 1—120, also "Prinsep's Tables," pp. 101—104.

[1] "Kasyapa," observes Professor Wilson, (As. Res., vol. xvi. p. 455,) in speaking of the eight deified Budha teachers, or human Buddhas, "is a name known to the orthodox system, and perhaps had once existence. He seems to have been the chief instrument in extending civilisation along the Himalayan and Caucasian mountains, as far as we may judge from the traditions of Nepal and Cashmere, and the many traces of his name to be met with along those ranges."

[2] Devos, the Greek Θεος, is the ordinary name of a religious teacher, or priest.

Attica, the Tettigẽs, the Cor-Inthians, and the Megareans, that by the same emigration Hellas was gifted with the noblest and the most lovely forms that ever graced the Temple of Creation.

We have seen Soo-Meros, Pambur-des, and Doda, flanking Cashmir on the East, and represented in Epirus by To-Maros, Pambo-'tis, and Dodon; we have yet to contemplate, mirrored forth on the western slopes of the Pindus, a southern province of Cashmir. That province is MATAN; and the new sojourners in Hellas, who have left the verdant plains of their father-land, are called "METAN-ASTÆ," or "PEOPLE OF MATAN."[1] Matan is "a Karywa, or table land, extending from the town of Islamabad to the base of the range, enclosing the valley on the east. Notwithstanding its situation below those vast mountain masses, it is devoid of streams, or other natural means of irrigation, but consisting, almost entirely, of very fertile alluvial earth; it bears, when cultivated, abundant crops of wheat, barley, and most kinds of grain, excepting rice. The great depopulation of Cashmire, however, has rendered it for the most part a waste, presenting a surface of the finest verdure, unbroken by tree, shrub, or human habitation. . . . Hügel assigns to it a breadth of four or five miles in every direction. He also mentions the solitude and unbroken silence of this fertile plain, which formerly was irrigated by means of a great aqueduct, now completely ruined. This table-land is elevated from 250 to 300 feet above the great alluvial plain of Kashmir. On a slight eminence, at its western extremity, are situated the ruins of a very ancient building, which excites in all spectators feelings of admiration,

[1] "*Matan*, and *Vásti*, dwellers; from the verb *vas*, to dwell; Vasti, plural only."—*Wilson's Sans. Lex., s.v.* This "v" is the old Greek, or rather Sanscrit sound, called digamma; sounded by the old Greeks, but dropped by their descendants.

approaching to awe, by the elaborate skill displayed in its construction, and the simple, massive, and sublime character of its architecture. It is built of huge blocks of hard compact limestone, the black colour of which adds to its gloomy grandeur.[1] This extraordinary monument of early civilisation consists of an outer colonnade, inclosing an area, in which stands the principal building, detached. There are four great gateways; one in the middle of each side, and facing the four cardinal points; those facing east and west being much finer than the others. Within the enclosure made by this peristyle, and equidistant from the side walls, is a magnificent temple, of a rectangular outline, seventy feet long, sixty feet wide, and in its present state, about forty feet high. The whole character of the building, like that of the enclosing colonnade, is massive, simple, and severe, yet in excellent taste. Some notion of the style may be formed by imagining a combination of the Egyptian, Tuscan, and Saxon. The tradition of the Cashmirian pundits, assigns it to an antiquity of about two thousand five hundred years: with them it bears the name Korau Pandau, and is attributed to Kooroo and Pandoo, two kings, who figure in the remote legends of Hindoo mythology. It is also known by the name of the 'City of the Sun.' Hügel observes, 'My description, unfortunately, gives little conception of the impression produced by this simple majestic structure, which I class among the finest ruins of the world. The forms are throughout noble, and the embellishments often tasteful; but it is peculiarly characterised by the huge masses of which it is constructed; and the effect of these is heightened by the dark hue of the marble, and the desolation in which it stands, in the

[1] Jacquemont observes: "Il est construit dans toute son étendue de tranches, posées successivement les unes au-dessus des autres, sans ciment."

most fruitful valley in the world.'"[1] Let the reader turn his eyes towards the province lying immediately to the west of Cashmir—it is "Attac," the parent Attica—the solution of the architectural problem of the temple of the Cooroos and Pandoo is easy: let him know that a line of Cashmirian princes ruled in Attica—the Attica of Greece, as their ancestors had ruled over the parent states of the Attac and Cashmir; let him know that the descendants of that noble race still exist on the north-western frontier of Cashmir. Let him farther know, that PANDION sprang from the chiefs of the Attoc, a clan of the great Yadoo tribe; that the descendants of that Yadoo tribe yet linger round the Y' Elumyo-des or Yelum-land,[2] between the Indian Attica, and the Casyo-pas of the Punjab; that Cecropos was a chief of the Pelasga race; that the Pelasga are "the people of Pelasa," part of which vast people are to be seen on the northern skirts of Cashmir;[3] that a temple, reared to the deified Pandoo, still stands mid the people of Metan, or the Metan-astæ; that the chief town among the Cassiopæi, in Greece, is PAND'OSIA, PANDOO TOWN;[4] that, on the "Royal River,"[5] and near the "Royal Lake,"[6] in Greece, is again founded by these exiles of Cashmir the city of their great tribe "Coocuroos;"[7] that this city is built at the confluence of the "Royal River" (Acheron), and the Co-cootus;[8] that the

[1] These ruins are situate in lat. 33° 45′, long. 75° 8′.—Thornton's Matan, vol. ii. p. 42, Punjab.

[2] Elymiotis (Elumyŏ-des), and the Cashmirians.

[3] Pulaza, lat. 45°, long. 71° 15′.

[4] Pandoo-vusia, from *vus*, "to dwell." The "oo" and "v" coalesce; thus Pand'wusia, the "w" English, forming the "ῶ" Greek.

[5] Ache-Ron; *Aca*, water; *Rana* (for *Rajan*), the king.

[6] Ache-Rusia; *Aca*, water; *Rajyu* (*Regius*), royal.

[7] Chichurus, Greek form of Coocosrus.

[8] Cocootus Riv.; from *Coh*, a hill; and *Coth*, the city. Coth or Koth, (called also Kotli), lat. 33° 29′, long. 73° 47′.

parent city, "Coh-cothus," or "Coth-on-the-hill," notwithstanding the lapse of ages, still stands close to the Casyopas, or Cashmirians; that the still more ancient name of "Cichurus," was E-Phure, "The Hiya Town," or "Hi-pur,"[1] once the capital of HE-PAIRA (Epeiros), or "The Hiya-chiefs land," laved by the waters of the Hi-yanian (Ionian) Sea, or the "Sea of the Horse Tribes." Let him again direct his glance across the waters that separate the land of the Hellenes, those "Chiefs of the Hela," from south-western Italy; let him again behold, rising beneath the same meridian as its predecessor in Greece, another royal town of the Pandoos—"Pandosia;"[2] another "Royal River," "Ache Ron." But why disguise the fact? These Pandoos are an exiled race; they are essentially "Su-Budhas;" emphatically "The Budhas," and the river which flows through this, their western settlement, announces the fact in language the most distinct.[3] But I cannot here abandon the noble exiles of the House of Pandava, without observing that not only are the Chiefs of Cashmir, of Egypt, and of Attica, and the Pandion and Pandarus of Greece, bound up with the geography of Hellas, and of India, but also the Bharatas and the land of the Bharatas, and the history of the "Maha Bharata."

Bhárataversha is the classical name for India proper, so called from Bharata, the son of Dushyanta, whose patrimony it was;[4] his descendants were called the Bharatas, amongst the rival clans of whom named the Cooroos and Pandoos, arose the fierce rivalry which was decided on the fatal field of Coorookshetra, in the

[1] The Hiya, Hi, or Aswa, was the grand Rajpoot tribe of N. W. Asia; so called from their equestrian renown. *Hiya*, *Aswa*, and *Asp*, signify "a horse."

[2] *Pandoo*, and *vus*, to dwell.

[3] Sabbatus Riv. Read: "Su-Buddhas" R. See Rule, "oo" and "a" broad.

[4] Wilson's Sans. Lex. *s. v.*

neighbourhood of Delhi. It was this gigantic struggle, which continued to rage for eighteen successive days, which forms the subject of the magnificent poem of the Mahabharata,[1] which I shall shortly have occasion to notice.

As the reader will now be convinced that the geography of north-western India is the geography of northern Greece, so will he also find that their early histories are one and indivisible. The great heroes of India are the gods of Greece. They are, in fact, as they have been often rationally affirmed, and as plausibly but not as rationally denied, deified chiefs and heroes; and this same process of deification, both among Greeks and Romans—the descendants of colonists from India, continued, especially among the latter people, down to and throughout the most historical periods. I regret that I cannot subscribe to the theories propounded by several writers of high and deserved celebrity, in Germany, relative to the foundation of the Greek mythology; still less, that I cannot accede to the doctrine of Greek *invention*, and Greek mythopœic propensities, as laid down by Mr. Grote, in his otherwise valuable History of Greece, as the exponent of that wide and crowded panorama, which has been styled Greek legend, and Greek mythology; a panorama painted by foreign artists.

I regret the tendency of this theory so much the more, because its dictum not only rests upon an arbitrary basis, but because its doctrine, if correct, must for ever preclude all independent and vigorous research—because we are required to accede to that which has not been proved, viz., that the mythology of the Greeks rests upon a foundation purely inventive. I believe the

[1] "*Maha*, 'great,' and Bharata. A name derived from Bharata, among whose descendants this great war occurred."—WILSON, *s. v. Bharata.*

ordinary sense of mankind, will allow, that there is nothing less mythological than geography securely settled by latitude and longitude; and further, that if to this geography there should be found inseparably attached, names proved to be historical, as well as geographical, by the mutual plain and practical harmony of their relations, —that then we are furnished with a document of the most trustworthy character; because, in fact, the *very geography*—which cannot be shaken—is the *very history* of which we are in search. If, therefore, I demonstrate the latitude and longitude of TARTARUS, exhibit by the same means, the native land of Erectheus, Erecthonius, Poseidon, the Centaurs, the Autocthons, and the Tettiges,[1] their *historical*, must be considered as powerful as their *geographical* evidence. The observations of Col. Mure, in his admirable "History of Greek Literature," form so correct a commentary upon the theory that would attribute Greek mythology to Greek invention, that I shall make no apology for introducing it in this place.[2] "The principle of human apotheosis, or in other words, of awarding divine honours to mortals, is not only one of the most prominent characteristics of Helleno-Pelasgic superstition, but one which distinguishes it from every other ancient form of Paganism . . . . . Among the Greeks the practice can be traced with singular consistency, from the earliest period of which tradition has presented any memorial, down to the final extinction of classical paganism. But the principle was too inveterate to give way even to a change of religion. It was transferred from the temple to the Church, from the heathen to the Roman Catholic mythology, in which system the canonised saints and martyrs offer the closest analogy to the deified Pagan heroes. The analogy is admitted and aptly expressed in the title 'Divi,' common to both Pagan and

[1] Τεττῖγες, the Athenian Grasshoppers.

[2] Col. Mure's Hist. of Gr. Lit., vol. i. p. 28.

Roman Catholic demigods." The Divi, in fact, of the early Roman Pontiffs were the Sanscrit "Devas," Brahmins, or "religious teachers,"—Deva expressing both "God," and him who was looked upon as a god by the inhabitants of Hellas and of Rome; for we are not to suppose that the term "Divi" took its rise in the so-called historical periods of Rome.

I have been thus explicit on the diametrically opposite doctrines of "Deification," and "Mythopœic Invention," because each will shortly be brought to the test of truth; when it will be found that both the prime deities of Northern India (and, necessarily, on geographical grounds, of Greece and of Egypt), are the deified heroes of the Ramayuna, and the Mahabharatha, and other venerable Indian records, as well those records now in existence, as those preserved in Puranic compilations. And these observations are of a tendency so purely *historical* as to be indissolubly bound up with the very name of GRÄKOI, or GREEKS.[1] "We must," sagaciously observes Col. Tod, "discard the idea that the history of Rama, the Mahabharat of Krishna, and the five Pandora brothers, are mere allegory; an idea supported by some, although their race, their cities, and their coins still exist."[2] There is a scepticism founded upon simple doubt, and there is a scepticism founded upon a pre-determined theory. The first may be overcome, because it is amenable to the doctrine of rational probabilities; the second is most difficult to vanquish, because, being founded upon a mythological fiction of its own, rational probabilities are discarded, as abhorrent to that fiction. To doubt well,

[1] Dr. Mill the learned Principal of Bishops' College, observes in his notes to the inscription on an Indian temple (*Ben. As. Journ.*, July, 1835, p. 394):—"It is a favourite practice of the Hindoos, to represent their great religious teachers as incarnations of particular divinities." See also in the same article, his illustrations of *Sanscrit prosody*, by that of the Greek.

[2] Tod's Rajasthan, vol. i. p. 44.

and to doubt much, are things widely different; the former often constitutes the integrity of justice—the latter would totally discard all circumstantial evidence, and demand conviction or acquittal upon nothing less than mathematical evidence. As the *geography* of Epirus and Attica, is necessarily connected with the Indo-Grecian *histories* of those countries, as well as other parts of Greece, I shall here introduce the account, both of the war of the Mahabharata, as related by Colonel Tod, and the sound reflexions of the same clear-sighted writer; who in common with other authors of still higher literary talent, though not of superior judgment, has been looked upon as rash, in attempting to establish the connection of the east and the west; and those very points of discussion which he has raised, forcibly and rationally urging this connection, have been those the most condemned by men who, while thus speaking, *ex cathedrâ*, had never gone into those geographical evidences, by which alone the truth of this connection could be tested.

Now that this problem is solved, I am impelled as a matter of justice to the memory of those talented orientalists who, like Colonels Tod and Wilford, nobly upheld the historical reality of the Indo-Greek connection, to bear my testimony to the soundness of their deductions, and the energy which supported them beneath much literary obloquy. Is it not astonishing, that reason should so halt half way in its deductions as to allow the derivation of the Greek from an Indian language, and yet deny the personality of those who spoke it; or, in other words, deny the settlement of an Indian race in Greece? "The affinity," observes the learned Dr. Prichard,[1] "between the Greek language, and the old Parsee, and Sanscrit, is certain and essential. The use of cognate idioms proves the nations who used them to have

[1] Physical History of Man, vol. i. p. 502.

descended from one stock. That the religion of the Greeks emanated from an eastern source no one will deny. We must, therefore, suppose the religion, as well as the language of Greece to have been derived, in great part, immediately from the east." The language of Colonel Tod, on the historical reality of the Pandavas, is so full of honest enthusiasm, and abounds with such just reflexions, and gives so clear an epitome of the war of the Mahabharata, that I shall here introduce it. "Arrian," he remarks,[1] "who sketches the history of the family ruling on the Jumna, in Alexander's reign, clearly indicates that he had access to the genealogies of the Pandoo race; a branch of which ruled in those regions eight centuries subsequent to the memorable conflict of the Mahabahrata, which forms an era in the very dawn of Hindoo history.[2] There is no name so widely disseminated in the local traditions of India as that of Pandoo; from the snowy Himachil to Cape Comorin, every nation and tribe has some memorial to exhibit of this celebrated race. Yet, although the name has been perpetuated through the lapse of ages, in the geographical nomenclature of the regions they inhabited; and although nations far remote, and without intercourse, possess monuments which they attribute to the race; and although one peculiar character forms the inscription of all such monuments, still there are sceptics as to their existence, who imagine the 'Great War' as fabulous as the Trojan.[3] For such there is no law of historic evidence short of mathematical demonstration that will suffice. The triumphal column of the

[1] Dissertation on the Hindu and Theban Hercules. *Roy. As. Trans.*, vol. iii. pp. 139, 140.—On a Hindu Intaglio, found at Montrose in Scotland: read Dec., 1830.

[2] Wilson places this at B.C. 1430.

[3] That the war of Troy has nothing fabulous in it, will be seen in the sequel, when I treat upon this portion of Greek history.

Yadoos,[1] at Delhi, mentioned by the bard 'Chund,' seven centuries ago; that at Praga, the first seat of their power; the form of Bhīma,[2] in the valley of Mokunderra;[3] the caves of Dhoomnar, of Nasuk, and Girnar, with their various rock-inscriptions; the sepulchral mounts of Pandu-mandalan,[4] in the Carnatic, and many other places, separated a thousand miles from each other, might in vain be appealed to."

The scene of the outbreak of the first burst of passion between the rival clans of the Cooroos and the Pandus, is placed at Hastinapoor, the modern Delhi. "On the death of Pandu," observes Col. Tod, "Duryodhana, nephew of Pandu, asserted the illegitimacy of the Pandus, before the assembled kin. With the aid, however, of the priesthood, and the blind Dhertarashtra, his nephew Yoodishtra, eldest son of Pandu, was invested by him with the seal of royalty, in the capital Hastinapoor. Duryodhana's plots against the Pandu and his partisans, were so numerous, that the five brothers determined to leave, for awhile, their ancestral abodes on the Ganges: they sought shelter in foreign countries about the Indus, and were first protected by Drupdeva, king of Panchalica, at whose capital, Panchalinagara, the surrounding princes had arrived, as suitors for the hand of his daughter, Drupdevi. But the prize was destined for the exiled Pandu, and the skill of Arjoona in archery, obtained the fair, who threw round his neck the garland of marriage, (Burmala). The disappointed princes indulged their resentment against the

[1] I shall distinctly show the tribes of the Yadoos contiguous to the northern boundary of Thessaly.

[2] One of the Pandoo leaders.

[3] The "Pass" (Durra, or Dwarra of Mokund, an epithet of Heri).

[4] The Pandionis Regio, of Ptolemy, having Madura as a capital; which yields conviction that the Pandoos colonised this region, and gave the name of this old seat of power, Mathura on the Jumna, to this new settlement.

exile, but by Arjoona's bow they suffered the fate of Penelope's suitors, and the Pandu brought home his bride, who became in common the wife of three brothers—manners decisively Scythic. The deeds of the brothers abroad were bruited in Hastinapoor, and the blind Dhertarashtra's influence effected their recal. To stop, however, their intestine feuds, he partitioned the Pandu sovereignty; and while his son Duryodhana retained Hastinapoor, Yoodishtra founded the new capital of Indraprest'ha . . . On the division of the Pandu sovereignty, the new kingdom of Indraprest'ha eclipsed that of Hastinapoor. The brothers reduced to obedience the surrounding nations, and compelled their princes to sign tributary engagements. Yoodishtra, firmly seated on his throne, determined to signalise his reign and his sovereignty, by the imposing and solemn rites of Aswamedha and Rajsoo. In these magnificent ceremonies, in which princes alone officiate, every duty, down to that of porter, is performed by royalty.

"The steed of sacrifice,[1] liberated under Arjoona's care, having wandered whither he listed for twelve months, and none daring to accept this challenge of supremacy, he was reconducted to Indraprest'ha, where, in the meanwhile, the hall of sacrifice was prepared, and all the princes of the land were summoned to attend. The hearts of the Cooroos, burned with envy at the assumption of supremacy by the Pandus, for the Prince of Hastinapoor's office was to serve out the sacred food. The rivalry between the races burst forth afresh; but Duryodhana, who so often failed in his schemes against the safety of his antagonists, determined to make the virtue of Yoodishtra the instrument of his success. He availed himself of the national propensity for play, in which the Rajpoot continues to preserve his Scythic resemblance. Yoodishtra fell into

[1] Aswamedha, from *Aswa*, a horse, and *Medha*, a sacrifice.

the snare prepared for him. He lost his kingdom, his wife, and even his personal liberty, and that of his brothers, for twelve years, and became an exile from the plains of the Yamuna.

"The traditional history of these wanderers, their many lurking-places, now sacred,—the return to their ancestral abode, and the grand battle (Mahabharat) which ensued, form highly interesting episodes in the legends of Hindoo antiquity.[1] To decide this civil strife, every tribe and chief of fame, from the Caucasus to the ocean, assembled on Curu-Khetu, the field on which the empire of India has since, more than once, been contested and lost.[2] This combat was fatal to the dominant influence of 'the fifty-six tribes of Yadu.' On each of its eighteen days' combat, myriads were slain; for 'the father knew not the son, nor the disciple the preceptor.' Victory brought no happiness to Yoodishtra. The slaughter of his friends disgusted him with the world, and he determined to withdraw from it; previously performing at Hastinapoor funeral rites for Duryodhana (slain by the hand of Bhima), whose ambition and bad faith had originated this exterminating war.

[1] "In detailing the lists of the Maghada kings, the Vishnu Purana states that from the birth of Parikshit to the coronation of Nanda, 1015 years elapsed. Nanda preceded Chandragupta 1000 years; and Chandragupta, as identified with Sandracoptus, ascended the throne, B.C. 315. Parikshit was the grandson of Arjuna, consequently the war of the Mahabbarat, occurred 1430 years before the Christian era. Wilford reduces this by sixty years, and places the conclusion of the Great War, B.C. 1370. The difference is not very material; and either date may present an approximation to the truth."—PROF. WILSON'S *Analysis of the Puranas*. *As. Journ.*, vol. xiii. p. 81.

[2] At the moment the combatants are about to make the onset, Arjuna feels a melancholy compunction at the idea of wading to the throne, through the blood of his brothers, kinsmen and friends, whom he recognises in the ranks of the enemy. He opens his mind to his companion (Crishna) who chiding him for his tameness of spirit, tells him that he belongs to the caste of warriors, that war is his element and his duty, and that for him now to recede, would be to lose both empire and honour. Upon

Yoodishtra, Baldeva, and Crishna, having retired with the wreck of this ill-fated struggle to Dwarica, the two former had soon to lament the death of Crishna, slain by the aboriginal tribes of Bhils, against whom, from their shattered condition, they were unable to contend. After this event, Yoodishtra, with Baldeva and a few followers, entirely withdrew from India, and emigrating northwards by Sinde, to the Himalayan mountains, are there abandoned by Hindoo traditional history, and are supposed to have perished in the snows."

These heroes will again be found in Greece, as deified beings; and as such they will distinctly appear. In perfect harmony with the religious faith of the Bud'histic settlers in Phthiotis and the Othrys, the Himalayas of Greece,—in harmony with the creed of the Cashmirian colonists of that country, they are the subjects of a saintly invocation, and a saintly ascription of power over the elements, identical with the present Bud'histic creed of

Arjuna's still testifying his reluctance to begin the work of death, Crishna replies to him in a strain, the terrible sublime of the Sanchya doctrine of fatalism; thus beautifully rendered by Milman :—

"'Ne'er was the time when I was not, nor thou, nor yonder kings of earth :
Hereafter ne'er shall be the time, when one of us shall cease to be.
The soul, within its mortal frame, glides on through childhood, youth and age,
Then in another form renewed, renews its stated course again.—
All indestructible is he that spread the living universe;
And who is he that shall destroy the work of the Indestructible?
Corruptible these bodies are, that wrap the everlasting soul—
The eternal, unimaginable soul. Whence, on to battle Bharata !
For he that thinks to slay the soul, or he that thinks the soul is slain,
Are fondly both alike deceived. It is not slain—it slayeth not,
It is not born—it doth not die; past, present, future know it not;
'Ancient, eternal, and unchanged, it dies not with the dying frame.'"*

Such are the savages that first peopled Greece, "feeding upon acorns."

* See Adeling's Sketch of Sans. Lit., by Talboys, p. 157.

Rome. While therefore the marvels wrought by these ancient saints and their Italian successors may be allowed to repose in the same medieval escrutoire, the fact of their existence as men of the same passions with ourselves, will be taken as historical, their miracles as poetical.

I have already pointed out the great settlement of the "Hiya tribes," or the "Ionians," in western Greece, and I have adverted to the term Ionian as applied to the sea which laves the shores of that country. It was from the clans of one of the Pandava brothers—these warlike chiefs whom I have just noticed, that the great eastern sea of Hellas,—the Ægaian, derived its appellation. "Vijaya," or "Victory," was the proud designation of Arjoona, the third of the Pandavas; his martial bands were, from this title of "Vijaya," by the regular patronymic form, designated the "Vaijaya," or "the clans of Vijaya;" an appellation that took firm root in the Greek language as 'Aigaios.[1] These warlike tribes I look upon as the relics of the great conflict recorded in the Mahabharata, an event fixed at about B.C. 1430; which, from connecting circumstances, I am inclined to place about fifty years previous to this date. The 'Aigaians undoubtedly formed a part of the Himalayan emigration, more especially in connection with the people of Cashmir. Vigi-para, a corruption of "Vijaya-pur," or "Vijaya-town," still standing in Cashmir, taken in connection with the temple of the Pandoos (of whom Arjoona or Vijaya was one), and the settlement in Greece of the Cashmirians and Himalayans (Xynia and Othrys), throw a powerful light upon this ancient emigration, and supply, in the great conflict of the

[1] As usual the ancient digammated sound of the "v" was lost; a practice prevalent throughout the structure of the Greek. The name "Vaijaya," thus became "Aijaia," whence the adjective "aigai-os-a-on." The "j" and "g" are constantly commutable; hence "Agaios." The Pali form is *Wijjayo.*

"MAHABHARATA," an adequate motive for this extensive settlement.

The name of the martial Arjoona, the chief of the Aigaians, is well preserved in a northern district of Thessaly, called from him, "PELAGONIA," properly "PHALGOONIA," from "PHALGOONUS," a name of Arjoona.[1]

The classical student will remember that the Ionians were called "PELASGOI AIGIALES;" the latter term supposed to be Greek and translated "Shores-men."[2] With the idea of *the sea*, however, it has no connection; it simply means that the Ionians, or horse-tribes, were "AIJYALEIS PELASKA," or "ARJUNA'S—CLANS of PELASA." The connection between the Attac and Benares has already been noticed, and nothing is more clear than that there existed in the earliest times the most intimate connection between north-western India and the eastern Gangetic provinces. Of this, no more direct and powerful evidence can be found, than that the Pali forms of the Sanscrit constitute the base of the Ionic dialect, while the source of the Doric is to be sought for in the rough northern Sanscrit, once spoken by the tribes bordering on Little Thibet.

While the clans of Arjoona, the "AIGAIANS," settled in a powerful body on the eastern shores of Hellas, another large band of the same martial chiefs, colonised a considerable portion of Epirus. These were the "KSHETRYAS," or "warrior caste;" who gave to their new abode the designation of "KSHETR'INE," or the "KSHETRA-CHIEFS,"[3] a name which appears in the Greek form of "KESTR-INE," and supplied to the Romans the term "CASTRA." These renowned clans were "DES-B'RATI"[4] ("THES-PR'OTI"),

[1] Wilson's Sans. Lex.—*Phalgoona*. [2] Ἀιγίαλες.

[3] From *Kshetrya*, a warrior, and *ina*, a king or chief.

[4] The full form is Bharata. The "h" being pronounced almost simultaneously with the "B," and the short vowel totally eclipsed by the usual

i.e. of the "LAND of BHARATA;" the same Bharatas,[1] be it remembered, who gave a title to the "Maha-BHARATA," the record of the tremendous war, which thus gave an additional population to northern Greece. The "Des-Bh'ratians," or "Thes-Protians," the reader will observe, are found in Hipairus, immediately in connection with the Cashmirians and people of Draus,[2] just as the Aigaians, the other division of the Pandari clans, are found contiguous to the same people in Thessaly. But yet this survey of the Pandavas and the Bharatas is far from being complete. They appear again across the southern channel of the Adriatic (Himalayan) waters, under the name of "B'rootii" (B'RUTII), with the royal town PANDOSIA. Their clans are again distinctly seen in Macedonia, as the Dassaretii,[3] or Yádoo tribes; so called from "Yadoo," the country on the west of the Jumna river, about Mathura and Vrindavan, over which Yadoo ruled.[4] Again, bringing these people in connection with the Himalayan provinces, Crishna, one of the great warriors in the memorable conflict of the Mahabharata, is styled the Yadu-Nath, or "Yadu-Lord," being descended from Yadoo, the eldest son of Yăyate, the fifth sovereign of the Lunar race."[5] He also will be

clipping style of the Greeks, left nothing but "Brata," identical in sound with Brŏta (Rule i. Appendix); the "p" and "b" are ordinary commutations. *Des-Bharat,* Land of Bharata.

[1] Mr. Grote remarks upon the Thesprotians, "We do not find the name Thesprotians in Italy, but we find there a town named Pandosea."—*Hist. Greece,* vol. iii. p. 553. It will now be evident, that it is of the utmost importance not to take Greek definitions at second-hand. Had Mr. Grote been aware that THES-PROTIA was a corrupt form of DES-BHARATYA, meaning the "Land of the Bharata," and that BROOTII (Brutii) was another corrupt form for the last member of the compound, the case would have been distinctly seen; since the form "Bruttii" would have been found to be analogous to the "Poles," and "Thes-Protia," to "Pole-land" or Poland.

[2] The Cassopæi and Dryopes.

[3] "Dasarhah, the Yadavas, or people of Dasarha."—WILSON'S *Sans. Lex.* —*Dashara.*

[4] Wilson's Sans. Lex.—*Yadu.*

[5] Wilson, *s. v.*

found acting a most important part in Grecian history.[1] I would here point out a singular specimen of the Greek system of recording names, by which history was made to assume the garb of fable; it occurs in connection with these early colonists of Greeee. Evemerus, the Messenian, we are told, derived the parentage of a chief, called "Brotos," from "a certain Brotos, an Autochthon;" while Hesiod deduced it from Brotos, the son of Aither and Hēmera; on which subject, misled by his Grecian guide, Mr. Grote has very naturally remarked that, "This Brotos must probably be intended as the *first* of men."[2] This strange piece of Greek travesty is, however, soon restored to its original text, by geographical evidence.

"Brotos," the "Autochthon" of Evemerus, is "Bhratas," a chief of "Barata;" an "Atac-than," (Autochthon), or hero of the Atac-land; Barata being situated about fifteen miles from the Atacthans, or Autochthons, as will be seen by the map of the Punjab; while Hesiod's genealogy comes nearly to the same point, since he makes his hero "the son of Bharatas, the

[1] Les Yadavas subdivisés en un grand nombre de tribus toutes alliées entr' elles et avec d'autres, occupent le vaste champ de l'histoire ancienne; c'est à cause de cette parenté si étendue, que les mêmes noms avec les mêmes faits qui s'y rattachent, et qui sont attribués à différents personages, *se retrouvent partout, depuis le Cachmir jusqu' à Ceylon;* on dirait que les actions ainsi que toute chose dans l'Inde, sont considérées comme une propriété de famille possédé en commun. Le Mahabarat, semble avoir été une guerre de l'Inde orientale et centrale, contre l'Inde de l'Orient et du Nord. C'est sur le champ de Kuru près de Hastinapoor, qu'elle fut amenée, moins à une issue, qu' à une pause, par la déstruction mutuelle, des combatants; à une grande pause dis-je, après laquelle, comme d'une source qui paraît tarie pour un instant, et qui se déborde de nouveau, eut son cours dans une nouvelle série d'évenements importants, semblable à ceux qui suivirent la guerre de Troie: soulèvements de peuples, migrations, construction de villes, formations de nouveaux états, changements de religion, et des innovations de toute sorte." — Troyer's *Exam. Crit. Raj. Tar.* vol. ii. p. 294.

[2] Hist. Greece, vol. i. p. 88, note 1.

HAI-THE'RO[1] (Αἰ-θερος), or HAYA[2] PRIEST, and of HEM-ARA, that is, the HIMALAYAN MOUNTAINS.[3] Notwithstanding these orthographical errors, however, the important fact of the careful preservation of the Hellenic genealogies is clearly established, as we shall repeatedly have occasion to remark; so carefully treasured in fact are they, that they will, as we progress, afford the most interesting, as well as convincing proofs that, whether these genealogies ascend to the gods, or to heroes, or to men, they are equally trustworthy, as a thoroughly sound basis for history. The error is theirs who, translating Sanscrit names by homogeneous Greek sounds, and very naturally discrediting the absurdities thereby produced, have upon this foundation been led to deny the existence of any historical basis upon which these errors repose.

A little to the north-west of the Cassopæi or Cashmirians, was the island of KORK-URAS, so called from its colonists, the "KORK-WARAS" or people of Kerku[4] in Little Thibet; while being also a settlement of the "P'HAYA-KES (P'Haia-kes) or HAYA CHIEFS,[5] its inhabitants were called Phœaces. The name of "SCHERIA," it also received from the settlers from SH'KER,[6] situate on the

[1] THÉRO, the appellation of the Bud'hist priest. *See* Mahavanso, *passim.*

[2] *Hai*, or *Hi;* the Horse Tribe.

[3] HĔM-ERA, "a" day, HIM-ARA; HIMALAYAN MOUNTAIN.—*Ara*, a mountain, is a term common to Rajpootana and other districts (the ὄρος of the Greek and the *Hor* of the Hebrews). *Vide* Col. Tod's account of Ara-boodh or the Jamant Aboo.

[4] Kerku, lat. 35° 8′, long. 76° 10′. *Awur* signifies a stronghold, or fort; as *Peshawur*, frontier fort; *Kerk'awur* (Kork'oorus), the fort of Kerku. The respective vowels "u, a," blend with "w," and form the long "u" in Corcūros and Corcȳrus. (*See* Rule xvi. Appendix.)

[5] *Pa*, a chief, and *Hayaka*, derivative of *Haya*, the horse. The Hayanian (Ionian) or Horse Chiefs.

[6] Properly Shaker. Lat. 34° 10′, long. 68° 45′.—Thornton, *s. v.* Spelt also Shakar. (*See* Rule i. Appendix.)

right bank of the Jailum, while a section of the Bullini, or the people of the Bolan, called the DREBAN,[1] having been the first colonists of the island, gave to it the name of DREPANE. Still farther to the south lay the "CEPHALLINI," (Gopal-ini) or "chiefs of Crishna,"[2] who had emigrated from "CABUL," the Asiatic corruption of "GOPAL,"[3] while immediately to the west and north-west the clans of "CARNA," prince of Angadesa, took up their abode in the province of "A'CARNANIA," a name derived from the usual Greek euphonic affix of the "a," and "Carnāri," the plural form of Carna. The small settlement, "CARNOS ISLE," lies to the central west of "Acarnania."

Karna himself, the elder brother of the Pandoo princes, by the mother's side, being the son of "Suryă," ("the Sun,") having taken the part of the Cooroos in the great conflict of the Mahabharata, had been slain by Vijaya (Ægæus), or Arjuna, the third of the Pandavas, who hence obtained the title of "KARNA-JIT," or "Conqueror of Carna." The history of Carna the "Sun-born"[4] will be again noticed in its proper place. The source of this Greek settlement is still seen in "KARNA," a north-western district of Cashmir. The Suryatanyas,[5] (Eurytanes,) or the Karnas, the clans of the Jumna, are to be seen on the southern base of the Ætolici Montes, or the mountains of Oude, while the AGRÆI or people of AGRA, lie

[1] The usual form is Drubbee; the pl. Drubban. (*See* Rule ii.—ŭ, ă ŏ, ĕ.)

[2] *Gopala*, Krishna, and *ina*, a chief.

[3] THE KOPHENES, River of Arran, is very properly allowed to be the River Cabul. Koph-enes is the Greek way of writing Gop-ina, or the Gopa-King, *i. e.* Go-pala (Ca-bul-a) or Krishna. See Rule vi., in Appendix, for the constant interchange of the Greek "a" with the Sanscrit "oo," "u," and "o." This also shows that the Greek "a" must have been sounded as broadly as the Scotch.

[4] Surya-ja, epithet of Carna.

[5] Eu is the ordinary Greek form for Su. *Surya*, the Sun, and *tanya*, a child,—the Children of the Sun. *Suryatanyā*, the Jumna R.

immediately to the north. Flanking the Agræans on the west, are the "AM-BHILOCHIANS," (AM-PHILŌCHIANS) or BHILOOCHS of AM, "a stronghold on the north-western bank of the Indus, enclosed between the river and the lofty and thickly wooded range of the Mabeen hills, an off-set of the Himalaya."[1] The Bomienses, or "Bamian tribes," have already been noticed. Among the "AIT-ALY'ANS,[2] ŒT-ALAYAN or OUDE-DWELLERS," essentially the "children of the Sun," are to be found also the "OPHIENSES," a name interesting both to the philologist and the historian.

They are the AFGHANS. *The* term Ophi-'ensa,[3] "Serpent tribe," or SNAKE-TRIBE, viz. the "TAG, or TACSHAK, is but the reflected Sanscrit of OPH-GANA,[4] or AF-GHAN; 'Ahis,' Sanscrit, 'Op-his,' Greek, and 'Aphia,' Cashmirian, being the corresponding equivalents of the first member of the compound. Yet this is the term 'AFGHAN,' which the natives of that country, in the same spirit with the Greeks, their descendants, derived from the Persian 'AFGHAN,' 'lamentation,' given to the race, say they, on account of their *lamenting* their expulsion from Judæa." The historian thus learns, that the Tacshak or Serpent Tribe, (OPHIENSA) at the era of the Scindian emigration into Greece, formed but an insignificant portion of that nation, of which it has now usurped both the name and the power.

Then, the Hellenes and the Helopes, or chiefs of the Hela, were the dominant clans; while both the people of

[1] Thornton's Punjab, vol. i. p. 52. Am is about fifty miles north-east of Attock, and in lat. 34° 17', long. 72° 54'.

[2] *Ait,* a contraction for *aditya,* the sun, and *alaya,* a dwelling; ὅυλιον of the Greeks. The people of Oude (also called Ayoodhia) are the 'Οιτει of the Greek geographers.

[3] *Vensa,* a tribe; the digammated "v" lost as usual.

[4] *Gana,* a tribe. *Aph-gana,* the serpent tribe; is the same with *Aphivensa,* serpent tribe, or Afghan.

the Dāmam (Athamania) and those of Cahun (Chaonia), the latter now comparatively an insignificant people, made a far more important appearance on the map of Greece, than the then slender tribe of the Ophienses or Afghans.

I shall now rapidly bring this geographical sketch to a close; nor should I have taxed the patience of the reader to this extent, had it not been indispensable to demonstrate irrefutably primitive Greece as being primitive India. On the "GOORKHA" Hills (the "CORAKOS[1] Mons" of Ætolia,) are the "GOORKHA CALLI-ENSES,"[2] or "GOORKHA WAR-TRIBES;" to their south the "HYAN-TES,"[3] or "LAND of the HYAS," who are situated along the banks of the "E-VENUS,"[4] so called from its having been a settlement of the HYA BRAHMINS. The COUREETES,[5] or "people of the LAND of the ÇORĒE," those founders of "C'RĒ-TA," and nurses of Zeus, are, in accordance with the sea-faring habits of their old country, situated near the southern shore of Ætolia. There is one characteristic of Indian society stamped irrevocably and unmistakeably upon the map of Greece, viz, the distinct provinces which are dotted over its surface. This separation it was that produced the civil wars, and ultimately the ruin of Greece. This it was, which, under the form of the Heptarchy, proved the weakness of England; and this it is, which with the same narrow feeling of a puny nationality, is still desired for Great Britain by the ignorant or the ambitious, as the best mode of forming an "*United Kingdom*." The same system was evident in the Indo-Saurian settlements of Palestine, where the children of Israel found the numerous tribes of the Hivite, Amorite, Perizzite, Jebusite, and many

[1] The genitive of Corax is given, as showing the source of the term.

[2] From *Cali*, war.

[3] *Hyan*, plural of *Hya*, and *des* (*tis*), land.

[4] *E-Venus* is *Hi-vena*,—Vena, Brahma. *See* "E-phura, E-pirus;" "Hi-pur, Hi-pairos." "E-Bud-es" (He-Bud-des).

[5] Couretes, a derivative form of Coree; Gr. form Κουρῆτες,—Eng. Curetes.

others, exactly analogous to the habits of these same Indians, whether under the name of Britons, Sachas, or Saca-soos (Saxons). "The whole of India," writes Colonel Wilks,[1] "is nothing more than one vast congeries of such republics. The inhabitants, ever in war, are dependent upon their respective Potails, who are at the same time magistrates, collectors, and principal farmers. They trouble themselves very little about the fall and dismemberment of empires; and provided the township with its limits, which are exactly marked out by a boundary line, remain intact, it is a matter of perfect indifference to them who becomes sovereign of the country."[1]

[1] Sketches of the South of India, vol. i. p. 117.

XIII.

THE HELIADÆ.

"FOUNTAIN OF LIGHT! that from thy golden urn
Shedst the bright streams that flood the circling year,
Or glow'st within yon living gems that burn
Throughout the blue of GLORY's hallowed sphere;
As is 'the voice of many waters,'[1] thine
Hymns a SIRE's might from an eternal shrine!"—E. P.

THE same tendency to an adoration of the visible powers of nature, which debased humanity; from the worshipper of the sun, to the worshipper of the Vicar-gods of the east and the west; very early gave a distinctive title to the hierarchies of the "SOLAR" and the "LUNAR" race, a title applied to the primeval inhabitants of the world, and derived from their specific worship of the Sun and the Moon. These titles became the distinctive appellations of two vast sections of the human family. When, therefore, we read of ancient tribes, represented as "CHILDREN OF THE SUN," or "CHILDREN OF THE MOON," we shall by no means consider such appellations as mythological, but as the correct and precise designation of these primitive idolators. This distinction will have its full weight in the venerable annals of the Apian Land, and of Egypt and Rome, and Peru. In Bharata Versha, or India, agreeably to this practice, the two great dynasties of the land, were divided into the Surya Vansa, or Solar dynasty, and the Chandra Vansa, or Lunar dynasty. The former were the earliest settlers in Greece; and the religious exponents of

[1] Rev., chap. i. v. 15.

this people appear to have been the DODAN, or Brahminical priests of the great tribe, DODA.

The earliest records we possess of the Brahminical worship, or, indeed, of the Brahminical literature, are those Vedas[1] which consist of invocations to the Sun, the Moon, the winds, and the most obvious agents of nature. These are exempt from the puerile interpolations which disfigure the Puranas.

A time came, however, when the Lunar Race (of which Bud'ha was considered the great head), adopted the worship of the ONE GOD. This change was followed by centuries of religious warfare, in which the hostile races of the Surya Vansa and the Chandra Vansa were the mighty champions. The same errors of record which have disfigured the annals of primeval Greece, have not spared those of Asiatic countries. Thus we are told in the ancient chronicles of Persia, of the long wars which raged between "Iran and Turan," without our obtaining thereby any just idea of the distinctive religion of these embittered foes. A correct interpretation of these important names, received by Persians of the present day as Persian—just as the Greeks of antiquity conceived Sanscrit vocables to be Greek—will give an insight into fact as the foundation of fable. AIRA[2], the name of Pururavas, the son of Bud'ha, the great Bud'hist patriarch, was so denominated from "IRA," the wife of Bud'ha, chief of the Lunar race. Hence the plural form, "AIRAN," the people of Bud'ha and their land, "IRAN and IRANIA."

Their opponents were the TURAN, a corrupt form of SURAN. SURA, the "Sun," SURĀN, the "Suns, or Sun Tribes."

Here, then, we have a distinct view of the respective

[1] See the Reg. Veda Sanhita, translated by Professor Wilson.

[2] More commonly written Aila; "l" and "r" are commutable.

champions of, and the causes for, a furious and protracted contest.

These foes of the Airanians, or Bud'hists, are mentioned under the designation of Diws, the Deus of the Romans, and the Devas of the Sanscrit. Thus, at length, we obtain the definition of the term. The Devas are BRAHMINS, for such is the ordinary acceptation of the title; hence, such too, is the signification of the term "DIU."[1] Further, to prove that this long conflict, noticed by Ferdousi, is between these rival sects, another error of the same author is sufficient; for even an error, submitted to a patient enquirer, will often prove a most valuable authority. The "DIW SUFEED," with whom the heroic Rustam fights long in a doubtful contest, is the "DIW SU-VED," or "The High Caste Brahminical Vedantist." It is thus, that sounds and forms are transmitted for centuries, when all idea of their true signification has long been swallowed up by time.

So, also, when Mohsan talks of the work "Timsar DASATER," or the "Venerable Desatir," he means Timsar "DAS-SOOTRA," or the Ten Sootras.

I would now take a rapid survey of the vast "Tribes of the Sun," whose influence and religious practices very early penetrated to the remotest regions. In a general point of view, we may look upon Oude, as having been the first great and ancient focus of the region of the Children of the Sun, of whom Rama was the patriarch. The prevalence of the Solar tribes in Egypt, Palestine, Peru, and Rome, will be evident in the course of the following rapid survey, for it will be impossible to do more than give a sketch of this widely spread people. In Egypt, where they are found to hold the chief sway, the religious system was so far tolerant, as freely to permit of

[1] Dio, Deo, Diu, Dyu, Diw, Dew, Deva, Deu, Do, are but various forms of the same words.

the worship of Bud'ha, the great head of the Lunar Race, and the incorporation into their religious system of much of his philosophy. In fact, the hierarchic constitution of Egypt embraced and freely permitted rituals and forms of worship of the most diverse character, with the exception of some few, which were peculiarly objectionable to the national sensibilities.

The children of the great Surya race of Northern India, are, throughout the world, to be recognised by their gigantic buildings, and still more distinctly, by those massive walls, and great public works, which strike the beholder with astonishment alike in Rome, Italy, Greece, Peru, Egypt, and Ceylon. They may with great propriety in all these instances be termed Cyclopæan, *i. e.* the style of building adopted by those Guklo-pes (Κύκλωπες) or chiefs of the north-Jumna, as well as the countries adjacent to the Rama tribes of Oude. This race early formed settlements in Greece to the south of Achaia: they were the Arcadians, and proudly styled themselve "PRO SELENOI," "BEFORE the LUNAR RACE." Their name was expressive of the fact of their being distinguished as coming from the "ARCA-DES,"[1] or of the LAND of the SUN; the more immediate district whence they emigrated, being the "ARAC-DES," or Arac land, in the vicinity of Akeha;[2] the form "ARAK," and the IRAK of the district of Babylon, being varieties of the same word. The very early prevalence of the Sun tribes in the Peloponnesus is clear. It was this people who gave to that large division of Greece the name of the "APIĀN Land;" a term which has constituted the standard literary enigma of ancient and modern times. They were the "APIĀN," or the "THE SUNS."[3] The reader

[1] *Arca*, the sun, and *des*, land. [2] *Vide* Map of the Indian Settlements.

[3] *Abi*, the Sun; Persian plural *Abi-an*, Suns. The usual Sanscrit form is Avi; the "v," "b," and "p," commutable: hence Apiān.

will remember that Ais-cul-apius was the son of Apollo,[1] or the Sun; that is quite correct. He was the offspring of the "THE GREAT SUN," and consequently the "AIS-CUL-APIUS,[2] or "CHIEF of the SUN TRIBE,"[3] a title which no more throws doubt on his personality or medical capacity, than that of the "Sons of the Mist," as applied to the Edinburgh school of medicine. "The princes of Mewar," writes Colonel Tod,[4] "are the elder branch of the Surya Vansa, or Children of the Sun. Another patronymic is Raghoovansa, derived from a predecessor of Rama, the focal point of each scion of the Solar race. The prince of Mewar is styled "Hindoo Sooraj," (Sun of the Hindoos). This descendant of one hundred kings shows himself in cloudy weather from the "Soorya Gokra," or Balcony of the Sun. The great object of adoration among the Egyptians was "APIS," (Abis,) *i. e.*, "THE SUN," and their connection both with Oude and the Solar worship is as distinctly seen from the appellation of their land, "AETIA."[5] both "the land of Oude," and "the land of the Sun," while the "RAMAS" of Oude, are as self-evident in "RAMES-ES,"[6] or "CHIEF OF THE RAMAS."

Another ancient name of the Peloponnesus, was "INACHIA," or the "land of the Suns,"[7] whence also the Inachus River, the Inachidæ and the Inachi-enses, or Sun tribes. The most venerable name to be met with in the Argive genealogies is Inachus, or the "Sun-king," both of whose sons were Autochthons, or the descendants of the Chiefs of the Attock."[8] The race of Inachus, or more

1 The A' Pollo of the Greeks, and Baal of the Scriptures, are merely various forms of the same name: they will be duly noticed.

2 As from Heri-cul-es the Greeks made the corrupt form Hera-c'les, so did they clip the form Ais-cul-apyus into As-c'lepios. (*See* Rule i. Appendix.)

3 *Ais*, a chief; *cul*, a tribe; *Api*, the sun.

4 Rajasth., vol. i. p. 211.

5 *Aetia;* a contracted form of *Aditya*, the sun.

6 From *Rama* and *es*, a chief.

7 *Inaca*, the sun; derivative form of *Ina*, the sun,—*Inach-ia*, Sol-land.

8 See chap. vii. p. 58.

correctly speaking, the INACAS, was co-extensive with the world, both old and new. They were the IN'CAS of PERU,[1] a term signifying the land of "The Sun," whose people were "Peruvians," or "people of the Sun." Here also the same vast public works are the characteristic of the Cyclopæan Ramas, who are still further demonstrated by their festival of the Rama-Sitva, or Rama and Setá, his wife. "From Rama," observes Colonel Tod,[2] "all the tribes termed Surya Vansa, or Race of the Sun, claim descent; as the princes of Méwar, Jeipoor, Merwar, Bekanér, and other numerous clans." "Ayodia" was the first city founded by the race of Soorya. Like other capitals, its importance must have risen by slow degrees; yet, making every allowance for exaggeration, it must have attained great splendour long anterior to Rama. Its site is well known at this day under the contracted name of Oude. . . . . Overgrown greatness characterised all the ancient Asiatic capitals, and that of Ayodia was immense. Lucknow, the present capital, is traditionally asserted to have been one of the suburbs of ancient Oude, and so named by Rama, in compliment to his brother, Lacshman.[3]

The names of Lacmon, the mountains of Oude, the fourteen tribes of Oude Ramas ("Call-id-Romos"), the "tribe of Lova," son of Rama, and the Canalovii Montes, have already been brought before the reader. This is the ancient race that reared such grand structures in Greece. Of these, Colonel Mure[4] has justly observed: "It is difficult to class the men who erected or inhabited the noble structures of Mycenæ, and who certainly preceded the Dorian Conquest, in the same rank of mythical nonentity as the barbarous semi-demons who figure in

[1] *Pāru,* the sun. Paruvyu-a-um, derivative form of Pāru (the Solar Race). [2] Rajasthan, p. 45. [3] Rajasthan, p. 38.
[4] Hist. of Gr. Lit., vol. i. p. 24.

northern romances. We feel as if the existence of the former ought to have been as intimately associated with their residence, even in the popular legend, as that of the Egyptian kings, with their pyramids and palaces." They *are* the men of Egypt, they are the men of Peru, they are the men of RŌMA, *i. e.* RĀMA![1] They are the same race. "That Rome," writes Niebuhr, "was not a Latin name, was assumed to be self-evident, and there can be no doubt that the city had another of an Italian form, which was used in the sacred books, like the mysterious name of the Tiber. The name Roma, which has a Greek look,[2] like that of the neighbouring town of Pyrgi, belonged to the city at the time when all the towns round about it were Pelasgian." Again, in another remarkable passage displaying that sagacity for which he was so distinguished, Niebuhr remarks: "This western world was connected with that primeval and extinct world which we call the New. The ancient Aztecans, whose calendar was the most perfect which was anywhere used for civil purposes before the Gregorian, had a great year, consisting of 104 solar years. Their mode of dividing it accorded with their system of numeration, in which twenty-five was the base. During this period they, too, introduced two intercalations, making up twenty-five days between them; and when we read of the Mexican festivals of the New Fire at the beginning of a new secular period, it is impossible not to be reminded of the Roman, or properly speaking, the Etruscan secular festivals; more especially as at Rome a new fire was kindled in the temple of Vesta on every first of March."[3]

1 The evidences of the settlements, clans, and early history of Rome, are even more distinct than the primitive history of Greece. On the subject of the early history of Rome, I have made considerable progress.

2 Vol. i. p. 287. Niebuhr was very naturally led to imagine this celebrated name to be derived from Ῥώμη "strength." The Sanscrit long "ā" very frequently replaces the "ō" and "ω" of the Greek; just as the dialectic change in Poseidōn and Poseidān.

3 Niebuhr's Rome, vol. i. p. 281.

The identity of practice in Rome and Peru under numerous points of view, I shall shortly have occasion to notice. But I shall now firmly rivet the chain of evidence that connects the children of "PERU," that is, the children of "THE SUN," with the Soorya Vansa, or Sun tribe of Oude. They are then, both the people of the "UN-DES" and the "AN-DES." "Undes" "is the general name of the tract of country situated between the Cailas and Himalaya ranges of mountains west of Lake Ravanas Hrad, and intersected by the course of the Sutlej river, which, issuing from that lake, flows to the north-west."[1] "To this day," observes Colonel Tod,[2] "AN-DES still designates the Alpine regions of Thibet, bordering on Chinese Tartary." Here, then, we have the Ramas of Oude directly connected with the Andes, and the people of Peru with the Cuclopes (Cyclopes), or "Chiefs of the Jumna;" the same tribes which we shall find characterised, both in Greece and Rome, as the Cyclopes, or owners of vast "Guk'la," or "herds of cattle." Hence the constant allusion of the early writers to the "Oxen of the Sun," and the immense flocks of sheep which covered the country of the "Ar-cades," or "Land of the Sun." Nor are the people of Mexico less connected with this race; their language, a dialect of the Sanscrit, at once betrays them. If the land of Peru derived that name from "the Suns" (Peru), not less did that of Mexico from the abundance of its gold and silver, MAKSHICO.[3] But our evidences of the

[1] Hamilton's E. Ind. Gaz., vol. ii. p. 692. Un-des is the local form for Urna-des.

[2] Rajasth., vol. i. p. 44. Col. Tod however derives the term from Anga, the country of Karna, the son of Soorya.

[3] "Makshika, is a mineral substance, of which two kinds are described. The *Svărnămăkshĭka*, or '*gold* Makshika,' of a bright yellow colour, apparently the common pyritic iron ore; and the *Rupyămāshĭka*, or '*silver* Makshika.' They are, however, perhaps rather synonymous of the gold and silver ore respectively, than the names of species."—WILSON'S *Sans. Lex.* Clavigero incorrectly derives Mexico from their war-god Mexitli.

identity of the race which peopled this country, do not rest simply upon language; the great monuments of this ancient people equally demonstrate their origin. Let us hear one who has had access to the most authentic documents connected with the ancient races of Peru. "The walls of many of the houses have remained unaltered for centuries; the great size of the stones, the variety of their shapes, and the inimitable workmanship they display, give to the city (Cuzco), that interesting air of antiquity and romance, which fills the mind with pleasing though painful veneration."[1]

Again, speaking of the fortress of Cuzco, he writes: "The fortress, walls, and galleries were all built of stone: the heavy blocks of which were not laid in regular courses, but so displayed that the small ones might fill up the interstices between the great. These formed a sort of rustic work, being rough hewn, except towards the edges, which were finely wrought. Many of these stones were of vast size, some of them being full thirty-eight feet long, by eighteen broad, and six feet thick."[2] Like the vast remains of the Guk'cla race, in Greece, and the marvels of architectural power in Ceylon, "the traveller still meets, especially in the central regions of the table land, with memorials of the past, remains of temples, palaces, fortresses, terraced mountains, great military roads, aqueducts, and other public works, which, whatever degree of science they may display in their execution, astonish him by their number, the massive character of the materials, and the grandeur of the design."[3] Nor does this writer's account of the united enterprise and industry required to construct a road over the grand plateaux, afford an inferior idea of the resources of these "Children of the Sun," the ancient people of the Rāmas.

[1] Prescott' Peru, vol. i. p. 15; from Mem. of Gen. Müller, vol. ii. 225.

[2] Prescott's Peru, vol. i. p. 15.

[3] Ibid., p. 59.

"It was conducted," remarks Mr. Prescott,[1] "over pathless sierras buried in snow; galleries were cut for leagues, through the living rock; rivers were crossed by means of bridges, that hung suspended in the air; precipices were scaled by stairways, hewn out of the native bed; ravines of hideous depth were filled up with solid masonry. In short, all the difficulties that beset a wild and mountainous region, and which might appal the most courageous engineer of modern times, were encountered and successfully overcome. . . . . The broken portions that still survive here and there, like the fragments of the great Roman roads scattered over Europe, bear evidence to their primitive grandeur, and have drawn forth the eulogium of a discriminating traveller, usually not too profuse in his panygeric, that the roads of the Incas, were amongst the most useful and stupendous works, ever executed by man.'"[2] If the mighty industry of this wonderful people has so powerfully excited the admiration of the traveller in America, the ancient achievements of the same RAMAS in ROMA, have not less called forth the astonishment of the most sagacious critic of modern times. I allude to the illustrious Niebuhr, whose perspicuous view of antiquity, unaided save by the glimmering light of the Greek and Roman historian, took in, in its just proportions, the venerable Temple of Time. "The reign of Tarquinius," writes that great man, "I have already remarked, is probably separated by a great chasm from the preceding period; for under him Rome presents quite a different appearance from what it had before presented. The conquests ascribed to Ancus Marcius are confined to a very small extent of country: he made himself master of the mouth of the Tiber, and fortified Ostia.

"But after him a state of things is described by historians

[1] Prescott s Peru, vol. i. p. 59.

[2] From Humboldt's Vue des Cordillères, p. 294.

of which traces are still visible. Even at the present day there stands unchanged the great sewer, the Cloaca Maxima, the object of which, it may be observed, was not merely to carry away the refuse of the city, *but chiefly to drain the large lake, which was formed by the Tiber,* between the Capitoline, Aventine, and Palatine, and then extended between the Capitoline and Aventine, and reached, as a swamp, as far as the district between the Quirinal and the Viminal.

"This work, consisting of three semicircles of immense square blocks, which though *without mortar,* have not to this day moved a knife's breadth from one another, drew the water from the surface, conducted it into the Tiber, and thus changed the lake into solid ground; but as the Tiber itself had a marshy bank, a large wall was built, as an embankment, the greater part of which still exists. This structure, equalling the Pyramids in extent and massiveness (and Niebuhr might have added, built by the same people), far surpasses them in the difficulty of its execution. It is so gigantic that the more you examine it the more inconceivable it becomes, how even a large and powerful State could have executed it. In comparison with it, the aqueducts of the emperors cannot be considered grand; for they were built of bricks, with cement in the inner parts; but in the more ancient work, everything is made of square blocks of hewn Alban stone, and the foundations are immensely deep."[1] These are the people who constructed the ancient Catabothra of Bœotia, drained the valleys of Cashmir and Thessaly, constructed the magnificent tanks and canals of Ceylon, the venerable walls of Mycenæ, reared the gloomy grandeur of the Egyptian Thebes, and the magnificence of the Temple of Solomon. True it is that the whole of this race did not continue in the region of the "Children of the Sun," but

[1] Niebuhr's Hist. of Rome, vol. i. p. 66.

not the less were they the identical people of the same land. The same tribe, who from the vicinity of Cashmir colonised the "LUN-CES-TIS," or "Lancas Land," of the Macedonians, and the MAGADHAS of Greece, gave the name to the most southerly part of Hindostan, viz., the island of Ceylon, to which appellation, but for this emigration it had no claim. And not the least interesting result of the geographical evidences already advanced of the original localities, which gave a population to Hellas, is the confirmation of the wide-spread Hindoo idea, that the island of Ceylon had originally no just claim to the name of Lanca; an evidence brought out by the fact that all the members of the Hellenic emigration surrounding Lyncestis or Lancas Land, are of a high northerly latitude. Speaking of Lanca, the Honourable G. Turnour, observes, in his "Epitome of the History of Ceylon," when alluding to a Hindu traveller, in the last century: "The testimony of this Hindu is the more valuable, as the identification of Ceylon with Lanca is not admitted by the Indian Pundits;" or, rather, to use Tod's words, it is "an idea scouted by the Hindoos, who transfer Lanca to a very distant region." The comprehensive views of the Old World, held by the illustrious Niebuhr, and the traditional belief of the Hindoos, relative to Lanca's land, (Lynces-tis),[1] will be both amply justified to the attentive student, by the venerable genius of antiquity, who with one hand reaches to Thrace, with the other to the Cis-Alpine rocks.

The Lanca people, both of Thrace, Macedonia, and Italy, were undoubtedly the people bordering on the northern frontiers of the Himalaya; more especially those in the neighbourhood of Ravans Roodh, or Ravana's Lake, about ten miles from that "MANASA-LEH," or "MEN-ZALEH," which I have lately noticed in Egypt, and in the Himalayas. Hence it was, that Ravana, the rival lord-

[1] Lunces-des.

paramount of India, was expelled by Rama, the sovereign of Oude, his warlike opponent, who has been already noticed as the great patriarch of the Surya Vansa. The tribes of Ravana are the fitting Bud'histic accompaniments to the emigrants from Thibet. A still larger body of this people, from their settlements in Thrace, moved forward into Italy. The bands of "I'Scardoh," and the Himalaya, as we have already seen, formed settlements upon Mount Scardus and Adrius. The population of the Draus gave its name to the large confluent of the Danube, called the Drave, and by the Romans, the Draus, or Dravus, (a mere variation of the same term), taking its rise to the north of the Carnic Alps. Not far from the north-western shores of the Adriatic, the people of Lanca formed one of their earliest settlements, that of "PATAVI-UM," or the "BUD'HAS TOWN;"[1] while the record of the old country was faithfully preserved in the foundation of the neighbouring town, "Adria," "HIMAL 'TAN,"[2] or "HAMIL-TON." Immediately to the south of this flowed the important river, PADUS, that is, "BUDHA'S" River, contiguous to which were the very people, whose history we are discussing. They appear in the Roman form of LINGONES, that is, in plain terms, LANC-GŎNĔS,[3] or LANCA TRIBES.

And now we are about to arrive at the crowning certificate of history. Behold the memory of their chief, RAVANA, still preserved in the city of RAVENNA, and see on the western coast of Italia, its great rival RĀMA, or ROMA. How that great city of the Solar Rajpoots—the "GENA TAGA-TA," or "GENS TOGA-TA,"[4] that is, the TĀG RACE[5]

[1] *Pata,* Bud'ha; *Patavi,* Budhavi,—or people of Bud'ha. (*See* Rule vi.)

[2] *Tān,* a land: properly spelt *t'hān.*

[3] *Gana,* a tribe. Short vowel in the various forms "ă, ĕ, ŏ, ŭ." (*See* Rule ii. Appendix.)

[4] *Gena,* a tribe.

[5] The Tāg is a renowned Rajpoot Tribe. The Toga of the Rāmas, was the dress worn by this tribe. The race was of the TAGA-DES (TOGA-TUS), that is, Tag-land.

gradually reduced, by the combined powers of policy and war, the once mighty 'TOROOSHCAS and HOOSCAS, (E 'TRUSCA's and OSCANS), a people of Cashmirian origin, is well known to the student of history. He may not, however, as clearly understand the internal structure of the society of Rome, and her domestic policy; for this he must exercise independent and energetic research. That city had its CURULE, chair of *ivory*, from the royal chair of the CURUS, the opponents of the Pandus (Pandusia) its tribe of "PLEB's"[1]—(PLEBE-IANS,) from the Soodras of India, and its "SEN-ATORS;" more correctly, "SEN-NĀT WARS,"[2] or "WAR-CHIEFS," from the same land. The reader will perceive that the knowledge of the Romans, relative to the sources of their own language, was about as correct as that of the Greeks, when speaking the old Hellenic tongue. The office of the "Sen-nath-war" had nothing to do with a "*Senex*." As I have a work in progress on the early history of Rome, I reserve any further remarks on that subject for a future period. But let us, ere we close the survey of this energetic race, in connection with its great architectural achievements, listen to the remarks of Bertolacci,[3] relative to the surprising works constructed in what I would call *southern* Lanka, or Ceylon, near the lake of Condeley, distant about sixteen miles from the lake of Trincomalee. "This lake," says the writer, "which comprehends nearly fifteen miles in circumference, is embanked in several places by a wall of large stones, each from twelve to fifteen feet long, broad and thick in proportion, lying one over the other, in the most masterly manner, so as to form a parapet of immense strength. At what time, or under what Government this

[1] *Plĕbas*—A man of a degraded tribe—an outcast.

[2] *Sén*, an army; *nat'h*, a chief, or lord: *war*, Persian attributive. (*See* Rule xvi. Appendix.)

[3] In the Hon. G. Turnour's Sketch of the Hist. of Ceylon.

surprising work was constructed, there is no satisfactory account to be obtained; but its magnitude evinces a very numerous population, with a strong government, possessing the power of putting it in action, and of guiding its strength and industry; as well as of exhibiting at the same time a degree of civilisation from which the present inhabitants are far removed. That part of this majestic work particularly deserves attention, where, by a parapet of nearly one hundred and fifty feet in breadth at the base, and thirty in the summit, two hills are made to join, in order to encompass and keep in the waters of this lake. In this work, then, we find the incontestible signs of an immense population, and of an extensive agriculture. It is apparently the most ancient of all other works extant in Ceylon; so ancient, that it cannot be traced to any of the Governments or kingdoms of the Brahmins. We must therefore say, that *the further back we go towards the remotest antiquity*, we find the island rising in the ideas it impresses upon our minds, respecting its civilisation and prosperity."

The same might be, undoubtedly, asserted of various parts of Greece, particularly of Bœotia, where the ancient Catabothra, by which that country had at one time been effectually drained, were in the historical times of Greece, allowed to fall into ruinous neglect. If we turn again to Peru, other evidences arise to mark the identity of this great people, of which nothing can be a stronger proof than the identity of especial social usage. The Peruvians, and their ancestors, the Indians, are in this point of view at once seen to be the same people. "The leaves of the Cuca," writes Prescott,[1] "when gathered, are dried in the sun, and being mixed with a little lime, form a preparation for chewing, much like the betel-leaf of the east; the pungent leaf of the betel was in like manner

[1] Prescott's Peru, vol. i. p. 133.

mixed with lime when chewed. *The similarity of this social indulgence in the remote east and west is singular.*"

Again; let us hear a most careful observer, when travelling in the neighbourhood of Cashmir, a very little north of the true Cyclops of India. "Ahmed Shah approached me, bareheaded, and when near he frequently stopped and salaamed, by bowing low, and touching the ground with the back of his hand, and then carrying it to his forehead."[1] Vigne then adds this allusion, from "Robertson's History of America," "Montezuma returned the salutation of Cortes, by touching the earth with his hand, and then kissing it."

The Chasquis, or runners of that country, are at once the Indian "Cossids," and the "Hemerodromoi," of the Spartans; while the Peruvian provision made for a ready communication with the capital, may remind one of the similar institution of ancient Rome, when under the Cæsars she was mistress of half the world.[2] Again: "the the flocks of lamas, or Peruvian sheep, were appropriated exclusively to the Sun, and to the Inca; their number was immense, they were scattered over the different provinces, chiefly in the colder regions of the country, where they were entrusted to the care of experienced shepherds, who conducted them to different pastures, according to the change of seasons."[3] These, then, are the "Arcades," or "Suns," of Greece, with their vast flocks and herds; these are the "Oxen of the Sun," which the ancient poets of Greece celebrated as being sacred to Helios—these are the Inachi-enses,[4] or In'ca-tribes of the "Hel'-īnes," or "Sun-kings,"—these are the "Apian," or "Sun tribes;" called also "Api-dones" (Api-tanyas),[5] or "Sons of the Sun;" these are, in fine, the northern Soorya-vansa of

[1] Vigne's Cashmir, vol. ii. p. 225.

[2] Prescott's Peru, vol. i. p. 66.

[3] Ibid, p. 48.

[4] *Inca*, the sun, and '*ensa*, a tribe.

[5] *Api*, the sun, and *tanaya*, a son.

India, who looked forward to the "Sun, as their abode," after death; that is, the Hellenic "El-ysium."[1] Of the magnificence of this worship of the God of the East, both in Egypt, Assyria, Greece, and Persia, as well as in Peru, we have no reason to doubt. In the latter country, particularly, it appears to have been the object of his worshippers, to imitate, as far as possible, the magnificent splendours of this deity of the rayed majesty.

> But, oh! what pencil of a living star
> Could paint that gorgeous car,
> In which as in an ark supremely bright,
> The Lord of boundless light
> Ascending calm o'er the Empyreum sails,
> And with ten thousand beams his awful beauty veils.[2]

"The most renowned of the Peruvian temples," says Prescott,[3] "the pride of the capital, and the wonder of the empire, was at Cuzco, where, under the munificence of successive sovereigns, it had been so enriched that it received the name of Coricancha,[4] or the place of gold. The interior of the temple was the most worthy of admiration. It was totally a mine of gold. On the western wall was emblazoned a representation of the deity, consisting of a human countenance, looking forth amidst innumerable rays of light, which emanated from it in every direction, in the same manner as the sun is often personified with us. The figure was engraved on a massive plate of gold, of enormous dimensions, thickly powdered with emeralds and precious stones. It was so situated in front of the great eastern portal, that the rays of the morning sun fell directly upon it, and at its rising, lighted

[1] From *Heli*, the sun, and *vusi*, an abode; forming by the blending of the Sanscrit "v" with its accompanying vowels, the Greek "υ," as El-usium. (*See* Rule xvi. Appendix.)

[2] Hymn to Surya, translated by Sir W. Jones.

[3] Vol. i. p. 91.

[4] Read—Ghur-i-cancha. *Ghur*, a horse; *-i*, of; *Cancha*,—gold. Ghur is the present Hindoostani for Griha: *cancha*, is pure Sanscrit for gold.

up the whole of the apartment with an effulgence that seemed more than natural, and which was reflected back from the golden ornaments with which the walls and ceiling were everywhere encrusted. Gold, in the figurative language of the people, was the tears wept by the Sun, and every part of the interior of the temple glowed with burnished plates and studs of the precious metal. The cornices which surrounded the walls of the sanctuary were of the same costly material, and a broad belt of gold work, let into the stone work, encompassed the whole exterior of the edifice." How little do we know of that gorgeous pomp, or solemn grandeur, which we have good reason to believe attended in every region of the ancient world the adoration of the glorious orb of day, since we find that a nation totally secluded from all intercourse with our own hemisphere, had arrived at such a state of civilisation.

Let us now, from Peru, direct our glance towards north-western India, where we cannot but be delighted with the guidance of Colonel Tod, the accomplished annalist of the martial Rajpoots, the children of the Sun. "At the Jeipoor Court," writes this energetic officer, "whose princes claim descent from CUSH, the second son of RAMA, the *Bha'n* Septimi [1] is peculiarly sacred. The chariot of the sun, drawn by eight horses, is taken from the temple dedicated to that orb, and moves in procession. In the mythology of the Rajpoots, of which we have a better idea from their heroic poetry than from the legends of the Brahmins, the Sun-god is the deity they are most anxious to propitiate; and in his honour they fearlessly expend their blood in battle from the hope of being received into his mansion. Their highest heaven is, accordingly, the *B'hant'han*, or 'B'hanu-loca,' The region of the Sun." [2] At Oodipoor the Sun has universal preference, his

[1] The seventh day of the sun; called also the birth of the sun.

[2] Rajast., vol. i. p. 563.

portal[1] is the chief entrance to the city; his name gives dignity to the chief hall of the palace;[2] and from the balcony of the Sun[3] the descendant of Rama shows himself, in the dark monsoon, as the Sun's representative. A huge painted sun, of gypsum, in high relief, with gilded rays, adorns the hall of audience, and in front of it is the throne. As already mentioned, the sacred standard bears his image, as does that Scythic part of the regalia, called *changi*, a disc of black felt, or ostrich feathers, with a plate of gold, to represent the sun, in its centre, borne upon a pole. The royal parasol is termed Kernia, in allusion to its shape, like a ray (Karna) of the orb.[4] That a system of Hinduism pervaded the whole Babylonian and Assyrian empires, Scripture furnishes abundant proofs, in the mention of the various types of the Sun-god, Bal-nat'h, whose pillar adorned "every mount," and "every grove;" and to whose other representative, the brazen calf,[5] the fifteenth of each month was especially sacred.[6]

Bal-nat'h, the deity worshipped in Puttun Somnat'h, "the city of the Lord of the Moon," was the Sun-god Ba'l. Hence the tribe of the dynasties which ruled this region, "BAL-CA-RAE," the Princes of Bal, and hence the capital "BALI-CAPOOR," the city of the Sun, familiarly written "Balabhi."[7] The reader will not readily forget the renowned "City of the Sun," "Heliopolis;" nor Menes, the first Egyptian king of the race of the Sun, the Menu Vaiviswata, or patriarch of the Solar race; nor his statue, that of "The Great Menoo,"[8] whose voice was said to salute the rising sun. In Peru, the most magnificent national solemnity "was the Feast of Raymi,"

1 Surya-pol. 2 Surya-mahal. 3 Surya-Gokra.

4 Rajast., vol. i. p. 565. 5 Nanda. 6 Rajast., vol. i. p. 605.

7 Rajast., Appendix iv., p. 801. Gr. *Helios* and *polis*, Sans. *Heli*, the sun; and *palli*, a village or city; a common terminative, as Trichino-poly.

8 The Greek Me'-M'noo, as a corruption of M'ha-Menoo, *i. e.* the Great Menoo.

(read Rāma). At this feast the priest, after opening the body of his victim, sought in the appearances it exhibited, to read the lesson of the mysterious future,[1] a practice, the reader need not be reminded, of the "Rōmani," (read "Ramani,") of Italy, as well as the northern tribes of the "TOOROOSCHI," and "HOOSCHIS," incorrectly written "ETRUSCANS" and "OSCANS," by the Romans.

I would here simply remark, that her great deified heroes were the chiefs of CASTWAR and BALIK[2]—CASTOR and POLLUK's; the former the son of LEDA, and brother of Pollox: that is, both the Cashmīrians and the people of Balk sprang from LEDA—or LADAKH. I might multiply the evidences of this great Cyclopic branch of the human race, the patriarchal idolators of the Sun; but enough has, I doubt not, been already said, to prove its vast extent, its origin, and its gigantic ambition to conquer time itself, by its architectural power, and its extraordinary mode of sepulture. The martial bands of the Surya Vansa will now be briefly contemplated, in their Syrian settlements; more especially those in which they acted so prominent a part, as the fierce and warlike opponents of the favoured Children of Israel.

Prescott has so judiciously pointed out the striking points of similarity between the Roman and Peruvian system of Solar worship, that I cannot do better than avail myself of his able remarks:—

"The sacred flame," he observes, speaking of Peru, "was entrusted to the care of the Virgins of the Sun; and if by any neglect it was suffered to go out, in the course of the year, the event was regarded as a calamity that boded some strange disaster to the monarchy."[3] Nor has

[1] Prescott, vol. i. p. 101.

[2] Castwar, Cashmir, and Nepal; Balika, Balikha, Vahlika, Balk. For the Latin form "Castor," *see* Rule xvi. Appendix.

[3] "Vigilemque sacraverat ignem
Excubias divum eternas."

the same author omitted to point out the several features which at once mark the common parentage of the ancient and modern followers of the rites of Rama; for Rome, like Egypt, was colonised by a conflux of the Solar as well as Lunar races; hence the pomp of her pontifices has always partaken of the ritual of each. "Another singular analogy with Roman Catholic institutions," he remarks, "is presented by the Virgins of the Sun; the 'Elect,' as they are called, to whom I have already had occasion to refer. These were young maidens, dedicated to the service of the deity, who at a tender age were taken from their homes, and introduced into convents, where they were placed under the care of certain elderly matrons, 'Mamaconas,' (read Mama-Canyas),[1] who had grown grey within their walls.

"Under these venerable guides, the holy virgins were instructed in the nature of their religious duties. They were employed in spinning and embroidery, and with the fine hair of the vicuna wove the hangings for the temples, and the apparel for the Incas and the household. It was their duty, above all, to watch over the sacred fire obtained at the festival of Raymi. From the moment they entered the establishmennt, they were cut off from all connection with the world, even with their own family and friends. No one but the Inca and the Coya, or queen, might enter the consecrated precincts. The greatest attention was paid to their morals, and visitors were sent every year to inspect the institutions, and to report the state of their discipline. Woe to the unhappy maiden who was detected in an intrigue! By the stern law of the Incas she was *buried alive*, her lover was to be strangled, and the town or village to which he belonged was to be razed to the ground, and sowed with stones, as if to efface every

[1] *Mama-Canyas*, Mothers of the Virgins. *Canya*, a pure Sanscrit word for "virgin."

memorial of his existence. One is astonished to find so close a resemblance between the institutions of the American Indian, the ancient Romans, and the modern Catholic."[1]

Had this writer been aware of the extent and modified worship of the idolaters of the Race of RĀMA—had he marked from the most distant periods to the present day the gradual fusion of its worship with the Lamaic rites of Bud'ha, who was called the "ARCA-BANDHA," or KINSMAN OF THE SUN, he would have found a just solution of this simple problem. He would have marked how the hoary Pontifices of the city of RĀMA (RŌMA), when the keys of power were about to be wrested from their grasp by the nascent vigour of Christianity, strove to save their tottering gods by persecutions unparalleled save by those of their successors; he would have marked how that priesthood, effete of everything but subtle craft, used as an engine of political power that very Christianity it could no longer oppose, by tenaciously preserving every rite that could bow down the mind to the sense. Then, armed with these powers, as with a host seduced from its allegiance, he would have marked these successors of Attus Nævius and his marvellous whetstone, first striving to out-miracle the human judgment, then crushing that TRUTH, by the adoption of whose name and forms alone, itself, the Lamaism of the West, was saved from utter annihilation.

[1] Prescott's Peru, vol. i. p. 105.

XIV.

THE BUDHA SIVAS.

I ask'd of *Time* for whom *those* temples rose,
That prostrate by his hand in silence lie;
His lips disdain'd the myst'ry to disclose,
And borne on swifter wing, he hurried by!
The broken columns, *whose?* I ask'd of *Fame:*
Her kindling breath gives life to works sublime;
With downcast looks of mingled grief and shame,
She heaved the uncertain sigh, and follow'd *Time.*
Wrapt in amazement o'er the mouldering pile,
I saw *Oblivion* pass with giant stride;
And while his visage wore *Pride's* scornful smile,
Haply *thou know'st,* then tell me, whose I cried,
Whose these vast domes that ev'n in ruin shine?
I reck not whose, he said, they *now are mine.*—BYRON.

WHO could have imagined that latitudes so northerly as the line of the Oxus and the northern Indus would have sent forth the inhabitants of their frozen domains to colonise the sultry clime of Egypt and Palestine! Yet so it was. These were the Indian tribes that, under the appellation of "SURYA," or "the Sun," gave its enduring name to the vast province of "SURIA," now Syria. It is in Palestine that this martial race will be found settled in the greatest force. The land called by the Greeks "AI-GUPTIA," (Ægypt) derives its name from its colonists, the "h'AI-GOPATI," a term at once revealing their original land and the object of their worship. They are settlers from the same land with the "HYA," or "HORSE TRIBES," most of whom are the "Children of the Sun," and worshippers of "*Gopati,*" a term which at once signifies "*the Sun*," "*the Bull*," and "*Siva*."[1] Hence their designation as "Hyas of the Solar Race," or "H'AI-GOP'-TAI" (Ai-Guptai); "Gop'tai" being the derivative from Gop'ti, expressing "the descendants of, or people of Gop'ti," a large section of whom were the "SONS OF CUSH;" hence the term "CUSHITES," as applied to the "AITIO-PAS" (Aithio-Pas), or "Chiefs of Oude." CUSHA was one of the sons of Rama,—sovereign of Oude,—in whose honour the dynasty of "RAMES-ES," or "RAMA'S CHIEF," took its rise; the members of the same Solar dynasty giving the title to "RAMOTH-GILEAD," one of its settlements in Syria. "Rameses," writes Colonel Tod, "chief of the 'Suryas,' or 'Sun-born Race,' was king of the city designated, from his mother, 'Cushali,' of which, 'Ayodhia' was the capital. His sons were Lova and Cush, who originated the races we may term 'LAVITES,' and 'CUSHITES,' or 'Cushwas' of India."

"Was then Cushali, the mother of Ramesa, a native of Æthiopia, or 'Cusha Dwipa,' the land of Cush? Rama and Crishna are both painted blue, (nila,) holding the Lotus, emblematic of the Nile. Their names are often identified; Ram Crishna; 'the bird-headed divinity,' is painted as the messenger of each, and the historians of each were contemporary. That both were real princes there is no doubt, though Crishna assumed to be an incarnation of Vishnu, as Rama was of the sun. Of Rama's family was Trisankha, mother of the great apostle of Bud'ha, whose symbol was the serpent; and the followers of Bud'ha assert that Crishna and his apostles, whose statues are facsimiles of those of Memnon, were cousins."

The great divisions of this ancient system of colonisation were "ABUS-SINIA" (Abyssinia,) a name derived from the

[1] I need not here remind the reader, of the far-famed chariots and horses of the Egyptians, nor of the importation of this celebrated breed into Judæa in the time of Solomon.

great river in their old land already noticed, viz. the "ABUA SIN" or the "INDUS," and the people of the river "NUBRA," a more northerly confluent of the Abuasin, which gave the name of "NUBIA" to the neighbouring division of Africa. "The chiefs of Oude," or "AITYO-PA,"[1] were the colonists who gave the name of "AITHIO-PIA" to another section of the land, while the "NIL,"[2] or "Blue River," once more reappeared in Africa as the "NILE." Thus, then, by the simple, yet conclusive nomenclature of land and water, have we reached the introductory evidences of the Indian colonisation of Egypt. But we pause not here—in fact the mass of these evidences is so overpowering, that the great difficulty is that of making a selection.

By the Hebrews this land of Egypt was called Misra-im, their way of writing "Mahes'ra-im,"[3] the latter termination being the Hebrew plural of "Mahes'ra," the name of "Siva," already demonstrated in the terms "Gop'ti, Siva, and Haigoptai," the descendants or "people of Siva." A very ancient name also was that of Eëria, an appellation given likewise to Thessaly, which in the usual etymological style of Greek antiquaries, is said to signify, "darkness, and blackness," from a supposed allusion to the colour of the soil, being thought to be a translation of the Egyptian word "*Chemia*," which Plutarch gravely observed, signified *the black part of the eye*, and was applied to Egypt in consequence of its dark soil! The old Greek term "E-ERIA" is simply "HE-HERI-A,"[4] that

[1] The Hai-thoo-phoo, or Hayas of Thoo-phoo, or Thibet, a province bordering on the Nubra, formed a part of the emigrating bands, who are also to be found in Palestine.

[2] More generally the *Nil-Ab*, or blue waters.

[3] Properly Mahesvra (Siva). The "v" is lost by the usual digammated process, and the "a" and "i" rapidly blend together. The Sanscrit "Mahi" always reappears in Greek as "Mai."

[4] See Hi-pairos, Hi-phure, &c.—Hi-Bud-des.

is, the "Hya Budha's Land," or the land of the "Ionian worshippers of Budha," and the term "Kamĉ," has nothing to do with "Chemia," or the black of the eye. It is simply, "KAMA," the name of that district of Kama, which the reader has already remarked, formed a component part of "CAM-BUNII" Montes; both the colonists of the Cam-bunian mountains, and the "KAME" of Egypt, being one and the same people, both being Hiyanian or Ionian, equivalent to the "Aswán" or the "Horse tribes," which name of "ASWAN," they gave to the cataracts of Syene, just as their chiefs ("pos,") gave the title of Aswapos (Asopos) to the chief Bœotian River. The same reverential regard for the holy mountain of Meroo, which characterised the primitive Hindu in his old country, accompanied him to the distant land of Æthiopia. To this distant spot, he transferred the name of the awe-inspiring peaks of the holy mountain of Meroo. In the land of his adoption, this hallowed appellation appeared as MEROE, the seat of a high sacerdotal caste. Thus it was that, in Hellas, this great physical and religious feature of the Indian land and the Indian Creed, was zealously preserved, as I have already shown under the form of To-MAR-os.

Heliopolis, a name at once Sanscrit and Greek[2] was, as I have observed one of their chief towns; called also ON, *i.e.* "O'M," the great triune symbol of the Creator. The sacred syllable spelt O'M, is pronounced A O M, or A U M, signifying Brahma the Supreme Being, under his three great attributes of the Creator, the Preserver, and the Destroyer; the letters standing in succession for the attributes as they are here described. The Gayatri, called by Sir W. Jones, the mother of the Vedas, is expressed by the triliteral syllable "AUM." Sir W. Jones thus translates it:—"Let us adore the supremacy of that

¹ Hi- (Hĕri, Siva).

² From *Hēli*, the sun (Helios), and *pŏli* (πολις), a city; as Trichino-poly.

Divine Sun, the Godhead who illumines all, delights all, and from whom all proceeds, to whom all must return, whom we invoke to direct our understandings aright in our progress towards his holy seat." Mr. Colebrooke again explains it. "On that effulgent power which is Brahma himself, and is called the light of the radiant sun, do I meditate; governed by the mysterious light which resides within me for the purpose of thought: I myself, an irradiated manifestation of the supreme Brahma. There is only one Deity, the great soul, (Mahamátmá). He is called the SUN, for he is the soul of all beings."[1] We are thus brought back to the great tribe noticed by the Hebrew legislator; viz., the DODAN-IM; that is, the worshippers of the "DEO-DEO," or "DO-DO," THE GOD OF GODS—("BRAHMA.") Consequently the Dodanim were "Brahims," as I have already shown by the term "AINEANES."[2] This people, as well as the "Selli,"[3] both in Epirus and Thessaly, are found grouped around the oracle. The classical reader will recollect the singular term applied to Delphi, or strictly to the round stone in the Delphic temple; a term at once showing the antiquity of the Hindoo mythology, and the venerable parentage, yet juvenile position of the Greek. It is "OM-PHALOS," "the Navel;" a term imagined by the Greeks to be so applied from its being the centre of the earth. With this idea it had no connexion. It was so called by the early Indian colonists, from being "OM-PHALOS,"[4] a Sanscrit reflex of "Nabhi-ja," or "Brahma."[5] The same people

[1] See Coleman's Hindoo Myth., p. 136. From Colebrook, *As. Res.*

[2] See page 105. [3] See page 127.

[4] From *Om*, Brahma, and *phalŏs*, fruit.

[5] *Om-phalos* (Ὀμφαλός), the navel. *Om-phŭlŏs*, the fruit of O'M, *i.e.* BRAHMA; a form equal to *Nabhi-ja*, "Navel-born," the name of Brahma: Brahma appearing from the lotus, which sprung from the navel of Vishnu. (*See* Nabhija.) Hence the equally *Brahminical* O'M-nis, or the "Great ALL," of the settlers in the city of Rāma or Rōma.

of the City of the Sun, the people of Rama, when settled in Peru, named their most sacred city, "Cuzco," or "the Navel," a fact which again unites them with the tribes of Oude, the people of Delphi, and the city of Heliopolis, or "Om."

But Egypt and the neighbouring provinces are the representatives of the countries not only of the high northerly latitudes of the Himalayas, Thibet, and Oude, but also of the more southerly provinces of the Indus. The grand abode of the Bhils, or Bhiloi, has already been shown in "Philai," both town and island, placed opposite Syene, or "Aswa," that is, "the Aswas," or worshippers of Baal, or "The Sun." This magnificent offspring of its parent city, in India, has by the grandeur of its enduring monuments excited the admiration of successive ages. That city was "Luxor," so named from "Lukshur," in Beloochistan, a place situated on the route from Bela to Kedjee, forty miles west of the former town.[1] While this parent town remains in obscurity, the splendour of the architectural remains, and the obelisk of the Luxor of Egypt, still form the wonder of the astonished spectator. For what a sultry African climate did the "Nasamones," another people of the Punjab, exchange their ancient land! They appear in the pages of Herodotus, as it were in a fabulous position. They are, however, the descendants of the Nasumones, or people of "Nasumon," in the northern Punjab, situate on the north bank of the Chenab, on the great route from India to Cashmir.[2] Two border districts of the latter country, both in the neighbourhood of the northern Aboa-Sinians, or people of the northern Indus, gave a name to important parts of the African settlements of the people. They are "Karna," the parent name of the grand structures of "Karna-k;"

[1] Lat. 26° 14′, long. 65° 52′. Thornton's Punjab, vol. ii. p. 26.

[2] Nasumon is in lat. 32° 2′, long. 75° 11′.

and CUSH-ali, whence the Egyptian "CUS."[1] The district of Karna, the source of this part of the Egyptian population, is distinctly seen, by reference to the map of the Punjab, accompanying this work. The people of KARNA emigrated from the northern frontier of Cashmir; they are the same Solar tribes that appear in Hellas as "A-CARNANIANS," and the colonists of "Carno's" Isle, on the coast of Acarnania. TU-PHONIA, placed by Strabo near the canal which leads to Coptos, was the representative of the sect opposed to the Karnas, or Surya Vansa, it being a colony of the TU-PHĀN, or people of TU-PHOU, that is Thibet, whose population nearly all held the Bud'histic faith.

"GURNA," another remarkable spot in the vast field of Egyptian antiquities, was a colony from the district of "GIRNAR," a place as remarkable for its Indian antiquities, as its African colony was for its Egyptian wonders. "The Yadu from Joonaghur (Girnar,)" observes Colonel Tod, "was of the race of Crishna, and appeared long to have had possession of this territory: and the names of the Khengars of this tribe will remain as long as the stupendous monuments they reared on this sacred hill."[2]

"The allegory of Crishna's eagle pursuing the serpent (Bud'ha), and recovering the books of science and religion, with which he had fled, is an important historical fact disguised. . . . . The gulf of Cutch, the point where the serpent attempted to escape, has been, from time immemorial to the present day, the entrepôt for the commerce of Sofala, the Red Sea, Egypt, and Arabia. There Bud'ha Trivicrama, or Mercury, has been, and yet is invoked by the pirates of Dwarica. Did Bud'ha, or Mercury, come from, or escape to the Nile? Is he the Hermes of Egypt, to whom the four books of science, the Vedas of the

[1] The Kos-birbir of the Egyptians, the Apollinopolis Parva, of the Greeks.

[2] Rajast., vol. i. p. 250.

Hindoos, were sacred? The representative of Bud'ha, at the period of Crishna, was Nema-Nath; he is of a black complexion,[1] and his statues exactly resemble in feature the bust of young Memnon. His symbol was the snake. I have already observed that Crishna, before his deification, worshipped Bud'ha; and his temple at Dwarica rose over the ancient shrine of the latter, which yet stands. In an inscription from the cave of Gaya, their characters are conjoined, '*Heri*, who is *Bud'ha*.'"

The sagacious conjectures of Colonel Tod prove to be perfectly correct. I have already shown that the land of the Nile was not only possessed by the worshippers of the Sun, but by the "HI-HERIANS," or "HIYA BUD'HAS," just as Hi-Heria (E-ëria), was the denomination of Thessaly, the land of "Pheræ," (Peeræ, or Saints,) and as "HI-BUDES" (E-budes), in Great Britain, were so called from the Hiya or Yadoo Bud'hists, mentioned by Colonel Tod. The "Ophienses," whom I have noticed in Greece, are He-Herians, or Hyas, of the *Serpent* tribe (Ophis), of Bud'ha, to the south of whom appear the "A-PODOTI,"[2] ("non-Bud'hists.") That the settlers from Nubra (the Nubians), the Aboa-sin-ians and the people of Leh, or Ledakh, firmly fixed the Bud'histic faith in Africa, will not for a moment be doubted, from even a rapid view of the case. "BUTO," a very simple disguise for "BUD'HA,"[3] was the oracle of Leto, or LATONA, the true form of which is "LEH-TĀN," or the "COUNTRY OF LEH," or Ladahk, from whose immediate neighbourhood I have already shown the emigration of the people of the "Ph ( ) thiotis," or "Bud'has land;" that is, the "Bhutias," the same people who in their colonisation of Africa gave the name to that lake, which

[1] As. Trans., vol. ii. p. 304.

[2] Read: A-Boodhati.

[3] See at the close of this work, the great variety of forms assumed by this name, in various parts of the world.

has come down to us through ages as "Menza Leh," properly, "Mánasa-Leh," or Lake "Manasa," in Leh, or "Ladakh."[1] Can there be a more striking demonstration of the ancient intimate connection subsisting between the people of the "Menza Leh" (Manasa Leh), of Egypt, and the Himalayas of India, and of Thessaly (Othrys.) Le, in Ladakh, or Middle Thibet, of which it is the capital, is situated about two miles from the right or northern bank of the Indus, here called Sin-kah-bab. A narrow sandy plain stretches between the river and a chain of mountains, which rise on the north about two thousand feet, and on this level space the town is built. It is enclosed by a wall, surmounted at intervals with conical or square towers, and extending on each side to the summit of the mountains. Le is important as the great rendezvous for the intercourse between the Punjab and Chinese Tartary, and the principal mart for the sale of shawl-wool, brought from the latter region. It has about five hundred houses, and probably four thousand inhabitants.[2] Its elevation above the sea is stated by Moorcraft

[1] "The Manasa Lake, or Manasarovara, is named by the inhabitants of the Un-des and Chinese Tartars (Choo-Mapang). It is bounded on the south by the great Himalaya range; on the east by a prolongation of the Cailos range, and on the north and west by a very high land, under the forms of a table, a ravine, and a slope, all declining towards the lake. Manasarovara is considered the most sacred of all the Hindoo places of pilgrimage, not merely on account of its remoteness, and the rugged dangers of the journey, but also from the necessity which compels the pilgrim to bring with him both money and provisions, which last he most frequently eats uncooked owing to the want of fuel. It has never been ascertained why the Chinese Tartars, and inhabitants of the Undes, call it Choo-Mapang, but they consider it an act of religious duty to carry the ashes of their deceased relations to the lake, there to be mixed with its sacred waters. On different parts surrounding the lake are the huts of lamas and gylums, (priests and monks,) placed in romantic spots, and decorated with streamers of different coloured cloth and hair, flying from long poles fixed at the corners and on the roofs of the houses."—*Hamilton*, vol. ii. p. 203.

[2] Thornton's Punjab, vol. ii. pp. 21, 22.

to be more than 11,000 feet; and by Vigne to be about 10,000. Lat. 34°, 11′; long. 72°, 14.′

"BUD'HA," (Buto), the oracle of "LEH-TAN,"[1] (La-tona, or Ludakh), may still be traced in the marshes on the south side of the lake "*Burullos*," another name which has escaped the ravages of time, being the settlement of the people of "BURULU," a celebrated pass, at an immense altitude, situated a little to the south of "LEHTAN." Bud'ha was the capital of a name called "PH ( ) THE-NOTHES," by Ptolemy,[2] a somewhat singular way, certainly, of writing "B (*u*) DH-NAT'HES,"[3] or "The Bud'ha Lord." This is the same deified being whom the Greeks considered synonymous with "Hephaistos." In this they were correctly informed by the Egyptians, whose fore-fathers were the fellow-countrymen of the Hiya Bud'has, or Hi-Herians (Eeria) of Thessaly. "HE-PHA-IS-TOS," is a term not badly preserved by the Greeks, nor their informants. HI-PA-IS-DES,[4] or ("The Lord of the Hiya chiefs' land,") that is, as Colonel Tod has correctly observed, "Heri," who is "Bud'ha." That the Lamaic system of Bud'ha also came in with, or was more prominently put forward with the dynasties of the Ptolemies, is clear, since "Ptolemy"—a name received through the Greeks as "PTOLEMAIOS," is merely a title expressive of the sovereign's office; that king being "P ( ) TO-LEMA-IOS," a Greek way of writing "B (*u*) DHA-LAMA-HYŎS," or "BUD'HA'S HYA LAMA." Nor need I remind the reader that the Ptolemies pursued, down to the time of Cæsar, the custom of intermarrying with their sisters, a practice running up to the ancient era of Okka'ko, (the Icshwaca of the Hindus,) one of the venerable Bud'has of

[1] *Tān, t'han,* and *st'han,* country, land. LEH is the name of Ludakh, so called from its capital Leh.

[2] Ptolemy, Geog. iv. 5.

[3] *Nat'ha,* "a lord;" with short vowel "ĕ" and visarga as in Nat'hĕs. (*See* Rule ii. Appendix.)

[4] *Hi, Hya, Pa,* chiefs; *Is,* lord; *Des,* land.

antiquity. Thus the same race in Peru, though of the Solar branch, practised the custom of the HAI-GOP'TAI (Αἴγυπται.) "The heir-apparent, according to Garcilasso, always married a sister, thus securing an heir to the crown of the pure heaven-born race, uncontaminated by any mixture of earthly mould."[1] The origin of this custom amongst the Sakyas (Bud'hist Princes), is of vast antiquity, as it proceeds from an authentic Bud'hist source, furnished by the most distinguished Pali scholar of his time. I give the passage at length:—

"I shall now only adduce the following extracts from the Tíká, containing the names of the capitals at which the different dynasties reigned; and giving a distinct account of Okkáko (Icskwaku of Indus) and of his descendants, as well as the derivation of the royal patronymic 'Sakya,' to which no clue could be obtained in Hindu annals; but which is nearly identical with the account extracted by Mr. Csoma de Koros from the Tibetan 'Kahgyur,' and published in the Bengal Asiatic Journal, of August, 1833. Those nineteen capitals were—Kusáwati, Ayojjhapura, Báránasi, Kapila, Hatthipura, Ekachckkhu, Wajirawutti, Madhura, Aritthapura, Ikdapatta, Kósambi, Kannagóchha, Rojá, Champá, Mithila, Rájagaha, Takkasillá, Kusnárá, Támalitti.

"The eldest son of Okkáko was Okkakamukho. The portion of the royal dynasty from Okkakamukho to Suddhódano (the father of Gótamo Buddho), who reigned at Kapilo, was called the Okkáko dynasty. Okkáko had five consorts, named Hatthá, Chittá, Jantu, Pálini and Wisákhá. Each had retinue of five hundred females. The eldest had four sons, named Okkákamukho, Karakando, Hatthinéko, and Nipuro; and five daughters, Piyá, Sapiyá, Anandá, Sanandá, and Wiyitaséná. After giving birth to these nine children, she died, and the raja then raised a lovely and youthful princess to the station

[1] See Prescott's Peru.

of queen consort. She had a son named Jantu, bearing also his father's title. This infant, on the fifth day after his nativity, was presented to the rája sumptuously clad. The delighted monarch promised to grant any prayer of hers (his mother) she might prefer. She, having consulted her relations, prayed that the sovereignty might be resigned to her son. Enraged, he thus reproached her:—'Thou outcast! dost thou seek to destroy my (other) children?' She, however, taking every private opportunity of lavishing her caresses on him, and reproaching him at the same time with—'Ra'ja! it is unworthy of thee to utter an untruth;' continued to importune. At last the king, assembling his sons, thus addressed them:—'My beloved, in an unguarded moment, on first seeing your younger brother, Jantu, I committed myself in a promise to his mother. She insists upon my resigning, in fulfilment of that promise, the sovereignty to her son. Whatever may be the number of state elephants and state carriages ye may desire, taking them, as well as a military force of elephants, horses, and chariots, depart. On my demise, return and resume your rightful kingdom.' With these injunctions, he sent them forth in charge of eight officers of state. They, weeping and lamenting, replied, 'Beloved parent, grant us forgiveness for any fault (we may have committed'). Receiving the blessing of the rája, as well as of the other members of the court, and taking with them their sisters, who had also prepared to depart,—having announced their intention to the king in these words, 'We accompany our brothers'—they quitted the capital with their army, composed of four constituent hosts. Great crowds of people, convinced that on the death of the king they would return to resume their right, resolved to adhere to their cause, and accompanied them in their exile. On the first day this multitude marched one yójana only; the second day, two; and the third day, three yójanas. The princes thus consulted together:—'The concourse of people has become very great; were we to subdue some minor rája, and take his territory, that proceeding also would be unworthy of us. What benefit results from inflicting misery on others? Let us, therefore, raise a city in the midst of the wilderness, in Jambudi'po.' Having decided accordingly, repairing to the frontier of Himawanto, they sought a site for their city.

"At that period our Bódhisatto, who was born in an illustrious Bráhman family, and was called Kapilo Bráhman, leaving that family, and assuming the sacerdotal character in the Isi' sect, sojourned in the Himawanto country in a 'pannasála,' (leaf hut), built on the borders of a pond, in a forest of sal trees. This individual was endowed with the gift called the 'bhómilakkhanan;' and could discern good from evil for eighty cubits down into the earth, and the same distance up into the air. In a certain country, where the grass, bushes, and creepers had a tendency in their growth, taking a southerly direction then to face the east; where lions, tigers, and other beasts of prey, which chased deer and hog; and cats and snakes, which pursued rats and frogs, on reaching that division, were incapacitated from persevering in their pursuit; while, on the other hand, each of the pursued creatures, by their growl or screech only, could arrest their pursuers; there, this (Kapila Isi) satisfied of the superiority of that land, constructed this pannasála.

"On a certain occasion, seeing the princes who had come to his hut in their search of a site for a city, and having by inquiring ascertained what their object was, out of compassion towards them, he thus prophesied:—'A city founded on the site of this pannasála will become an illustrious capital in Jambudípo. Amongst the men born here, each will be able to contend with a hundred or a thousand (of those born elsewhere). Raise your city here, and construct the palace of your king on the site of my pannasála. On being established here, even a chandálo will become great like unto a Chakkawati rája.' 'Lord,' observed the princes, 'will there be no place reserved for the residence of Ayyo?' 'Do not trouble yourselves about this residence of mine; building a pannasála for me in a corner, found your city, giving it the name of Kapila.' They, conforming to his advice, settled there.

"The officers of state thus argued: 'If these children had grown up under their father's protection, he would have formed matrimonial alliances for them; they are now under our charge;' and then addressed themselves on this subject to the princes. The princes replied, 'We see no royal daughters equal in rank to ourselves, nor are there any princes of equal rank to wed our sisters. By forming unequal alliances, the children born to us, either by the father's or mother's side, will become degraded by the stain attached to their birth; let us therefore form matrimonial alliances with our own sisters.' Accordingly, recognising in their eldest sister the character and authority of a mother, in due seniority (the four brothers) wedded (the other four sisters).

"On their father being informed of this proceeding, he broke forth (addressing himself to his courtiers) into this exultation. 'My friends, most assuredly they are "SAKYA," my beloved, by the most solemn import of that term, they are unquestionably "SAKYA,"' (powerful, SELF-POTENTIAL.)

"From that time to the period of King Sudhódano, all who were descended (from those alliances) were (also) called SAKYA.

"As the city was founded on the site where the Bráhman Kapilo dwelt, it was called Kapilanagara."[1]

Again, the uniformity of practice connected with the rites of sepulture, subsisting among the tribes of Rama both in Egypt and Peru, is an evidence of identity not to be gainsayed. "The body of the deceased Inca," writes Prescott, "was *skilfully embalmed*, and removed to the great temple of the sun at Cuzco. There the Peruvian sovereigns, on entering the awful sanctuary might behold the effigies of his royal ancestors ranged in opposite files, the men on the right, and their queens on the left, of the great luminary which blazed in refulgent gold on the walls of the temple. The bodies clothed in the princely attire which they had been accustomed to wear, and placed on chairs of gold, sat with their heads inclined downwards, their hands placidly crossed over their bosoms, their countenances exhibiting their natural dusky hue—less liable to change than the fresher colouring of an European complexion; and their hair of raven black, or silvered over with age, according to the period at which they died. It seemed like a company of solemn worshippers, fixed in devotion,—so true were the forms and lineaments to life. The Peruvians were as successful as the Egyptians in the miserable attempt to perpetuate the existence of the body beyond the limits assigned to it by Nature."[2]

The long files of the representatives of the dead, shown to Herodotus,[3] by the Egyptian priests under the name of "Piromis," must at once occur to the classical reader. These PI-ROMIS" of Herodotus, were PI-RAMAS; "THE RAMAS;" the representatives of the race of the Incas or Sun-kings.

[1] Introd. to Mahawansa, p. 35: Hon. G. Turnour.

[2] Prescott's Peru, vol. i. p. 32.

[3] Herod., ii. 143.

The great patriarch "Bud'h," is he of whom Moses speaks under the name of "Phut." And it is with this family of Hierarchs, that the priestly "BUTES" of Attica, that people of the Attoc, and of HIYANIA (IONIA) will be found to be intimately connected, coming as both parties did, from the same land of north-western Asia.

The same corrupt method of transmitting Egyptian names through the Greek is constantly apparent. Thus we are told of "Sethos," priest of Hephaistos, who made himself master of Egypt, after the death of Amasis. This "SETHOS," is simply "SIDHOS," the title of the Bud'histic SIDHA or saint; the Ascetic, who by mystical or austere practices, has effected one, or all of five purposes: viz. the affluence, the form, or the society of the Gods, residence in the divine Locas, or identification with a Deity.[1] So again, "THOTH," the Mercury of the Egyptians, *i.e.* the Boodha of the east, and ultimately the Woden of the west, is equally a corruption of "SOODH;" the "Pure," of the English,[3] the "Purus" of the old Roman, and the "Peer" or saint of the old Persian.

Again: the great heroic chief of Egypt appears in the disguise of "SE-SOSTRIS,"[4] instead of Su-Sastra, or the great warrior "Su-Sastra;" "the great warrior," being the exact equivalent of "BHOO-C'TRIA" (BACTRIA.)[5] Then too we have "SHE-SHONK," for "SOO-SUNKA," or the chief of the "WAR CONCH," or "WAR SHELL," which the heroes of India sounded in battle. The other names of this chief, "Rameses," Ramas Chief, and SESOS-IS, the "SASŎ CHIEF,"[6] are well preserved.

[1] Wilson's Sans. Lex., *s. v.*

[2] Woden's day (Wednes-day) is thus well translated *Mercredi*, or Mercury's day, *i. e.* Bud'ha's day.

[3] *Soodhu*, signifies "Pure;" *Peer*, properly signifies "old," and it is only by implication that it means pure. It is now applied to Mahomedan saints and elders.

[4] From *Su*, well, and *Sastron*, arms.

[5] *Bhoo*, great; *Catrya* (a form of *Kshetrya*), warrior.

[6] The Săsŏ is one of the great Rajpoot tribes.

Again, "Tirtheka," of whom we are presented with a lively sketch by Rossellini, is the disguised representative of Tirthakar,[1] the title for a "sanctified Jaina teacher."

Then also we read of the "Hycsos," without thereby obtaining any idea of this people. We hear of them as a race of shepherds; their name will be found not only to imply this, but to tell the very place whence they came. The "HOOKSOS," then, are simply the tribes of the "OXUS," a name derived from the "Ookshas," those people whose wealth lay in the "OOKSH," *i.e.* the "Ox,"[2] the same martial bands who gave their name to the "Ooksh-ine," *i.e.* the sea of "the lords of the Oxus," or, "the EUX-INE." If the warlike tribes of the Oxus ruled the countries round the Euxine, penetrated into Egypt, then swept onwards to Palestine, (PALI-STAN[3],) the "land of the Palis or shepherds," and there effected more permanent settlements in Egypt, till dispossessed by the children of Israel,—the powerful people, immediately to their south, ultimately penetrated far to the European west; giving an abiding name to a sea of not less importance to the civilisation of mankind than the Euxine.

These were the Tartar bands of "Balti,"[4] who, as the BALTIKAS, or "people of Balti," carried to the BALTIC the fame of their ancient chiefs, the "BOODHAN," as "VODEN," or "Woden." The same warriors will again be found in Southern Greece, as constituting a part of its earliest population.

The presence of the chiefs of the Oxus, who have been already seen in Thessaly, as the Paen-i-oksh (Pene-i-os

[1] From *Tirtha,* holy.

[2] *Ookshan,* crude form of *Ooksha,* an ox. The Sanscrit and English are here but one word.

[3] *Pali,* a shepherd, and *s'than,* a land.

[4] "Balti,—written also Bulti and Bulti-stan,—is a small state north of Cashmir, bearing also the name of Little Thibet, by which prefix it is distinguished from Middle Thibet, or Ladakh, and Great Thibet, or Southern Tartary. Bulti is sometimes called Iskardoh, from the name

River,) or princes of the Oxus, will again be demonstrated in the Holy Land, as the fiercest, the most bitter, and the most warlike foes of the children of Israel; while tribes, drawn from regions far to the north and north-west, fill up the extraordinary picture of a population, issuing from the remote regions of a high northerly table-land, and pouring down like a torrent upon the plains and valleys below, overwhelming in their progress, and holding long in bondage a people of ancient civilisation.

Such were the "OOKSHAS," or "tribes of the Oxus," the "HUCSAS," of the Greek writers. They were the people who ultimately gave a name to a considerable district of Egypt, which appears in the sacred records, as "the land of Goshen," properly "Goshten," "the station for cow-herds."[1] Hence the instructions of Joseph to his brethren, and his application to Pha-raoh ("the king,") in their behalf. "My father, and my brethren, and their flocks, and their herds, and all that they have," said the youthful ruler of Egypt, "are come out of the land of Canaan, and *behold they are in the land of Goshen.*" Hence the reply of Joseph's brethren to the question of Pharaoh, "What is your occupation?" "Thy servants," said they, "are shepherds, we and also our fathers." "In the land of Goshen," said Pharaoh, to his young Vizier, "let them dwell, and if thou knowest any men of activity among them, then make them rulers over my cattle."[2] Were I to notice a tithe of the errors which we derive from the imperfect forms, in which the Egyptian mythology alone, has come down to us through the Greek, it would carry me entirely beyond the scope of the present work;

of the capital. It is bounded on the north by Chinese Tartary, from which it is separated by the Mustag or Mooz-Taugh (icy mountains) and the Karakorum Mountains, prolongations of the Hindoo Koosh to the eastward."—THORNTON'S *Punjab*, vol. i. p. 119.

[1] *Gō*, a cow; *Go-shtan*, a station for cowherds.

[2] Gen. xlvii. 1, 2, 6.

I will however just touch upon a part of Egyptian mythology, which, being only another name for Greek or Indian mythology—(for the identity of all three is established)—will be found to rest upon an historical basis.

The chief, called "The Great Sun," the head of the Rajpoot Solar race, in fact the great "Cuclo-pos," (Cyclops), or "Gok'la Prince," the patriarch of the vast bands of Inachienses—this "Great Sun" was deified at his death, and according to the Indian doctrine of the metempsychosis, his soul was supposed to have transmigrated into the bull "APIS," the "SERA-PIS" of the Greeks, and the "SOORA-PAS," or "SUN-CHIEF," of the Egyptians.[1]

The plain account of the wars carried on between the Solar chief, Oosras (Osiris), the Prince of the Guclas, and "TU-PHOO," is the simple historical fact of the wars of the Apians, or Sun-tribes of Oude, with the people of "TU-PHOO," or THIBET, who were, in fact, of the Lunar race, mostly Bud'hists, and opposed by Rama, and the "AITYO-PIAS," or people of Oude, subsequently the "AITH-IO-PIANS," of Africa.

I would now rapidly recapitulate the leading evidences of the colonisation of Africa, from North-western India and the Himalayan provinces.

First, from the provinces or rivers deriving their names from the great rivers of India, namely, the NILE, ABUSSINIA, and NUBIA; so called from the NIL and ABU SIN, (two names of the Indus), and the NUBRA.[2] Secondly, from the towns and provinces of India, or its northern frontiers; namely, the Oracle of AMMON, and the Oracle of LETO, in BUTO; the sacerdotal Meroë, the city and isle of

[1] *Osiris*, properly *Oosras*, signifies both "a bull," and "a ray of light." *Soora-pas* (SERA-PIS), the SUN-CHIEF.

[2] The letter "r" is resolved into "i" throughout the general structure of language.

PHILAI, the city of LUXOR, the land of E-ERIA, the land of TU-PHOO, the land of KAME, the land of MISRA-IM, the land of AI-GUPTOS, the land of CUSH, the children of CUSH, the cataracts of ASWAN, the city of KARNA-K, the city of GU'RNA, Lake MENZA LEH, and the Lake of BURULLOS; all borrowed from the lands of the Indus, where they stood as HAMMON, LEH-TAN, in BUDHA'S-land; the sacerdotal Mount MEROO, BHILA, LUKSHOR, HI-HERIA, KAMA, MAHESRA, HAI-GOP 'TA, CUSH, the land of ASWAN, the land of KARNA, the city of GURNAR, the city of NASUMON, the Lake of MANASA LEH, and the hills of BURULUS. Thirdly, from the ruling chiefs, styled RAMAS, (RAMESES); from the CHIEFS OF OUDE, (AITYA-PAS); from the Hiya B(*u*)D'HA LAMAS; (P ( ) TO LEMAI-OS); from the Oracle of BUTO, BUDHA, and from PH( )THA, (Bud'ha), being synonymous with "THE CHIEF OF THE HYA, OR IONIAN LAND," (HE-PHA-IS-DES), HE-PHA-IS-TOS. Fourthly.—Similarity in the objects of sepulture. Fifthly.—Architectural skill, and its grand and gigantic character. Sixthly, and finally.—The power of translating words, imagined to be Egyptian, through the medium of a modified Sanscrit. I shall now close these proofs, by two extracts, which arising from evidences drawn from sources widely differing from those which have formed the basis of my investigation, give a stamp of certainty, as decisive as any that can arise from circumstantial evidence,—an evidence admitted freely in our Courts of Law as equally valid with that which is direct.

The judicious compendium of the opinions expressed by men of sound judgment, here subjoined, in connection with the Indian colonisation of Egypt, will I doubt not rivet conviction on the minds of the most superficial observers.

"Besides the accounts published by the French literati and artists, the narrative of the British Captain Burr, attached to the Indian division sent to Egypt, deserves attention. He certainly visited only the temple of Denderah, but it cannot be uninteresting to hear the observations of a British traveller, more especially when just come from India, on the same subject which had just been examined by the French; as it will at least serve to convince us of the credit due to the statements and observations of the former. In the drapery of the figures he recognises the costume which still prevails in India. —'Often have I conjectured, and this conjecture was never so much strengthened as by the view of this temple, and the sculpture with which it is ornamented, that a greater resemblance in manners, and consequently a closer friendly connection, must formerly have existed among the nations of the East, when they were yet united by the same worship. The Indians who accompanied us regarded these ruins with a mixture of wonder and veneration, the effect of a resemblance which many of the figures which they saw here bore to their own deities, and still more of the opinion that this temple was the work of a rajah who had visited the land.'[1] He speaks of the statues of lions, as fountains, at Denderah; namely, couchant lions, whose jaws served for water-spouts, a circumstance which carries us back instinctively to India, and the remote East. Another traveller, Alvarez, found similar statues at Axum.[2] A striking analogy will be found to exist between the rock architecture of both countries; the grottos of Salsette, Elephantina, and Ellore, remind us strongly of the excavations in Egypt and Nubia, of the royal tombs at Thebes, and the splendid monument rescued from the sand and restored to the light of day by Belzoni at Ipsambul.

"The pagodas in the isle Ramiseram, between the con-

[1] Bibl. Britannica, v. 38. Literature, p. 208.

[2] Heeren, v. 179—2. 178.—Oxf.

tinent and Ceylon, are held in high estimation for antiquity and sacred character; the entrance of strangers is interdicted, and the statues of the divinities here worshipped; Rama, Sivà, Mahadeva, are washed in none other but the water of the Ganges, brought hither by the pilgrims and fakeers. A grand portal, under the form of a truncated pyramid, conducting to the principal pagoda, reminded Lord Valentia,[1] (from whom we have the above account,) of the monuments of ancient Egypt. Having thus shown a resemblance between the religious systems of Egypt and India, and consequently between those of Meroë and the latter country, we come at last to the final question. Did Meroë receive the civilisation from India, or India from Meroë? The latter of these suppositions would necessarily imply that the progress of civilisation in India was from south to north, since a colony from Meroë could only have come into India by sea; now if anything is well established about the early history of the Hindoo race, it is that the career of civilisation commenced from the north of India; the caste of the Brahmins identify themselves with this early civilisation, and appear to have come in as a conquering race among an ignorant population; their original country it is impossible to determine historically; one thing is conceded by all, that they spread themselves from north to south over the Indian peninsula. The traditions of the kingdom of Cashmire[2] name the Brahmins as the first who entered that country, and the researches of English travellers among the mountains of the Himalayan range throw additional light on this subject. In the heart of these mountains are found the residences of the earlier Brahmins, and more ancient temples of their gods; at the confluence of the two arms of the Ganges rises the holy

[1] Lord Valentia's Travels, vol. i. p. 340.

[2] Ayeen Akberri, ii. 157.

city Devaprajaga, 30° 8′ lat. inhabited by Brahmins; further on is seen the temple of Badri-Nuth, said to be extremely rich, and to possess as its domains more than seven hundred flourishing villages, placed in a state of dependence on the high priest of the temple; this pontiff also holds under his sway the city Mana, a place of trade on the route from Cashmire to Little Thibet, containing fifteen hundred inhabitants of Tartar origin. We find also another of these ancient temples on the borders of the country Gangutri, where the Ganges rolls amid these Asiatic Alps, the interior of which resembles a vast sea of ice. In every part of these regions the worship of Siva predominates without being exclusive; and the temples which still exist here after the lapse of so many ages, are sacred places, to which thousands of pilgrims from the more southern countries resort, and where trade allies itself to religion. Thus at periods unknown to history, and in regions safe from the inroads of conquerors, sacerdotal empires were formed, the influence of which was subsequently extended to all India, and probably to other parts of the globe in the east and west.

"The most ancient poems of India represent the countries of the Ganges as the cradle of those heroes, who afterwards carried their arms in the southern regions, even as far as Ceylon; everything, in a word, tends to show most clearly that civilisation followed in India a route diametrically opposite to the one which it pursued in Egypt, where the social movement was from south to north.[1] A confirmation of what has just been stated is to be found in the accounts of the Brahmins themselves; their books frequently mention two mountains, placed in the middle of Iambudwipa, (their name also for the habitable world,) remotely situated beyond the most northern boundary of India. One of them is designated

[1] Heeren, iii. 253.

Maha Meru, "Great Meru;" the other Mount Mandara: frequent allusions are made to them in the prayers of the Brahmins, their religious and civil ceremonies, and the principal occurrences of life. According to them and their books, this mountain is situated in the remotest quarter of the north, and from its bosom they still agree that its ancestors took their origin.[1] If, then, the route of civilisation was from north to south, we must bid farewell to the idea that this country received the germs of religion from the continent of Africa; and the only remaining supposition is, that *Meröe was indebted for its civilisation to India.* It may, perhaps, be urged, that some traces at least of such an event would be found in the ancient writers: waiving all exception to the unfairness of such a remark, in a matter of such remote antiquity, we may even here adduce authorities, which if not very weighty in themselves, yet derive great force from what has already been advanced. Philostratus[2] introduces the Brahmin Iarchus, stating to his auditor, that the Ethiopians were originally an *Indian race,* compelled to leave India for the impurity contracted by slaying a certain monarch, to whom they owed allegiance.[3] An Egyptian is made to remark that he had heard from his father, that the Indians were the wisest of men, and that the Ethiopians, a colony of the Indians, preserved the wisdom and usages of their fathers, and acknowledged their ancient origin. We find the same assertion made at a later period, in the third century, by Julius Africanus, from whom it has been preserved by Eusebius and Syncellus; thus Eusebius states, that "the Æthiopians, emigrating from the river Indus, settled[4] in the vicinity of Ægypt."[5]

[1] Dubois' India, i. 73. [2] V.A., iii. 6. [3] Ibid., vi. 8.

[4] "'Αιθίοπες ἀπὸ 'Ινδου ποταμοῦ ἀναστάντες, πρὸς τῇ 'Αιγύπτῳ ὤκησαν."—Chron. Can., 278. [5] Lemp., Barker's edit., "Meroë."

Of the distinct notices I have already given of the high northerly sources of Ægyptian, Æthiopian, and Abyssinian colonisation, all drawn from geographical evidence, demonstrating the Cashmirian and Thibetian aggregate, which shed the light of primitive civilisation in Africa, Thrace, Northern Greece, Northern Italy, Peru, and Rome, the extracts just quoted offer a singular confirmation.

I now present other evidences, equally powerful, deduced from the most rigid anatomical science. It is an able *resumé* of the result of European opinion on this momentous question, which the author has placed in a luminous point of view.

"The Asiatic origin of the first dwellers in the Nilotic Valley, is clearly demonstrated by concurrent and independent testimony. Cuvier and Blumenbach affirm, that all the skulls of mummies which they had an opportunity of examining, presented the Caucasian type. A recent American physiologist (Dr. Morton), has also argued for the same conclusions. The following is the result of his examination of one hundred Egyptian crania:[1]—

"The Table speaks for itself. 'It shows that more than eight-tenths of the crania pertain to the mixed Caucasian race; that the Pelasgic form is as one to one and two-thirds, and the Semitic form, one to eight, as compared to the Egyptian; that one-twentieth of the whole is composed of heads in which there is a trace of Negro and other exotic lineage; that the Negroid confirmation exists in eight instances, thus constituting about one-twentieth part of the whole; and finally, that the series contains only a single unmixed negro.

[1] Crania Ægyptiaca: Philadelphia, 1844.

"'ETHNOGRAPHIC TABLE OF ONE HUNDRED ANCIENT EGYPTIAN CRANIA.

Sepulchral Localities.	No.	Egyptian.	Pelasgic.	Semitic.	Mixed.	Negroid.	Negro.	Idiot.
Memphis . .	26	7	16	1	1	1	—	—
Maabdeh . .	4	1	1	—	—	2	—	—
Abydos . .	4	2	1	1	—	—	—	—
Thebes . .	55	30	10	4	4	5	—	2
Ombos . . .	3	3	—	—	—	—	—	—
Philæ . . .	4	2	1	—	—	—	1	—
Debôd . . .	4	4	—	—	—	—	—	—
	100	49	29	6	5	8	1	2

"From these, and a variety of other details, Dr. Morton has drawn the following among other conclusions:—

"The Valley of the Nile, both in Egypt and Nubia, was originally peopled by a branch of the Caucasian race.

"These primeval people, since called the Egyptians, were the Mizraimites of Scripture, the posterity of Ham, and directly affiliated with the Libyan family of nations.

"The Austral-Egyptian, or Meröite communities were an Indo-Arabian stock, engrafted on the primitive Lybian inhabitants.

"Besides these exotic sources of population, the Egyptian race was at different periods modified by the influx of the Caucasian nations of Asia and Europe—Pelasgi, or Hellenes, Scythians and Phœnicians.

"The Copts, in part at least, are a mixture of the Caucasian and the Negro, in extremely variable proportions.

"Negroes were numerous in Egypt, but their social position in ancient times was the same as it now is, that of servants and slaves.

"The present Fellahs are the lineal and least mixed descendants of the ancient Egyptians; and the latter are collaterally represented by the Tuariks, Kabyles, Siwahs, and other remains of the Libyan family of nations.

"The modern Nubians, with a few exceptions, are not the descendants of the monumental Ethiopians, but a variously mixed race of Arabs and Negroes."

"Again, Lepsius, Beufey, Meyer, Bunsen, Birch, and other philologists have proved that the ancient Egyptian tongue is full of affinities with the Shemitic or Syro-Arabic languages, and that it occupies a kind of middle place between them and the Indo-Germanic dialects. Quâtremere showed the relation of the present Coptic to the early tongue, and we find it in sisterly contact with these classes of languages which have spread so widely over the world. The first book of Bunsen exhibits this relationship in a variety of illustrations, and he had been preceded by Lepsius, in his famous 'Essay on the Egyptian numerals.' It is only of late years that any relationship was allowed between Hebrew and Sanscrit, but Fürst and Delitzsch have abundantly proved it, and it is now universally acknowledged. The old language of Egypt is found to be a connecting link between all these great varieties of human speech; and even the Celtic, in points where it differs from the Sanscrit, nearly corresponds with the ancient Coptic—the language of the pyramids and monuments. If the old Egyptian tongue have so many analogies with other and remote tongues; if they often resemble it in forms and flexions where they do not bear much likeness to one another, the plain inference is, that it is older than any of them, and has retained much of its original shape and character, while they were constantly subject to a process of development. 'The Egyptian language,' Bunsen affirms, 'is as certainly the primitive formation of the Euphrates and Tigris territory fixed in that island.'[1] There are also many points of analogy between the temple ceremonies and mythology of Egypt and those of Asia. Juba, as quoted by Pliny,[2] was of opinion "that

[1] Report on Ethnology. British Association, 1847.

[2] Lib. iv. 34.

the dwellers in Egypt, from Syene to Meroë, were not Ethiopians but Arabs."

"It seems to us, therefore, the only rational opinion to suppose that Mizraim, the son of Ham, and the first colonists, passed out of Asia into Lower Egypt, and settling at Heliopolis or Memphis, laid the formation of that marvellous kingdom, whose wisdom, arts, and labour have given to it a singular and imperishable fame. The pyramids in the vicinity of Memphis are the most ancient of the monuments, while those of its rival Thebes scarcely go beyond the eighteenth dynasty. Besides, the Isthmus of Suez offers the most natural and probable passage from Asia into Africa, (it has been the pathway between the continents for every important expedition,) and it plainly would conduct the emigrants into Lower Egypt.[1] The most distinguished Egyptologers now adopt this or a similar view, such as Bunsen in his recent and popular production.[2] Hieroglyphical records show that Egypt was named the "land of Ham" from the earliest period, and Egypt and Cairo are universally named Misr or Musr, at the present day. Phœnician story speaks also of Miser, who is evidently Mizraim, being the ancestor of Tautus, Thoth, or Hermes-Trismegistus. Nay, more, one of the gods of the first class was named Kham, whose name and mystic attributes seem to identify him with Ham, the father of the Egyptians.

"The long periods of chronology to which the ancient history of Egypt lays positive claim are sufficiently startling. Manetho demands many thousands of years as the prior period of his country's duration, while Herodotus, in referring to the alluvial deposit which the Nile had spread over the country, speaks of its accumulation as capable of being effected during twenty thousand years,

[1] See Wilkinson, vol. i. p. 2.

[2] Egyptens Stellung in der Welt-geschichte.

a period which he plainly reckons as nearly equal to the ages which had preceded his own birth. Definite epochs cannot be ascertained with satisfactory precision. That Egypt arrived at comparative civilisation at a very early period cannot be questioned, and that it was far advanced in social order as early as Abraham's days, is now universally admitted. That patriarch found in it a king —a Pharaoh, with a court, nobility, harem, and great wealth, joined to other indications of a fixed state of society."[1]

I now pass on to survey this race as the great opponents of the children of Israel in the LAND OF PROMISE.

[1] Illustrated Early Oriental History, by J. Eadie, D.D., L.L.D.—Encyclopædia Metropolitana, vol. xviii. p. 64.

XV.

THE PROMISED LAND.

"Who smote great nations and slew mighty kings. Sihon, king of the Amorites, and Og, king of Bashan, and all the kingdoms of Canaan. And gave their land for an heritage unto Israel, his people."—Ps. cxxxv. 10—12.

It is with a profound feeling of gratitude to the Great Author of Truth, that I approach this sacred subject. Whatever light I may throw upon the momentous theme, I would in all humility ascribe to the only source of light, and thankfully preface my remarks with that "Laus Deo," which characterised the conclusions of the literary labours of our forefathers.

The marvellous history of that people who were hallowed by the blessing of Jehovah for the holy work of regenerating the human race, is perhaps the grandest monument of Divine compassion and justice, in connexion with any single nation upon earth. The land which was "flowing with milk and honey," a "land of vineyards and olives," was an especial inheritance, granted for an especial act of faith, to the descendants of the Father of the Faithful.

But it would have been utterly impossible for the children of the great Patriarch, to realise this rich token of Almighty benevolence, had not the same Gracious Being who had "caused the lines to fall to them in pleasant places," vouchsafed the might of *His* arm to dispossess the warlike tribes which had secure possession of this fertile territory at the period of their entrance upon it.

The long slavery of His chosen people in Egypt, was closed by a miracle as striking as the providence which had introduced Joseph its youthful ruler. A dynasty which "knew not Joseph," had taken possession of the Egyptian throne, and the bondage of the Hebrews had become bitter and constant. The ambition which prompted the Solar Race to attempt, in spite of the intentions of Providence, an eternity of existence for the body, induced the same people to rear grand and gigantic structures to ensure a perpetuity of renown.

Works such as these could not possibly have been constructed in those early times without a body of men urged on to the task by princes, who moved a large portion of their subjects as a gigantic living machinery, uniform in its action, having no volition, and set in motion by the vapour of a Despot's ambition. By such means were constructed the grand aqueducts of Rome —her highways, and the pyramids of Egypt. The rearing of these last named gigantic masses of masonry had pressed heavily upon the strength of the Hebrews. The misery of their existence is forcibly depicted in the sacred writings. At length the day of deliverance dawned. By the special intervention of the Almighty, they were enabled to depart from that land, which to this day bears the traces of their forced slavery. But such valuable auxiliaries could not be tamely resigned by a warlike people; who while they scorned the arts of peace themselves, found it indispensable to maintain around them a large body of slaves to aid them in the objects of their ambition. The pursuit of the Hebrews was resolved upon, and hastily put into execution. Already the martial bands of these Solar Rajpoots were upon their track, and the advance of the fugitives seemed completely barred by the arm of the sea which rolled directly in their front. It was at this critical moment that the cavalry and chariot force of Pharaoh made its appearance immediately in their rear, and nothing but the intervention of a miracle could have saved them from utter destruction. That miracle was vouchsafed through the instrumentality of the great Hebrew lawgiver.

"Forthwith
Dilate in form, and radiant to the sight
Of all that host, the god-like Hebrew stood;
Then, spake the VOICE ETERNAL. Amram's son,
Whose eye with heav'nly pity beamed on all
That wide expanse of Innocence and Age,
His staff attenuate, with virtues rare
Surcharged, calm o'er the flood extending, glanced
To HEAVEN. The waves the incumbent GOD confess,
And in dread homage bow their heads; then wide
Disparting, as with voice of thunder, hymn
HIS praise. So,—semblance weak and faint,—
Some victor-king to distant conquest bound,
A chosen band full sorely tried, leads on
Through the vast pomp of all his marshalled realms;
Wide they roll back to give the victor way,
And as his serried files their glorious line
Hold on, in Pæans high they shout his praise."[1]

To the Biblical reader, the long sojourn of the people of God in the wilderness, and the series of marvellous events by which the authority of the Hebrew lawgiver was promoted and upheld, are well known. He is not, however, aware of the extraordinary difficulties which the Israelites had to encounter and overcome on their entrance into the land of promise. There the fiercest and most warlike of the Solar and Lunar race had early taken up their abode; in all probability composing a part of the identical vast array of the human family which helped to colonise Egypt, who moved onward to still farther conquests and a still wider series of settlements. The ample evidences about to be laid before the reader will, I doubt not,

[1] From MS. Poem.—E. P.

establish this fact. He has already remarked the extraordinary spectacle of a people of a high northerly latitude, in the vicinity of the Himalayan mountains, and the province of Ladakh, settled in the fertile land of Egypt, and bringing thither its religious rites and the various usages of a society that stamp an Indian original. That population is again to be distinctly seen in Palestine, so that both identity of nationality and identity of the era of colonisation, become almost self-evident. The Tartarian population, which flowed in upon the northern part of the rich country of Palestine, formed a considerable proportion of the inhabitants of that country, which will be shortly noticed; while the tribes of the Oxus, who have been already contemplated in PAEN-I-OKSH, or PENE-I-OS of Thessaly, as well as in the HOOCSHAS, or HYCSOS, of Egypt, will again be found resting like a war-cloud over that country, then passing onward to lord it over the rich champaign of the Holy Land. The most ancient name of that renowned region, so early the seat of civilisation, is CANYA, a name received by us as CANAA, through the Hebrew form,[1] and by them applied as to a nation of CANAANITES, or Traders. The appellation, however, is that of Canya, classically called Apollo.

Its other name, *Palæstine,* it derived from the term "PALI STAN," or, the LAND of SHEPHERDS, those very HYCSOS, or OXUS tribes, who have been lately noticed as overpowering, and for a long time holding in bondage the Egyptians. I shall now rapidly pass through the main points of this

[1] I would here make this general remark; that those etymologies which we receive through the medium of the non-inspired Hebrews, often rest upon the same foundation with those of the Greeks and Romans. On the other hand, definitions of names, given in the sacred writings, while having application to the history related by the inspired penman, at the same time that they are undoubtedly true, do not invalidate the nomenclature of the same places, previously given, having an homogeneous sound.

colonisation, more especially in connection with the people of Israel. On the north of the favoured Land of Promise, the people of Ladakh, who have already been contemplated in Egypt, in the neighbourhood of Menzaleh, effected a powerful settlement. They were the LE BANĀN.[1] or the TRIBES of LEH. The Tribes of LEH (LE-BANĀN) are again distinctly marked by their great river, bearing the name of the LEON-TES (LEHĀN-DES), "Land of the people of LEH," close to which is found the district of CŒLE (CAILE), the CAILA of the Himalaya Mountains. About ten miles from the banks of the river of LE-LAND (LEONTES), was the city of LASHE-m, or LAIS, named from LAHSA, the capital of TUB-et (TOB). TUBET is a name which gave rise to the celebrated TOPHET, and its various applications in Holy Writ.

Immediately to their south, on the east part of the River Jordan, were the warlike HERMEN, whose settlement was on the HER-MON mountains, at whose western slopes commenced the kingdom of the martial Tartar Prince, OGZ (OG), King of BASHAN. BASHAN, as the reader will observe, by referring to the Hyperborean Punjab, will be found immediately to the north of Cashmir. Close to the country of the Cashmirian Bashan, he will not fail to remark the land of GILID, which country he will again find contiguous to the kingdom of BASHAN in Palestine, appearing as "GALID," and GILEAD. Here, too, he will find the river GILGIT, which gave a name to the Gilghites of Palestine. The fierce and gigantic Og, or Oguz, as it is generally written, with his Tartar horde, is one of the most notable foes mentioned by Moses as being encountered and defeated. "Only Og, king of Bashan," says the sacred historian, "remained of the remnant of the giants; behold his bedstead was a bed of iron: is it not in

[1] From *Leh* and *Bănă*, a tribe; Persian plural, *Banān*. *Bana* is the Rajpootana form of the Sanscrit *Varna*; "p, b, v," locally commutable.

Rabbath, of the children of Ammon? Nine cubits was the length thereof, and four cubits the breadth of it, after the cubit of a man."[1] The cities of this formidable frontier prince were many and well defended; but notwithstanding, they all fell into the hands of the Children of Israel, by the irresistible power of the Almighty. "We smote him," says the sacred historian, "until none was left to him remaining. And we took all his cities at that time; there was not a city which we took not from them; threescore cities, all the region of Argob, the kingdom of Og, in Bashan." Then follows the decided testimony of Moses to the advanced state of military polity, which was found existing in the land, at the period of the entrance of the Hebrews. "All these cities were fenced with high walls, gates, and bars; beside unwalled towers a great many."

The scene of the defeat of this giant Tartar was the neighbourhood of the forest of Ephraim, near ASHTAROTH CARNAIM; the parent city ASTOR will be seen in the old kingdom of BASHAN, north of Cashmir. The sacred historian has called the city by the name of ASHTOR-ETH CARNA-IM,[2] from its being the "CITY OF THE CARNAS OF ASTOR." The province of CARNA, in Cashmir, is in juxta-position with ASTOR, in Cashmirian Bashan; hence these tribes, with the strong feeling that ever bound this patriarchal form of society, had emigrated from, and settled down in, the immediate vicinity of each other. Both OIN and HAZOR, too, frontier towns of the kingdom of Bashan, in Palestine, are as true to their original position in the parent country, as their inhabitants were to the feeling of fatherland. Both OIN and HAZOR, in the *old land*, are as near to each other as in the *new*; these towns being situated, the one to the east, the other

[1] Deut., iii. 2.

[2] Carnaim, is the ordinary Hebrew plural of Karna.

to the west of the CARNAS of Cashmir, and nearly equidistant about thirty miles. Immediately to the west of the Bashan of the Hebrews, was the land of TOB, the Hebrew way of writing "TUB-ET," in which that people had considerable settlements, lying along the eastern slopes of the Hermon range, and reaching to Rabbat. The Bud'histic colonisation of this region cannot for a moment be doubted; but as I shall again notice this fact, in conjunction with the grand Bud'histic era of Greece, I pass on to remark on HAMM-ĀN (HAMM-ON),[1] that is, the tribe of HAM, who not only fixed their oracle in the deserts of Africa, but were also in great force in the land of Canaan. The Ammonites took up their abode on the south-eastern frontier of Bashan, while the AMOR-ITES, or Rajpoots of the Oxus, colonised the country, to the south-west.[2]

But it is evident that the land which once sent forth to distant conquest, and to the foundation of such thriving settlements, these Tartarian tribes, must have vastly retrograded in the scale of civilisation. What can be said of the present semi-barbarous land, which produced the HIV-ITES, for these were the people of KHIVA! It is but too evident, that an immense retrogression in civilised life, and in the arts of war and peace, must have taken place in the Tartarian regions; for we have no right to assume that any of these great families of mankind were less civilised than the Egyptians, who formed a component part of the same great emigration. The people of Khiva, however, seem to have been scattered over the surface of Cama, though they are found principally in the vicinity of Gaza. What an extraordinary change must it have been from the cold chilly climate of Khiva, and its sparse

[1] *Ham-ān*, plural of Ham, "the people of Ham."

[2] Amoo, "the Oxus;" *Amoo-war* (AMO'RI), the people of the Amoo or Oxus.

produce, to the rich warmth and luxurious fertility of the Land of Promise. We have no better evidence of the strong contrast of the first and second home of this Tartarian people, than the animated description of one who experienced the rigour of this climate in all its severity:—

"In England," writes Capt. Abbot, "nothing is known approaching to the chill of the Khiva winter. My towel, hung up to dry in the small room warmed with a large fire of charcoal, instantly became a mass of ice. If the door was left open, the passage of the wind was detected, as it blew over any liquid, by its sudden conversion to a solid form, and there was no thaw excepting in spots where the sun-beams accumulated. In the shade, the snow always lay feathery and granulated, incompressible into masses, so that snow-balls could not be formed."[1]

Let us now take a view of the maritime portion of this remarkable country, where the most interesting monuments still remain, establishing the fact of that ancient Greek connexion with Phœnicia, so often alluded to by early writers, so pertinaciously denied by some, so suspected by others. There to the north, dwelt the singularly ingenious and enterprising people of Phœnicia. Their first home was Afghanistan, that is, the land of the OPHI-ENSES or Serpent tribe, the people of Bud'ha, whose symbol was the Serpent. This merchant race, the figure-heads of whose ships the classical reader will remember to have been adorned with the Pat-aikoi, were of the same stock with the early colonists of Corcyra, which island was peopled by the P'Hayakas, or the Hayas. The images which these ancient mariners placed on the prow of their vessels, called PAT-AÏKOI, were BUDH-HAYAKOI, or the effigies of the Haya Bud'ha, the patriarch and religious teacher of these great secessionists from the Brahminical or

[1] Abbot's Khīva and Heraut, vol. i., chap. v. p. 77.

state religion of the day. Hence this people were styled BHAINIKOI (PHAINIKOI,)[1] or "THE HYAS." The original seat of this energetic race was in a district closely connected with the Hellenic emigration—hence the supposed mythology of Greece is mixed up with their history. I shall notice this fact with all the brevity consistent with the short space allowed by the extent of my investigation. The history of the Cabeiri has a tolerably mythological appearance; that history, a plain matter of fact, will now be placed in a clear point of view, occurring as it does, in connexion with the Phœnicians; but for this, I should have left the so-called fable for future investigation. The PHAINICAS or the Hiyas (PHŒNICIANS), were emigrants from a district near Logurh, in Afghanistan, called BHĪNĪ BADĀM, (read BHĪNĪ BUD'HĀN,) the "HYA BUD'HISTS," whence, as I have shown, is the derivative form Phainika. One of the principal towns of Bhīnī, as the reader will observe, is SAIDĀN, a name adopted by the settlers in the new land of Phainica, as SIDON. The term Saidan is simply the plural of SIDHA, a "SAINT;"[2] hence Saidan, Sid-ān or Sid-on, is properly "ALL-SAINTS TOWN," just as DAMASTIUM was so named in Epīrus, and DAMASCUS (DAMAS-KAS)[3] in the Land of TOB, or TUBET, the head quarters (as will shortly be shown) of the Budh-'istic Propaganda, at a most important era of Greece.

Creuzer has very justly traced to the Phœnicians the worship of the Cabeiri, with whom he has identified the Pataïkoi, and he has shown that the worship of the Cabeiri was associated with that of Lunus.

[1] *P'Haien,* "the Hayas," plural of *Hai.* P'Hainika, a derivative form, with the same meaning. The Hayas (P'Hainicas, P'Hœnicians) were the colonists of Ireland. Hence the quasi-identity of the Irish and Phœnicians. The Irish are HI-BERNAS Hya-tribes, (*berna,* a tribe,) and their land *Hi-bernia,* Land of the Hya tribes.

[2] *Sidha,* a saint; *Sidhān,* saints.

[3] Dhamas-kas, derivative form of Dhamas.

If the reader will only refer to the territory in connexion with the Hiyanian, (Ionians,) or Horse Tribes, he will have no difficulty in comprehending the plain facts of the case. Not only are the Pat-aikoi identified with the Cabeiri, but the Corubantes also.

Behold now the simple fact. The CABEIRI are the KHYBERI, or people of the KHYBER; the CORUBANTES are the GHOR-BAND-DES, or people of GHOR-BUND LAND; all of whom are PAT-AIKOI, or Lunar tribes, that is, Bud'hists. HE-PHA-IS-TOS, the "Lord of the Hya Chiefs land" (BUD'HA,) was said to be their father, that is, their great parent and teacher, which was a fact. The Roman account produces nearly the same results—by this nation Hephaistos is identified with VULCAN, that is, BALKAN, the people of BALK, from which Tartarian regions they considered Bud'hism as emanating. Others of the Cabeiri (Khyberi,) were AXIEROS and CASMILLUS, in plain terms, AKSHYĔ-RAJ, and CASMIR-RAJ, the OXUS KING, and the CASHMIR KING —facts perfectly in accordance with the original head quarters of Budhism in Lancas Land. Again they are often confounded with the DIOS-CUROI, (DWYOS-CUROI,) TWO CURUS, or CASTOR and POLLUX, or, as I have shown, CASHMIR and BALK.

The same system of personification sank deep into the Hindoo cosmogony, and in fact the whole of what is called their mythology. The Cabeiri are, as Wilford has endeavoured to prove, CUVERA, the Hindoo god of wealth and regent of the north,—that is, in simple language, the Khyber; its region is wealthy and abounds with rubies; gold is found in the rivers in its vicinity, and it was likewise the ruling northern power in these early days. The Hindoos, like the Greeks, have their own derivation for Cuvera; and alluding to the deformity of the god, who is represented as having three legs, and eight teeth, they derive his name from "Cu," vile, and "vera," a body.[1] Here

[1] Wilson's Sans. Lex., *in v.*

then, the CUVERA of the Hindoos, the PATAIKOI of the Phœnicians, the CABEIRI OF THE GREEKS, are simply distorted records and distorted comments upon the plain facts of Bud'hist worship, Bud'hist industry, and Bud'hist wealth, abounding in the regions of the KHIAIBER, and its relative vicinity.

The Roman Augurs ignorantly styled the Khyberi, (Cabeiri,) DII POTES, instead of DII BODHES, or BUD'HA GODS. Sometimes they are as ignorantly called Κόβαλοι, (COBALOI,) instead of CABULOI, or CABUL Deities. Their worship resembled that of Cybele, (CUBELE,) and no wonder, since this is again but a transparent disguise for "CABUL-E;" hence "CYBELE," or CABUL, is often represented as a female with a turretted coronet. We have then, in the Cabeiri, the representatives of a form of Bud'histic worship and Bud'histic chiefs, extending from the Logurh district (Locri) to Cashmir, the object of worship of the Hya, and the Phœnician race, for they are but one. There is yet another most important point of view in which the KHAIBERI are to be considered. They are the KHEBREW-I, or Hebrews. The name A-BRAHAM, (properly "BRAHM," in the Indian dialects,) is considered by some Hebrew antiquarians to be derived from "HAIBRI," signifying "passenger," in allusion to his emigrating from Mesopotamia. The tribe of YUDAH is in fact the very YADU, of which considerable notice has been taken in my previous remarks. The people of God therefore were literally taken out from amongst the other tribes, to be especially sanctified for the important work of the moral and religious regeneration of mankind.

Hence it is, that among the Greek writers of antiquity such a stress is always laid on the piety of the "HYPERPOREANS," that is the people of KHAIBER, or the HEBREWS. It is only within the last few years that any connexion between the Indo-Germanic and the Shemitic dialects has been admitted. I have no doubt whatever, that the northern limits of Afghanistan will be demonstrated to be the parting point of these two great families of language, and consequently of nations. The Afghans have claimed descent from the Jews, or IOUDAIOI (YOUDAI-OI); the reverse is the case. The HAIBREWS, or KHAIBREWS, are descended from the YADOOS. In that very land of the Yadoos, or Afghans—DAN and GAD, still remain as the feeble remnants of Jewish antiquity. But I must now pass on to the further consideration of the maritime division of Canaan.

The energetic people whose fleets traversed the ocean, on the most distant voyages, and who, in fact, long before the days of Solomon, were in the habit of sailing to India, the parent land, were a considerable time before they experienced the maritime rivalry of Hellas. That India was the point whence came the gold and the luxurious appliances of Solomon's court is clear; both the length of the voyage, and the nature of the commercial imports, and the original land of the Phœnicians, establish this fact. It was a coasting voyage of THREE YEARS. "For the king had at sea a navy of Tarshish,"[1] with the navy of Hiram; once in three years came the navy of Tarshish, bringing gold and silver, IVORY, and APES, and PEACOCKS. It is evident that in the absence of the compass, the navigators of antiquity would acquire peculiar skill and hardihood in the practical training required for long coasting voyages; nor have I the slightest doubt that the three years' navigation noticed by the sacred historian was the great coasting voyage to Ceylon. A most singular correspondence in a group of settlements has lately been noticed, in speaking of BASHAN, GILEAD, ASHTORETH-CARNAIM, and HAZOR, so wonderfully the counterpart of the parent Indian sects of BASHAN, of GILID, and of the CARNAS of ASTORE and HUZARA.

[1] 1 Kings, x. 22. 2 Chron., ix. 21.

Another coincidence, equally marvellous, is to be seen on the shores of Canaan. There, following in the exact order in which they stand in the mother country from north to south, are ACHO, the river KISHON, CARMEL, and DOR, in the original land of the settlers, standing as ACO, KISHEN, CARMEL, and DOR. Aco, in the parent land, is situated on a branch of the Indus, near Bashan; the river Kishen, or the Kishen Gunga, that is, Krishna river, flows immediately to the south, encircling the north-western frontiers of Cashmir. The river Dor (whence the Dorians) is on the west; while the town of Carmel is at a comparatively short distance to the south. Directly to the south of the river Kishon, "that ancient river," is the far-famed MEGIDDO, which has been already noticed in India as MAGADHA, and in Greece as MAGHEDAN (MAKEDONIA). The vicinity of this spot was the scene of the disastrous defeat of Sisera, the great Rajpoot prince, the "captain of the host of Jabin, King of Canaan, who dwelt in Harosheth of the Gentiles." The worship of Bál by the Surya Vansa, or Solar tribes, has already been noticed. Into this idolatry the children of Israel had fallen, and had moreover adopted the worship of the bull, which was characteristic of the solar idolatry. They "served Baalim, and they forsook the Lord God of their fathers, which brought them out of the land of Egypt, and followed other gods, of the people that were round about them, and bowed themselves unto them, and provoked the LORD to anger. And they forsook the LORD, and served Baal and Ashtaroth."[1] The clear views held by Colonel Tod of ancient society throughout the whole of the primeval civilised world, is a subject that does honour to his name. His views were comprehensive, yet true to nature and history. "The 'BUL-dan,' or gift of the Bull to the Sun," says this energetic writer, "is well recorded. There are

[1] Judges ii. 11—13.

in Rajasthan numerous temples of BAALIM and BALPOOR. Mahadeo has several in Saurashtra. All represent the SUN.

> 'Peor his other name, when he enticed
> Israel in Sittim, on their march from Nile.'
>
> *Paradise Lost*, b. i.

. . . . . . All the idolators of that day seem to have held the grosser tenets of Hinduism."[1] Again:—"When Judah did evil in the sight of the Lord, and 'built them high places, and images, and groves, on every high hill, and under every tree,' the object was Bál; and the pillar, (the lingam) was his symbol. It was on his altar they burned incense, and 'sacrificed unto the Calf on the fifteenth day of the month,' the sacred Amavus of the Hindus. The Calf of Israel is the Bull (nanda) of Bâlcésar, or Iswara; the Apis of the Egyptian Osiris."[2] Again: —"Mahadeva, or Iswara, is the tutelary divinity of the Rajpoots in Mewar; and, from the early annals of the dynasty, appears to have been, with his consort Isa, the sole object of Gehlote adoration. Iswara is adored under the epithet of Ek-linga, and is either worshipped in his monolithic symbol, or as Iswara Chaomukhi, the quadriform divinity represented by a bust with four faces. The sacred Bull, Nanda, has his altar attached to all the shrines of Iswara, as was that of Menes, or Apis, to those of the Egyptian Osiris.

"Nanda has occasionally his separate shrines, and there is one in the Valley of Oodipoor, which has the reputation of being oracular as regards the seasons. The Bull was the steed of Iswara, and carried him to battle; he is often represented upon it with his consort Isa, at full speed. The Bull was offered to Mithras by the Persian, and opposed as it now appears to Hindu faith, he formerly bled on the altars of the Sun-god, on which not only the

[1] Rajasth., vol. i. p. 76. [2] Rajasth., vol. i. p. 79.

Buld-dan (*offering of the bull*) was made, but human sacrifices. We do not learn that the Egyptian priesthood presented the kindred of Apis to Osiris, but as they were not prohibited from eating beef, they may have done so. The shrine of Eklinga is situated in a defile, about six miles north of Oodipoor. The hills towering around on all sides are of the primitive formation, and their scarped summits are clustered with honeycombs. There are abundant small springs of water, which keep verdant numerous shrubs, the flowers of which are acceptable to the deity, especially the Kinér or Oleander, which grows in great luxuriance on the Aravulli. Groves of bamboo and mango were formerly common, according to tradition; but although it is deemed sacrilege to thin the groves of Bál, the bamboo has been nearly destroyed: there are, however, still many trees sacred to the deity scattered around. It would be difficult to convey a just idea of a temple so complicated in its details. It is of the form commonly styled pagoda, and, like all the ancient temples of Siva, its *sikra*, or pinnacle, is pyramidal. The various orders of Hindu sacred architecture are distinguished by the form of the *sikra*, which is the portion springing from and surmounting the perpendicular walls of the body of the temple. The *sikra* of those of Siva is invariably pyramidal, and its sides vary with the base, whether square or oblong. The apex is crowned with an ornamental figure, as a sphynx, an urn, a ball, or a lion, which is called the *kulhis*. When the *sikra* is but the frustum of a pyramid, it is often surmounted by a row of lions, as at Biolli. The fane of Eklinga is of white marble, and of ample dimensions. Under an open vaulted temple, supported by columns, and fronting the four-faced divinity, is the brazen bull Nanda, of the natural size; it is cast, and of excellent proportions. The figure is perfect, except where the shot or hammer of an infidel invader has penetrated its hollow flank in search of treasure. Within the quadrangle are miniature shrines, containing some of the minor divinities."[1]

Again:—"Near where I crossed the river (Loony,) I visited a small temple dedicated to Balpoor-Siva, or the city of Bál; in front of the mythic emblem of the god, was the Vahan or the bull in brass; at one time apparently the sole object of worship of the Saura peninsula; a land, which there can hardly be a doubt, *was in communication with the shores of the Red Sea, Egypt, and Palestine, in the earliest periods of history, probably long before Hiram and the mariners of Tyre were carriers to the wise King of Jerusalem.* What are Baal and the brazen calf, to which especial honours were paid, on the fifteenth of the month, but the Bâl-Eswar and bull (nanda) of India? . . . . . . Balpoor, or the city of Bel, is therefore the same as Baltec, or Heliopolis of Syria; coincidences in names, rites, and symbols, all denoting one universal natural religion, namely, the worship of the sun, and his type the bull, emblematical of fertility and production."[2]

Such is a faithful description of that idolatry into which the children of Israel fell,—a description in exact keeping with that population, which I have exhibited as colonising the land of Canaan. "HARO-SHETH of the Gentiles," the residence of the Rajpoot war chief, is exactly descriptive of a military post, being the grand city for the HAROS, (the HEEROS, of the Greeks,) and the town of HAR, the Hindu god of war already noticed. Jabin had "nine hundred chariots of iron," the usual description of force of the old Hellenic and Indian war caste, and "he mightily oppressed the people." On the total discomfiture of his martial bands, through Almighty intervention, by which a panic was made to fall upon these

[1] Tod's Rajasth., vol. i. p. 515.

[2] Tod's Western Asia, p. 54.

fierce warriors, Sisera, the solitary relic of the slaughter, had escaped on foot from the scene of havoc.

Trusting implicitly to the sacred rights of hospitality always accorded by the Rajpoots and held inviolable, and utterly worn out by the fierce conflict and the rapid flight on foot, he entered the tent of the wife of a Chief with whom he was at peace. This apparently inviolable sanctuary, however, only proved the scene of his miserable assassination; he fell by a contemptible death,—his destruction was to be ignominious; he perished in a tent by a nail, driven into his temples by the feeble hand of a woman, when he was "fast asleep and weary; and so he died." Nothing can exceed the combined sublimity and noble expansion of gratitude which characterise the song of praise that burst forth from the heart, and flowed from the lips of the prophetess "who judged Israel at that time."

"Praise ye the Lord for the avenging of Israel, when the people willingly offered themselves . . . .

"Lord, when thou wentest out of Seir, when thou marchedst out of the field of Edom, the earth trembled, and the heavens dropped, the clouds also dropped water.

"The mountains melted from before the Lord, even that Sinai from before the Lord God of Israel. . . . .

"*They chose new gods, then* was war in the gates: was there a shield or spear seen among forty thousand in Israel?

"My heart is toward the governors of Israel that offered themselves willingly among the people. Bless ye the Lord. Speak, ye that ride on white asses, ye that sit in judgment, and walk by the way.

"They that are delivered from the noise of archers in the places of drawing water, there shall they rehearse the righteous acts of the Lord, even the righteous acts toward the inhabitants of his villages in Israel: then shall the people of the Lord go down to the gates.

"Awake, awake, Deborah; awake, awake, utter a song; arise, Barak, and lead thy captivity captive, thou son of Abinoam. . . .

"Zebulun and Naphtali were a people that jeoparded their lives unto the death in the high places of the field.

"The kings came, and fought; then fought the Kings of Canaan in Taanach, by the waters of MEGIDDO; they took no gain of money.

"They fought from heaven; *the stars in their courses fought against Sisera.*

"The river of KISHON swept them away, that ancient river, the river Kishon.[1] O, my soul, thou hast trodden down strength.

"Then were the horse-hoofs broken by the means of the prancings; the prancings of their mighty ones.

"Curse ye Meroz, said the angel of the Lord; curse ye bitterly the inhabitants thereof; because they came not to the help of the Lord, to the help of the Lord against the mighty.

"Blessed above women shall Jael, the wife of Heber the Kenite, be: blessed shall she be above women in the tent.

"He asked water, and she gave him milk: she brought forth butter, in a lordly dish.

"She put her hand to the nail, and her right hand to the workman's hammer, and with the hammer she smote Sisera; she smote off his head, when she had pierced and stricken through his temples.

"At her feet he bowed, he fell, he lay down; at her feet he bowed, he fell: where he bowed, there he fell down dead. . . . So let all thine enemies perish, O Lord; but let them that love Him, be as the sun when he goeth forth in his might."[2]

[1] From the Kishen, or Krishna River of Cashmir, the old country.

[2] Judges, v. 2—31.

"The loss of a battle," says Colonel Tod, "or the capture of a city, is a signal to avoid captivity and its horrors, which to the Rajpootni[1] are worse than death. . . We can enter into the feeling which insured the preservation of honour by the fatal *Johur*,[2] when the foe was the brutalised Tartar. But the practice was common to the international wars of the Rajpoots; and I possess numerous inscriptions on stone, and on brass, which record as the first token of victory, the captive wives of the foemen. When the mother of Sisera looked out of the window, and cried through the lattice, 'Why tarry the wheels of his chariot—have they not sped? Have they not divided the prey, to every man a damsel or two?'—WE HAVE A PERFECT PICTURE OF THE RAJPOOT MOTHER EXPECTING HER SON FROM THE FRAY."[3]

Nothing can more strongly mark the admirable discrimination of this clear-sighted writer, who has been too often set down as visionary in some of his notions, by men whom nothing but chapter and line will satisfy, forgetting that there is yet a surer historian than the most scrupulous chronicler, in the transmitted customs, rites, and even disguised language of the most venerable antiquity; they will accept nothing less than *direct* evidence, and will deny authenticity or proof to *circumstantial evidence*,—a line of demonstration freely admitted and acted upon in the most important Courts of Law. Colonel Tod proves to be correct to the letter. "SISE-RA" is the Rajpoot name for the SĔSĔ-PRINCE, or Chief of the SĔSĔ, or HARE TRIBE, one of the Royal Rajpoot Tribes, which Colonel Tod has so admirably described in the "Raja-cula," or Royal Races of the Surya Vansa.

Thus, then, at length, are distinctly seen:—First, the identical localities in the Indian and Tartarian provinces,

[1] Female Rajpoot.

[2] The immolation of the females of the tribe.

[3] Rajast., p. 640.

whence Palestine was colonised. Secondly, identity of idolatry is proved between India—the old country, and Palestine—the new. Thirdly, the ever-prevailing use of the war-car, both in the provinces of India and those of Syria. Fourthly, the identity of the Rajpoot of India and of Palestine. Fifthly, the positive notification of the distinct tribe which the Israelites encountered and overthrew.

I shall now rapidly pass forward to sketch some of the remaining provinces or people, of Palestine.

The exact point whence the colony of Phœnicia set out has been clearly shown, as well as the parent town of Sidon. The reader will by the accompanying map of Afghanistan distinctly see the position of the Phainicas, or Phœnicians.

He will now understand the bitter sarcasm contained in that eastern play upon words, which induced the contemptuous question of Hiram, on receiving his reward for building the temple of Solomon. "Hiram," the sacred writer tells us, "came out of Tyre, to see the cities which Solomon had given him; and they pleased him not. And he said, What cities are these which thou hast given me, my brother? And he called them the LAND of CABUL unto this day."[1] By reference to the map of the Punjab, the reader will perceive that the parent CABUL, is in the land of the BHAINIKAS (PHŒNICIANS), as also SIDON; which cities he will find in the PHŒNICIA of *both* countries.

The term "CABUL," then, signifying "*displeasing*," or "*dirty*," is a sarcastic play upon the name of the ancient country of Hiram's ancestors. Not far from the Kishon, or "Krishna river" of Palestine, and a little to the south of Dor and Megiddo, already noticed, is the sacred hill of "SA-MAR-ia," the "SOO-MERU" of the Indian settlers in Palestine, and the SO-MARO-S of the Hellenic colonists. It had, long before the arrival of the Israelites, been a

[1] 1 Kings, ix. 13. Cabul signifies dirty, or displeasing.

holy mount for the Bud'histic worship, and it had continued a kind of rival establishment to the temple of Jerusalem. "Sir," said the Samaritan woman to our Saviour, "I perceive that thou art a prophet. *Our fathers worshipped in this mountain;* and ye say, that in Jerusalem is the place where men ought to worship."[1] We are thus presented with the indubitable proof of the strong ties of that primitive patriarchal society, by which, after families had expanded into tribes, and tribes into nations, the same first strong feeling of unity continued to subsist. Hence the reader cannot fail to have been struck with the extraordinary harmony of emigration and settlement which have been demonstrated in all the movements of mountain tribes. Thus are at once seen, in the CITY of DOR, the KISHON, MEGIDDO, and MOUNT SAMARIA of Palestine, the same northerly people of the DOR RIVER, the KISHEN, the MAGADHAS, and SU-MERU of the Cashmirian district. What can be a stronger evidence of those primitive ties by which the most venerable societies were knit together!

The more southerly inhabitants, both of Afghanistan and Palestine, now begin to come into view. SARON is the frontier province of Samaria towards the south. Its parent district will be easily recognised as the SARAWĀN, the same people who have been noticed as the SARONICAS, or settlers in the SARONIC Gulf. As in the old, so in the new country, their chief town is SARON, with a trifling variation of form. Again is brought into prominent and marked distinction the feature of society so lately noticed. In the Sarawan district of Afghanistan, is the land of Shāl, or Shāli;[2] in SARON of Palestine, is the same, under the name of the land of "SHALISH-a;" whilst the renowned city of GAZA of Palestine, is to this day, under the identical name of GAZA, found in the districts of SHĀL and SARAWAN, in the land of Afghanistan!

[1] St. John, iv. 19, 20.

[2] Pronounced Shawl.

We are now amongst the fiercest foes of the people of God; they are warriors not inferior to any who raised the war-yell[1] against the bands of Israel.

The PHILIS-TINES or the BHILI-STANS, the people of the LAND of the BHILS, are of the most ancient original tribes of India.[2] They are a branch of the people of Hamon, of whose lineage was the BHIL-PRINCE (PHIL-POS), of Macedon. By classical writers these people were converted to ALLO-PHULI, in lieu of the true name HALA-PHULA, or the tribes of the HALA MOUNTAIN, also written "HELA," who have been already noticed as the ancestors of the HEL-LENES, or CHIEFS of the HELA. We are now brought into actual contact from the coasts of Phœnicia, with the Hellenes, their brethren in Greece; and we shall now, I trust, not be disinclined to receive the reports of their early historians relative to the intercourse, colonisation, and affinity, once subsisting between these two countries—countries easy of mutual access, to or by those mariners to whom the coasting voyage from Phœnicia to Ceylon presented no insuperable difficulties. It is with regret that I quit the interesting theme of that land which has sent forth the harbingers of peace and good-will towards men. The nature, however, of the following investigation, demands immediate consideration.

[1] The "*Boēn agathos* Diomedes" of Homer is the present North American Indian: his powers of endurance and indomitable valour will be noticed at a future period.

[2] See Malcolm's Central India.

XVI.

TIME, THE BASIS OF ERROR AND TRUTH.

KĀLĂ moolămidăn sărvăn bhāvābhāvou sookhāsookhē;
KĀLĂ srijăti bhootāni: KĀLĂ sănhărite prăjnāh.
Nirdăhăti prăjnāh Kālăh: KĀLĂH samăyăte poonăh.
KĀLĂ sănkshipăte sărvā prăjnā visrijăte poonăh.
KĀLĂ soopteshoo jāgărte: Kālo hi doorătikrămăh.

Mhabar. Adiparv.

TIME is the root of all created beings,
And uncreate; of pleasure and of pain.
TIME doth create Existence. TIME destroys.
TIME shatters all, and all again renews.
TIME watches while all sleeps. Unvanquished TIME!

FROM the extensive view already taken of the vast primitive families of mankind, and their ramifications in those regions to which they have already been traced, it must be evident that any partial view of local religious faith, assumed on the mere dictum of the historian of such a venerable antiquity, is entitled to little credit, unless it harmonise with the great principle of patriarchal government and teaching. As the component members of the northern colonisation have been already traced to their primæval settlements, and as those settlements have, together with their geographical definitions, produced a distinct historical result, and as that result is founded on the interpretation of the actual language of the colonists, it would be just to consider facts, so evolved, as the basis of an argumentative process, on which to found an inferential course of history. Yet, as such a process might seem to rest too much upon theoretical principles, I purpose to adhere for the present, at least, to that system of investigation which has already been attended with such beneficial results. That investigation has evolved facts which through the ordinary records of Hellenic historians would have been perfectly unattainable; for it has been already demonstrated, in the course of this work, that these writers were totally incapacitated for obtaining any such information. It is not necessary in this place to recapitulate the numerous instances of misapprehension which have been already found to obscure the plainest historical truths. Such instances might easily be multiplied tenfold. That, however, which now presses upon the attention of the inquirer after truth, is the necessity of acquiring a series of facts, all of which must be in perfect harmony with that state of society which has been already demonstrated to have existed in Hellas at the period of primæval antiquity; an antiquity, in fact, so venerable, as to precede the formation of that language and that state of society which is usually called Grecian.

Of the origin of the term Graikos, which we through the medium of the Romans have at length received as the term "Greek," I purpose giving a brief notice; the more especially as it is in intimate connexion with what is generally considered a mythological portion of Hellenic record.

For the present, however, it will be necessary to review some of the most salient features in the primitive Hellenic society; for, until this be done, the accounts already received through the false medium presented by Hellenic histories, will be apt not only to bias, but to lead us astray.

Whatever facilities for locomotion may be presented at the present day by improved mechanical facilities, it is very clear that it would be impossible in the existing state of civilised society to set in motion, and to find subsistence for such vast masses of men, as, in the state of primitive society, moved unobstructed, over wide tracts, attended by flocks and herds, almost innumerable,—as being the subsistence of a nation. Movements of such magnitude it is clear, would not be permitted, through the territories of a civilised power of the present day. Such a jealousy however did not subsist in primitive society. The patriarchal system had produced families which had grown into nations, who looked back upon the memory of their venerable founder, with a feeling of the deepest reverence;—that feeling amounted to adoration. The father of a nation became its god. The same effect was produced by the successful warrior, and the true or fictitious ascetic, and to this kind of worship the Lunar race was especially addicted. Although the Solar tribes first introduced into Greece the worship of the sun, yet, in process of time, both that race and that worship were entirely supplanted by the Lunar system, which will be hereafter noticed, as forming ultimately the basis of the Hellenic worship. Before, however, I enter upon the consideration of this subject, it will be well to introduce the judicious reflections of Bishop Thirlwall, which contain a just summary of two important facts recorded by Herodotus. "In the Iliad," writes the learned prelate, "Agamemnon is calling on the gods to witness a solemn contract. Among those of Olympus, he names none but Jupiter; after him, he invokes the all-seeing, all-hearing sun, the rivers, the earth, and lastly the gods who punish perjured men in the realms below.

"In like manner we may suppose the Pelasgians to have worshipped the invisible powers, which, according to the primitive belief of the people, animated the various forms of the sensible world. That such was in fact the oldest form of religion which prevailed among the Pelasgian tribes, is both highly probable in itself, and confirmed by the example of the ancient Persians. In this sense, therefore, we both can understand, and may accept, the statement of Herodotus. But it is not quite so easy to follow him, when he attempts to trace the steps by which this simple creed was transformed into the complicated system of the Greek mythology. He seems to distinguish two great changes which the Greek religion underwent; one produced by the introduction of foreign deities and rites, the other by the invention of native poets. His researches had, as he says, convinced him that all the names of the Greek gods had been derived from the barbarians; and the result of the information which he had gathered in Egypt was, that, with a few exceptions, they had all been transplanted from that country. Some, the Egyptian priests themselves disclaimed; but the rest had, as they asserted, been always known among them; and hence Herodotus infers that the excepted names had been invented by the Pelasgians, all but that of Poseidon, the god of the sea, which had been brought over from Africa. It seems necessary to suppose that, by the names of the gods, both Herodotus and his instructors understood their nature and attributes, and that they conceived the Egyptian appellations to have been translated into equivalent Greek words. But this testimony, or judgment of Herodotus, combined with the various traditions of oriental colonies planted in Greece, at a time when its inhabitants are supposed to have wanted the first rudiments of civilisation, with the priestly institutions of the East, the presumed antiquity of the Greek mysteries, and of esoteric doctrines transmitted by them, and coincidences observed in several features of the Greek and the Egyptian mythology, has formed the ground of a hypothesis which is still a subject of earnest controversy. It assumes that the colonies which migrated into Greece in the darkness of the old Pelasgian period, were headed by priests, who long retained the supreme power in their new settlements.

"They brought with them the faith and the wisdom which they had inherited in their ancient seats, the knowledge of one God, the hidden spring of life and intelligence, but infinitely diversified in His attributes, functions, and emanations. These they proposed to the veneration of the ignorant multitudes, not in their naked simplicity, which would have dazzled and confounded those unenlightened minds, but through the veil of expressive symbols and ingenious fables, which were accepted by the people as literal truths, and were gradually wrought into a complicated mythological system. The sublime dogmas of the priestly religion were reserved for the chosen few, who were capable of contemplating them in their pure and simple form, and these alone understood the epithets and images which, in the poetry of the temples, conveyed the tenets of the ancient theology. When these priestly governments were everywhere forced to give way to the power of the heroic chieftains, as the priests themselves drew back into the shade, so their doctrines were more confined to the recesses of their sanctuaries, and were revealed only to those who were admitted to the rites there celebrated in awful obscurity. Meanwhile, a new race of poets started up, and gained the ear of the people —bards, who, blending heroic legends with religious fables, the original meaning of which had been lost, introduced fresh confusion into the mythical chaos. The troubles that accompanied the Dorian invasion contributed to widen the breach between the popular and the priestly religion; the latter, however, was preserved without any material alteration in the mysteries, which continued to be the vehicles of the more enlightened faith down to the latest days of paganism."[1]

[1] Thirlw. Hist. Gr. vol. 1. 210.

On this summary of a late celebrated German hypothesis, the learned prelate has many just observations. Still, the opinion of Herodotus will, in the sequel, be found to contain much valuable truth. The fusion of the Solar and Lunar forms of worship in Greece, though never complete, had yet left among the Hellenic population many doctrines and rites common to both. Notwithstanding, there ever remained a marked distinction between these races of worshippers; in nothing more clearly shown than in the opposite characteristics of the Spartans and Athenians, the deep-seated causes of whose mutual jealousy reposed upon religious grounds, as connected specially with the tribes of each.

The Tartarian element of the Greek nation has already been extensively noticed. A very considerable portion of this people was of the Bud'histic faith; and by their numbers and their martial prowess ultimately succeeded in expelling from northern Greece the clans of the Solar Race. This important event will be shortly noticed. Meanwhile, to elucidate the influences of the Bud'histic faith, or the members of the Lunar family, in the extraordinary care with which the primitive chieftains preserved their genealogy, even long after all true recollection of their original country had been lost, I shall briefly notice the first Attic genealogies. So far from being fabulous, they will be found, when rightly examined, to be historical documents of much importance. And it is not a little singular, that the very features of these genealogies, which have the most fabulous air, considered as Greek records, are of converse value, when expounded by the language and the geography of that country from which came the ancestors of the families whose records run up to such a vast antiquity.

It is on this very point, that I regret to find one of the ablest of modern Greek historians entirely led astray by the corrupt medium through which information has been handed down.

It will be seen in the sequel, that neither the peculiar faith nor the peculiar credulity of any nation, will warrant the affirmation of a non-historical basis to wild legend or cloudy fable. The very practices affirmed to be commemorative of certain events, have been attributed to an inventive source, as though the doctrine of invention could build columns, or construct the massive walls of Mycenæ.

It is clear that the historical canon, so far from being more rigidly interpreted, must be relaxed till it is placed upon a footing that shall harmonise with that state of society of which the historian is treating. To do otherwise would be to offer violence to the just feelings of our nature, and the practical tests of sound judgment. The existence of an agent may rationally be credited, while the machinery by which the agency is said to have been effected, may be purely poetical, or possibly inventive. In these cases of strange or fabulous record, it will be the duty of the patient enquirer after truth, to allow its full influence to the power of Time, which should as reasonably be supposed to have as much effect upon truth as upon the noblest structure reared by human hands.

After noticing the opinion of Milton relative to fabulous records, Mr. Grote remarks: "I presume that our great poet has proceeded upon mistaken views with respect to the old British fables, not less in that which he leaves out than in that which he retains. To omit the miraculous and the fantastic (it is that which he means by 'the impossible and the absurd'), is to suck the life-blood out of these once popular narratives, to divest them both of their genuine distinguishing mark, and of the charm by which they acted on the feelings of believers.

"Still less ought we to consent to break up and disenchant, in a similar manner, the myths of ancient

Greece; partly because they possess the mythical beauties and characteristics in far higher perfection, partly because they sank deeper into the mind of a Greek, and pervaded both the public and private sentiment of the country to a much greater degree than the British fables in England. Two courses, and two only, are open; either to pass over the myths altogether, which is the way in which modern historians treat the old British fables, or else to give an account of them as myths; to recognise and respect their specific nature, and to abstain from confounding them with ordinary and certifiable history. There are good reasons for pursuing this second method in reference to the Grecian myths; and when so considered, they constitute an important chapter in the history of the Grecian mind, and indeed, in that of the human race generally. The historical faith of the Greeks, as well as that of other people, in reference to early and unrecorded times, is as much subjective and peculiar to themselves as their religious faith: among the Greeks, especially, the two are confounded with an intimacy which nothing less than great violence can disjoin. Gods, heroes, and men—religion and patriotism—matters divine, heroic and human—were all woven together by the Greeks into one indivisible web, in which the threads of truth and reality, whatever they might originally have been, were neither intended to be, nor were actually distinguishable. Composed of such materials, and animated by the electric spark of genius, the mythical antiquities of Greece formed a whole at once trustworthy and captivating to the faith and feelings of the people; but neither trustworthy nor captivating, when we sever it from these subjective conditions, and expose its naked elements to the scrutiny of an objective criticism. Moreover, the separate portions of Grecian mythical foretime ought to be considered with reference to that aggregate of which they form a part: to detach the divine from the heroic legends, or some one of the heroic legends from the remainder, as if there were an essential and generic difference between them, is to present the whole under an erroneous point of view. The myths of Troy and Thêbes are no more to be handled objectively, with a view to detect an historical base, than those of Zeus in Krête, of Apollo and Artemis in Dêlos, of Hermês, or of Promêtheus. To single out the siege of Troy from the other myths, as if it were entitled to pre-eminence as an ascertained historical and chronological event, is a proceeding which destroys the true character and coherence of the mythical world; we only transfer the story (as has been remarked in the preceding chapter,) from a class with which it is connected by every tie both of common origin and fraternal affinity, to another with which it has no relationship, except such as violent and gratuitous criticism may enforce."[1] It will be seen from this passage that the rational mind is debarred the satisfaction of handling objectively, with a view to detect an historical basis, in the myths of Troy and Thebes, any more than in those of Zeus in Crete, or of Apollo, or of Prometheus.

But what if they should each be found historical—what if that which is denounced as "British fables in England" be Truth obscured? Would it be any satisfaction to the independent student of history, to be afterwards told that, such and such canons having been laid down, although the light of truth might beam upon the page of Time, the perusal of that page was of no avail because theory had decided that it was of no avail? The Autochthons (the Athenian Grasshoppers), the Centaurs, the Lapithæ, the Ozolæ, have been seen to disappear before the light of a searching investigation; and the Cabeiri and Corybantes are about to be placed in a category equally historical. I cannot, therefore, having

[1] Grote's Hist. Greece, vol. i. p. 651.

obtained these positive results, consent to be led by a doctrine which totally strikes at the root of all progress. If this canon be just, it may be as justly applied to the performances of legerdemain. But what is the result of that application? Simply that the senses of the spectator may be deceived, but that the personality of the ingenious actor will not be at all affected. Thus, though the positive performance of the miracle of Attus Nævius be denied, his existence will be permitted. Yet here both the fable and the fact centre in the same person. On the relative definition of the term "historical value," let us hear the opinion of the able translator of, and commentator upon, the Raja Tarangini.

"I cannot refrain from repeating what I said elsewhere (Raja Tarangini, vol. ii., p. 372), 1. That according to my firm persuasion, the epoch of the commencement of the Kali Yuga, B. C. 3102, is historical in the general sense I attach to the term; that is, after reducing to their lowest possible values, all the historical traditions and chronological data of the Chinese, Hindoos, Persians, Phœnicians, Egyptians, and other nations; and, after considering and appreciating the monuments of art, the sciences, and the religious and political institutions, a knowledge of which has reached us, I cannot refuse credence to this fact, namely, that great states, highly advanced in civilisation, existed at least 3000 years before our era. It is beyond that limit that I look for Rama, the hero of the Ramayuna.

"In the history of this country (Cashmere) we find 20 centuries B. C. there were religious troubles; the religion of the Vedas is opposed to that of the Budhists."[1] This opinion of Captain Troyer is amply corroborated by

[1] Capt. Troyer, Paris, 1840; pub. "Société Asiatique." See Asiatic Journal, 1841.

the sound judgment of the author to whom European history is so much indebted, not as the mere compiler of dry facts already prepared to hand, but as the eloquent and just expounder of the most venerable societies of the world. I allude to Colonel Tod, to whose able work I am deeply indebted for valuable corroborative proof, and distinct illustration of the geographical facts already adduced. He describes the great war of the Mahabharata, which I have already noticed as adding its contingent to the population of Hellas, as "a conflict, which was evidently religious as well as political, for supremacy between the houses of Hastinapoor and Indrapres'tha. Although the rival families were of one stock, it is evident that whatever were the tenets of the first, the latter had held those of Bud'ha till they accepted the modified system of Heri, 'who was Bud'ha.' Both houses were of the Lunar Race, and traced their origin to the first Boodha, who espoused Ella (Earth personified), daughter of the son of the Sun, or 'the sun-born Swam-Bhuva' (Lord of the Earth,) a Manu supposed to be the great post-diluvian patriarch; so that Budha has equal claims to antiquity with Manu, son of SURYA or the SUN. Now Budha (Mercury) being the son of the moon, his descendants are styled Chandra Vansa; while the descendants of the solar line were styled 'Surya Vansa,' children of the Sun. And hence all those countries where the worship of Mithras chiefly prevailed, are called Syria, Assyria, and the inhabitants, Saurondians or Heliadæ. Hence the city of Solomon Tad-mor, called Bàl, the son's type or power of production, was there worshipped 'when he bowed to the god of the Sidonians.' Such, therefore, is the earliest distinction of the two grand races, distinguished as those of Surya and Indu Badoha; the sun worshippers became idolators; the votaries of Mercury or the Moon adored 'THE ONE' only, as do their descendants.

There appears no doubt that the Solar Race first inhabited India Proper (well known in the Ramayuna,) their capital being ADITYA or Aetya-sthan,—'land of the Sun,' Ayodhia or Oude. . . The first Budha parent of the Lunar Race is stated to have come from a distant region. In all those countries where the worship of Budha prevailed, the Moon was held a male deity, and hence all the earlier tribes of Europe adored Woden, Boodha, or Mercury, and Ella or Ert'ha, their original parents. . . . Hence, too, their dread of eclipses when the monsters (Rahoo and Ketoo, ascending and descending nodes) swallowed their first parent; and hence the Scandinavians pursued the same system, as did the Scythians of old, and the Rajpoots still, of beating every noisy sort of instrument to frighten away the demons during an eclipse, and hence the mythological resemblances of each." The accuracy of these remarks will now be evident. These descendants of Bud'ha are the CORUBANTES, whom classical writers represent as wildly beating their cymbals, and whom I have shown to be the people of GHOR-BAND.[1] They are also the priests of CUBELE, CABUL; they are said to have first dwelt upon Mount Ida, a name which at once transports us not only to Asia Minor, but to that island of the Mediterranean which was colonised by these Haya tribes. That island, CYPRUS, was the settlement of the KHYBER population, and one of their chief towns was named SA LAMIS,[2] (or the HIGH LAMAS,) in like manner as the island to the south of Attica. IDA is the *wife* of BUD'HA, and daughter of Ichshwaka. Hence the history of the CORUBANTES, or people of GHORBAND, is found in classical writers, more or less mixed up with the history of the CABEIRI, or people of the KHEIBER.

The Afghan name "GHOR-BANDH" is itself a corruption

[1] *Vide* Map. [2] Su Lama. (*See* Append., Rule vi.)

of GOOROO-BANDHU,[1] "THE KINSMAN OF THE GOOROO."[2] Hence, the COROOBANTES were the KINSMEN of BUD'HA the GOOROO, whose wife was IDA, recorded in Mount IDA, and their people the KHYBERI, subsequently CYP'RI, the settlers in CYPRUS. Bud'ha was eminently the Gooru, or the GREAT TEACHER; hence he was deified and his memory adored. BAMIAN too, (BOMIENSES,) in the immediate vicinity of GHOR-BAND, as observed by Wilford, is considered by Bud'hist writers as the "source of all purity," while contiguous is the land of the PHEENE BADAM, or "THE HAYA BUDHAS," those who from this point colonised Phœnicia, which will be shortly seen as eminently Bud'histic. The Phœnician Astarte (ASHTORETH, the ASTORE of Cashmir) had usually the epithet CHABAR.[3] It is thus that the historical basis of one of the most cloudy mysteries of the land of Hellas is amply vindicated on the most rational grounds. After this, the Siege of Troy is not likely to oppose a very formidable obstruction to patient investigation.

The remarks of Colonel Mure, upon the relative value of special eras in Greece, as forming the just boundary between truth and fiction, are so convincing, that they are entitled to the ready assent of the unprejudiced. "It

[1] "*Bandhu*, a kinsman. The Bandhu is of three kinds; the kinsman of the person himself, of his father or his mother; as his father's brother's son, and his mother's sister's or brother's son; and the same reckoning upwards; as his father's father's sister's son."—WILSON'S *Sans. Lex.*, ' Bandhu."

[2] "The Brahminical Gooru is a spiritual parent, from whom the youth receives the initiatory *Mantra* or prayer, and who conducts the ceremonies necessary at various seasons of infancy and youth, up to the period of investiture with the characteristic thread or string; this person may be the natural parent or the religious preceptor."—WILSON'S *Sans. Lex.*

[3] Mistaken for the Arabic *Kabar*, Great. *Vide* Gabar (Khaiber), in Phœnicia; and Ashtoreth in Bashan. KHAIBER-NAYŒ, CAPER-NÆUM, is another derivative, implying the district of the Khaiber (Caper).

must indeed be apparent," observes that judicious writer, "to every intelligent reader who peruses Mr. Grote's elaborate commentary on Fynes Clinton's views, that there is a fallacy running through his argument; and that, as tested by the ultra-sceptical law of critical demonstration which he lays down, the admission of the Olympic register, as a genuine document, is as complete a *petitio principii,* as what he calls Mr. Clinton's unsupported conjecture, in favour of other Peloponnesian archives. The case of the former record, when divested of the arbitrary title to exclusive infallibility set up for it by Mr. Grote, reduces itself simply to this: that a certain Chronicle of Elis, professing to embody the quadrennial notation of the Olympic victors, from the year 776 B.C. downwards, but unknown to, or not valued by Herodotus, Thucydides, or any other earlier standard Greek historian, is first mentioned, or cited as valid chronology by the Greeks, about the year 260 B.C., or upwards of 500 years after its own assumed era. It is certainly not easy to see how, according to Mr. Grote's rule of judgment in such cases, this document could be worth more than the Spartan royal genealogies, which Charon and Herodotus knew, and quoted as an authority, and which Eratosthenes so highly appreciated."[1]

When the reader understands that the Royal Spartan genealogies, to which Colonel Mure alludes, are the productions of the family Senachies, bards of the identical class of men, and the identical people with whose customs and manners, from the most distant period, Colonel Tod was so well acquainted, and which he has so ably described, the value of such documents, as compared with the bare catalogue of Olympic victories or defeats, can be easily ascertained. Let it be remembered that this order of men had a particular jaghire, or estate, set apart for their

[1] Mure's Hist. of Greek Lit., Append. J., 502.

maintenance; that their office was carefully to preserve the genealogy of the prince whom they served, and whose praises they sang—that not only in the middle ages, but from the most distant period, it was necessary that the Bard should be enabled to compose and *record* the heroic achievements of the royal house from whose bounty he derived a rich subsistence;—that this genealogical and heroic record was ever considered of the utmost importance by the race who colonised Hellas, and we shall be enabled to give its just weight to the observations of Colonel Mure.

"Chund, or Chand," writes Colonel Tod, "called also Tri-cala, from his supposed prophetic spirit,[1] flourished towards the close of the twelfth century of the Christian era. He may be called the poet-laureate of the Prithi-raj.

"His work, consisting of sixty-nine books, comprising 100,000 stanzas, each book being devoted to a particular event in battle, is an immense chronicle[2] of the period, and is consequently highly valued by his countrymen, (and would be of vast use to the European antiquary) for its genealogical, historical, geographical, and mythological details, as well as for its pictures of manners. Of the gallantry of Tri-cala the plains of Canouge afforded a conspicuous instance. Chund was not one of those who merely inspired valour, like Timotheus, by precept and song; he was in his own person a *gay and preux chevalier*. He offers to us a perfect specimen of the bards of the times; gallant, bold, and a poet, in search of adventures, he accompanied his heroic master in at least half the perilous enterprises in which he was engaged. Whether to interpret the decrees of fate from the *flight of birds*, the chattering of a jay, or the hooting

[1] The bards of India, as well as of the west, were supposed to possess the gift of prescience.

[2] Tod, Asiat. Journ., vol. iii., 1840.

of an owl;—to detect the abode of beauty, or to praise it; to inspire contempt of death, by recounting the glories of the past, or by personal example, Chund was equally prepared, as well as to enliven the enjoyments of the 'festive cup.'" . . . . Again: "The north-west of India was divided, from very ancient times, into many small sovereignties of warlike princes, each of whose domains was parcelled out into feudal possessions, in which every vassal proprietor kept up a court, the miniature representation of his sovereign's, the chief ornament of each of which was the bard. It consequently became a primary object with every chief to possess a bard of talent, which was a distinction or jewel in his coronet; and the praise of a bard often conferred a name, while there was a barrenness in deeds. . . . Thus the Bards of Rajasthan were a numerous and distinct class of society, giving a tone and influence to the whole frame, political, religious, and social." . . . And again:—"With that supercilious contempt which many of our countrymen evince, consequent upon the confidence derived from the academical discipline of Europe, they will deem the mere mention of previous studies to form a Rajpoot bard's mind, a burlesque. Nothing can be more groundless. In the first place, the future bard must devote himself to the cultivation of a difficult classical language—the Sanscrit. In this rich tongue is combined all his literature. In this he must study the laws, the religion, and the manners of past ages, not in a few octavos, but throughout many folios. He must commence with the voluminous epics, the Ramayuna and the Mahabharata, whose authors, Valmike and Vyasa, are the Hesiod and Homer of India. . . . But these works are not accessible to the Bardi till after a long course of grammatical study, comprehending the complicated rules of prosody, and the mysteries of his own art; the formation of every species of stanza, from the short couplet (Doha), to the lengthened serpentine (Bhojunga). Possessed of such extensive acquirements, we cannot be surprised at the popular influence which the bard exercises over these martial races, who dread his satirical censures far more than the anathemas of the Brahmin."[1]

This history of the bard Chund,[2] or Tri-cala,[3] that is, "He of the three times," cannot fail to strike every classical scholar with the recollection of the Cal-chas of HOMĒRŎS, properly AMĒRŎS, for that is a Rajpoot name, not having the slightest connection with "Homēros," "Blind." In fact, the CAL-CHAS of AMĒRŎS is the CAL-CAS,[4] "SKILLED IN THE TIMES," of the Rajpoot DOLŎ-PES, and the ABANTIS of OUGEIN, who fought on the plains of T'RŌJA, T' RĀJYA,[5] *i. e.* "THE BUD'HA KINGDOM." And is this BUD'HA KINGDOM a fable? It is just as much a fable, and no more, than the existence of ODRYS, or HIMALAYA, in Greece; the existence of the DOLOPES, or CHIEFS of the HIMALAYAN DOLA, in Greece; the existence of the SPERCHĪUS, or GANGES, in Greece; and in very truth, as I have shown, the existence of INDIA IN GREECE.

Professor Wilson observes:—"The origin and development of the doctrine, traditions, and institutions (described in the Purans now extant) were not the work of a day; and the testimony that established their existence three centuries before Christianity carries us back to a much more remote antiquity,—to an antiquity that

1 Asiat. Journ., vol. xxxiii., 1840.

2 *Chund*, a Persian equivalent for *Cala*, "time."

3 *Tri*, three, and *Kala*, time.

4 *Cala*, time, and *cas*, one who is dexterous or clever.

5 *Ta*, a Bud'ha; *Rājya*, a sovereignty. (*See* Append., Rule i.)

is probably not surpassed by any of the prevailing fictions, institutions, or beliefs of the ancient world.[1] What says Colonel Tod on the history which lies buried beneath the vast weight of superincumbent Time?—

"If it be destined that any portion of the veil which covers these ancient mysteries, connecting those of the Ganges with the Nile, shall be removed, it will be from the interpretation of the expedition of Rama, hitherto deemed almost as allegorical as that of the *Arg'hanat'hs*. . . . . If Alexander, from the mouths of the Indus, ventured to navigate these seas with his frail fleet of barks, constructed in the Punjab, what might we not expect from the resources of the king of Cushala, the descendant of Sagara, emphatically called the *sea-king*, whose '60,000 sons' were so many mariners?"[2]

What says the clear-sighted and learned Sir W. Jones, many of whose theories, in common with those of Wilford, Tod, and others who have had the courage to step out of the beaten path of knowledge, have been condemned as rash and chimerical! Do they, or do they not, accord with that distinct notice I have given of the most venerable series of emigrations and colonisations of the human race? The conclusions of that elegant scholar, not less than those of the profound Colebrooke, will, as the reader accompanies me through the course of this demonstration, rivet indissolubly the chain of evidence of which each land has been the faithful chronicler:—

"Rama (the Indian Bacchus) is represented as a descendant from Surya, or the Sun, as the husband of Sita, and the son of a princess named Causelya. It is very remarkable that the Peruvians, whose Incas boasted of

[1] Vans Kennedy, Asiat. Journ., 1841.

[2] Col. Tod's Rajast'h, vol. i. p. 602.

the same descent, styled their greatest festival RAMA-SITVA; whence we may suppose that South America was peopled by the same race who imported into the farthest parts of Asia the rites and fabulous history of Rama."[1]

Again: "All these indubitable facts may induce no ill-grounded opinion, that Æthiopia and Hindustan were possessed or colonised by the same extraordinary race; in confirmation of which it may be added, that the mountaineers of Bengal and Behar (Pelasa) can hardly be distinguished in some of their features, particularly their lips and noses, from the modern Abyssinian, whom the Arabs call the children of Cush." Sir W. Jones concludes his observations by this singular but comprehensive remark: "Of the cursory observations on the Hindus, which it would require volumes to expand and illustrate, this is the result: *that they had an immemorial affinity with the old* PERSIANS, ETHIOPIANS, and EGYPTIANS, the PHŒNICIANS, GREEKS, and TUSCANS, the SCYTHIANS or Goths, and Celts, the Chinese, Japans, and PERUVIANS."[2]

Now, there is no one, who peruses with unbiassed mind the whole of this,—one of the first papers of Sir W. Jones,—but must confess, that in conjunction with the overpowering proofs I have already advanced of the actual sources and direction of a vast and most primitive emigration, this subject does not demand the ordinary proof of what is called chronological history. The language of a mighty people is its greatest history, and for the just development of this history, I have applied the most rigid tests, allowing, with the most jealous care, no theory—no mere similarity of sound, to lead me astray from that uniform process of investigation by which these results have been

[1] Sir W. Jones, As. Res., vol. i. p. 426.

[2] As. Res., vol. i. p. 426.

obtained. That process will be found to be based on no narrow nor imaginary foundation, but verified by results as uniform as they are copious. The ancient world is a physiological *Grammar of Fact,* by the study of which the great chart of the wanderings of the patriarchs of our race will yet be read with truth.

XVII.

HESIOD'S HISTORY OF GREECE.

"KONGX OM PAX."

It must not be forgotten that, in contemplating the geographical facts, recorded so distinctly and undeniably upon the very mountains and rivers of Hellas, we have been equally contemplating her *history*, as connected with those people who gave names to these rivers and mountains.[1] If, therefore, there be found in any of her early writers, records entirely discordant with such a state of society, it is evident that those writings must be either fabrications, grounded entirely upon pure inventions, or that they must be the perverted relics of an ancient history, which, the writers having lost the original language of the first settlers, were unable to comprehend. The travesty of language which runs through the whole circle of early Greek literature, has been amply elucidated in the geographical course which forms the substratum of this history. If, therefore, the Cyclopes, the Autochthons, the Athenian Grasshoppers, Cheiron, and many others have been found gross perversions of plain matter-of-fact, these names, and others which occur in the writings of Hesiod, and the Logographers, will justly come under the same category of corrupt orthography, and of corrupt history based upon that orthography; the representative to Hesiod of words apparently Greek, but in reality Sanscrit,

[1] *Vide* Postulates, p. 22.

Thibetan, or the Pehlavi dialects. The outline, however, of history, given by such writers, may be perfectly authentic, while the features of individuals, princes, or people represented may be exceedingly distorted. Hesiod's "History of Greece," generally conceived to be a Theogony, or an account of the Generation of the Gods, is of this nature. It may, however, not incorrectly, be compared to the celebrated Long Walls of Pericles, which tell not only their own history, but that of preceding years, and of an ancient people. Here we find a frieze, there an entablature; here is to be seen a sepulchral inscription, there the massive ornaments of a temple. Each disjointed piece worked into this wall tells, to a certain extent, its own tale: its relative age, the character of the people who wrought it, and many of the inscriptions still remaining may be read by the attentive and patient student of history. These observations, based upon a distinct view of the primitive population of Hellas, will prepare the mind for a description of Hellenic society, in perfect harmony with the members of that society. The great aggregate of the colonists of Greece has already been shown to consist of these two great bodies,—the Solar and the Lunar races; each following the peculiar tenets of that faith to which the heads of their respective races gave so strong a bias, viz., either the Solar or the Bud'histic forms of worship. The former was more ancient in its establishment, but the latter more durable. The Lamaic nations, springing up apparently upon the frontiers of the kingdoms of Cashmir and Thibet, have by the population, already shown in Thessaly, been proved to have existed in the latter countries in high antiquity, and the record of the life of Zeus, as drawn by Hesiod, is but a garbled statement of plain facts, in perfect harmony with the existing state of Lamaism in Tartary. Whatever variations may have been introduced into this account by Hesiod, of a cosmogonic nature, they all repose upon a false foundation, which I shall not unfrequently remove, to exhibit the ancient basis upon which his new temple was built. The presence of the people of the Himalayas, the population of Mons Adrius and Othrys, have been already shown; the immigration of the people of Balti and Skardo, and the adjoining provinces, has been distinctly seen; and now it will be necessary to contemplate the country of the "Great Lamas," "DAL-L'MATIA,"[1] lying contiguous to these denizens of the Adrius and Himalaya Mountains. The Lamaic system was, at the earliest periods of Greece, undoubtedly administered with great vigour. Its contests, however, for supremacy, were many, and vigorously conducted; and but for that Tartar population, which in common with the people of Lebanon, or the tribes of Leh, found so powerful an element in the colonisation of primeval Phœnician Egypt, it would have been impossible to insure its dominant influence over nearly the whole of Hellas. This system of religion will be found, as this history progresses, to have been so far modified, and so far compromised, as to be compelled to take its place in the asyla of the *mysteries* of Greece, in lieu of the open, and as it were state-position, it once occupied.

That Lamaic sovereignty, which was once wielded with the vigour of the triple crown in its most palmy days, had lost its imperial, and still more its despotic character; and an oligarchy of the Hellenic Bud'histic priesthood, had taken the place of the absolutism of one. That priesthood, too, was distributed over Greece, as a body influential not from its numbers, nor its special caste—for Brahminical caste never became established in Hellas—but from the ingenuity of its operations, acting by that principle of ancestral adoration which has ever distin-

[1] *Dalé Lamas*, or Great Lamas.

guished genuine Bud'hism, from Athens to China. It was thus that some of the best of the human affections were enlisted in the cause of a mild, though ingeniously politic, priesthood. Their faith, and the faith of those Athenians who were initiated at Eleusinian Mysteries, will in the sequel be shown to be identical with that of Pythagoras, of whom I propose giving some notices that will be of vital interest, as being corroborated by that admirable scholar and profound student, the late Mr. Colebrooke.

The Lamaic System, originating as I have before noticed, on the high tract of land in the vicinity of the Himalayan frontier of Thibet, had taken up a strong position to the north of Thessaly, on the Adrian or Himalayan Mountain, in whose neighbourhood the DALÉ LAMAS have been distinctly shown. From this point it descended into northern Greece, where a powerful body has been pointed out as the LAMIENSES or LAMA TRIBES. The main point, however, whence this gigantic system of ancient Hellas was administered, was from that lofty mountain which was called O-LUM-'POS by the Greeks, but "OOL-LAM-'POS," or "the High Lama Chiefs," by the settlers. Its chief town or fortress, as it has been considered, was PUTHUIM, *i. e.* BUDHYUM or BUDHATON, contiguous to which, on the west, was the town of SA-L'MON, that is, SU-L'MON,[1] "THE HIGH LAMA-TOWN." Immediately to the east lay the SRACĔS, called by the Greeks THRACES,[2] a sect of Bud'hists so ancient and so extensive as to give a name to a vast tract of country in which they had settled. The doctrines of the Sracas, as well as of the Jainas, of which they to this day compose a component part, will be duly noticed.

[1] *Su*, well, or high caste; *Lamān*, plural of *Lama*, "The Great Lamas." The "a" in Lama, lost. (*See* Appendix, Rules i. and vi.) Another settlement is at SA-LAMIS, SOO-LAMAS. (*See* Appendix, Rule vi.)

[2] *See* Appendix, Rule xxiii.

The country in which these Jainas or Sracas dwelt, was called "BIHĀRIA," PIERIA, "the Land of BIHARAS" or JAINA MONASTERIES, a very little to the south of which was the Castle of the L'HOPATOS, LAPITHA, or BHUTIAS, religionists of the Bud'hist or Jaina faith. The great head of this vast system of hierarchic domination, which in these ancient days extended over the known world with an uniformity and vigour unparalleled but by the same system of Bud'histic Rome during the middle ages, was termed "Jeenos" by the Greeks, written "Zeenos," an appellation given to the Bud'ha Pontiffs of antiquity as well in Phœnicia as in Greece.[1] The Greek term "ZEUS" has been generally considered to be a form of Deva, Deus, and Theos. This, however, is not the case. It is simply the form "JEYUS," "The VICTORIOUS ZEUS," inflected by the Greeks as Zeus, Zēnos (Jĕyŭs, Jeenos).[2]

The "Jino" is the generic name of the personage peculiar to the Jaina sect, who is ranked by them as superior to the gods of other sects,[3] and is the special term always employed in the most authentic Bud'hist writings to express the ruling saintly Pontiff of his day.[4] Such was the JÆNOS (ZEENOS) or JAINA PONTIFF, "the King of Gods and Men," that is, of the Devas (Priests) and people in Greece, long before the Homeric days. In

[1] *Z'aan-im*, xix. 33; Judges, iv. 2; Micah, i. 11. "Adopted into the Hebrew expression of the 'Jainas;' like the 'Srakes' (Thrakes), of the Greeks. Hesychius observes that the chiefs of ancient Greece were styled Zani-des, and Pausanias remarks that certain ancient statues near Mount Cronius were called 'Zanes.'"—*Paus.* i. v., p. 430.

[2] The derivative or genitive case—as Zeenos (Jeenos)—at once shows its source. Zeus, Dios, exhibits the source, as Deva, Deos, Theos,—Zeus, Zeenos, exhibiting the Jĕŭs, Jeenos, or Jaina, *Bud'hist* Pontiffs; and Zeus *Dios* (Deva), the *Brahminical* sway in Greece. This name of the supreme pontiff of the Bud'hists is now more generally written Jino, and in ancient days pronounced Jinos. The Greeks not having the sound of the letter "j" in their language, substituted the letter "z."

[3] Wilson's Sans. Lex.—*Jino*.

[4] See the Mahawanso, *passim*.

the BIHARIAN (PIERIAN) Heights, formerly the site of numerous Biharas, or Jaina monasteries, which are very generally built on such commanding eminences, dwelt the "GREAT SAGES," called MOW'SEE,[1] the MOUSEE of the Greeks, and MUSA of the Romans, a name highly expressive of the "Sage with subdued passions." These were the Pierian muses, the Jaina poets, and the monastic chanters in the Biharas or Bud'hist monasteries surrounding the chief residence of "Oo'Lāmpos" or the High Lama Chief, whose supreme Pontiff was JĔYŬS or ZEUS, and two of whose chief towns were PUTHIUM, BUDHA'S town, and SA L'MON, or the High Lamas, whom I have lately pointed out in great force to the north as the DA'L'MA-TI, DALÉ LAMAS, or GRAND LAMAS, in the neighbourhood of the sources of this Bud'hist emigration, namely, the Himalayans, ADRIANS, and SKARDOS MONS; the people of Skardo being again distinctly visible on the river AS-CORDUS, that is, ISKARDUS, another form of the same word. The settlers of Iskardus are contiguous both to the BHOOTIAS, or BOTTIÆI, and the BIHARIAN (PIERIAN) mountains. A section of these SRACĂS, THRACES, had settled in BŒOTIA, a circumstance which, together with other religious influences, tended to give that meditative tone to the writings of the learned of that province which is so distinctly to be perceived in the writings of Pindar and of Hesiod. The observations of the learned Bishop Thirlwall,[2] relative to these Thracians of Bœotia and their connection with the Pierians, are marked

[1] M'ow, M'hausee, or M'hāoosee; formed by the Greeks into Mousai; from *Mahā*, great, and *vusee*, or *wusee*, a sage with subdued passions. The sound of the letter "h" and its short vowel "ă" or "ŭ," was entirely lost. (*See* Appendix, Rules i. and xxiv.) The Greeks being accustomed to pronounce and write *Mahi*, "great," as *Mai*. The long "ā" is sounded as "ā" in "lāw;" and the "ā" blending with "v" in "vusee" becomes "oo." (*See* Appendix, Rule xvi.) As *M'hāoosee*, identical with *Mowsee* or *Mousee* (Μοῦση).

[2] Hist. Greece, vol. i. p. 50.

with much distinctness, and are so applicable to the religious tendencies of their primitive Srācas, that I shall introduce them in this place.[1]

"These Bœotian Thracians were undoubtedly distinguished, not only by their name, but by a very peculiar character from the other Pelasgian tribes; and their relation to the Greeks appears to have been very similar to that of those Pelasgians who were most properly so called. Whether they were also in any degree related to the people who are known to us by the name of Thracians in later ages, is a question the more difficult, as the population of Thrace underwent great changes during the period when that of Greece was shifting, and even after the latter had finally settled; and it is not clear either how far the tribes which are said to have emigrated from Thrace into Asia Minor, and to have established themselves there under various names—as Mysians, Bithynians, Mariandyians—were allied to the subsequent possessors of their European seats, or these among one another.—— Strabo observes, that the worship of the Muses on Mount Helicon, and the cave there dedicated to the Leibethrian Nymphs, proved that this region had been occupied by Thracians, and that these Thracians were Pierians; the people who consecrated the land of Pieria at the northern foot of Olympus, and Leibethrum and Pimpleia, to the same powers.[1] But it does not appear why the Pierians are called Thracians; for Homer describes Thrace as beginning far from Pieria; so that Herē when she descends from the Thessalian Olympus, to seek Lemnos, lights upon Pieria, and Emathia, before she bounds towards the snowy mountains of the Thracians.

"The Pierians may have been the genuine Thracians, from whom the name was extended to the foreign tribes

[1] Thirl. Hist. Gr., vol. i, p. 50.

that surrounded them;[1] or, if they emigrated from the north to the land at the foot of Olympus, they may have brought with them a name derived from the seats they had left. Though the Bœotian Thracians belong to a mythical period, and none of the legends relating to them can claim to be considered as historical traditions, still their existence, and their affinity with the northern Pierians, are well attested; and the same evidence that proves these points, justifies us in attributing several important consequences to their presence in Greece. The worship of the Muses, which is uniformly acknowledged to have been peculiar to them, though it arose out of the same view of nature which is expressed in many popular creeds, appears to have afforded a groundwork for the earliest stage of intellectual culture among the Greeks. The belief that the invisible deities, who dwelt in the depths of caves and fountains, loved music and song, and would dispense the inspiration by which the human voice was modulated to tuneful numbers, implies a disposition to poetry, and some experience in its effects. This connexion between a popular form of religion, and the first strivings of political genius, does not indeed warrant any conclusion as to the character they assumed, or afford a ground for supposing that the earliest poetry of Greece was distinguished from that of a later period, by being exclusively dedicated to religious subjects. But it is probable enough, that the Greek oracles owed their origin to this source, even if that of Delphi was not founded by the Pierian Thracians,—the tribe which seems to have combined the various elements of the Greek mythology,

[1] This case would be analogous to that of the Etolians, a genuine Hellenic race, which in course of time imparted its name, together with a certain degree of civilisation, to a number of tribes which were very remote from it in their origin.

and to have moulded them nearly into the form they present in the Homeric poems."[1]

The religious tendencies engendered in the population of Hellas, Srākes (Thrakes), is certain; and notwithstanding the more popular and open system introduced by Homer, long maintained its sway in the mysteries of Greece. As the reader will find a distinct notice of the Sraca or Jaina system at the close of this work, I shall not farther enlarge upon it in this place.

The introduction of the Lamaic worship into north-eastern Hellas, is distinctly preserved by Hesiod, though possibly nothing was farther from his idea, when he penned that singular poem called the "Theogony." The ancient establishment of the solar tribes in Greece, and their corresponding forms of worship have already been noticed. The introduction of the Lamaic or Lunar race into Greece, was the signal for a renewal of that fierce conflict which had from the most distant period dyed deep in slaughter nearly all the nations of Asia. The dynastic establishment of the Solar race, represented by Hesiod as having been of far superior antiquity to that of the Jainas (Zeenos) is with the usual perverseness of the Greek form, written down as the Deva, or god Kronos, that is, Karnŏs, whose clans as Sun worshippers, and Surya-tanayas (Eurytanes), "Children of the Sun," or the tribes of Carna, have already been

[1] Müller (Prolegomena, z. c. w. M., p. 219.) thinks that this may be inferred from the single fact, that the *Pierian* Olympus, which is the seat of the gods, gives the Muses their epithet in Homer and Hesiod. The reader should, however, compare the two leading passages on the subject. Paus., ix. 29, 3; Strabo, ix. p. 410: on which Müller commented in his *Orchomenous*, p. 381, foll. An English translation of Müller's very valuable *Prolegomena* has just appeared under the title *Müller's Scientific Mythology, translated by J. Leitch;* in which the passage above referred to will be found (p. 159). There is an Appendix containing a translation of an Essay of Müller's on *Orion*, from the *Rheinisches Museum*, and of a small piece, the *Hyperboreisch-Roemische Studien* fuer Archæologie.

contemplated in the province of a'CARNANIA. This clan is the "CRONOS" of Hesiod. Not only is Carnos, metamorphosed into Cronos, but the distinguishing epithet of the Deified Indian chief, undergoes the same change.

Karna was the sovereign of Angadesa, that is, the district of Bhagalpoor, and part of Bengal. He was the elder brother to the Pandu princes, and the son of Surya, or the Sun. Hence, is at once seen a source of rivalry and warfare between the Pandians of the Lunar or Bud'histic race, and the Surya Vansa. A portion of Carnos clan has been already noticed as emigrating from that part of the frontiers of Cashmir, which to this day is indelibly stamped with the name of Carna.

But not only does the name of the Clan Carnas, become Cronos, chief of that clan, in lieu of the CARNOS ANG-KULŎ-MITRĔS,[1] that is, "CARNOS, THE SUN-CHIEF OF THE ANGA TRIBE," becomes CRONOS ANG-KULO-MEETES, or the INSCRUTABLE SATURN!—the GOC'LOPĔS, (GOCLA CHIEFS,) change to one-eyed monsters, and the SIRENS, or people of SĪRIN, Balarama, the half-brother of Krishna, become the Sirens of enchanting voice! Amid this disguise and singular perversion of names, the simple history of the establishment of the Jaina sect by the Jino Pontiff of Thessaly, and the overthrow of the Solar tribes, is distinctly to be seen. The Lama had grown up distinguished for political powers of a high order; and by combining in one great confederacy against the Surya Vansa the tribes of northern Greece, he had strong grounds for anticipating that victory which afterwards crowned his arms. He more particularly succeeded in gaining over to his side the CHIEFS OF THE JUMNA, the (CYCLOPES,)[2] and EKATAN-KAIRĔS,[3] HECATONCHEIRES, or the sect of the "MEDI-

[1] Anga-kula: *Anga*, tribe; *Mitra*, the sun; *es*, a chief.

[2] See page 40.

[3] *Ekaton*, having the mind fixed on one (*ek*) object; *Kaira*, people of Cashmir.

TATIVES OF CASHMIR," seen in Greece as EKATOM-PEDON, (EKATAN BUDAAN), or Unitarian Bud'has. For ten years did this religious war rage in Thessaly; the Jaina Pontiff taking post on the mountain of the HIGH LAMA-CHIEFS, (OL'AMPOS,) and the people of the KARNA-DES, or LAND OF THE KERNAS, occupying the strong ground of the Hellenic HIMALAYAN, or OTHRYS. At length the KEROONAS,[1] or (KERAUNOS), the JAINAS of the great pontiff led on by the Gokla Chiefs[2], and the Bud'has of Cashmir[3] prevailed against the TITHYANS,[4] (TITANS,) or HERETICS. The tribes of the Sun were driven down to the TARTARAS, that is, the people of TARTARY, situated in the south-western extremity of THE HYA CHIEFS Land, or HIPAĪRUS. The HYA-PUTOS, or SONS OF THE HYAS, (IA-PETOS,) the clans of KARNŎS, (CRONOS,) and the remaining Heretics were imprisoned in this contracted point of land; PO-SAIDHAN, the CHIEF OF SAIDAN being placed to keep guard over them, in company with the ECATAN-KAIRES, or CASHMIRIAN Bud'hists. The DRUOPES, or CHIEFS OF THE DRAS, on the east, and the ELŒATIS, ELEUTHES, or ELUTHS, on the west, (both people of TARTARUS, or TARTARY,) with the KHALKAS, another great Tartarian tribe, placed to watch over them, sufficiently show the locality to which these chiefs were driven. This last tribe is "CHALKOS," the WALL OF BRASS of Hesiod!

A branch of the same great tribe was early in these Lamaic days settled to the north-west of Olympus, where their chief city appears as CHALKIS (KHALKAS), and their country as Chalk-idike (Chalk-adhicar) in the kingdom of the Khalkas. Another branch of their tribe is seen in the map of Greece, on the western slopes of Mount Œta,

[1] KEROONOS, JAINAS, or Bud'hists. KERAUNOS, THUNDER.

[2] Guklopes (Cyclopes).

[3] Ekatankaires.

[4] *Tithyān*, plural of *Tithya*, an heretic.

[5] χαλκός.

as CORAES, the CORAEN of the present day. They are the same tribe noticed by MM. Huc and Gabet in their late travels to Mongolia. "From the depths of this sanctuary" (the temple of the Great Lama) writes M. Gabet, "whose gilding and lively colours glitter on all sides, the Lama-King receives the perpetual homage of this crowd of worshippers incessantly prostrated before him. In this country he is called 'The Saint,' by way of eminence, and there is not a single KHALKA Tartar who does not consider himself honoured by styling 'himself his disciple.' When one meets with an inhabitant of Great COURAEN, if he is asked whence he comes, '*Koure Bokte-Ain Chabi*,' proudly replies he, 'I am a disciple of the holy Couraen.'" Here then, in Greece, in the most ancient times, are the same tribes of the ELUTHS (HELOTS), CORAEN, and KHALKAS.

In the great conflict just noticed, the Jaina Pontiff had gained over to his cause one of the great Solar Tribes, who have been already contemplated in Thessaly, namely, the CATTIS. These are the COTTYS of Hesiod, which tribe, as well as the GOOKLOPES, CUCLOPES, fought in the ranks of the KERAUNOS, those "thunderbolts" of war. The last foe which fell beneath the power of the Lamaic system, in Northern Greece, was the heretical party of THIBET, or TOU-PHOO; the TU-PHO of Hesiod. This body, also, was driven down to Tartarus by the CERAUNOS, or JAINAS, of the Pontiff JĔYŬS. A new order of things succeeded the tumult of this gigantic conflict. The supreme Lama administered the grand directing power over all the provinces of Northern Greece, as well as the control of HAI-THEROS,[1] the "Priests of the Hayas." PO-SAIDON, the "CHIEF OF SAIDON," (which territory will be distinctly seen in the map of Afghanistan), took the direction of

[1] *Hai-Thēros*, Haya Priests; *Ai-thēros*, the ether.

mercantile affairs, and of the maritime force of the country, in which latter capacity he greatly distinguished himself in the Lamaic war by the pursuit of the heretical squadron of the Sun tribes, and the destruction of their admiral, the "PALA-POT-ES" (POLU-BOT-ES[1]), "LORD OF THE SEA KINGS."

The succession of the Lamaic rulers in Greece appears, judging by the accounts left us by Hesiod, to have been settled by the pure decision of the ruling Pontiff, in lieu of the method at present adopted in Tartary, where, on the death of the Grand Lama, he is supposed to be incarnated at his sovereign will and pleasure in any child throughout those vast regions. "There is one new personage begotten by Zeus (Jĕyŭs), who stands pre-eminently marked in the Orphic Theogony, and whose adventures constitute one of its peculiar features. Zagreus[2] (Chakr'as) 'the horned child,' is the son of Zeus by his own daughter, PERSEPHONE (PAR'SOO-PANI).[3] He is the favourite of his father; a child of magnificent promise, and predestined to grow up to succeed to supreme dominion." He is also to have the sovereign control of the KAROONAS (KERAUNAS) or JAINAS. "The Horned Child," thus described as the successor of the Lamaic sovereignty, was clothed in the Tartarian head-dress, the horns being the usual distinctive mark of the sovereigns of Thibet. He was, in fact, the same TARTARIAN JUPITER HAMMON

[1] Apollod. i. 6, 2. (Polybotes) *Pāla,* a protector; *Pot* (pronounced *pote*), a boat, and *Es,* a chief or king.

[2] "ZAGREUS, a corruption of CHAKRAS. The Greeks not having the sound of 'ch' or 'j' in their language, wrote these by 'z.' Hence Jeyŭs and Chakras, became Zeus and Zagreus. *Chakras* should be properly *Chakravarti,* a sovereign of the world, the ruler of a *Chakra,* or country described as extending from sea to sea."—WILSON's *Sans. Lex., s. v.* Hence the Orphic destination of *supreme dominion* for Zagreus (Chakras).

[3] Grote, vol. i. p. 25. *Parasoo-pani,* a name of Durga, called also *Coree* (Sans. *Gouree*).

whose Lamaic worship accompanied the emigrants of Tartary to Egypt. This intended successor to the Pontificate of Tartary, appears to have been murdered by the TITHYAS (TITANS), or HERETICS. With the usual Bud'histic belief, however, of transmigration, the young Lama is described as being born again from the consort of the Jaina Pontiff, the SOO-LAMEE (SE-MELE), or GREAT LAMA QUEEN. Other accounts represent this new incarnation, who had the name of "Dio-Nausos," as being born upon the holy mountain of "MEROO," a history converted by the Greeks to the "MEROS," or "thigh" of Zeus!

The ELEUS-INE, properly ELEUTH-INI, or ELEUTH-CHIEFS, a part of the same Tartar race who have already been surveyed as accompanying the COCAUNS or CAUCONES to Greece, were the chief instruments by which the propagation of the Lamaic doctrines were spread in the Attic territory. The usual ingenuity, however, of their hierarchy, did not desert them in this missionary enterprise; the same skilful means seem to have been adopted, which, centuries after this event, crowned with success the ambitious designs of Peisistratus. A female of surpassing beauty, attired in that garb which early superstition attributed to the inhabitants of heaven, suddenly made her appearance in the neighbourhood of Athens. Her sacred character was at once recognised, and the whole of her after conduct was of such a nature, as to confirm her claim to divine origin.

This effect, even at the distance of centuries, seems to have been produced upon the mind of the poet, who has thus caught some slight glow of that enthusiasm, which was at once poetical and religious. He makes her to speak thus, "I am the venerated Demeter, the joy and help of gods and men. But come—let the united people erect my temple and my altars above the fount Callichorus; I myself will order the method of their sacrifice, and the means of propitiating my favour." The supposed heavenly being now ended, and revealed hersel in all her majestic grandeur.

> "Changed form and stature now,
> Age vanished from her brow,
> And beauty breathed around.
> Forth from her fragrant robes sweet perfumes flowing,
> Far flashed the heavenly form with splendour glowing,
> Whilst golden o'er her shoulders flow
> These radiant locks unbound;
> And as the lightnings blind the gaze,
> So filled those halls the frequent blaze!"[1]

Such was the captivating messenger who ushered in the Lamaic faith in the vicinity of Athens, whose forms of worship and Tartar ceremonials composed the staple of the celebrated Eleusinian Mysteries. Nothing more clearly proves the antiquity of the Eleusinian temple worship than the discordant accounts of the founders of the sacred rites handed down to us, although each is perfectly consistent with the long prevalent Bud'hism of the country in all its branches.

It appears to have existed already in the time of Cecrops.[2] The intimation of the highest antiquity given to this establishment, is in Aristides, who notices its foundation by a son of OGUGOS, where, perhaps, we should rather read "OKAKOS," the great Bud'histic Pontiff, styled Ikshwaka by the Hindoos.

All the ancients who have had occasion to mention the Eleusinian Mysteries, or the Mysteries, as they were

[1] . . . . . *μέγεθος καὶ εἶδος ἄμεψεν.*
Γῆρας ἀπωσαμένη περί τ' ἀμφί τε κάλλος ἄητο
Ὀδμὴ δ' ιμερόεσσα θυηέντων ἀπὸ πέπλων
Σκίδνατο τῆλε δὲ φέγγος ἀπὸ χροὸς αθανάτοιο
Λάμπῑ θεᾶς, ξανθαὶ δὲ κομαὶ κατενήνοθεν ὤμοος·
Αὐγῆς δ' ἐπλησθη πυκινὸς δόμος, ἀστεροπῆς ὥς.

[2] Strabo, 387.

sometimes called, agree that they were the holiest and most venerable of all that were celebrated in Greece. I shall not embarrass the reader with the contending accounts of the different individuals said to have introduced this worship of the venerable Bud'hist family, my object being at this time to show the nature of this religion; and as small space remains for me to unmask the disguise of names, places, and things, handed down by the Homerid of Chios, I shall merely touch on the outlines of his history. It is a history connected with the Rharian Plain and with Celeus. There is every reason to believe, from the position and characters of the agents employed in the founding of the Eleusinian worship, as well as the localities noted by the poet, that this portion of Attica had been more or less affected by the form of the Brahminical worship. The difficulties met with by the holy visitant of the Attic land, and the subsequent political troubles induced in that vicinity, point very distinctly to a change of local worship.

The Rharian Plain, which appears in juxtaposition with this history of Demeter in the account of Homer, is not without its connexion with the celebrated Rarhya division of the five principal Brahminical tribes, however comparatively modern that distribution may appear in the Hindoo chronicles.

Before the departure of the sacred visitant, she is said to have communicated to CELEUS (CULYUS[1]), the ruler of the land of the RARHYA, the system of worship, and the solemnities to be observed in her honour. And thus, is said to have begun the Venerable Mysteries, at her especial

[1] CULYUS, "high-born," is but another word for CULĪN. "A Culīn is a Brahmin of one of the twenty-two RARHIYA divisions of the five principal tribes, as established by Balal Sén, king of Bengal."—WILSON'S *Sans. Lex.* The Culinī Brahmins appear in the greatest force in the Mont Cullenius (Cyllenius).

command. These were divided into the Greater and the Lesser; the latter celebrated in February, in honour of PARASOOPANI (PERSEPHONE), or DURGA, called also CALI, and the greater in August, in honour of the Bud'hist missionary Demeter. The month in which the greater festival was held, was called BHĀDRŎ-MĪYŎM (BOËDRO-MION), "THE GREAT B'HĀDRĂ," the Hindoo month B'hadra, being August-September, in fact, the very BOËDRO-MEON (August) of the Greeks.

To continue the worship introduced in this captivating guise, three sacred individaals were specially appointed, who may be distinctly recognised as the representatives of the Brahminical and Bud'histic power, in the vicinity of Athens in the most ancient times. These hierarchs were, —SRI-B'DHŎ-LEMOS, "The sacred BUD'HA LAMA" (TRI-P'TO-LEMOS[1]); SU-MOL-BOODHA (EU-MOL-PODOS), "THE VERY GREAT BUDHA," and the DEO-C'L-ES (DIO-CLES), the Deva, or "BRAHMIN TRIBES' CHIEF." The Deva did not long continue to enjoy his quasi-regal position. He was obliged to surrender his country to the TRI-P'TO-LEMOS, whose political weapons were very possibly keener than those of his adversary. Both at Eleusis and Athens, however, conspicuous temples and statues declared his deity. The GEPHU-RAE ("GOPHA-RAE," or "LORDS OF THE CAVE," sometimes called SROO[2]-CULA-DUTÆ), TRO-G'LO-DUTÆ,

[1] *Sri*, (the Greek interchange for *Tri*, *see* Appendix, Rule xxiii.,) a prefix to the names of deities. It is also used as a token of religious respect as "The Rev.—The Right Rev.," in England. *P'to*, is a very common Greek contraction for *Bodh*. See the varieties of this name in Appendix: Lema, is Lama; P'to-Lema is Bud'ha-Lama. *Su-mal*, very great; Podos (Boodhas) is the original form of the last member of the compound. *Deva* or *Dev*, a Brahmin; *cul*, a tribe; *es*, a chief. The "u" suffers the ordinary apocope. (*See* Appendix, Rule i.)

[2] Sroo-cula. The tribe of *Sroos*, or Hearers, *i. e.* Jainas, a sect of the Bud'hists. Of this the Greeks made Tro-g'lee, a hole or cave, the place of worship for this sect. Troglodutos, a Troglodyte, properly a Hermit of the Cave, and one of the SROO-CULA (TROG'LO). *See* "Sraces," and Appendix, Rule xxiii.

the special ministers of the Bud'histic faith, who kept their mysteries closely concealed, being a particular gens at Athens, were the genuine cave-hermits, and Jainas, of the highest antiquity. Perhaps in nothing were the different phases of ancient Indo-Hellenic society so distinctly marked, as in the enduring records of the Greek language.

Thus the Brahminical influence is seen in one of the most ordinary vocables. The KA-KOS or Bad-man, is the "GO-GHŎ-S" or COW-KILLER; the latter member of which compound, as indicative of the worst of beings, again permeates into the language of the SACA-SOOS or SAC-SONS, as BAD, from the Indian source, BADH, to "KILL." So too, the SO-PHOS or the WISE-MAN is the representative of the "SOO-BHOO-YA," or the high abstract meditation, by which humanity was supposed to be absorbed into the divinity. Then again, the DES-POTES or the LAND-LORD, (DES-PATI'S)[1] became synonymous with an "OPPRESSOR," and strongly marked the struggles through which one portion of Hellas had gone, in establishing a more extensive system of representative power, in which effort it passed from one extreme of Oligarchic to the opposite limits of Democratic tyranny.

In the reign of Erectheus, which will be shortly noticed, a war arose between the rival sects of the Eleusinians, and the subjects of that prince. The former being defeated, acknowledged the supremacy of Athens in every particular, save their own sacred rites, which they obtained permission to regulate themselves.[2] The EU-MOL-PIDES, that is the descendants of "THE HIGH BUD'HA PRIEST," were now appointed to the administration of the holy rites, with an inferior order of priests, under the general name of KEERUKES,[3] or BUD'HISTS, aided by the

[1] *Des*, land; *pa*, a lord or ruler. [2] Thucyd. ii. 15.

[3] Ceryces,—from "KEERUKA," A BUD'HIST; whence the KEERUKOS (KEERUX) or *sacred* Herald of the Greeks.

daughters of the late Eleusinian high-caste king COOLYUS (CELEUS.) By the more modern Greek writers who treat the Eleusinian worship rather as mysteries than the old national form of worship, we are informed that the candidates admitted to the Lesser Mysteries, bore the name of MUSTAI, (MOKSH'TAI,) or, "EMANCIPATED," a title derived from the well-known Bud'hist MOKSHA,—final and eternal happiness,—the liberation of the soul from the body, and its exemption from further transmigration.

But it was necessary for them to wait yet another year, before they could be admitted to the Greater Mysteries. One of the chief rites of the initiatory stage, was evidently emblematic. It consisted in the washing of a sow in the Holy River, called KANT-HARUS, or KAND-ARHA-S, or LAND OF WORSHIP.[1] To this sacrifice succeeded purification. Those who were, Moksh'tai, (Mustai,) took an oath of secresy, which was in fact absolutely necessary for the preservation of the old religion of the country in these sanctuaries, where alone it could preserve its ground against the more attractive heresy of Homer and his popular gods. The initiated were styled ĕbāptoi (ἐπόπται); they were not, however, admitted into the sanctuary of Demeter, but remained during the solemnities in the vestibule.[2]

The fourth, fifth, and sixth days, appear to have been the most important. On the fourth day a grand procession set out, with a basket containing pomegranates and poppy seeds. This was carried on a waggon, drawn by oxen, followed by women, who were seen carrying small mystical cases. "The Torch Day" was the fifth. A procession headed by the torch-bearer, Dadouchos,

[1] *Arha*, worship; *Arhata*, a worshipper, or Jaina.

[2] *Avaptoi*, literally "obtaining, or getting."

repaired with torches to the temple of Demeter, remaining there during the ensuing night.

The sixth day which was the most solemn, was ushered in with great pomp. It was called Iākchos, properly "YOGÉS," the title of a Mooni, or Saint. The Yogi, is defined as a devout man, who performs worldly actions and ceremonies, without regard to their results, and keeps his mind fixed on Brahma.[1] But the "Yoges" of the Eleusinians, is the name of the celebrated Dio Nausho, (Dio-Nusos,) a sovereign of great power in north-western India, called the son of the Jaina Pontiff, (JEYUS,) and the Great Lama Queen, SOO LAMEE, (SE-MELEE.) Ignorant of the real origin of the term "KOUROS," which was a term especially given to "Iacchos," Sophocles represents the young god, at the breast of the Eleusinian Demeter; which idea is strengthened by a long train of classical authorities to repeat, and of still more persuasive statuary to confirm this idea. The "COUROO's" of Sophocles, is no other than "GOOROO-S", a "GOOROO," or teacher of spiritual things. Hence, Demeter is styled by the Greeks, "COURO-TROPHOS," ("GOOROO-TROPHOS,") or nurse of Gooros. The statue of IACCHOS, (YOGES,) adorned with a garland of myrtle, and bearing a torch in his hand, was carried along the sacred road, amidst joyful shouts. The interval between the night of the sixth and seventh day witnessed the initiation of those pilgrims into the most important mysteries; those, meanwhile, who were neither BELIEVERS nor EMANCIPATED, being sent away by herald. A new purification having been gone through, and a repetition of the oath of secrecy taken, they were admitted to the innermost sanctuary. After the initiation of each individual, he was dismissed with those solemn words, the very mystery of mysteries to Europeans, and the torment of orientalists, for ages. They are

[1] *Răma*, beloved.

the words of a Tartarian priesthood, and the language is Tibetian.

ΚΟΓΞ	ΟΜ	ΠΑΞ.
Kongx	om	Pax.
Dkon	qsum	phag-hts.[1]

"Salutation to the Three Holy Ones."[2]

The present Lamaic doctrines relative to the incarnation of successive Bud'has, will throw some light upon the history of Zagreus, the "Horned Child," and demonstrate the doctrine of the impossibility of the non-existence of a supreme Jaina Pontiff. The passage is from the popular work of Mr. Prinsep, on the social and political condition of Thibet, Tartary, and Mongolia. The Lamaic ideas are as follows:—

"Everything proceeds from God, and will return to him; but the soul passes, in transmigration, to inferior or superior animals, according to its desert. There are six grades of animals vested with souls. Angels, demons, men, quadrupeds, birds, and reptiles. A soul in each state has its means of attaining perfection; the highest of all is to be absorbed into the Divinity, whence again living Boodhs are detached, to take a human shape, in order to recall men from errors, and teach the road to perfection. The highest of existing regenerate Boodhs are the Delai Lama of Lassa; the Band-shan Remboochi, of Teeshoo-Loomboo, the same who was visited by Captain Turner, in the time of Warren Hastings; and the Geesoo Tamba of Grand Kooren, Oorga, on the borders of Siberia; and the C'hangkia-fo, or great almoner of the court of Pekin. Of all these, the Delai Lama of Lassa is the pope, or

[1] The full formula, is Dkon (Mch'og)—Qsum-(la) p'hag—Hts (-'hal-lo). *See* Csoma de Cooroos, *As. Res.*, vol. xx. p. 45.

[2] *Om*, with Brahmins, is Brahma, Vishnu, and Mahesa; with Bud'hists, it is, Bud'ha, Dherma, and Sanga; generally conceived to be typical of Bud'ha—the Law and the Clergy. The Sanscrit formula is Namo Ratna Triyaya.

spiritual guide of all Boodhists. He was only nine years old when our missionaries were there, and had been recognised pope for six years, having been taken from an obscure family of Sifans, in the province of Ming-chen-tou-tse. When this Boodhist dies everybody falls to meditation and prayer to discover the new birth. Prayer-barrels[1] turn with redoubled vigour. All who fancy they have a regenerate Boodh in their families give notice, and a council of holy ones, that is, of Kotooktoos, sits, and selects three infants, who are sent for to Lassa to be examined. For six days they are shut up, and the examiners devote themselves this while to earnest meditation and prayer. On the seventh day they write the names of the three infants on golden plates, and place them in an urn. The senior Kotooktoo draws the lot; and the child whose name is drawn is immediately proclaimed Delai Lama, and carried in state through the town; while the two rejected children are returned to their families, with liberal pensions."[2]

The Bud'histic faith, notwithstanding the depression under which it ultimately laboured as the state religion of Hellas, permeated every branch of society, maintaining, in extraordinary vigour, the ever-present idea of the visibility and non-visibility of the deified saints, according to their own volition. Hence, Poseidon is sometimes represented as a chief engaged to build the walls of Troy: thus he is in his grosser capacity of substantial agent. On the other hand, Ares is wounded, and a celestial ichor

[1] Every Lama has his prayer-barrel. Prayer and meditation being regarded as the only effectual means of attaining sanctification, the continued repetition of the mystical "Om mani padme hom," is considered as the first essential of faith. Hence the number of repetitions is the test of merit, and for multiplication of them the devise of turning a barrel, on which the words are written, has been imagined, and obtains universal credence in its efficacy.

[2] Prinsep, "Mongolia," p. 107.

flows from the wound. Apollo transforms himself into a dolphin; and, in fact, the power of the saints of the middle ages over the elements is a very general characteristic of the Budha deities.

At length the strongest peculiarities of each deified hero became, as it were, the stereotyped characteristics of each divinity. Thus, the Chief of Sidon, that is, Chief of the Saints[1] (Bud'ha), having been both in Phœnicia and at Dwarica, and generally on the coasts of Sinde, recognised as the patron of the Vaisya or Mercantile Caste (so much so in the former country as to have his memory preserved by his image on the figure-heads of the Phœnician vessels), was the object of adoration as the special protecting divinity of the sea. The faith of his adherents was as lively as that of the pilgrims to Apollo's shrine; and their thorough belief in his ever-living personality as the heavenly guardian of a special cosmogonic trust was as active and confiding as the faith of the pilgrims to Loretto's shrine; and while the more subtle philosophic principles, held by the Bud'hists of antiquity, were lost sight of, a faith more lively and more personifying supplied its place. Thus, whilst the Hindoo of the Himalaya could realise upon a substantial Meru, an unsubstantial Indra, the Indo-Greek of Thessaly could perceive his Budha on Tomarus—the Greek of subsequent ages could just as strongly fix for Poseidon, the great Patriarch guardian of Merchants, a fitting palace and sovereignty in the depths of the sea. Hence, with the Homerid of Chios, the vital action of the old Bud'histic principle is at work, as it was centuries previous to his time, to personify the power of Poseidon, the Lord of the sea-faring mariner. Ægæ, in Eubœa, boasted the dignity of providing a palace for the Phœnician ruler of the waves,

[1] *Sidha*, a saint; *Sidhan*, saints; *Pa-Sidhan*, chief of the saints.

in whose depths was situated the goodly structure. Here were his steeds, glorious with their golden manes and brazen hoofs. Borne along in his chariot by those swift ministers of his will, he passes over the tumbling billows of the deep, whose waving crest sinks to perfect stillness on his approach, and whose monsters, recognising their sovereign lord, gambol in a thousand varying gaieties around his gliding car.

> "In the deeps of ocean flood,
> Where his glorious palace stood,
> Golden, dazzling, undecaying,
> Entereth now the Ocean-god.
> He his fleet-footed steeds in their car is arraying;
> All brazen their hoofs;—see their shoulders, that laves
> The gold of their mane that so gloriously waves.
> See, gold the god's form in a vesture of light;
> See, gold is the lash which he holds in his right;
> As he mounts in his chariot so bright.
> Now over the ocean his coursers on-urging,
> Forth gambol wild crowds of her monsters up-surging.
> As they rise from the lair of their watery night
> They hail him their lord,
> And wide smiles the ocean with joy at his sight!" [1]
>
> *Select. from MS.*—E. P.

This vital and energetic faith, however, will not account for the *basis* of fable; it will only tend to show its own tendencies and intensity. In the patriarchal system of deification, already largely noticed, will be found the sum and substance of the whole system; as wide as the world, as craving as ambition, and as strong as the ties of kindred.

[1] . . . ἔνθα δὲ οἱ κλυτὰ δώματα βένθεσι λίμνης
Χρύσεα, μαρμαίροντα τετεύχαται, ἄφθιτα αἰεί
Ἔνθ' ἐλθὼν ὑπ' ὄχεσφι τιτύσκετο καλχόποδ' ἵππω,
Ὠκυπέτα, χρυέησιν ἐθείρησιν κομόωντε.
Χρυσὸν δ' αὐτὸς ἔδυνε περὶ χροΐ· γέντο δ' ἱμάσθλην.
Χρυσείην, εὔτυκτον, ἑοῦ δ' ἐπεβήσετο δίφρου
Βῆ δ' ἐλάαν ἐπὶ κύματ' ἄταλλε δὲ κήτε' ὑπ' αὐτοῦ
Πάντοθεν, ἐκ κευθμῶν, οὐδ' ἠγνοίησεν ἄνακτα·
Γηθοσύνῃ δὲ θάλασσα διίστατο· . . *Hom. Il.*, xiii. 21—29.

XVIII.

PHŒNICIAN BUD'HISM.

Κάδμος απυργώτοιο θεμελεία πεγνυε Θήβης
'Επταπορῳ πυλεῶνι, περίδρομον αστυ χαράξας.—*Dionys.* v. 50.

"Son origine est placé dans les temps les plus reculés, dans des temps mêmes anté-historiques. Le nom de Bud'ha est rapporté à plusieurs ages, dans différens pays. Une longue suite de Bud'has est donnée, non seulement d'un commun accord par tous les Bud'histes, mais mêmes par d'autres, à qui cette religion est indifférente, ou odieuse."—TROYER's *Raja. Tarangini*, vol. ii. 399.

THE reader will not fail to remember the Tartarian population I have already pointed out in the province of Bashan, and the "LEBANAN," (LEBANON), or the "TRIBES OF LEH." How thoroughly Lamaic these and other provinces were, on the entrance of the Children of Israel into Palestine, may be proved in a variety of ways. I shall mention one circumstance only as establishing this fact,—namely the Chaonim or Cakes offered to the Queen of Heaven, a Tartar rite that runs up to the most remote periods.

"We arrived at *Chaborté*," observes M. Huc, "on the fifteenth day of the eighth moon, an epoch of great rejoicing for the Chinese. This festival known under the name of the *Yué-Ping*, 'Cakes of the Moon,' runs up to the highest antiquity. It was established to honour the moon with a superstitious worship. During this solemnity all labours are suspended; workmen receive from their masters a pecuniary gratification; every one is appareled in his best clothes, and very shortly, in the midst of games and feasts, the joy becomes universal.

Relations and friends mutually send to each other cakes of different size, on which is imprinted the figure of the Moon."[1]

Such was the same practice, followed by the same Tartar people at the time of the Hebrew settlement in the Promised Land. The settlement of the Bud'hist "DHAMMOS," or Priests at Damas-cus, has already been noticed. That fact will now receive additional confirmation, by its position in the CADMON-I-TIS (GAUD'MAN-E-DES), the LAND OF THE GAUTAMAS, that is the BUD'HISTS, a term derived from Gautama, a title of the founder of this vast sect.

The connection between Greece and Phœnicia, peopled as both were by the same nation, leaves us no reason to doubt of the far-famed settlement of Cadmus, (for so the Greeks wrote the name,) in Thebes. "Gauteme Boudha," observes M. Joinville,[2] "is generally called Saman Gauteme, Boudhou Vahanse, 'The Lord Saint Gouteme Bud'h.' It has been justly observed, that the Samonocodum of the people of Siam is the same as the Boudhou of the Cinghalese. . . . We see that Samono and Saman resemble each other, and that Codom can easily be taken for Gauteme."

A thorough familiarity with the ancient phonetic and orthographic systems will be of the utmost value, in establishing or refuting the historical claims of various writers, in various parts of the world. The existence or non-existence of certain forms of expression, as the equivalent of names foreign to the nation of the historian, will pave the way for much valuable history, which at present lies buried beneath the ruins of ancient languages, and of a once mighty people. The colony of the Phœnician Cadmus comes particularly under this category.

[1] Souvenirs d'un Voyage dans la Tartarie, par M. Huc, vol. i. p. 84.

[2] *As. Res.*, vol. vii. p. 415.

"There is a curious coincidence," writes Keightley, "between the name of Cadmus and the Semitic term for the east, Keddam, and this may in reality be the sole foundation of the notion of a Phœnician colony at Thebes; for none of the usual evidences of colonisation are to be found. We do not, for example, meet with the slightest trace of Phœnician influence in the language or institutions of Bœotia. It is, further, a thing most incredible, that a sea-faring commercial people, like the Phœnicians, should have selected as the site of their very earliest foreign settlement, a place situated in a rich fertile valley, away from the sea, and only adapted for agriculture, without mines, or any of those objects of trade that might tempt a people of that character. It is also strange, that the descendants of these colonists should have so entirely put off the Phœnician character, as to become noted in after ages for their dislike of trade of every kind. We may, therefore, we think, now venture to dismiss this theory, and seek a Grecian origin for Cadmus."[1]

These observations are characterised by that sound judgment which everywhere distinguishes the author of the Greek Mythology. At the same time, it evinces the necessity of a thorough revision of early Greek history, based upon the foundation of a secure geographical system. The Phœnician language, of which the author of the Mythology is speaking, had not, at the era of Cadmus, received that distinctive character as a separate dialect which afterwards marked it; it was but commencing its transition to a more decided form of the Shemitic, and to that gradual union with the Celtic, which, in after ages, almost identified the Celtic with the Phœnician. The power of free and unrestrained communication, therefore, with the Greeks, without the aid of interpreters, distinguished the era of Gautamas (Cadmus) and his

[1] Keightley's Mythology, vol. i. p. 327.

disciples. There can remain no shadow of a doubt to those who are acquainted with the missionary efforts of the early Bud'hists, as recorded in their most ancient and most authentic writers, that this settlement of Cadmus in Greece, was the vanguard of a series of Bud'histic propagandism. A perusal of the pages of the "Mahawanso" alone, independently of the valuable records received from the various columns in India, bearing the edicts of Bud'histic emperors, will be sufficient to establish this important fact. The historical value, derived from the marvellous harmony subsisting between the north of Palestine aud the north of the Punjab—between the Jaina religion of the one country, identical with the Lamaic system of the other, cannot be gainsayed.

As usual, on the introduction of a designing creed, disastrous political results ensued. It is but too evident that the city of Thebes and Bœotia at large were the scene of bloodshed and violence which ill-beseemed the propagation of any religion that deserved that name. The Gautamăs (Cadmus), the Bud'hist propagandist of the day, was but too truly said to have sown the dragon's[1] teeth in Bœotia; the crop arose on a wide field of slaughter, which long continued to bear the most deadly fruits. He appears to have introduced and urged, not only the Bud'histic faith, but to have mingled in his doctrines many Brahminical practices unpalatable to the laity generally.

Hence he is said to have spread abróad the VEDANTAS, or ODONTAS, of the BRAHMINS.[2] The Greek Logographers tell us that those who survived the dreadful slaughter which characterised this religious war, were said to be of the family of the SPARTOI; that is, say they, of those who

[1] DRAKON, a SERPENT; DROOGON, BRAHMA.

[2] ODONTES, "teeth;" VEDANTAS, "precepts of the Vedas. The "v" and "o" commutable. (*See* Appendix, Rule xvi.)

were *Sown.* The plain fact is evident: that those who embraced the doctrines of Gautamăs, were of the race of So-PUR, their country being called So-PUR-TAN, whence the Greek contracted form S'PURTAN, and SPARTAN.[1] "SOPUR, is a small town in Cashmir, at the point where the Jailum, (here two hundred yards wide,) flows from the Wulur Lake, and commences that rapid course which it holds downwards, until it enters the plain of the Punjab, above the town of Jailum."[2] These were the S'POORTANS, who, as military chiefs, became in the sequel so formidable to the rest of Greece. Coming partly from the north of Cashmir, but the great bulk of their nation from Ladac, whence they were called LADAC-I-MEN, and LADACAI-MEN, (LACADAI-MEN,)[3] they formed a perpetual subject of banter to their more polished neighbours of the south. The Spartan Hellenic dialect was too Tartarian to please the tasteful native of the Attoc, whose commercial bias, grafted into the HYANIAN, (IONIAN) stock, by the great Patriarch Vaisya of the Attoc, (that is, Bud'ha,) formed from the most remote period the cause of national disgust and antipathies.

Notwithstanding any Brahminical bias in the doctrines of GAUTAMAS, (CADMUS,) that the Bud'histic doctrine and deities were mainly inculcated is clear; for Gautamas is said to have named one of the gates of the new city of the DEBAI, "THEBAI:"[4] that is, the city of the PRIESTS, or BRAHMINS, after the title of a celebrated Bud'ha Sacti, so called, who is looked upon as the female personification of divine energy. That name was ONGKA-RA; by the Greeks called ONGKA; and hence the mysterious name of

[1] *See* Appendix, Rule i.

[2] Thornton's Gazetteer. Punjab, vol. ii. p. 250.

[3] From *Ladaci*, a native of *Ladac*, is regularly formed *Ladacai;* the compound *man* has been noticed before. Hence the Latin form *Lacedæmon.*

[4] *Devai;* locally pronounced *Debai.*

ONGKA ATHENE; a name derived from Om, the mystical name of Brahma, which has already been contemplated.

The indiscreet religious zeal with which the Bud'hist envoy acted, appears to have been displeasing to the reigning Chakraverti, or Jaina pontiff of the day; since GAUTAMAS is described as being condemned to an expiatory servitude of eight years. The marriage of GAUTAMUS forms a brilliant episode in the almost poetical narrative of the logographer. It appears to have been of such a nature as to befit the high rank of the Lamaic envoy, being graced by all that was dignified and noble in Bœotia. Agreeably to oriental custom, magnificent presents were bestowed upon Gautamas, all in perfect keeping with the existing Indo-Hellenic population. Amongst other precious gifts, the consort of the Bud'histic missionary received a magnificent necklace from the GRAND LAMA (JEYUS), made by the skilful Bud'hist chief of the Hya Land.[1]

The disasters which accompanied the first appearance of Gautamas in the "City of the Devas," long continued to run parallel with the existence of that unhappy town. The religious disputes which sprang up between the disciples of the Bud'hist and Vedantic factions raged vehemently till, in the time of the ETYO-C'L-ES[2] (ETEO-C'L-ES), THE CHIEF OF THE BRAHMINICAL TRIBE, and PALA-NAG-ES[3] (POLU-NEIK-ES), THE PRINCE OF THE NAGA CHIEFS, a devastating war broke forth, and ultimately embroiled not only the City of the Devas, but also Argos.

Like the military priests of the middle ages, the Bud'histic and Brahminical factions mutually sent forth

[1] HE-PHA-IS-DES, HE-PHA-IS-TOS.

[2] *Etyŏ*, attributivè form of *Eta*, a Brahmin; *cul*, a tribe, (*see* Appendix, Rule i.,) and *es*, a chief.

[3] *Pala*, a protector; *Naga*, a serpent (Bud'hist), *Es*, a chief.

their well-equipped champions to many a holy war. One of the combatants in the great struggle, Amphiaräus, the priestly warrior-prophet, enters upon, and disappears from the scene of the gigantic contest before the walls of Thebes, in a manner so striking that I cannot resist the temptation of portraying the admirable Bud'histic feeling of saintly and military grandeur which descended even to the days of Æschylus. It conveys a singular warning of the necessity of separating positive agents from fictitious agency, and demonstrates, in common with the thousand miracles, claimed both by Bud'histic Rome and Bud'histic Greece, that the miracle is a dogma, and the wonder-worker a fact. It was after the death of the great VEDANTIST,[1] that the curse uttered by their spiritual parent upon the ambitious chiefs, Eteocles and Polyneices, descended upon them. It was but too soon apparent in the fierce discord of the two chiefs who had agreed each to rule in the City of the Devas annually. Eteocles having tasted the sweets of power, refused to resign the throne to Polyneices, whom he expelled. The exiled prince repaired to the court of Adrastus, King of Argos, whose daughter, Argeia, he had married, and sought to engage that prince in his quarrel.

"On proposing the expedition to the Argeian chiefs around him, he found most of them willing auxiliaries; but Amphiaräus, formerly his bitter opponent, but now

[1] OIDI-POS, 'AIDYA-POS. The VEDA LORD. *Vaidyh*, a follower of the Vedas. The digammated "v," lost as usual. (*See* Appendix, Rule vii.) This is the prince who is described as unravelling the knotty riddle of the SBANGAS, SPHINGOS (SPHINX), *i. e.* the abstruse Anga, Su-anga: by the rules of combination, Suvanga; by local pronunciation, Subanga; and by loss of short vowel, S'banga (Sphingos). (*See* Appendix, Rules i. and xix.) The Anga is a division of Hindu learning, comprehending such science as is considered dependant upon the Vedas, hence also called *Védánga*. Works on six subjects came under this description; viz. Pronunciation, Grammar, Prosody, explanation of obscure terms, description of religious rites, and Astronomy.

reconciled to him, and husband of his sister Eriphylê, strongly opposed him. He denounced the enterprise as unjust, and contrary to the will of the gods. Again, being of a prophetic stock, descended from Melampus, he foretold the certain death both of himself and of the principal leaders, should they involve themselves as accomplices in the mad violence of Tydeus, or the criminal ambition of Polynikês. Amphiaräus, already distinguished both in the Kalydonian boar-hunt and in the funeral games of Pelias, was in the Thêban war the most conspicuous of all the heroes, and absolutely indispensable to its success. But his reluctance to engage in it was invincible, nor was it possible to prevail upon him except through the influence of his wife Eriphylê. Polynikês, having brought with him from Thêbes the splendid robe and *necklace* given by the gods [Devas] to Harmonia, on her marriage with Kadmus, offered it as a bribe to Eriphylê, on condition that she would influence the determination of Amphiaräus. The sordid wife, seduced by so matchless a present, betrayed the lurking-place of her husband, and involved him in the fatal expedition. Amphiaräus, reluctantly dragged forth, and foreknowing the disastrous issue of the expedition, both to himself and to his associates, addressed his last injunctions at the moment of mounting his chariot to his sons, Alkmæôn and Amphilochus, commanding Alkmæôn to revenge his death by killing the venal Eriphylê, and by undertaking a second expedition against Thêbes."[1]

The Argive army soon made its appearance before the walls of that city, headed by the seven chiefs, Adrastus, Capaneus, Amphiaräus, Hippomedōn, Tydeus, Parthenopæus, and the exile Polyneices, a number which gave rise to the celebrated tragedy of Æschylus, "The Seven

[1] Grote's Hist. Greece, vol. i. p. 369.

against Thebes." On the approach of this mighty force, preceded by clouds of cavalry, terror reigned within the city :—

> "Hark to the tramp
> From the hostile camp!
> Like the crested steeds of Ocean,
> Flowing vast in motion,
> Their waving horse appears and heads the wild array!
> And the earth-clouds that rise
> Vast and silent to the skies,
> Their faithful message say.
> And the thunder of the clanging hoof that startles our repose,
> Near and more near is rolling through the air
> O'er the plain from our foes,
> With deepening roar,
> As checkless pour
> The Torrent Hosts, that through their mountain channel tear."[1]
> *Select. from MS.—E. P.*

Before these terrors of the citizens Eteocles maintained a resolute countenance. "What!" said he, "does the mariner gain safety by quitting the helm, and flying to the prow, when his bark is labouring amid the ocean billows?" And his resolute advice was at length effectual in calming their fears. A messenger now entered, giving a terrific description of the Seven Chiefs, who had posted themselves each before one of the seven gates; Tydeus faced the Prœtean gate.

> "His triple plumes dark waving fly,
> And crest his helm, o'erarching high:
> The brazen bells within his shield
> The note of terror wildly yield.

---

[1] Μεθεῖται στρατὸς στρατόπεδον λιπὼν
Ῥεῖ πολὺς ὅδε λεὼς πρόδρομος ἱππότας
Ἀιθερία κόνις με πέιθει φανεῖς,
Ἄναυδος, σαφὴς ἔτυμος ἄγγελος·
Ἐλεδεμνὰς πεδιπλόκτυπός τ'
Ἐγκρίμπτεται βοὰ, ποτᾶται,
Βρέμει δ' ἀμαχέτου
Δίκαν ὕδατος οροκτύπου.—*Sept. cont. Theb.*, 79, 86.

That shield a haughty bearing shows—
A sky with stars that blazoned glows—
Shines in mid-orb the full moon bright,
That boast of heaven and eye of night.
Such vaunting bearing of his arms
He madly shows mid war's alarms;
Rings wildly through the crowded ranks
His war-cry on the river's banks.
As champs the bit, to be at large
Some war-horse, ere the battle-charge,
And marks the piercing trumpet bray,
So burns he for the desperate fray." [1]—*E. P.*

Previous to this assault of the town, the united force of the Cadmeians, Phlegyæ, and Phocæans had marched out to meet their invaders; but being defeated in a battle near the heights of Ismenus, they were driven back within their walls. Menætius, the son of Creon, having heard from Tiresias, the blind prophet, that should he offer himself up as a sacrifice to HAR-ES,[2] victory would declare for Thebes, went forth from the city, and slew himself before the gates. The storming of the town now began. Parthenopæus was killed by a stone from Periclymenus, and the warlike Capaneus, who had already mounted the wall, by a scaling-ladder, was smitten down by a thunder-bolt from Zeus. Terror-struck at this interposition of divine power, Adrastus and his Argive

1 . . . . τρεῖς κατασκίους λόφους
Σείει κράνους καίτομ', ὑπ' ἀσπίδος δὲ τῷ
Χαλκήλατοι κλάζουσι κώδωνες φόβον·
"Εχει δ' ὑπέρφρον σῆμ' ἐπ ἀσπίδος, τόδε,
Φλέγονθ' υπ' ἄστροις οὐρανὸν τετυγμένον·
Λαμπρὰ δὲ πανσέληνος ἐν μέσῳ σακει
Πρέσβιστον ἄστρων, νυκτὸς ὀφθαλμὸς,
Τοιαῦτ' ἀλύων ταῖς ὑπερκόμπαις σάγαις,
Βοᾷ παρ' ὄχθαις ποταμίαις μάχης ἐρῶν,
"Ιππος χαλινῶν ὣς κατασθμαίνων μένει
"Οστις βοὴν σάλπιγγος ὁρμαίνει μένων."
Æschyl. Sept. ap. Theb., 384, 394.

2 HAR-ES (ARES), THE WAR-PRINCE.

bands drew off from the walls, and the Thebans, sallying forth in pursuit, a single combat ensued between the rival chiefs, who were so exasperated by fury, that intent only upon inflicting mutual death, and regardless of self-defence, they both fell lifeless upon the spot:—

> "A deadly kindred, they
> All hate-dissevered lay,
> In anger's frenzy 'mid the closing strife
> That hate has ceased, and, true to kindred birth,
> Lies reeking on the sod the blood of life,
> Commingling in the earth."[1]

Amphiaräus, though struggling hard to stem the tide of battle, was carried away by the fugitives, and being closely pursued by Periclymenus, would have been pierced by the spear of that warrior, had not the omnipresent JAINA SAINT (JEYUS) miraculously rescued him, by receiving within the bosom of the opening earth the hero, with his chariot and horses uninjured.[2] An incident so memorable was vouched for by a sacred tomb, built on the spot, and shown by the Thebans even in historic times.

All the Argive chiefs had perished in the disastrous fight. Adrastus, now bereft of the Prophet Warrior, left alone in his flight, and saved solely by the matchless speed of his horse, Areion, reached Argos, bringing with him—

> "Saved by his mighty courser's speed,
> Nought but his garb of woe, and black-maned steed."[3]

Such is one of these magnificent episodes in the

[1] Ὁμόσποροι δῆτα καὶ πανώλεθροι,
Διατομαῖς οὐ φίλαις,
Ἔριδι μαινομένᾳ,
Νείκεος ἐν τελευτᾷ
Πέπαυται δ' ἔχθος
Ἐν δὲ γαία ζωὰ
Φονοῤῥύτῳ μέμικται·
Κάρτα δ' εις' ὅμαιμοι.—*Æchyl. Sept. ap. Theb.* 933, 940.

[2] Pind. Ol., vi. 21. Plut., par. 6.

[3] Paus., viii. 25, 5.

Bud'histic annals, written centuries after the course of action described; written too by a poet, whose vivid conception and living faith in the magnificent heroes which graced the gloomy grandeur of the age of Thebes, fully realised the Brahmino-Bud'histic creed of the historian, whose narrative, orally or in a written form, descended to the days of Æschylus,[1] an author pre-eminently oriental in his imagery, and gigantic in his conceptions.

[1] 'AIS-CUL-ES (Vais-cul-es), CHIEF OF THE VAISYA OR MERCANTILE TRIBE (ÆSCHYLUS). (*See* Appendix, Rule vii.)

XIX.

APOLLO.—THE BUD'HISM OF LADAC AND THE LADACAI-MEN (LACADÆ-MON).

STAND UP! I MYSELF ALSO AM A MAN.—*Acts* xv. 26.

WHEN the pious centurion of the Italian band influenced by the lingering relics of Roman Bud'hism, fell down prostrate in the presence of St. Peter and worshipped him as a deity, that great apostle, with the humility of a Christian, reprobated any such homage; at the same time virtually remarking, that his sacred functions did not make him a vicarious god, nor rank him with a distinct and unapproachable caste.

He was still a man—a man with the noblest yet the basest feelings;[1] one not to be adored, for he was still a fallible and a weak being, as evinced by his cowardice in the Prætorian Hall. Cornelius thus firmly reproved, thenceforward considered him not as Christ's vicar upon earth. An envoy so faithful to his MASTER, perhaps never addressed the Lama-gods of the east and west. Hence both these divinities of earth still sway the impulses of myriads of their fellow-creatures. Alas! human ambition is of a nature so vitreous as to be easily seen through, though screened by the exotics of spiritual pride.

Such mighty godships existed for centuries in Greece. Much silver and much gold did the arch-priests of these

[1] Jer. xvii. 9; Luke xxi. 31, 62; Galat. ii. 11—14; 1 Cor. ix. 27.

ingenious deities gather up from the confiding pilgrims, whose offerings personally or by deputy ranged from the golden image of the Jaina Prince Apollo, to the obolus of Charon; and such was the unbounded confidence in the vivifying powers of this dexterous fraternity, that had the lot of these pilgrims been cast in modern days, the dedication of a silver cradle at the fitting shrine, would have been considered the happy fore-runner of a numerous progeny. Nor was the rock-crowned throne of the Pilgrim-god inferior to the majesty of his claims as the interpreter of the will of the supreme ruler of the universe. Everything which could affect the senses with a feeling of the sublime, was connected with this favourite abode; the statue for the deity—the magnificent prospect for the eye—the choral chaunt for the ear—and the incense for the nose—all pleaded with frail humanity for *the god.*—That must be indeed a vital religion, that will thrive upon whitewashed walls. Oh, HUMANITY! it is *thee* we adore, and not our GOD.

The national god of the LADACAI-MEN (LACADAI-MEN) had fixed his abode in a situation well calculated to impress the mind with a fitting awe of his unseen presence. "The site," writes Hughes, "is compared by Strabo to a vast natural theatre; and the comparison is just, even to the minutest details, for the city (Delphi) was not only built upon a fine semicircular sweep of the mountain, but suspended as it were upon regular gradations of terraces, built in the Cyclopean style of masonry. Such was the colossal theatre where deities and their satellites composed the drama! How great must have been the astonishment of the ancient pilgrim after he had toiled over many a wearisome stade to view this solemn sanctuary—this common altar of all nations—when the splendid scene burst upon his sight, with all the decoration of pomp and sacrifice, whilst the hollow rocks reverberated with the clang of trumpets, the neighing of steeds, and the shouts of assembled multitudes. And what a scene does this spot still present to the painter who would raise his ideas to the sublime association with which it is connected!"[1]

Such is the admirable description of an eye-witness of the favoured abode of this prophetic God; the God of the ancient Hindoo—of his progeny, the Hindoo Greek—and his offspring, the Greek of Homeric song. That God was CRISHNA; and from his rock throne, and from his town, Crissa (Crishna), could be seen glittering, like burnished gold in the setting sun, the waters of the CRISSÆAN, or CRISHNÆAN BAY. The city, sacred to the deified Hindu, was named DELPHOI,[2] being the abode of the DELBHAI,[3] or clans of DELBHI, a name of ARJUNA, the third of the Pandava princes, whose martial bands, under the name of VAIJAYAN (AIGAIAN) have already been contemplated as settling on, and giving a name to the ÆGÆAN Sea, on whose north was the gulf of THERMA, so called from Dherma,[4] another name of the same prince Arjuna. Both Arjuna and Crishna are the great heroes of the war of the Mahabharata, which has already been noticed. DELBHI, or ARJUNA, was the bosom friend of CRISHNA (CRISSA); hence the name of that town, which afterwards became a shrine so wealthy.

The name A'POLLŌNO-s is the Greek euphonic term of A'BALĀNO-j, a name of Crishna.[5] This name Crishna or Krishna, is in the local dialects, particularly of the neighbourhood of Cashmir, called Kishen, a name

[1] Hughes's Travels in Greece, vol. i. p. 358. [2] Lat. *Delphi.*

[3] *Delbhi:* Arjuna. *Delbhai*, descendants or people of Arjuna.

[4] *Dherma*, Raja.

[5] Derived from *Bala*, *Bala-rama*, and *anoja*. younger-born. Bala Rama was the half-brother of Crishna, and third of the Ramas, considered the eighth avatar of Vishnu. *Bala-deva* (the god of strength), was the elder brother of Crishna.

given as we have seen, both to KISHEN of Cashmir, and the KISHON of Palestine. In the latter country 'BALĀNO-j (A'POLLŌNO-s) was called, (as in India) SAMA, or SHAMA, from his dark complexion, which is also expressed by the word "CRISHNA." The CANAANITES,[1] or people of CANYA, *another* name of CRISHNA, (BALANO-J, or A'POLLONO-S), particularly saluted him by this title.[2]

The people of Ladaci, or the Ladacai-men (LACEDAIMON) especially reverenced his memory, and Canya was, as it were, the national god of this Tartarian tribe. Hence their name LA'CANYAN (LA-CONIAN)[3] or THE PEOPLE OF CANYA.

Let us now for a short space visit the primitive shrine of the same god, guided by that admirable writer Colonel Tod. It is to the magnificent rocky heights of Aboo, in Rajpootana, that he is conducting us; a place of pilgrimage, not less celebrated than the Parnassus of the West—so much so, indeed, as to be called the SAINT'S PINNACLE. The staffs of pilgrims were heaped in piles around the footsteps of the saint, as memorials of their successful intrepidity.

"Caves innumerable were seen in various parts of the mountain, indicative of a Troglodyte population in former ages, and there were many curious orbicular holes, which could only be compared to cannon-shot. I patiently awaited the termination of the struggle between the powers of light and darkness, in conversation with the recluse. He told me that during the Bursat, or rainy season, when the atmosphere is cleared of all impurities, the citadel of Jodpoor, and the desert plain, as far as Balotia on the Loony were visible. It was some time before I could test this assertion, though during occasional out-breakings of

1 *Canyān*, plural of *Canya*.

2 "Ouranou Kurion, BAAL SAMEN, kalountes."—*Phil. ap. Eus.*, b. i. c. x.

3 *Lao*, people, and Canya (La'conya, pl. Laconiān).

the sun, we discerned the rich valley termed Bheetul, extending to Sarchi, and nearly twenty miles to the east, the far-famed shrine of Ambá-Bhavani, amongst the cloud-capped peaks of the Aravulli. At length, however, Surya burst forth in all his majesty, and chasing away the sable masses, the eye swept over the desert, until vision was lost in the blending of the dark blue vault with the dusky, arid soil. All that was required to form the sublime was at hand, and silence confirmed the charm.

"If the eye diverted from the vast abyss beneath, turned but half a circle to the right, it rested on the remains of the castle of the Pramars, whose dusky walls refused to reflect the sun-beams, while the slender palmyra, as if in mockery of their decay, fluttered its ensign-like leaves amidst the ruined courts of a race who once deemed their sway eternal.

"A little further to the right, rose the clustering domes of Dailwarra, backed by noble woods, and buttressed on all sides by fantastic pinnacles, shooting like needles from the crest of the plateau, on whose surface were seen meandering several rills, pursuing their devious course over the precipitous face of the mountains. All was contrast—the blue sky and sandy plain, the marble fanes, and humble wigwam, the stately woods, and rugged rocks. In spite of the cold blast, it required an effort to withdraw from the state of contemplative indolence which overcomes one amidst such scenes, where, as if brought into the immediate presence of the Creator of such grandeur, the mind feels oppressed by a sense of its own insignificance.

"While my eye rested with delight on these Argosies of the Hindoos, it was gratified by finding, amidst details often too mystical for a western intellect, something that savoured of a more classical Pantheon. Here, amidst a mingled crew, appeared the Greek Pan, his lower extremities goat-like, with a reed in his mouth. To the east, the inter-columniations of the piazza have been built up, and in the centre is a procession of elephants, with their riders, drums, and caparisons, each cut from a single block of marble, of tolerable execution, and about four feet high. Fronting this is a column, similar to that noticed in the other temple, rising from a circular base. The various cells, their altars and their occupants, and the different Jineswars[1] (each about four feet high), in the usual sitting posture, are objects eminently worthy of admiration."[2]

But it is now fitting to contemplate the thoroughly historical foundation upon which repose the whole history of this deified chief, who exhibits in a remarkable manner the soundness of the judgment formed by the learned Principal of Bishop's College, lately quoted. Colebrooke also held the same opinion; Colonel Sleeman likewise, is equally correct on this point,—his opinion is not a *theory* but a *fact*. "The Hindoos," he observes, "think that the incarnation of their three great divinities, were beings infinitely superior to prophets, being in all their attributes and prerogatives equal to the divinities themselves. But we are disposed to think that these incarnations were nothing more than great men, whom their flatterers and poets have exalted into gods. This was the way in which men made their gods in ancient Greece and Egypt. All that the poets have sung of the actions of these men, is now received as revelation from heaven; though nothing can be more monstrous than the actions ascribed to the best incarnation, Crishna, of the best of the gods, Vishnu."[3]

This opinion will be found correct to the letter. Be it remembered that the recording historian of antiquity was the Bhat, or Bard, who received preferment, honour, and wealth, from his royal master. With the death of his prince, or the expulsion of his clans from the once splendid

[1] Statues of the Jaina Pontiffs. [2] Tod's Western Asia, p. 111.
[3] Col. Sleeman's Rambles of an Indian Official, vol. i. p. 61.

seat of their power, all his hopes perished. He who had been to him a god, was for ever removed from him. The sources of princely munificence had become dried up for ever. What wonder then, that gratitude and the saddening memory of the past, should draw forth the lay of homage to the spirit of the chief, whose banners had floated over the soldier-bard, in the fury of that battle storm, which had swept away the last scion of a line of kings.

The history of CRISHNÆUS A'BALANO-J, (CRISSÆUS A' POLLONO-S,) is as thoroughly free from what is called "Myth," as the term GRAIKOI, GRÆCI, or GREEKS. In fact they are bound up with each other. I shall give a brief summary of this Indian Prince and Greek deity, drawn from undoubted sources. The first will be found in the admirable treatise of Professor Wilson, on the History of Cashmir, as drawn from the Raja Tarangini; displaying profound and various learning, guided by sound judgment.

The Raja Tarangini notices the remarkable fact of the intercourse and alliance, political and domestic, which often subsisted between the kings of Cashmir, and the Gangetic provinces; and likewise the facility with which royal retinues, or royal armies, moved from one end of India to another. This fact should be borne in mind, because it will satisfactorily account for many apparent discrepancies in Indian writers. It will be necessary to preface the history of Crishna, with the history of the Graikoi, or Greeks. In the province of the PELASKAS, (PELASGAS,) or people of BIHAR, (PIERIANS,) about ten miles to the south of the latter city, was situated a magnificent, and even in the days of Crishna, an ancient city. It was the Royal city of the MAGEDHANIANS, (MAKEDONIANS,) or kings of MAGADHA; hence its title of the "Raja Griha," or "Royal Mansion." The "people, or clans of Griha," were, according to the regular patronymic form of their language, styled "Grahika," whence the ordinary derivative, "GRAIHAK-ŏs," (GRAIK-OS,) GRÆCUS, or GREEK. "The kings of Magad'ha were Lords Paramount and emperors of India, for above two thousand years, and their country the seat of learning, civilisation, and trade."[1] Raja Griha, was the abode of Jarasandha, the noblest of the Magad'ha kings, a hero, whose name and memory were cherished by the Bud'hists, whose great champion he was. This is the prince whose name is for ever united to the destinies of imperial TROYA, (TROJA,) "THE BUD'HIST KINGDOM;" called also "ILYON," ILION, "OR THE CITY OF THE ILAS," or the Bud'has.[2] The far-famed stream of ZANTHUS, that flowed near the walls of Trājya, was "SANDHUS," the martial chief of the GRAIHAKES, (Greeks,) or clans of Raja Griha. "Nonnus, in his Dionysiacs shows, that Jara SANDHA, literally, old Sanda,[3] Maharaja of India, and whom he well describes, when he says, that Marrheus, [the Greek way of writing Maha-Raj',] the emperor of India, who was called Sandes, was contemporary with Minos, and his Bacchus is the same with Bhagwan in the character of Crishna."[4]

Again: "Rajagriha was the abode of Jarasandha, the first of the Magad'ha kings, who was slain by the sons of Pandu, Arjuna, and Balarama. Rajagriha is described as situated amongst five mountains, which formed as it were its walls. It was described at the time of Fa Hian's visit, A. D. 393. And we need not be surprised therefore, if fifteen centuries should have effaced all traces of a city which was one of the most ancient and celebrated in the India of the Hindus."[5]

[1] Col. Wilford, *As. Res.*, vol. ix. 82.

[2] *Ila*, the son of Budha. Ilyān (Ilion), the sons of Budha.

[3] The poetical derivation is from *Jara*, a female demon, and *sandha*, connection. "He was born in two halves, which were put together by the Raksha Jara."—WILSON'S *Sans. Lex.*

[4] Wilford, *As. Res.*—"On the Kings of Magadha."

[5] Profess. Wilson on Early Hindu Navigation, in his account of Remusat's Trans. of Foe Kue Kí; being the Travels of Fa Hian.

I cannot more clearly portray the course of events connected with the Raja GRÆHAKOI, (GRÆCI,) Jara SANDHUS, (ZANTHUS,) and CRISHNA, (CRISSA,) or A' BALANO-J, (APOLLONO-S,) than by presenting the reader with a notice of them contained in the masterly summary of the Raja Tarangini, of Professor Wilson. It will be found in the 15th Vol. of Asiatic Besearches, where Gonerda the king of Cashmir, and son-in-law of Jarasandha, is noticed in connection with the latter prince.

"Although the name of Gonerda does not appear in the Mahabharat, yet there is an account of an inveterate and sanguinary war between Jarasandha and Crishna, in the course of which a battle on the Yamuna took place, when Hamsa and Dimbica, two princes in alliance with the former, were killed. Hamsa was defeated by Balarama, driven into the Yamuna, and drowned. The cause and course of this war are narrated in the Mahabharat with great appearance of probability, and throw considerable light on the history of Crishna, and of India in his time; its substance may therefore not be unacceptable. Jarasandha, King of Magadha, is described as a powerful prince; he held in alliance or subjection Sisupala, King of Chedi; Vacra, or Vacradanta, King of Carusha, the powerful prince of the Yavanas; Bhagadatta King of the South and West; the Kings of Banga and Pundra, of the Surasenas, Bhadracaras, Bodhus, Salwas, Parawaras, Sust'halas, Mucutas, Pulindas, Salwayanas, Cuntyas, Southern Panchalas, and Eastern Cosalas, and he had driven eighteen families of the Northern Bhojas to the westward, and the Matsyas to the south. Cansa, King of Mat'hura, was married to the daughter of Jarasandha, and it was to revenge the murder of his son-in-law that the latter levied war upon Crishna. According to the Mahabharat, this war continued for three years, and in the Bhaghavat it is said that Jarasandha besieged

Mat'hura eighteen times. Both authorities agree in the result. Crishna was obliged to fly, and take refuge with his family and followers in a strong place on the west coast of India, where he built the city of Dwaraca. Jarasandha's power was an insuperable obstacle to the performance of the Rajasuya sacrifice, or in other words to his pretensions to be considered supreme monarch of India. This impediment was sagaciously interwoven by Crishna with his own quarrel, and induced the Pandava princes to arm in his behalf. Accompanied by Bhima and Arjuna, Crishna entered Behar by a circuitous route, passing under the hills by Gorakhapura and Tirhut, and he thence appears to have taken Jarasandha unprepared for defence; the text, when reduced to common sense, importing that the monarch was surprised in his capital, and, after a conflict of some days, killed in a single combat by Bhima. The occurrence does not appear to have produced the expected consequence, as it was undoubtedly one of the causes of the great war between the Pandava and Caurava princes; one of the effects of which was to prevent Crishna from recovering the territory he had murdered his uncle to obtain; Karna, the illegitimate son of Koonti, the daughter of Sura, King of Mathura, who appears to have held that territory after Jarasandha's death, being probably placed, and undoubtedly maintained in it by the Caurava princes, to whom he was a faithful and valuable ally. These occurrences furnish a satisfactory clue to the close confederacy that subsisted between Crishna and the Pandava brethren."

Agreeably to the whole tenor of ancient clanship, the process of deification forthwith began with Jarasandha, as it did in the case of Crishna. Nor is this difficult to account for. The population of Griha, or the Graihakas, were Bud'hists, one of whose doctrines was the transmigration of souls; to be the king of a Bud'hist land, implied the being a Bud'hist Saint—and a Bud'hist Saint completely answers to that ardent wish of the oriental vizier, "Oh king, LIVE FOR EVER!" Martial games and solemn festivals long cherished the memory of the Emperor of the GRAIHAKAS, as they did the record of their chiefs, after their emigration to Europe, and their settlement in Greece. "There among the Raja Griha Mountains, the unfortunate Jarasandha had a palace, near some hot springs, where he generally resided; some remains of it are to be seen to this day, and it is considered as a place of worship. The Puja is there performed, first in honour of Crishna and the five Pandavas; then with flowers, in honour of old Sandha, and his son, Lahadeva. There, in memory of the unfortunate hero, martial games are annually exhibited. They were celebrated with great solemnity; people came from distant parts; and during the time they lasted a fair was held there. The games, the fair, and the place were famous throughout all India."[1]

Here, then, the historian is presented with a primitive population in Hellas, not only from the Himalayas, but from Pelasa, Maghada, or Bahar, with corresponding clans to enter Greece, and the cherished memory of their chiefs, as the foundation of one of the godships of Hellas. Though Baladeva, the elder brother of Crishna, who was supposed to have perished in crossing the Himalayan mountains, succeeded ultimately in reaching Greece, where his renown became great, Crishna was doomed to perish in a land far distant from that country. Baladeva, Yudishtra, and Crishna are represented, after their expulsion from India, as feeling all the pangs of sorrow and repentance for the blood their ambition had shed, though in defence of their right.

[1] Col. Wilford, *As. Res.*, vol. x. p. 8.

"Thus wandering from one *teerut*, or place of pilgrimage, to another, he with his friends, Arjuna, Yudishtra (the abdicated paramount sovereign of India), and Baldeva, approached the sacred soil around the shrine of Somnath. Having performed his ablutions in the holy *Triveni* Kanya, he took shelter from the noon-tide heat under an umbrageous Pepul, and while he slept, a forester, Bhil, (says the legend), mistaking the Padma, or lotus-like mark, on the sole of his feet, for the eye of a deer, sped an arrow to the mark. When his kinsmen returned, they found that life was extinct. For a long time Baldeva would not part from the corpse, but at length they gave it sepulture at the point of juncture of the three streams. A Pepul sapling, averred to be 'a scion of the original tree,' marks the spot where the Hindu Apollo expired, and a flight of steps conducts to the bed of the 'golden' Hiranya for the pilgrim to lustrate himself. This place of purification bears the name of Swerga Dwarra, or door of bliss, and contends with that of Deva Puttun for superior efficacy in absolving from sin."[1] Thus far have I conducted the hero of the clans of the LADACAI-MEN (LACADÆ-MON), till, from the adored chief of his tribe, he has become the adored divinity of a people. In fact it was essential, on Bud'histic principles, that this should be the case—the Jaina Prince, or son of JEYUS, the great Jeenos (Zeenos) or Victor over self and over all the world, could never be mortal. He might be removed from their sight—his image only might remain—but somewhere he, the saintly prince, *did* exist: and his invisible power was to be invoked and to be obtained. The war of the Cooroos and the Pandoos, though ostensibly political, was in *reality* a struggle between the Bud'histic and Brahminical party. The success of the latter was complete. Crishna, Baladeva, and Yudishtra, the champions of the Heri or Bud'hist Faith, had become

[1] Tod's Western Asia.

exiles; one of this race of priestly warriors—Crishna—we have seen sinking deeply lamented in a foreign land. "All the traditions of the Hindus," says Troyer, "are filled with wars, in which religion certainly had its share. I have shown this sufficiently already, without being obliged to go back so far as the contests between the Suras and the Asuras, the gods and the demons. At the commencement of the Kali Yuga, we see the nations in the west in arms against those of Central Asia. This variety of creeds prevailing in the Panjab especially, by no means excludes Buddhism,[1] traces of which are detected in the early portion of the history of Cashmere."[2] To the LAO-CANYIANS, (LA'CONIANS,) Crishna was the ever "præsens divus." His priest, with the aid of the DELBHAI (DELPHOI), the clan of ARJUNA, or the 'Aegeans, succeeded in rearing a wealthy shrine favourable at once to their own aggrandisement and their saint's renown. Its situation could not be more imposing. Dwarica, near the COR 'INDUS, was one of the last strongholds to which Crishna, the Yadu Nat'h, or Lord of the Yadus, retreated, and it is in connection with the Sinus CORINTHIACUS that the name, Crissæus Sinus or the Crishnæan Bay, constantly recurs to our minds. The grandeur, beauty, and romantic scenery surrounding the immediate locality of Crissa and the Crissæan Bay cannot be surpassed. "Of the beauty of this scene," writes Wordsworth,[3] "and of the peculiar features which distinguish it, no better or more accurate description can be given than that which is contained in the following lines of Milton, to whose imagination, when he composed them, a landscape presented itself similar to that which

[1] The ancient Budha of Mr. Charles Ritter (Die Vorhalle Europæischer Völkergeschichten) finds support in the historial legends of the Hindus.

[2] Troyer on the Ramayuna, *As. Journ.*; Oct., 1844, p. 514.

[3] Greece, Pictorial and Descriptive, by C. Wordsworth, D.D., p. 23.

the traveller beholds from the ruins of the citadel of Crisso:—

> "It was a mountain at whose verdant feet,
> A spacious plain, outstretch'd in circuit wide,
> Lay pleasant: from his side two rivers flow'd,
> The one winding, the other straight, and left between
> Fair champaign with less rivers intervein'd,
> Then meeting join'd their tribute to the sea;
> Fertile of corn the glebe, of oil and wine;
> With herds the pastures throng'd, with flocks the hills;
> Huge cities and high tower'd, that well might seem
> The seats of mightiest monarchs."

The very presence of the terrestrial divinities of PARNASSUS, the Jaina Saints of the neighbourhood of Bamian (afterwards the BOMIENSES of Hellas), would show the future destination of the mountain. Part of the PAR-O-PAMISUS (the HILL OF BAMIAN), is called PARNASSUS. "These mountains are called Devanica, because they are so full of devas or gods, called 'Gods of the Earth,' Bhu Devas. They lived according to the Puranas, in bowers or huts, called PARNASAS, because they were made of leaves"[1] (PARNAS). A day soon came, however, when a magnificent shrine was to rise over the humble Parnasas of the primitive hermit of the cave.

In the devotional feeling of Hellas, however secondary might have been the state and dignity of APOLLO,[2] no deity so prominently called forth the piety of his votaries, and none ever elicited such mingled sympathy and awe. From the first settlement, the innate elegance of Hellenic genius was called forth by the patron god of music and of poetry: by the latter, faith in the oracles of "THE HAYA LORD" (PHŒBUS),[3] was made more implicit, and devotion more profound. This twofold character of graceful dignity

[1] Col. Wilford, *As. Res.*, vol. vi. p. 497.

[2] See my Preliminary view of Greek Mythology, in Vol. i. Hist. Greece, Ency—clopædia Metropolitana.

[3] *Pi-Hya-pus*, the Hya-chief.

and religious force is beautifully portrayed by the blind bard of the Isle of Delos, at whose inspiring note creation gives forth the trumpet-call of glorious praise. After struggling with the majesty of his theme, the poet bursts forth with a magnificent exordium, to which it is difficult to do justice in a translation.

> "With thee each Rock, each Headland Brow
> Of Lofty Mountains rang;
> While Rivers in their seaward flow,
> And Toppling Cliffs with waves below,
> And Creeks, thy praises sang." [1]

But how came it to pass, that a deity of such majesty and power should be born in so rugged a spot as the Isle of Delos?[2] This the poet proceeds to explain, and that explanation is in perfect harmony with the history already given of the prior antiquity of the Solar worship in Hellas. This son of LETO or of the LEH-TĀN[3] (LA-TON-A), this divinised Jaina Lord of the LADACAI-MEN (LACEDAI-MON), the "people of CANYA (LA'CONYANS") was with great difficulty accepted as the prophetic-god of Hellas. The rugged Isle of Delos was the only asylum that could be gained for the worship of the Ladaki deity and hero. When once, however, that religious system had a fair opportunity of gaining proselytes, its progress was rapid. The same ingenuity which was so profitable in the case of Demeter and Peisistratus again came to the aid of the priesthood of Delphi, while their poets spread his fame as a potentate possessed of power over the elements. They sang how the Princely Jaina Saint advanced towards the verge of Parnassus amid lofty and impending cliffs, where

[1] "Πᾶσαι δε σκοπιαί τοι ἅδον καὶ πρώονες ἆκροι
Ὑψηλῶν ὀρέων, ποταμοί θ' ἅλαδε προρέοντες,
Ἀκταί τ' είς ἅλα κεκλιμέναι, λιμενές τε θαλάσσης."
Hymn, Apoll. 22—24.

[2] V. 27, *ut supra.*

[3] The land of Leh, or Ladac.

reigned an awful silence,—how he approached the deep recesses of that hallowed region, to select the spot destined for his sacred shrine,—how he found its rocky fountain guarded by a tremendous Naga PUTHA,[1] or BUD'HA of the Serpent race;—and of the god's triumph over the monster did they sing likewise. It was the very Priest of the Serpent Tribe[2] that had trained to Heretical practices the impious faction of TU-PHON (TU-PHO) or TIBET! The identical renegade who had been driven down to the Tartar's Land by the CERAUNAS of the GRAND LAMA (SALMON), and the GREAT LAMA CHIEFS (OLĀM-POS)! But the crowning triumph of the god was the establishment of a priesthood for his wealthy shrine. If we are guided by the Jaina poet, it was as miraculous a display of his divinity as any to be met with in the history of the saints in the middle ages. The deity, from his lofty throne, beholds a company of mariners plying their busy way from the coasts of Crete, and bound to the Peloponnesus. Exerting that miraculous power which was ever his, from incarnation to incarnation, the form of the Lama Prince instantly changes. He rends the air in his rapid flight from the mountain brow, and, plunging in the sparkling waves, becomes a huge dolphin. He throws the foam on high, and shakes the vessel to its centre.

Lo! the god drives the ship with a mighty hurricane along the rugged coast of the Peloponnesus. On, on she glides with resistless power through the foaming Corinthian gulf, till she reaches the harbour of Crissa, where she grounds. A youth of glorious form is seen on the shore: he observes the terror of the crew, and soothingly enquires whence they came, and their object. The Cretan captain

[1] *Putho* (Pytha), *Bud'ha*; *Naga* (snakes) are used in contradistinction to the pious or good.

[2] Heri, or Bud'hi, carries, as his distinctive mark, a serpent twined round a staff. *Ceraunos*, thunder; *Cerunas*, Jainas.

relates how his voyage had been marvellous—irresistible! The Princely Minstrel-Saint now reveals himself, declaring his own agency in the miraculous voyage and their future exalted functions. To their loved native land never are they to think of returning: all is to be given up to the honour of his glorious shrine. They show a cheerful obedience—the sails are furled—the ship drawn high upon the beach. By the side of their sable bark is reared an altar, and, pouring out a libation to the ever-present Jaina Saints, they indulge the genial banquet, till it beseems their princely entertainer to intimate their departure.

> "Now nobly feasted, cheered with wine,
> Led by the Jaina Prince divine,
> That wondrous Harper, Lyre in hand,
> Strode grandly on: the Cretan band
> Danced following to the Holy Land.
> Crete's Pæan-minstrels hymn'd the god;
> Within whose breasts the mellow flood
> Of song the goddess Muse had pour'd:
> Their step untoil'd that upwards soar'd,
> Soon scaled Parnassus' crested hill,
> The lovely spot where they should dwell,
> By crowding pilgrims honour'd still.[1]

All this and more sings the poet in his firm conviction of the god-like might of his great divinity. Then follows

> [1] Αὐτὰρ ἐπεὶ πόσιος καὶ ἐδητύος ἐξ ἔρον ἕντο
> Βάν ῥ' ἴμεν· ἦρχε δ' ἄρα σφιν ἄναξ, Διος υἱὸς, 'Απόλλων·
> Φόρμιγγ' ἐν χείρεσσιν ἔχων, ἀγατὸν κιθαρίζων,
> Καλὰ καὶ ὕψι βιβάς οἱ δὲ ῥήσσοντες ἕποντο
> Κρῆτες πρὸς Πυθώ, καὶ ἰηπαήον' ἄειδον
> Οἷοι τε Κρητῶν παιήονες, δισίτε Μοῦσα
> 'Εν στήθεσσιν ἔθηκε θεὰ μελίγηρυν ἀοιδήν
> ῎Ακμητοι δὲ λόφον προσέβαν ποσίν, αἶψα δ' ἵκοντο
> Παρνησὸν καὶ χῶρον ἐπήρατον, ἔνθ' ἀρ' ἔμελλον
> Οἰκήσεν πολλοῖσι τε τετιμένοι ἀνθρωπόισιν.

[1] See my Mythology of Greece, in Vol. i. of Hist. of Greece,—Encyclopædia Metropolitana.

the procession of the pilgrim bands, and the inauguration of the most ancient monastic foundation of Hellas, and the establishment of the Lamaic Mission.

Such in behalf of his saintly patron, such for the glory of that dignified being, is the record of the Jaina poet of Greece. The miracles effected by this exalted saint are poetical; the establishment of a wealthy shrine, historical. To request a rational being to "go into the *evidences*" of the *poetical*, to the utter neglect of the *historical*, is a melancholy compliment to the understanding. Yet such is the Lamaism of the East and of the West. Men who beg of their fellows this mental prostration, may enlarge the sacella of mythology,—may make silver shrines for Diana, but can never rear the temple of History. It is this very feature, common to the Bud'hism of Greece and to the Bud'hism of Rome, to the Delphi of the blind Greek, and the Vatican of the blind Roman,[1] that has cast a veil over the truth of time. The super-naturalist claims all, and injured reason grants none. And yet the truth of *personality* remains, while the legend is utterly fabulous. Let this be tested by the parent Theological Institutes of the city of Rāma. The *agency* of an ingenious priesthood will not be doubted—that is clear; the evidence, however, of the actual performance of the wonderful miracles said to have been performed, rests upon a foundation no deeper than that of an hierarchic corporation. I present the reader with an extract of one of those abundant miracles with which the Bud'hist Church is absolutely hung from end to end. It is taken from the Mahawanso, a work of authentic standing in the Bud'histic sacred books of Ceylon. It is the history of the inauguration of a relic, and the building of a shrine for its reception; acts of imaginary piety, for which the

[1] Τυφλὸς ἀνὴρ, οἰκεῖ δε Χίῳ ἐνὶ παιπαλόεσσῃ.—*Hymn. Apoll.* 172.

Bud'hists, in the highest antiquity, as well as in more modern time, have been celebrated.

"The vanquisher of foes, (Dutthagámini,) having perfected the works to be executed within the relic receptacle, convening an assembly of the priesthood, thus addressed them: 'The works that were to be executed by me in the relic receptacle, are completed; to-morrow I shall enshrine the relics. Lords, bear in mind the relics.' The monarch having thus delivered himself, returned to the city. Thereupon the priesthood consulted together, as to the priest to be selected to bring relics; and they assigned the office of escorting the relics to the disciple named Sónuttaro, who resided in the Pìyá Parawéno, and was master of the six departments of doctrinal knowledge.

"During the pilgrimage (on earth of Budho), the compassionating saviour of the world, this personage had (in a former existence) been a youth of the name Nanduttáro, who having invited his supreme Budho, with his disciples, had entertained them on the banks of the river (Ganges). The divine teacher, with his sacerdotal retinue, embarked there at Payágapattana in a vessel; and the théro Bhaddaji (one of these disciples), master of the six branches of doctrinal knowledge, and endowed with supernatural powers, observing a great whirlpool in the river, thus spoke to the fraternity:—'Here is submerged the golden palace, twenty-five yójanas in extent, which had been occupied by me, in my existence as King Mahápánado,' at the commencement of the "kappo."

"The incredulous among the priests (on board), on approaching the whirlpool in the river, reported the circumstance to the divine teacher. The said divine teacher, addressing himself to the Bhaddaji, said, 'Remove this scepticism of the priesthood.' Thereupon by his supernatural gift, springing up into the air, to the height of seven palmira trees, and stretching out his arm brought to the spot where he was poised, the Dussathúpo in which the dress laid aside by Budho, as Prince Siddhatto, on his entering into priesthood, was enshrined in the Brahmalóka heaven, *for its spiritual welfare,* and exhibited it to the people. Thereafter, having restored it to its former position, returning to the vessel on the river, by his supernatural powers he raised from the bed of the river the submerged palace, by laying hold of it by a pinnacle with his toes, and having exhibited it to the people, threw it back there. The youth Nanduttáro seeing the miracle spontaneously, arrived at this conviction, 'It will be permitted to me to bring away a relic appropriated by another.'"

The procession now sets out, attended with the most gorgeous accompaniments; the pomp of military music, and the admiring homage of myriads.

"The priest Sónuttaro, while yet at his parieweno, hearing for the first time the burst of the musical sounds which announced the procession to be in motion, instantly diving into the earth, and proceeding subterraneously to the Land of Nágas, there presented himself to the Nága Rája. The Nága king, rising from his throne, and reverentially bowing down to him, seated him thereon; and, having shown him every mark of respect, inquired from what land he had come. On his having explained himself, he then asked the théro for what purpose he had come; who, after detailing all the principal objects, then delivered the message of the priesthood:—'For the purpose of enshrining at the Mahá Thupo, pursuant to the predictive injunction of Buddho; 'do thou surrender to me the relics which have fallen into thy hands.' On hearing this demand, the Nága Rája, plunged into the deepest consternation, thus thought, 'surely this sanctified character is endowed with power to obtain them by forcible means; therefore it is expedient that the relics should be transferred to some other place;' and secretly signified to his nephew, who was standing by, 'By some means or other, let this be done.' That individual, whose name was Wásuladatto, understanding his uncle's intention, hastening to the relic apartment, swallowed the relic casket; and, repairing to the foot of Mount Méru and by his supernatural powers extending his own dimensions, to three hundred yójanas broad, coiling himself up, remained there. This preternaturally gifted Nága, spreading out thousands of hoods, and retaining his coiled-up position, emitted smoke and lightning; and calling forth thousands of snakes similar to himself, and encircling himself with them, remained coiled there. On this occasion numerous déwos and nágas assembled at this place, saying, 'Let us witness the contest between these two parties, the snakes and the théro.'

"The uncle, satisfying himself that the relics had been removed by his nephew, thus replied to the théro, 'the relics are not in my possession.' The said théro revealing to the Nága Rája the travels of these relics from the commencement to their arrival in the Land of Nágas, said, 'Give up those relics to me.' The ophite king, in order that he might indicate to the théro that he must search elsewhere, escorting and conducting him to the relic apartment, proved that point to him. The priest, beholding the chétiyo and the chétiyo apartments, both exquisitely constructed, and superbly ornamented in various ways, with every description of treasure, exclaimed, 'All the accumulated treasures in Lanká would fall short of the value of the last step of the stair of this apartment; who shall describe the rest.' The Nága king, forgetting his previous declaration, that the relics were not there, retorted. 'Priest, the removal of a relic from a place where it is preserved in so perfect a manner, to a place inferior in the means of doing honour to it, surely cannot be right?' Sónattero replied: 'Nága, it is not vouchsafed unto you nágas to attain the four superior grades of sanctification; it is quite right, therefore, to remove the relics to a place where the four superior grades of sanctification are attainable. Tatthágatas (Buddhos) are born to redeem beings endowed with existence from the miseries inseparable from sangsára (interminable transmigration). In the present case, also, there is an object of Buddho's to be accomplished. In fulfilment thereof, I remove these relics. On this very day the monarch of Lanká is to effect the enshrinement of the relics. Therefore, without causing unavailing delays, instantly surrender the relics.'

"The Nága insidiously rejoined, 'Lord, as thou of course seest the relics, taking them, begone.' The théro made him repeat that declaration three times. Thereupon, the théro, without moving from that spot, miraculously creating an invisibly attenuated arm, and thrusting its hand down the mouth of the nephew at Mount Méru, instantly possessed himself of the relic casket. Then saying to Kálo, 'Nága, rest thou here,' rending the earth, he reascended at his pariwéno at Anurádhapura.

"The Nága Rája then sent a message to his nephew to bring back the relics, informing him at the same time, 'the priest is gone, completely deceived by us.' In the mean time, the nephew being conscious that the casket was no longer in his stomach, returning, imparted the same to his uncle, with loud lamentations. Then it was that the Nága Rája, exclaiming, 'It is we who are deceived,' wept. The afflicted nágas also all mourned the loss of the relic.

"The déwos assembled at Méru, to witness the conflict, exulting at the priest's victory over the nága, and making offerings to the relics, accompanied him thither.

"The nágas, who were in the deepest affliction at the

removal of the relics, also, presenting themselves, full of lamentation, to the théro (at Anurádhapura), wept. The priesthood, out of compassion to them, bestowed on them a trifling relic. They delighted thereat, departing to the Land of Nágas, brought back treasures worthy of being presented as offerings."[1]

Passages innumerable might be multiplied, illustrative of this marvellous power of working miracles, as a standing proof of the existence of a True Church amongst that nation which is favoured by such popular exhibitions. The very recondite faculty of cleaving the earth, and thereby producing an extemporaneous as well as subterraneous passage for substantial flesh and blood —the still more recondite faculty of creating an invisible arm, an ingenious forceps, to extract a casket of relics from within the clay walls of humanity, are poetical performances, such as have been, and are the standard means of upholding the divinity of Lamaism in the east and west. I cannot agree with Mr. Grote in his observation, that "the great religious movement of the Reformation, and the gradual formation of critical and philosophical habits in the modern mind, have caused these legends of the saints, once the charmed and cherished creed of a numerous public, to pass altogether out of credit, without even being regarded, among Protestants, at least, as worthy of a formal scrutiny into the evidence—a proof of the transitory value of public belief, however sincere and fervent, as a certificate of historical truth, if it be blended with religious predispositions."[2] The Bud'histic tribes, still living on the banks of the Isis, present a practical refutation of this remark, unless, possibly, their habits may not be so philosophical nor quite so critical as those described in the valuable work just quoted.

[1] Mahawanso, xxxi. p. 183—189.

[2] Grote's Hist. Greece, vol. i. p. 633.

How much indebted are some sections of the European population to the Lamaism of Ladac and the Ladacai-men (Lacademonians), those sons of Crishna, the Apollo of Greece, will be at once seen from the able treatise of H. T. Prinsep, Esq. That author thus writes:—

"The Boodhists of the west, accepting Christianity on its first announcement, at once introduced the rites and observances which for centuries had already existed in India. From that country Christianity derived its monarchical institutions, its forms of ritual, and Church service; its councils or convocations to settle schisms on points of faith; its worship of relics, and working of miracles through them; and much of the discipline and of the dress of the clergy, even to the shaven heads of the monks and friars. It would require an entire volume to compare in details the several points of similarity, and to trace divergence from the more ancient doctrine and practice in the creed and forms of ritual ultimately adopted by the Churches of the west. It is enough for our present purpose to establish the superior antiquity of the one, found to exhibit so many points of close correspondence. But, independently of the similarity of doctrine, of ritual, and of institutions, we find that Boodhism has run in the east a very analogous course with Romanism in the west. Having its classes of specially initiated and ordained teachers, it spread widely amongst the population before it was adopted and made a state religion by the reigning sovereigns. It was torn in pieces by heresies and schisms on trivial observances and doctrinal points, till one sect having enlisted the power of the state on its side, persecuted and expelled its opponents, to the weakening and ultimate ruin of the Church and its authority. The subserviency of the temporal to the spiritual power was universally preached by this separate initiated class; and by its presumptuous reliance on their influence over the populace, priests in the east, as in the west, have humbled and destroyed the kingly power, and occasionally, when circumstances favoured the pretension, have established a priestly government, such as we see in Tibet in entire supercession of the ordinary temporal authority, and have sought to reserve the administration of all affairs for the special class of initiated or ordained. But the consequence in the east has been the same as in the west. The priestly governments have been unable to maintain themselves without foreign support; priestly domination has been found quite incompatible with energetic military action, which always has been, and always must be, the source of real political power. The great Lamas of Tibet are the protected minions of China, just as the Pope of Rome is dependent to-day on France, and was recently on Austria, notwithstanding the reverence in which the Papal name and spiritual authority is still held by vast populations."[1]

The work just quoted contains a valuable though compendious view of the Lamaic establishments, which run up to an antiquity far surpassing that of which we have any conception from the ordinary sources of history. The races of which it treats have been already contemplated in Greece, Egypt, and Palestine. In another point of view, also, may they be contemplated, viz., as being the parent source of much of that artistic mode of devotion which appears in many parts of Europe. This point, however, has been brought forward in so interesting a way, that I shall make no apology in this place for its introduction.

It is contained in an able review of the Travels of MM. Huc and Gabet, in Mongolia and Tartary, whither they had gone to extend the sphere of their usefulness. "These volumes," writes the reviewer, "contain the most detailed and complete account of

[1] H. Prinsep, Esq., "Mongolia and Tartary."

Lamanism that we remember ever to have met with; and they confirm, on the authority of these Romish priests themselves, the astonishing resemblance that exists between the external rites and institutions of Bud'hism and those of the Church of Rome. Besides celibacy, fasting, and prayers for the dead, there are enshrined relics, holy water, incense, candles in broad day, rosaries of beads counted in praying, worship of saints, processions, and a monastic habit, resembling that of the mendicant orders. Although our worthy missionaries call the images of Lamanism *idols*, and the Romish idols *images*, we do not think the distinction is worth much, and therefore may throw in this item with the rest; the more especially, as on the summary principle of *inveniam viam aut faciam*, the commandment against idol worship has been thrust bodily out of *their* decalogue by the Romanists, as may be seen from any copy of the Missal. It is remarkable that these very missionaries had an image made for their own adoration, from a European model, at a place on their journey, where a huge image of Bud'ha had just been cast, and sent off to Lhassa. Thus the object of their worship was a molten image, the work not only of men's, but Pagan hands, employed indifferently for either Bud'hism or Romanism. It was at once curious, and an intrinsic lesson to unprejudiced minds, to observe that M. Huc, while he indulges in pleasantries, at the expense of the Bud'hists, entirely forgets how applicable his sarcasms are to his own side of the question. After describing an assembly in a college of Lamas, where the explanations given by the priests or professors on certain points of their religion, proved as vague and incomprehensible as the thing to be explained, he adds, 'On est, du reste, convaincu que la sublimité d'une doctrine est en raison directe de son obscurité et de son impénétrabilité.' Let us only suppose M. Huc expounding to these Lamas the dogma of Transubstantiation, and adding, in testimony of its truth, that St. Ignatius Loyola, with eye-sight sharpened by faith, declared he actually *saw* the farinaceous substance changing itself into flesh. 'Les hommes,' observes our author, in another place, 'sont partout les mêmes!' The jokes, in which M. Huc indulges against the devotees and recluses of Bud'hism, are similar to what have been repeated a thousand times with reference to those of Romanism:—'Ce jeune lama de vingt-quatre ans, était un gros gaillard bien membré, et dont la lourde et épaisse figure l'accusait de faire dans son étroit réduit une forte consommation de beurre. Nous ne pouvions jamais le voir mettre le nez à la porte de sa case, sans songer à ce rat de La Fontaine qui par dévotion s'etait retiré dans un fromage de Hollande.' The monasteries of the Lamas, resembling as they do in so many respects those of the Romanists, differ from them on some few points. The members are all subject to the same rule, and the same discipline, but they do not seem to live to the same extent in community; and exclusive rights of property prevail among them. Our missionaries passed some months in these establishments. Besides His Holiness the Supreme Lama, at Lhassa, there are Grand Lamas, who derive their investiture from him, and descend from past ages in uninterrupted succession. With reference to one of these, it is observed:—'Si la personne du grand Lama nous frappa peu, il n'en fut pas ainsi de son costume, qui était rigoureusement celui des évèques; il portait sur sa tête une mitre jaune; un long bâton en forme de crosse (crosier) était dans sa main droite; et ses épaules etáit recouvertes d'un manteau en taffetas violet, retenu sur la poitrine par une agraffe, et semblable en tout à une chape. Dans la suite, nous aurons à signaler de nombreux rapports entre le culte Catholique et les cérémonies Lamanesques.'

"M. Huc afterwards recapitulates as follows :—'La crosse, la mitre, la Dalmatique, la chape ou pluvial, que les Grands Lamas portent en voyage, ou lorsqu'ils font quelque cérémonie hors du temple ; l'office à deux choeurs, la psalmodie, les exorcismes, l'encensoir soutenu par cinq chaînes, et pouvant s'ouvrir et se fermer à volonté ; les bénédictions données par les Lamas en étendant la main droite sur la tête des fidèles ; le chapelet, le célibat ecclésiastique, les retraites spirituelles, le culte des saints, les jeûnes, les processions, les litanies, l'eau bénite ; voilà autant de rapports que les boudhistes ont avec nous.' He might have added, that they likewise have a goddess, whom they call Tienhow, literally *regina cœli*, 'Queen of Heaven ;' but with a different legend. Our author very naturally endeavours to persuade himself and his readers that by some process of diablerie these things have been borrowed from his own Church ; but why should we do such violence to the subject, when there is the much easier, more intelligible, and more straight-forward course of deriving both from something older than either ; and, remaining persuaded, as most of us must have been long ago, that the Pagan rites and Pontifex Maximus of the modern Rome represent, in outward fashion, the Paganism and Pontifex Maximus of the ancient ? Strange to say, instead of blinking the matter, a sort of parallel has often been studiously preserved and paraded, as when the Pantheon, the temple of 'all the gods,' was consecrated by Pope Boniface to 'all the Saints.' Is it necessary for us to compare the annual sprinkling of horses with holy water to the like process at the Circensian games—the costly gifts to Loretto to the like gifts at Delphi—the nuns to the *virgines sanctæ* of old Rome—the shrine of 'Maria in triviis' to the like rural shrines of more ancient idols—the flagellant (whose self-discipline Sancho so dexterously mitigated in his own case) to the practices of the priests of Isis? In running the parallel, the only difficulty is where to stop. It is impossible to look at innumerable votive pictures and tablets which conceal, without adorning, the walls and pillars of many a church at Rome, and not to think of

> 'nam posse mederi
> Picta docet templis multa tabella tuis.'

"To instance a higher department of art—as the old artist, in painting his Venus, is said to have combined 'each look that charmed him in the fair of Greece,' so the Italian painters have sometimes immortalised the features of their own mistresses in pictures of saints and martyrs, intended to adorn churches. In its modern traits, as well as in its ancient, Lamanism maintains its resemblance to Romanism. Prodigies and miracles of constant occurrence come to the aid of the priesthood and maintain their influence over the stupid multitude. Some of the instances adduced are palpable cases of ingenious jugglery; but M. Huc, with characteristic facility, believes in the fact while he attributes it to the agency of the devil:—'Une philosophie purement humaine rejettera sans doute des faits semblables, on les mettra sans balancer sur le compte des fourberies lamanesques. Pour nous, missionaires catholiques, nous croyons que le grand menteur qui trompa autrefois nos premiers parents dans le paradis terrestre, poursuit toujours dans le monde son système de mensonge; celui qui avait la puissance de soutenir dans les airs Simon le Magicien, peut bien encore aujourd'hui parler aux hommes par la bouche d'un enfant, a peu d'entretenir la foi de ses adorateurs.'

"Whatever Protestants may think and say of the means by which the Romish Church has maintained and extended its influence over the masses of mankind, it is impossible to deny the thorough knowledge of human nature, on which all its measures have been calculated. The same causes which have aided it so long against the reforms of a pure faith, are likely to aid it much longer; and we really see very little chance of a change. The priestly array, the lighted tapers, and the histrionic pantomime, are aided by smoking censers, graven images, and all the paraphernalia by which so many temples of so many different religions have been before distinguished. We entirely agree with M. Huc, that the Romish Church has a fair field for proselytism in the vast regions where Bud'hism at present prevails. In external forms, the transition is the easiest possible; and during his short residence at Lhassa, he remarked :—'Il nous semblait toujours que la beauté de nos cérémonies eût agi puissamment sur ce peuple, si avide de tout ce qui tient au *culte extérieur*.'

"If the new system cannot be made to supersede the old, it may at least be grafted upon it, as experience has already proved at our own colony of Ceylon; for Romanism has sometimes been satisfied with a part, where the whole was attainable. In a recent work by Sir Emerson Tennent, he observes of the early converts in that island to the Romish Church, 'there is no reason to doubt that, along with the profession of the new faith, the majority of them, like the Singalese of the present day, cherished with still closer attachment, the superstitions of Bud'hism; and he attributes the ease of their external conversion to the attractions of a religion, which, in point of pomp and magnificence, surpassed, without materially differing from, the pageantry and processions with which they were accustomed to celebrate the festivals of their own national worship. We may, however, charitably and reasonably suppose, that the present emissaries of Rome would stop short of the complaisant conformity of their Jesuit predecessors, who, according to the Abbé Dubois, conducted the images of the Virgin and Saviour on triumphal cars, imitated from the orgies of Jaggernath, and introduced the dancers of the Brahminical rites into the ceremonial of the Church."[1]

Let us hear another writer upon this subject of the Western Bud'hism and its ancient connection with Lamaism, as descending to the present days.

"Amongst the heathen, every shrine had its priest; and as these priests were generally maintained by the offerings brought to the altars of their respective patrons, they, of course, became deeply pledged to uphold a system which furnished them with the means of subsistence, if not of profusion.

"It is lamentable to observe in how many particulars this picture is true of modern Italy and Sicily; where, in spite of that knowledge of the one and only God which revelation has communicated, the same tendency to polytheism, (for the worship of saints has all the character of that creed in practice, however ingeniously it may be explained,) is still manifested; and where the same abuses as those which have been already enumerated, and from the same causes, abundantly prevail. On the one hand, impertinent and unworthy solicitations of divine interference; on the other, encouragement in such a practice by self-interested individuals. Priests ill paid, and hoards of friars, mendicants by profession, have been tempted to lay under heavy contribution the credulity of the public; and accordingly we find most cathedrals, as well as nearly all the chapels of the regular clergy, possessed of images or relics said to be endowed with miraculous virtues, while a box is at hand to receive the offerings of those, who, out of gratitude for the past, or hope for the future, are disposed to give their mite for the good of the Church.

"I have seen the poor fishermen at Catania regularly

[1] Edin. Review, April, 1851, p. 411.

greeted on their arrival at the coast with the produce of their day's toil, by the craving voice of a Capuchin, or Franciscan; nor has that been refused to the holy vagrant, which ordinary beggars, though wrung with distress, would have besought in vain. Indeed few persons are so poor as to escape subscribing their quota towards filling the satchels of these men, or so fearless of the consequent anger of heaven as to risk a denial.

"The general effects of this unhappy system have been, to degrade the worship of the Deity, to swell the calendar with saints, to extend the influence of charms, to instigate pilgrimages, to clothe the altar with votive tablets, and to give currency to numbers of miracles which have not a shadow of testimony to their truth. In short, it has made the countries of Italy and Sicily what they are, emblems of the churches in them, replete themselves with beauty, yet serving as vast magazines for objects calculated to excite the devotion of the superstitious; the pity of the wise and good; and the scoffs of the profane." [1]

I subjoin from the authentic source of the Mahawanso, a brief notice of this worship of Lanca; it relates a miracle effected by the celebrated Bo-tree, or Bud'ha tree. The different Bud'hist Saints were accustomed to select particular trees as their special favourites. Hence we read of Zeus selecting the Oak, Athene the Olive.

The Bo-branch is represented as being on a miraculous progress through the country, conferring many blessings, and performing many miracles. Take an instance of one of them. It is not wanting in picturesque effect. "The instant it (the Bo-branch) extricated itself from the hand of man, springing eighty cubits up into the air, self-poised and resplendent, it cast forth a halo of rays of six colours. These enchanting rays illuminating the land, ascended to the Brahma heavens, and continued visible

[1] Blunt's Vestiges of Antiquities, p. 4.

till the setting of the sun." Now mark the effect, for the interest of the Church. "Ten thousand men, stimulated by the sight of these miracles, increasing in sanctification, and attaining the arahat, (the subjugation of sinful passions,) consequently entered into the priesthood."[1] Take again the Apollonic doctrine of *salvation* by the grace of relics. It occurs in a passage, where the Bud'hist Missionary is desired to repair to one of the principal courts of that kingdom. The following was the argument to be urged by this Bud'hist envoy. "King of Devas, thou possessest the right canine tooth-relic, (of Bud'ha,) as well as the right collar bone of the divine teacher. Lord of Devas, demur not in *matters involving the salvation* of the Land of Lanka."[2] Again: "Thus the Saviour of the world, (Budha,) even after he had attained 'Parinibánan,'[3] by means of a corporeal relic, performed infinite acts to the utmost perfection, for the *spiritual comfort* and mundane prosperity of mankind. While the vanquisher [JEYUS,] yet lived, what must he not have done!"[4]

Again, "on the south-eastern branch" (this was after the descent of the sacred tree), "a fruit manifested itself, and ripened in the utmost perfection. The Théro,[5] taking up that fruit as it fell, gave it to the king to plant. The monarch planted it in a golden vase, filled with odoriferous soil, which was prepared at the Mahásano. While they were all still gazing at it, eight sprouting shoots were produced, and became vigorous plants, four cubits high each." This miracle was greatly to the advantage of the true Church of Lanka, since Anulá, together with her retinue of five hundred virgins, and five hundred women

[1] Mahawanso, 118.

[2] Ibid., p. 105.

[3] Final emancipation, the object of the MOKSH'TAI (MUSTAI), of the Eleusinian. Its general meaning here, is "after Bud'has death.

[4] Mahawanso, p. 109.

[5] Priest: *Hai-Théros* (aitheros), the Hya priest, governed by *Jinos* (Zeenos) or Jaina Pontiffs.

[6] Mahawanso, p. 109.

of the palace, entered into the order of priesthood, in the community of the Théri (Abbess) Sanghamittá, and attaining the sanctification of Arahat,[1] or the subjugation of sinful passions.

Let us now turn to the Western Lamaism. Here St. Columban employs a crow to bring back the gloves which he had lost; on another occasion he as miraculously prevents the beer from flowing from a cask which had been bored. On this, Mr. Grote justly remarks, "The miracle by which St. Columban employed the raven to fetch back his lost gloves, is exactly in the character of the Homeric and Hesiodic age: the earnest faith, as well as the reverential sympathy, between the Homeric man and Zeus, or Athênê, is indicated by the invocation of their aid, for his own sufferings, and in his own need of danger."[2]

The state of Lamaic society I have already exhibited in primitive Greece, and the Lamaic population, I have already shown, especially in Thessaly, the land of miracles, will satisfactorily account for the legends of our Hierarchy of the Senses. Again, let us hear no mean authority for the Lamaism of the West. "St. Raymond was transported over the sea on his cloak; St. Andrew[3] shone *brightly* in the *dark*."[4] What says the Lama patriarch of the East?

"The Attock was formerly no barrier to the hierarchs of Bud'ha, who, blending fable and magic (a grand ingredient in their faith) with tradition, have it written that when Sur-Acharya used to visit his flocks west of the Indus, he floated himself across the stream upon his mantle."[5] Now observe the miracle of shining. "Many Asankyas (vast numbers) of paid labourers, in the course

[1] "From *ari*, foes, *i.e.* sinful passions; *Hattattá*, being destroyed or overcome."—*Mahawanso, Gloss.* p. 2.

[2] Grote's Hist. Greece, vol. i. p. 633.

[3] See Dr. Newman's Lectures, or Birmingham Mythology, pp. 286, 287.

[4] N.B. This miracle of *shining* in the *dark* has been since performed at Oxford very frequently. About one hundred cases have been already recorded.

[5] Tod's Western Asia, p. 277.

of the construction of the Thu'po (shrine for a relic), becoming converts to the faith, went to Sugato (Bud'ha). The wise man bearing in mind that by conversion alone to the faith, the supreme reward of being born in heaven is obtained, *should make offerings also at the Thu'po.* Two women who had worked for hire at this place, after the completion of the great Thu'po, were born in the Táwatinsa heavens. Both these women, endowed with the merits resulting from their piety in their previous existence, calling to mind what the act of piety of that previous existence was, and preparing fragrant flowers and other offerings, descended at a subsequent period to this Thu'po, to make oblations. Having made these flower, and other offerings, to the Chétiyo, they bowed down to worship. At the same instant, the Théro (Priest) Mahásíwo, resident at the Bhatiwanko Wiharo (Monastery), who had come in the night-time, saying, 'Let me pray at the great Thu'po,' seeing these females, concealing himself behind a great Sattapanni tree, and stationing himself unperceived, he gazed on their miraculous attributes. At the termination of their prayers, he addressed them thus: 'By the effulgence of the light proceeding from your persons, *the whole island has been illuminated.* By the performance of what act was it, that from hence ye were transferred to the world of Déwos?' These Dewátas replied to him, 'The work performed by us at the great Thu'po.' Such is the magnitude of the fruits derived from faith in the successor of former Bud'has."[1]

I make another extract from the valuable mythology, produced at the great manufacturing town just named. "St. Scholastica gained by her prayers a pouring rain."[2] What says the Lamaic Patriarch? "In his reign, (Bud'hadásis,) the island was afflicted with drought, disease and distress. This benevolent person who was like a

[1] Mahawanso, p. 178. [2] Dr. Newman's Lectures, or Birm. Myth. p. 287.

luminary which expels the darkness of sin, thus inquired of the priests. 'Lords! when the world was overwhelmed with the misery and horrors of a drought, was there nothing done by Bud'ha in his time, for the alleviation of the world?'

"They then propounded the 'Gangáróhana Suttan,' of Bud'ha. Having listened thereto, causing a perfect image of Bud'ha to be made of gold, for the tooth-relic, and placing the stone or refection dish of the divine teacher filled with water, on the joined hands of that image, and raising it into his state car, he went through the ceremony of receiving 'Sila,' which confers consolation on all living beings; and made the multitude also submit to the same ceremony, and distributed alms. Having decorated the capital like to a heavenly city, surrounded by all the priests resident in the island, he descended into the main street. There, the assembled priests, chanting forth the 'Ratanasuttan,' and at the same time sprinkling water, arranged themselves in the street at the end of which the palace was situated, and continued throughout the three great divisions of the night, to perambulate round its enclosing wall. At the rising of the sun, *a torrent of rain descended as it would cleave the earth. All the sick and crippled sported about with joy.* The king then issued the following command: 'Should there, at any time, be another affliction of drought and sickness in this island, do ye observe the like ceremonies.'"[1] One more instance of the Lamaism of the west, from the excellent authority lately quoted. "Relics are ever touching the sick, the diseased, the wounded, sometimes with no result at all, at other times with marked and undeniable efficacy."[2] What says the Bud'hism of LYNCES-TIS, (Lanca's Land,[3]) and

[1] Mahawanso, pp. 248, 249.

[2] Dr. Newman's Lectures, or Birm. Myth., p. 286.

[3] Ceylon and the Himalayas.

the Bud'hism of the LINGONES, (LANCA-TRIBES,)[1] and the Budhism of the GENS TOGA-TA, or the Tackshak tribe? "King of Dévos," says the Budhist envoy, "thou possessest the right canine tooth-relic, as well as the right collar-bone relic of the Deity, worthily worshipped by the three worlds: continue to worship that tooth-relic, but bestow the collar-bone of the divine teacher. Lord of Dévos! demur not in matters involving the salvation of the land of Lanká."[2]

The request was granted, and the relics and the sacred dish obtained. "The populace, congregating from all quarters, assembled to witness its arrival. The relic rose up spontaneously to the height of seven palmira trees, and, remaining self-poised in the air, displayed itself, and astonished the populace till their hair stood on end, by performing a two-fold miracle. From it proceeded at one and the same time flames of fire and streams of water. The whole of Lanka was illuminated by its effulgence, and was saturated by its moisture."[3] And now observe the signs of a true (Lamaic) church. "Witnessing this miracle, the people were *converted to the faith* of the Vanquisher (Zēnos Jinos).[4] The younger brother of the king, the royal prince Mattábhayo, being also a convert to the lord of Munis,[5] entreating of the lord of men (the king) for permission, together with a thousand persons, was ordained a minister of that religion.

"Thus the saviour of the world," (Budha,) by *means of a corporeal relic,* performed infinite acts, to the utmost perfection, for the spiritual comfort, and *mundane prosperity* of mankind."[6]

Protestants have no authority for doubting the authen-

[1] Gana, a tribe. [2] Mahawanso. [3] Ibid., p. 108.

[4] JĒYUS (ZEUS), "the victorious;" JINO, idem; JEYU-PITI (JU-PITER), "VICTORIOUS LORD." [5] Saints. [6] Mahawanso.

ticity of these miracles; they come recommended to every "amiable and candid mind," with the strongest testimony and vouchers of pious men. It would be unreasonable to doubt; for "Miracles to the (Bud'hist) are historical *facts*, and nothing short of this; and they are to be regarded and dealt with like other *facts;* and as natural facts, under circumstances, do not startle Protestants, so supernatural, under circumstances, do not startle the (Bud'hist). They *may* or *may not* have taken place in particular cases; he may be unable to determine which; he may have no distinct evidence; he may suspend his judgment, but he will say 'it is *very* possible!!' He never will say, 'I cannot believe it.'"[1]

To those who assume this, "their *first* principle" to be an historical canon, I recommend the adoption of a fitting corollary, from the Mahawanso; it is as follows:—

"Thus, the Budhists are incomprehensible: their doctrines are incomprehensible; and the *magnitude of the fruits of faith,* to those who *have faith* in these INCOMPREHENSIBLES, is also INCOMPREHENSIBLE!!"[2]

[1] Dr. Newman's Lectures, or Birm. Myth., p. 294.

[2] Mahawanso, p. 108. This is a commentary on a passage of the "Pitakkattava."

XX.

THE ATTAC-THANS.

ΔΗΜΟΝ 'ΕΡΕΧ-ΘΗΟΣ ΜΕΓΑΛ—ΗΤΟΡΟΣ.—*Hom.*

"SUBJECTS OF GREAT-HEART, EREC-PRIEST, WERE THEY."

THE fallacy which runs through the whole supposed mythological legend of the Autochthons, has been now laid bare—the remainder of the same series will be found equally amenable to the same geographical evidence, which has already thrown a light upon the mistaken travesties of Greek writers. Erectheus is a name as mythological as could well be imagined. He belongs to the earth—to the earth he has been consigned, with all that contempt which the haughty Autochthon merited. But should he come before us in more humble guise, with the humility befitting a being of flesh and blood, it may be an inducement to investigate his claims to historical consideration. The district of the Erac, often written Arak, will be seen in the neighbourhood of the Haya-Budhos (Bheene Budam), or the P'HAYAKES, those who have been already contemplated as the colonists of *Phoenicia*, PHŒN-ICIA and HI-BERN-IA. ERECH-THEUS is simply ERAC-DEUS, or the Deva (PRIEST) of Erac. Erechthonius has been rightly conjectured to be the same individual; that is, merely a variation of the term. It is ERECH-THĀN-YUS,[1] "OF THE ERAC-LAND." He is the most eminent specimen of the genus homo to be found

[1] *Erac* and *t'hān,* land (-yus, -a, -um).

in Attic records. The Butadæ, one of the most ancient and dignified families at Athens, were proud of boasting of him as their ancestor. "The genealogy of the great Athenian orator, Lykurgus," observes Grote, "a member of this family, drawn up by his son Abrôn (read Abram), and painted on a public tablet in the Erectheion, contained as its first and highest name, Erectheus, son of Hêphæstos and the earth."[1] Lycurgus was perfectly justified in claiming from Erectheus. Lycurgus simply designates his family title, from his family landed property or royalty, just as "Simon de Montfort, or Peter de Roches." LUKUR-GUS is in fact nothing but LOGURH-KUS, "of Logurh;" and the Athenian orator's great ancestor was "ERAC-THEUS (DEUS)," THE PRIEST OF ERAC, IN THE VICINITY OF LOGURH.[2] The Erac-Priest was also a son of "THE LORD OF THE HYA-CHIEFS' LAND,"[3] that is, he was a son of Bud'ha, or a Bud'hist. Hence the Butadæ (Budhists), boasted of the Erac Priest as their ancestor. Bheene Budam, the Logurh, the Arac-land, will be all found in the vicinity of each other—a vicinity, I need not remind the reader, most decidedly Bud'histic.

Again: "Erectheus was identified with the God Poseidôn, and bore the denomination of Poseidôn Erectheus."[4] Justly so, on the same geographical authority, Po-seidōn, is simply "the CHIEF OF SAIDAN;"[5] Saidan, the Erac-land, and the P'hainicas (Phœnicians), all being in close contiguity in Afghanistan; and Sidan, as I have before shown, is repeated in the Phœnicia of Palestine.

But again: Erectheus, as identical with Poseidon, was worshipped with Athenē. This is again an historical fact. Po-Sidhān is "the PRINCE OF THE SAINTS,"

[1] Grote's Hist. Greece, vol. i. p. 263. [2] *Vide* map.

[3] HE-PHA-IS-TUS (HI-PA-IS-DES). *Hi*, Haya; *pa*, a chief; *is*, the lord; *des*, a land.

[4] Grote's Hist. Greece, vol. i. p. 263. [5] *Pŏ*, a chief, and *Saidan*.

as well as the "Prince of Sidon."[1] In fact, as the western Bud'hism styles it, he was a "Prince of the Church," or "a Cardinal," and somewhat inferior to the Pontiff, ZEUS (JEYUS). He was "worshipped conjointly with Athene."[2] That is but natural. The reader has not forgotten the fact of a Tartar population in Thessaly, nor of a Tartar priesthood at Athens, in the Eleusinian Mysteries; nor the visit of the ingenious Theri, or priestess called Demeter; nor the ELEUTH-INI (ELEUS-INI), or ELEUTH-CHIEFS, who founded these mysteries; nor has he forgotten the Tartar festival, both in Palestine and Tibet, of the cakes offered to the Virgin Queen of Heaven.

Her name is ATHĒNĒ, the Greek way of writing "ADHEENE,"[3] "THE QUEEN ABOVE." The Egyptians worshipped the same deified being as "NEETI," or "POLICY," corruptly written "NEITH." "The Queen of Heaven," then, and the "Prince of the Saints," were "Paredroi," or companion deities. Like other Bud'hist saints, they could be corporeal and incorporeal; could perch, like a fly, on the slenderest blade of grass; could swell to the heavens, or could totally vanish. They could hover in the air, or, as we have lately seen, could cleave a subterranean path through the earth. In fact, there is no power, whatsoever, claimed for their saints by the Lamaic Churches of the East and the West, that was not claimed, testified to, and believed in by the primitive Bud'hists of Hellas. Why should it not be so, since "miracles to the (Bud'hist) are historical facts, and nothing

[1] *Sidha*, a saint; *Sidhān*, saints; *Po-Sidhan*, the chief of the saints. SIDHĀN (SIDŌN), DHAMAS-KAS, DAMASTI-UM, have only one meaning; *viz.*, "Saints'-town" or "All-Saints."

[2] Grote's Hist. Greece, vol. i. p. 263.

[3] From *Adhi*, above, and *inee*, a queen; by the rules of combination *Adheenee*—exactly *Atheenee*—where the Greek long "e" is equal to "ī" or to "ee." *Athēnē* is, by the Tartars of the present day, called *Tien-How*, the Queen of Heaven.

short of this; and as natural facts, under circumstances, do not startle Protestants, so supernatural, under circumstances (did) not startle (Budhists)?"[1] "Certainly, the (Budhist) Church, from East to West, from North to South, is, according to (their) conceptions, hung with miracles. The store of relics is inexhaustible; they are multiplied through all lands."[2]

I come now to an Attic dynasty that has been considered as mythological as the Autochthons themselves. It is so, exactly, but not more. The reader will not fail to remember the race of the Yadus, Crishna, or Apollo, who was styled Yadu-Nat'h, or the Yadu Lord, and their brave allies, the Pandus, the theme of the magnificent poem of the Mahabharata. Cecropos,[3] whom the Greeks call half-man and half-serpent, was of this splendid race. "Cec'ropos," as the name implies, was the "CEC'ROO-POS," or "KING OF THE CECEROO, KEKERS, or COOKEROOS, one of the mightiest of the Yadu tribes. The race of the Cookeroos, sometimes called Guikers, are still to be found in their most ancient seats in the vicinity of the Attoc. Hence is at once seen the propriety of a Prince of the Attoc, ruling over the people of the Attoc, or the AUTOCHTHONS. From that prince, and from his clans and chief, the COOC'-ROO-POS, a portion of Attica, received the name of CECROPIA.

It was in the reign of this prince, that the coast of Attica was ravaged by the pirates of Corĩ origin, by the Greeks called Carians. The clans of Arjuna, one of the Pandava Princes, have already been contemplated as forming a settlement upon the western coast of Thessaly, and as giving a name to the sea lying contiguous to that settlement, viz., the 'Aigæan, a name derived from the 'Aijayas, or clans of 'Ijaya,[4] a title of the Pandava Prince, Arjuna. The same martial colonists have been surveyed

[1] Dr. Newman's Lectures, or Birm. Myth., p. 294. [2] Ibid., p. 285.

[3] Cecooroo, the Coocooroo tribe; and Pos, a chief. *See* Append., Rules 1, 2.

[4] *See* Append., Rule 7.

in the vicinity of Athens, as "Aigiales," not "The Coastmen," but "The Arjuna Pandavas." The bands of these Pandavas have again been identified as DELBHAI, or the men of DELBHI, another name of that "Ægæan" or "Victorious" Chief, Arjuna. Another scion of this royal stock has been demonstrated to be the deified CRISHNA of the LADACÆ-MEN (LACEDÆMON), whose name was also (A)BALONO-J, APOLLONOS, or APOLLO. THE ÆGÆAN, THE ÆGÆALES, DELPHI, CRISSA, and APOLLO, are all connected with the family of the Pandavas, who are written down by Greek historians as "PANDIONS." The connection of the PANDIONS with the CEC'ROO-PAS, or CEC'ROO-CHIEFS, a branch of the Yadu tribe, is self-evident, since APOLLO, or CRISHNA, is emphatically styled "THE YADU CHIEF." The connection with the Bharata Chiefs in Athens will also be as clear. In order to obtain a concise, as well as a most trustworthy view of the Pandavas, and the opinions held both by ancient Hindoo and classical authorities relative to this Indo-Hellenic family, I here present the reader with the masterly summary of Professor Wilson, drawn from his admirable essay on the History of Cashmir :—

"We may here pause to notice the concurrence of this account with that which we have already extracted from Hindu authority, of the subjection of Cashmir to a long series of Caurava princes, as these are, in the estimation of the Hindus, the offspring of a common ancestor, and virtually the same with the Pandava race. This position of the family in the north-west of India, is referred to in many works, and the chief scene of their early exploits is the Punjab and its vicinity; and these traditions, therefore, although much embarrassed by uncertainty and fiction, seem to support the idea that this part of India was the native seat of the Pandavas. Besides the positive assertions to this effect in the history of Cashmir as the birthplace of the Pandavas upon Hindu authority, and we find in classical authors the realm or city of Panda, or of the Pandavas, in a similar direction, although not precisely the same position; at the same time, it is true, that Curu, the progenitor of the Caurava and Pandava races, is placed by the Pauranic writers in a more central part of India, and made King of Hastinapur; the five supposititious sons of Pandu were, however, according to the same authorities, actually born in the Himalaya mountains, whither Pandu, with his wife Cunti, had accompanied the Rishis, and where the gods descended to rear posterity for the prince; there can be little doubt, therefore, that either the original Caurava family, or a very important branch of it, came from the north-west and mountainous parts of India."[1]

The whole of the geographical evidences, already contemplated in Hellas, demonstrate the correctness of these views. The very title of Apollo marks him, both as a Pandava, and as a Hya Chief, and a Yadu Lord. He is emphatically Koontius (Kynthius), Apollo, that is, the son of Koonti, the wife of Pandu, the mother of the three elder Pandava princes. He is also P'hai-pus (P'hœ-bus), or The Haya-Chief. Again:

"The accounts gathered by Megasthenes, which are adopted by Arrian and Pliny, of the customs of this country, and its traditionary history, are obviously to be traced to Indian sources, and are connected with the history of the Pandavas.

"It was the only Indian country governed by queens, they observe. We have a Stri Rajyam, or feminine Government, frequently noticed in the west, but this lay to the east. The notion seems really to have originated in a practice prevailing still throughout the Himalaya, and of an antiquity prior to the marriage of the five Pandava

[1] As. Res., vol. xv. p. 11.

brethren to Draupadi; Yudhishthir observing, in answer to the objection urged by her father, Drupada, that they only follow, in this polyandrian marriage, the path trod by other princes.

"Arrian says the Pandæan region was denominated after Pandæa, the daughter of Hercules, it being the country in which she was born, and which he governed, but he does not indicate its locality, beyond the remark that Hercules was particularly venerated by the Suraseni, the people on the Jobares, whose chief cities were Methora and Kleisobora, these being, in fact, the Surasenas, on the Yamuna, one of whose capital cities was Mat'hura, and we might consequently suppose he meant by the Pandæa regio, the country along the western bank of the Yamuna. The next authority, and who first speaks with precision of the situation of the northern Pandyans (for we need not here advert to the Pandion of the Peninsula) is Ptolemy; he fixes them at once in the Punjab, about the Hydaspes, the Vitasta, or river of Cashmir."[1]

We have thus a distinct view of this family, and its members in Cashmir and its immediate vicinity, an adequate cause for a vast immigration in the war of the Mahabharat, and the positive geographical evidence of these identical clans in Greece. The dynasty of the CECR'OOPAS, or CEC'ROO-CHIEFS, continued long to rule at Athens. Of these, some of the most distinguished seem to have been the Pandions of the Greek historians, the Pandavas of the Attac-thans. The kingly and priestly Bud'histic power continued centred in the great families of the Hyanians (Ionians). After the death of Pandion, one of the successors of the Cecr'oo Chief, the Lord of Erac (Erectheus) succeeded to the kingdom; and his brother, the Bud'ha Priest,[2] became the chief hierarchic official, a position ever after held by the Butadæ, that is, the Bud'hist Priests.

[1] Prof. Wilson.

[2] But-es: *Bud'ha*, lord.

The diversity of characters in which Erectheus appears has been not a little puzzling to the historical student. "Erectheus," writes Mr. Grote, "seems to appear in three characters, in the fabulous history of Athens,—as a god, Poseidon Erectheus—as a hero, Erectheus, son of the Earth—and now as a king, son of Pandiôn: so much did the ideas of divine and human rule become confounded and blended together in the imagination of the Greeks, in reviewing their early times."[1]

This obscurity, I trust, will now disappear. Erectheus, or, "The Lord of Erac," appears as a god—(a Bud'hist term, equivalent to saint,) as PO-SIDHAN, ERAC-DEUS, "THE ERAC-PRIEST, THE CHIEF OF THE SAINTS." As a "SON OF THE EARTH," he is an ATTAC-T'HAN, one of the ATTAC CHIEFS. "AS A KING," he is a son of PANDION, or a CHIEF of the PANDAVA RACE. All these characters, and many more, are and would have been perfectly compatible with the Bud'histic tenets held by the Hiyanians. In fact, that very confusion of divine and human rule, noticed by Mr. Grote, is an essential consequence of the Lamaic doctrines, which acknowledge not only the gift of saintly power over the universe, but the gift of inspiration and omniscience. The Bud'hist saint is at once present and not present,—a god and a man, a visibility and an invisibility. In fact, he is gifted with the attributes of omnipotence.

But, not only are the Lords of the Erac recognised as ruling in Attica, in a princely and hierarchic capacity, but the Bharata chiefs are as distinctly seen. These have been already contemplated in Des-Bh'ratia, Thes-Protia, or, the Land of the Bharatas. They have been contemplated as the BRUTII, and they will now be as apparent in the PROOT-AN-ES, (PRYTANES, or the BHARATA CHIEFS.)[2] The term "Prutanes," is often equivalent to Basileis, or Kings.[3]

[1] Grote's Hist. Greece, vol. i. p. 271.

[2] *Bh'ratān*, plural of *Bh'rata*: *Bh'ratan-es* (*Prytanes*). Bharata chiefs.

[3] Smith's Antiq., p. 970.

On the altar of the PRUTANEIUM, or "HALL OF THE BHARATAS," according to the Indian custom of their forefathers, a perpetual fire[1] was kept burning.

The successive chiefs of this noble race, and all foreign envoys, were entertained in this ancient building. The convocation of the chiefs of the great Bharata clans, which was called the Boulē, or Council, subsisted with little alteration till the time of Solon, when this Senate consisted of five hundred individuals, divided into ten sections of fifty each, also from the same tribe of the PRUTAN-ES, or BHARATA CHIEFS.

As it is not my intention to follow up the whole range of classical functions connected with ante-Homeric names, I shall in this place merely quote the opinion of Müller on the nature of this office, as contrasted with ancient and Solonian Greece:—

"The striking dissimilarity in the duties of the Prytanes, in the Athenian, and in the early constitutions of Greece, and a conviction that the democracy of Athens, although relatively modern, had so completely thrown into oblivion the former institutions, that they can be only recognised in insulated traces and *names which had lost their ancient meaning*, encourage me to offer some conjectures on the original nature of the office held by the Prytanes of Athens. There was at Athens a court of justice in the Prytaneum (ἐπὶ πρυτανείῳ), which in the times of which we have an historical account, only possessed the remnants of a formerly extensive criminal jurisdiction. Now, that this had been once the chief court in Athens, is proved by the name Prytanea, which were fees deposited by the parties before each lawsuit, according to the amount of value in question, and which served for the maintenance of the judges. The name proves that these moneys had at one time been the pay

[1] Πῦρ ἄσβεστον.

of the Prytanes in their judicial capacity, like the gifts in Homer and Hesiod. Furthermore, we know that the ancient financial office of the Colacrete, at one time (as their name testifies), collected their share of the animals sacrificed (which exactly resembles the perquisites of the kings of Sparta), and that they always continued to manage the banquets in the Prytaneum, and collected the justice fees; for example, these very Prytanea."[1]

It has now been seen, both from Hindu and classical sources, as well as distinctly marked by geographical nomenclature, that the Cecroo-pas, or Cooc'roo-Chiefs, the Bharata clans, and the Pandavas, ruled in Athens; that they came from the Attock, and the vicinity of Cashmir, where they have been always placed by the best Hindoo authorities. The BHARATAS have also been shown as the PROTIANS, in the immediate vicinity of their fellow emigrants, the CASSIOPÆI, or people of Cashmir, and in the immediate vicinity of the CEC'ROOS, under the name CICUROS,[2] where also has been pointed out PANDOSIA, or the town of Pandoo.

These, then, are the Clans of the Attock and the BHARATAS, and the CEC'ROO-PAS, and the VAIJAYAS, and the DELBHOIS, and the BALĀNOJ, whom the Greeks, totally ignorant of the sources of their own language, wrote down as AUTOCHTHONS, THES-PROTIANS, CECROPS, the ÆGÆAN, DELPHOI, and APOLLO.

I shall now rapidly draw to a close this outline of primitive Attic History, which, however slight in extent, will yet have the certain result, of demonstrating the state of darkness in which we have been compelled to grope our way, in consequence partly of the vanity, and partly of the singular religious views held by Hellas generally. Before I conclude this sketch, I shall briefly review the main

[1] Müller's Dorians, vol. ii. p. 141. [2] *Cichyros.*

incident in the history of the heroic Theseus. And here we are still closely connected with the dynasty of Cashmir and the Attock. Theseus is the son of Ægeus, or a prince of the family name of Arjuna. Ægeus or Arjuna, is again described as being the son of Pandion.

The history of Theseus, in whom so much of political contrivance appears mingled with romance, has led to a belief, that the former quality is the gratuitous graft of Grecian statesmen, and that "the jovial knight-errant" is the genuine form of the first record. The fact is, that both points of view are consistent. There was indeed a knight-errantry in the movements of Theseus, but it was both military and saintly. As a devotee to the Jaina doctrines, and the Red Cross knight of antiquity, it was his glory to extend their sway, and by every means in his power gain additional proselytes to his religious system. That the accounts left us by the historians of the complete remodelling of the Athenian state—of the establishment of a well organised government by this Jaina prince, are in the main perfectly correct, I have no doubt—his very name implies in a remarkable manner the political changes wrought, and the benefits secured by his instrumentality. He is essentially "THE INTELLECTUAL SAGE," "DHEES-YUJ" (THĒS-EUS).

The evils of a state broken up into a number of petty independent townships, could not fail to force themselves upon his attention. This intelligent chief therefore, abolished all separate political jurisdiction, and erected others into the capital of a compact kingdom. Two remarkable facts, both wearing a most fabulous appearance in the Greek narrative, characterised his career. One was the expedition against the Minotaur of Crete; the other, the celebrated encounter with the Amazons.

The history of the Minotaur and Theseus, calmly considered in reference to the high civilisation and power of Crete at the period in connection with this far-famed record, will clearly demonstrate the feeble state of the kingdom of Athens. Under the influence of the maxims and laws of the celebrated Sage Menu, the kingdom of Crete appears to have risen to an unexampled state of prosperity; and even in the time of Homer, when its power was already on the decline, ninety cities were the flourishing evidences of its vast prosperity. Judging from no scanty evidences still preserved in the geographical features of that once wealthy state, many strong features of the Brahminical system appear to point to the true cause of the tributary position of Athens in the days of Theseus. While Athens was yet struggling for that compact form of government, by which alone her political existence could be fostered and maintained, Crete seems to have been under the powerful influences of a quasi-Brahminical priesthood.

A tribute was demanded from the then feeble state of Attica; viz., the annual sacrifice of seven youths and seven maidens, to be offered up to the MENOO-TAURA,[1] (MENO-TAUROS,) or the Menoo-Durga. Durga, in the character of Cali, the awful goddess of destruction, is perhaps the most sanguinary of the Hindoo deities. She is represented as wearing a necklace of skulls, and with ferocious joy, trampling upon a prostrate human body. Her ritual is equally sanguinary. From this peril the young Athenian monarch escaped by gaining the affections of the priestess of the idol. The other event, which occurring in the military career of Theseus, has given rise to grave doubt and copious speculation, I trust will now take its place in the category of History. I allude to the Thesean combats with the Amazons, and more especially to that part of the supposed legend which assigns the scene of the last great conflict to Athens itself.

[1] *Tāra* (pronounced *Taura*), Durga; *Menoo-Tāra*, the Menu-Durga.

"Attic antiquaries," observes Mr. Grote, "confidently pointed out the exact position of the two contending armies; the left wing of the Amazons rested upon the spot occupied by the commemorative monument called the Amazoneion; the right wing touched the Pnyx, the place in which the public assemblies of the Athenian democracy were afterwards held. The details and fluctuations of the combat, as well as the final triumph and consequent truce, were recounted by these authors with as complete faith and as much circumstantiality as those of the battle of Platæa, by Herodotus. The sepulchral edifice called the Amazoneion, the tomb or pillar of Antiopê near the western gate of the city—the spot called the Horkomosion, near the temple of Theseus itself, and the sacrifices which it was customary to offer to the Amazons at the periodical festival of the Thêsia—were all so many religious mementos of this victory, which was moreover a favourite subject of art both with the sculptor and the painter at Athens, as well as in other parts of Greece.

"No portion of the anti-historical epic appears to have been more deeply worked into the national mind of Greece than the invasion and defeat of the Amazons. It was not only a constant theme of the logographers, but was also familiarly appealed to by the popular orators along, with Marathon and Salamis, among those antique exploits of which their fellow-citizens might justly be proud. It formed a part of the retrospective faith of Herodotus, Lysias, Plato, and Isokratês, and the exact date of the event was settled by the chronologists. Nor did the Athenians stand alone in such a belief. Throughout many other regions of Greece, both European and Asiatic, traditions and memorials of the Amazons were found. At Megara, at Trœzen in Laconia, near Cape Tænarus, at Chœroneia in Bœôtia, and in more than one part of Thessaly, sepulchres or monuments of the Amazons were preserved. The warlike women (it was said,) on their way to Attica, had not traversed those countries without leaving some evidences of their passage."[1] Here is another instance of the ill-effects produced upon Greek History, by Greek Etymology.

The term "Amazon," will be found to have no more connexion with the idea of "Breast-less" females, than that of the Autochthons" with the "Earth." When these Amazons made their terrific onslaught into the territory of Athens, the Greek form of "Amazons" was not in use amongst the then inhabitants of Attica. These "AMAZONES" were plainly and simply "UMA-SOONS," or UMA'S-SONS; UMA-SOONA, signifying UMA'S-DAUGHTER. UMA, is the appellation of Parvati, or Durga, the consort of Mahadeva, or Siva. "UM-ES, UMA'S LORD," is the title of Siva, and "UMA-SOOT," the same word with "UMA-SOON-OO,"[2] signifies CARTIKEYA, the GOD OF WAR, who has been already noticed, as the name given to the CARTI-CEYAN, or WAR CHIEFS, of MOUNT CERCETIUS.

Here then, by the plain practical means of a *translation from the language* of the AMAZONS, in lieu of *Greek conjecture*, we arrive at a positive *Historical Fact*. That not only Stree Rajyam, or Female Governments existed of old, as in the case of Semiramis, but that large bodies of women adopted the use of arms, (as we have lately seen in the war of the African Amazons) will now be set beyond a doubt. Their settlements are marked with the utmost precision. Their well known abode was on and near the Thermodon. There still remains their record, on the Gulf of "AMI-SENUS," *i.e.* UMA-SENA, "DURGAS' WARRIORS."[3] Again, to the west on the same coast of the

[1] Grote's Hist. Greece, vol. i. pp. 289, 290.

[2] SOONOO and SOOTĂ, "A SON;" SOONA, "A DAUGHTER."

[3] *Uma*, wife of Siva, and *sena*, an army. "*Sena*," a goddess; the personified armament of the gods, the wife of Kartikéya."—WILSON'S *Sans. Lex.*

Euxine, is another settlement, viz., AMA-STRIS, that is "UMAS'-WOMEN."[1] Once more, to the north of the Thermaic Gulf we have their tribe, viz., CHALA-STRA, "CULA-STRI[2] TRIBE OF WOMEN." We have then at length a test by which hypercriticism on the one hand, and extreme credulity on the other, may be rationally tested. It is not without some just cause, undoubtedly, that certain traditions have obtained a wide, a deep, and a most durable foundation. These traditions deserve to be respected, so long as we have no better argument than *theory* to deny their historical foundation.

Hence, in the remarks just quoted, there is scarcely one out of the numerous category adduced, that does not tend to prove the fact, instead of the fable, of the warrior caste of Amasoon. Having once demolished the corrupt Greek version, and restored the true text, all the cases advanced by Mr. Grote are perfectly natural. The crossing of the Cimmerian Bosphorus, the fight in the very heart of Athens, are just what we should expect from hordes of daring and warlike clans, and the very circumstance of recording the exact positions of the two contending parties, one of which was the Pnyx, a word that cannot be explained from the ordinary Greek,[3] but runs up to and beyond the time of Theseus. So far from assuming as inventions the offering of sacrifices to the Amazons at the festival of the Theseia and the memento of the Areiopagus,[4] which explains itself,—I consider them as positive proofs of facts, handed down from generation to generation. For, having now got to the historical fact of the warlike

[1] From *Uma* and *Stri*, a woman. [2] *Cala*, a tribe, and *stri*, a woman.

[3] PNUX (Pnyx) has nothing to do with PUKNOS, "CROWDED." PUKNOS is emphatically BUGNOOS, "THE SPEAKER." Usual form Vuknoos; locally Bugnos, equivalent to Vaktri.

[4] HARYA-BHAGAS, "HAR'S OR HARO'S-DISTRICT.

Amazons, and having acknowledged the Indo-Athenian practice and opinions tallying with these matter of fact Amazons, in the erection of a column, of a sepulchral edifice, and the celebration of a periodical sacrifice, I can no more consider the latter inventions, than I consider the Umasoons, inventions—they must stand and fall together. Nay, the very ignorance, which, in union with these mementos of distant centuries—mementos thoroughly Indian in their periodical recurrence, and in the style of the recording structure—corrupted a *name*, but retained a *practice*—form an irresistible evidence of a *fact*. And while the sculptor, the painter, and the poet were producing artistic memorials of Greek Amazons, as the representatives of an *Indian Race*, they too were adding a testimony to their own ignorance, a basis for baseless theories, but at the same time an unwitting corroboration of FACT. It was not without good reason that historians, orators, and chronologists, felt concerning these Amazons, and spoke of them, as of no imaginary beings.

Let the subject, even as handled by the Greeks, divide itself into its two component parts, viz., impossible agents and possible acts,—which is the maximum and the minimum of the case;—place the impossible in one scale, and the possible in the other; the reasonable possible must outweigh the unreasonable impossible. Shall we then, to get rid of a difficulty, receive evidence of action, yet assign invention as the source of action? That would be to invent an invention for others. The whole product of my investigations, slender in amount, but mighty in principle, will, I trust, lead to a more practical system of determining evidence. It will demonstrate that we are not warranted in destroying the foundation of the building, because grotesque figures destroy the simplicity of the frontage.

It was not without reason that "the accomplished

intellect of Julius Cæsar acknowledged the Amasoons as having once conquered and held in dominion a large portion of Asia;" and if that great warrior, in common with the ancients, while believing the universal *form* of the Amazonian accounts, credited also the *results* of their prowess, I am well content, along with *historical* "AMASOONS," to receive as historical the achievements of the "AMAZONS."

As the BHARATA, VAIJAYA, PANDEA, CECROPIA, and other clans, under the name of PRUTANES, AIGIALES, PANDOOS, and CECROPS, have been distinctly shown in the colony of the Attock, it is but reasonable to anticipate a class of society exactly corresponding to the original immigrants; and if this be the case, most certainly those accounts of the early system of Attic government, which have come down to our times, through the medium of Greek writers, must be liable to misapprehension, unless those original names which have descended to our time, have been translated, as well as the general narrative, which stands in connection with those names. To demonstrate the thoroughly Indian character of the primitive population of Attica, and to exhibit that primitive feature in all its force, I cannot do better than present the reader with the excellent observations of the author just quoted. His testimony is the more valuable, because, throughout the whole of his (in many respects) admirable work, he appears to have had no suspicion of the original starting point of the inhabitants of Hellas, and consequently has treated of the Hellenes in their own primitive estate, upon the same principles as those which apply to the Homeric and Thucydidean Greek. I am happy to find that the *realities* of Attic society, in the most distant ages, are granted by Mr. Grote, although the personality of such individuals as Theseus, and the existence of such places as Troy, are treated as unreal.

The account he has given of the constituent parts of the Attic state, are so just and true to the habits and system of the tribes of the Attock, in the olden time, that I cannot but introduce them in this place.

"The Phratries and Gentēs themselves," says Mr. Grote, "were real, ancient, and durable associations among the Athenian people, highly important to be understood. The basis of the whole was the house, hearth, or family,—a number of which, greater or less, composed the Gens or Genos. This Gens was therefore a clan, sept, or enlarged, and partly factitious, brotherhood, bound together by,— 1. Common religious ceremonies, and exclusive privilege of priesthood, in honour of the same god, supposed to be the primitive ancestor, and characterised by a special surname. 2. By a common burial-place. 3. By mutual rights of succession to property. 4. By reciprocal obligations of help, defence, and redress of injuries. 5. By mutual right and obligation to intermarry in certain determinate cases, especially where there was an orphan daughter or heiress. 6. By possession, in some cases at least, of common property, an archon and a treasurer of their own. Such were the rights and obligations characterising the gentile union: the phratic union, binding together several gentes, was less intimate, but still included some mutual rights and obligations of an analogous character, and especially a communion of particular sacred rites and mutual privileges of prosecution, in the event of a phrator being slain. Each phratry was considered as belonging to one of the four tribes, and all the phratries of the same tribe enjoyed a certain periodical communion of sacred rites, under the presidency of a magistrate, called the Phylo-Basileus, or Tribe King, selected from the Eupatrids: Zeus Geleôn was in this manner the patron god of the tribe Geleôntes. Lastly, all the four tribes were linked together by the common worship of Apollo

Patrôus, as their divine father and guardian; for Apollo was the father of Iôn, and the Eponyms of all the four tribes were reputed sons of Iôn."[1] "Such was the primitive religious and social union of the population of Attica and of the Attock, in its gradually ascending scale, as distinguished from the political union, probably of later introduction, represented at first by the Trittyes and Demes. The religious and family bond of aggregation is the earlier of the two; but the political bond, though beginning later, will be found to acquire constantly increasing influence throughout the greater part of this history. In the former, personal relation is the essential and predominant characteristic—local relation being subordinate: in the latter property and residence become the chief considerations, and the personal element counts only as measured by these accompaniments. All these phratic and gentile associations, the larger as well as the smaller, were founded upon the same principles and tendencies of the Grecian mind, a coalescence of the idea of worship with that of ancestry, or of communion in certain special religious rites with communion of blood, real or supposed. The god or hero, to whom the assembled members offered their sacrifices, was conceived as the primitive ancestor to whom they owed their origin; often through a long list of intermediate names, as in the case of the Milesian Hekatæus, so often before adverted to. Each family had its own sacred rites and funeral commemoration of ancestors, celebrated by the master of the house, to which none but members of the family were admissible: the extinction of a family carrying with it the suspension of these religious rites, was held by the Greeks to be a misfortune, not merely from the loss of the citizens composing it, but also because the family gods and the manes of deceased citizens were thus deprived of their honours and

[1] Grote, Hist. Greece, vol. iii., p. 74.

might visit the country with displeasure. The larger associations, called Gens, (Phratry Tribe,) were formed by an extension of the same principle of the family, considered as a religious brotherhood, worshipping some common god or hero with an appropriate surname, and recognising him as their joint ancestor; and the festivals of Theoenia, and Apaturia, (the first Attic, and the second, common to all the Ionic race,) annually brought together the members of these phratries and gentes for worship, festivity, and maintenance of special sympathies; thus strengthening the larger ties without effacing the smaller."[1]

The "PHRATRIES," here noticed, are the "BHRATRIYA,"[2] or BHYADS, or BROTHERHOODS, embracing all the descendants of one and the same stock, which afterwards became of a military character, while the GANA,[3] was, as just described, a clan, but more strictly a tribe.

The custom of marriage among the Rajpoots, (Hyănians, Ionians,) in the case of heiresses or daughters, has been ably remarked upon by Colonel Todd.

"Rajpoots," says that author, "never intermarry with their own kin; the prohibition has no limit; it extends to the remotest degree. All these clans are resolvable into the generic term of the race, or Cúla Sesodia. A Sesodia man and woman cannot unite in wedlock—all these are therefore of the blood royal."

The "ZEUS GELEON," of the day of Theseus, was the Jaina GELONG, or GELUM, or GRAND LAMA, the Pontiff of the tribe GELONTES, or GELONGS; that is, of the LAMAIC PRIESTS, who still subsist to this very day under that name; while "APOLLO PAT-ROUS is A' BALONO-J, "BUDH-RAO," or the BUDHA KING; for Apollo, or Crishna, is "the father of the HYĀN," (ION,) or the HYA TRIBES. Hence, it will no longer surprise us, to find on the principles before laid down, that any nation or tribe should

[1] Grote's Hist. Greece, vol. iii., p. 74.

[2] *Bhratra*, a brother; *Bhratriya*, attributive form.

[3] *Gana*, a tribe.

look up to its parent stock, with such an amount of reverence and adoration, as to invest that Patriarch with the attributes of Divinity—especially, as this would, on Bud'histic principles, be the natural consequence.

Thus, having acknowledged that "the historian Hekatæus is a real man, and doubtless his father Hegesander also, I cannot subscribe to the doctrine that it would be unsafe to march up his genealogical ladder, fifteen steps, to the presence of the ancestorial god of whom he boasted; nor do I believe that the upper steps of the ladder will be found broken and unreal;"[1] on the contrary, I believe them to be quite sound and substantial. Lycurgus, who traced his pedigree to a source far more remote than that of Hekatæus, has, upon geographical evidence, in perfect harmony with the general history of his tribe and people, been found to be perfectly correct. Now, judging from the known care with which the ancient tribes of India preserved their genealogies, that genealogy of Hekatæus was perfectly correct, which traced his origin to some Deva or Bud'hist Saint; for this, as I have already shown, is the proper definition of the term "Theos," as used by the Indo-Hellenes.

The Apaturia of the Indo-Greek Theseus' time, was simply the Abatarya (Avatar) festival, to which all had access, while the Theo-enia were for the Bud'histic people of the Attock, who were Dev-'ena,[2] the Deva or Holy-tribe. The festival of the Avatars occurred in the month Bhavane-Pusyiăn (Puane-P'sian)[3] or Bhoowane and Pusoo; the festival of Parvati and Siva.[4] Such were the festivals, and such the rites that accompanied a considerable part of the first emigrants from the land of the

[1] Grote's Hist. Greece, vol. ii. p. 74.

[2] *Vĕna*, a tribe; "v" lost. (*See* Rule vii. Appendix.)

[3] *Πυανέ-ψιον*. Bhavane is generally spelt Bowanee.

[4] *Bhavane*, a form of *Parvati*. Păsoo, Siva. (*Vide* Appendix, *Durga* and *Siva*.)

Hela Mountains and the Attock. The same people introduced into Attica the political divisions of their fatherland, but those political divisions are amongst the most obscure in classical archæology. Thus, little is known of the nature of the "Naucrary," the name of a division of the inhabitants of Attica. How embarrassing this subject has proved to the very best antiquarians, will be seen from the following extract, from a most excellent work on classical antiquities:—

"What the Naucraries were, previous to the legislation of Solon, is not stated anywhere, but it is not improbable that they were political divisions similar to the Demes in the constitution of Cleisthenes. . . . At any rate, however, the Naucraries before the time of Solon can have had no connection with the navy; and the word Naukraros cannot be derived from 'Naus' a ship, but from Naiō; and Naukraros is only another form for Naukleros, in the sense of 'a householder,' as Naulon was used for the rent of a house."[1] When the classical reader learns that the term "NAUCRA-ROS" is a Greek disguise for NAUG'RA-RAJ,[2] or the HEAD CITIZEN of his division, or in Indian parlance, the DISTRICT POTAIL, he will at once have an insight into the whole question, as it bears upon the primitive population of Thesean and Cecropian Attica. The Bud'histic structure of that population is so well pourtrayed by Mr. Davis, that his remarks need only to be read to impress the stamp of conviction upon the unbiassed mind, as to the Indian origin of the primitive Greek population.

He observes, "Sons are considered in this country, where the power over them is so absolute through life, as a sure support, as well as a probable source

[1] Smith's Dict. of Greek and Roman Antiq.

[2] *Naugara* (spelt *Nāgara*), a citizen; *Nāgara-raj* (*Naukra-ros*), head of the citizens.

of wealth and dignities. But the grand object is the perpetuation of the race, to sacrifice at the family tombs. Without sons, a man lives without honour or satisfaction, and dies unhappy; and, as the only remedy, he is permitted to adopt those of his younger brothers. It is not during life only that a man looks for the service of his sons. It is his consolation in declining years, to think that they will continue the performance of the prescribed rites in the halls of ancestors, and at the family tombs, when he is no more; and it is the absence of this prospect which makes the childless doubly miserable. The superstition derives influence from the importance attached by the government to this species of posthumous duty; a neglect of which is punishable, as we have seen, by the laws. Indeed, of all the subjects of their care, there are none which the Chinese so religiously attend to as the tombs of their ancestors, conceiving that any neglect is sure to be followed by worldly misfortunes."[1]

To this I would only add one single remark, viz., that Colonel Tod, with his usual sagacity, has shown that the Chinese are connected with the Hya race, consequently with the Ionian.

[1] "The Chinese," by John Francis Davis, chap. ix. pp. 131—134: Ed. Knight, 1840.

XXI.

THE BUD'HIST MISSIONARY.

Ἑλλήνων οὐ τῷ ἀσθενεστάτῳ Σοφιστῇ Πυθαγόρῃ.

DURING the ages that had elapsed from the grand disruption of the Hindo-Hellenic elements of society at the war of Troy, to the era of the remarkable Bud'hist, whose history will now, I trust, be placed in a distinct point of view, the doctrines of the EKATAN-KAIRES, or MEDITATIVE UNITARIANS OF CASHMIR, appear to have slumbered.

Those Lamaic writings, monastic services, and long series of miraculous agencies which had for ages riveted the ascendancy of the Bud'hist priesthood, had at length succumbed to the united influence of a popular poetry, and still more to the expulsion of those DES-PATIS,[1] or LAND-LORDS, whose interest had ever, both in India and Greece, been exerted to uphold the splendour and the power of the Bud'hist Priesthood.

Henceforward a more humble sphere of action became the province of that once brilliant hierarchy. Its Melampuses of old, those marvel-working propagandists of ancient days, had well-nigh passed away, and the descendants of the Tartarian priesthood were now officiating in humble guise, in that land in which they once boasted a State Church, and State emoluments. The same ingenious teachers who had successfully trained the politico-

[1] Des-potes. Des, a land; pati, a lord or prince.

religious career of NŬMA,[1] "THE SPIRITUAL TEACHER," had in Hellas long since lost that influence in political affairs which once attended their movements. An individual at length arose, the Loyola of his day, who wrought a marvel in the restoration of the ancient power of the Lamaic order. Although preceded by many SOO-BHOO-YA (SO-PHOI), or "Meditationists who arrived at the exalted object of identification with the Divine Essence," he was the great and successful champion who was destined to revive Lamaism—not in Greece, for her present feelings were of a nature too buoyant to bear the dull weight of a monastic establishment, but in other lands where the plant of Bud'hism might shoot forth, flourish, and bear much fruit. The choice made was as admirable as the sagacious tact of the Lama missionary.

It was to the adopted land of the exiled Pandoos, those ancient champions of Bud'hism, that he now bent his steps, wearied with the gigantic labours of a thirty years' travel. In that country of the ancient BHARATI, a country which they had colonised centuries previous to his arrival, and which now appears on the map of Italy as "BRUTII," did he at length fix on the seat of action which was to crown with unprecedented success, the labours, forethought, and sagacity of many years. The Meditatives of Cashmir have been already pointed out in the land of the HEPAIRUS, as the Cassiopœi. The same Bud'histic bands had accompanied the Bharatas to Southern Italy, where the *town of* THE PANDOOS (PANDOSIA,) was again seen to rise in the vicinity of the River of the SU-BUDHAS (SABATUS RIVER,) immediately to the south of which was the LAMAIC settlement[2] of the HYA-CHIEFS.[3] It was, how-

[1] NŬMĂ-GURU, THE SPIRITUAL TEACHER. From *Nŭmăs*, reverence; from *Nŭm*, to bend.

[2] LAMETICUS SINUS, LAMAS' BAY.

[3] HI-PPONIA-TES (HI-PANYA-DES), HYA CHIEF'S LAND.

ever, on the Italian coast immediately in communication with the shores of Greece, that the zealous but clear-sighted Lamaic envoy took his position. Thus posted, his influence, if successful, would be felt not only in Italy, but in Western Hellas; while the maritime position of Crotona presented great facilities for communication with other emissaries from the Lamaic countries of the East. There is no one who is acquainted with the energetic enterprises of the Bud'hists of antiquity but must duly appreciate at once the difficulties and the success of Pythagoras. There is no doubt that many lingering influences of the old Lamaic establishments still had their unseen, though guiding influences in Southern Italy at the period of the arrival of that energetic and gifted individual, who, at one period, swayed the destinies of the greater part of Southern Italy, though the mighty hand which moved the complicated machine of government was an invisible hand. It was the master hand of that catholic Sakya, or universal Potentate,—MIND.

"Pythagoras," writes Mr. Grote, (who has certainly the clearest view of the character, objects, and system of the profound Samian, that has been hitherto drawn from purely classical sources,) "Pythagoras was founder of a brotherhood, originally brought together by a religious influence, and with observances approaching to monastic peculiarity, working in a direction at once religious, political, and scientific, and exercising for some time a real political ascendancy, but afterwards banished from government and state affairs into a sectarian privacy with scientific pursuits, not without, however, still producing some statesmen, individually distinguished. Amidst the multitude of false and apocryphal statements which circulated in antiquity respecting this celebrated man, we find a few important facts reasonably attested, and deserving credence. He was a native of Samos, son of an opulent merchant, named Mnesarchos,—or according to some of his later and more fervent admirers, of Apollo, born, as far as we can make out, about the fiftieth Olympiad, or 580 B.C. On the many marvels recounted respecting his youth it is unnecessary to dwell. Among them may be numbered his wide-reaching travels, said to have been prolonged for nearly thirty years, to visit the Arabians, the Syrians, the Phœnicians, the Chaldeans, the Indians, and the Gallic Druids. But there is reason to believe that he really visited Egypt, perhaps also Phœnicia, and Babylon, then Chaldæan and independent. At the time when he saw Egypt, between 560—540 B.C.; about one century earlier, it was under Amasis, the last of its own kings, with its peculiar native character yet unimpaired by foreign conquests, and only slightly modified by the admission during the preceding century of Grecian mercenary troops and traders. The spectacle of Egyptian habits, the conversation of the priests, and the initiation into various mysteries, or secret rites and stories not accessible to the general public, may very naturally have impressed the mind of Pythagoras, and given him that turn for mystic observance, asceticism, and peculiarity of diet and clothing, which manifested itself from the same cause among several of his contemporaries, but which was not a common phenomenon in the primitive Greek religion."[1] I have not the slightest doubt that all those countries mentioned as being visited by Pythagoras, were actually traversed by that ardent Apostle of Lamaism. Certain it is, that he visited India, which I trust I shall make self-evident.

It is not without cause that he is styled a "son of Apollo," since "Heri," a name of Crishna, or A' BALANO-J, (A'POLLON-OS,) is essentially the Yadu Lord and Bud'ha Chief.

[1] Grote's Hist. Greece, vol. iv. p. 529.

"Of the personal doctrines or opinions of Pythagoras," continues Mr. Grote, "whom we must distinguish from Philolaus and the subsequent Pythagoreans, we have little certain knowledge, though doubtless the first germ of their geometry, astronomy, &c., must have proceeded from him. But that he believed in the metempsychosis or transmigration of the souls of deceased men into other men as well as animals, we know, not only by other evidence, but also by the testimony of his contemporary, the philosophic Zenophanês of Elea. Pythagoras, seeing a dog beaten, and hearing him howl, desired the striker to desist, saying, 'It is the soul of a friend of mine, whom I recognised by his voice.' This, together with the general testimony of Hêrakleitus, that Pythagoras was a man of extensive research and acquired instruction, but artful for mischief and destitute of sound judgment—is all that we know about him from his contemporaries.

"Pythagoras combines the character of a sophist (a man of large observation, and clever, ascendent, inventive mind; the original sense of the word sophist, prior to the polemics of the Platonic school, and the only sense known to Herodotus), with that of an inspired teacher, prophet, and worker of miracles—approaching to, and sometimes even confounded with the gods, and employing all these gifts to found a new special order of brethren, bound together by religious rites and observations peculiar to themselves. In his prominent vocation, analogous to that of Epimenidês, Orpheus, or Melampus, he appears as the revealer of a mode of life, calculated to raise his disciples above the level of mankind, and to recommend them to the favour of the gods; the Pythagorean life, like the Orphic life, being intended as the exclusive prerogative of the brotherhood, approached only by probation and initiatory ceremonies, which were adapted to select enthusiasts, rather than to an indiscriminate crowd, and exacting active mental devotion to the master. In these lofty pretensions the Agrigentine Empedoclês seems to have greatly copied him, though with some varieties, about half a century afterwards. While Aristotle tells us, that the Krotoniates identified Pythagoras with the Hyperborean Apollo, the satirical Timon pronounced him to have been 'a juggler of solemn speech, engaged in fishing for men.'"[1]

The identification of Pythagoras by the Krotoniates, with the CRISHNA (Apollo) of KHYBER-POOR, is exactly that which might reasonably be expected from those who held the Lamaic doctrines. Pythagoras was undoubtedly looked upon as the incarnation of Crishna, or Heri, in which point of view, he would necessarily be considered as the HERI-CUL-ES, or "The Chief of Bud'ha's Tribe."

The succession of the incarnations of Bud'ha has become thoroughly interwoven with the very nature of the Lama priesthood and laity. Of its existence at the present day in all its primitive force, ample evidence is supplied by the narrative of MM. Huc and Gabet :—

"After several days' journey across the sandy plains of the Ortous, we observed on our way a small Lama monastery built in a wild and picturesque situation. We passed on, however, without stopping. We were already distant from it about a gun-shot, when we heard behind us, as it were, the galloping of a horse. We turned round, and perceived a Lama, who was hurrying towards us with great eagerness. 'Brother,' said he, 'you have passed before our monastery without stopping: are you in such a hurry that you cannot rest one day and offer your adorations to our saint?'

"'Yes! we are in a great hurry; our journey is not one of a few days only; we are going towards the west.' 'By your physiognomy,' replied he, 'I knew very well that you were not of the Mongolian race; I know that you are

[1] Grote's Hist. of Greece, vol. iv. p. 531.

from the west; but since you are about to take so long a journey, you would be doing well to prostrate yourself before our saint; that would bring you good luck.' 'We never bow down before men; the true doctrines of the west are opposed to that practice.' '*Our saint is not merely* a man; perhaps you are not aware that in our small monastery we have the good fortune to possess a Chaberon, a living Bud'ha. It is two years since he condescended to come hither from the holy mountains of Thibet; in fact, he is seven years of age. In one of his former existences, he was the Grand Lama of a magnificent monastery, situated in this valley, which was destroyed in the time of the wars of Gengis Khan. The saint having re-appeared a few years since, we have hastily constructed a small monastery. Come, brethren, our saint will extend his right hand over your heads, and good fortune will attend your steps.'"[1]

Such is a picture of the universal belief in the ever-existing personality of the successors of the ancient Bud'ha. The effects produced among the Crotoniates by the arrival of Pythagoras, are said to have been truly marvellous; being nothing less than a moral and political reform in their most powerful sense. Luxury was abandoned, simplicity took the place of seductive attire. At the very first discourse of the illustrious missionary of morality, two thousand individuals were converted; and the Supreme Council, penetrated with the noble powers of the great apostle of Lamaism, offered him the exalted post of their President, and placed at the head of the religious female processions, his wife and daughter. The extensive nature of these conversions is in exact keeping with the Bud'histic accounts contained in the Mahawanso, where the conversion of many thousands is but the work of a day.

"To trace these tales to a true foundation," writes

[1] Souvenirs d'un Voyage dans la Tartarie, par M. Huc, vol. i. p. 276.

Mr. Grote, "is impossible; but we may entertain reasonable belief that the success of Pythagoras, as a person favoured by the gods, and patentee of divine secrets, was very great; that he procured to himself both the reverence of the multitude and the peculiar attachment and obedience of many devoted adherents chiefly belonging to the wealthy and powerful classes; that a select body of these adherents, three hundred in number, bound themselves by a sort of vow, both to Pythagoras and to each other, and adopted a peculiar diet, ritual, and observances, as a token of union, though without anything like community of property, which some have ascribed to them. Such a band of men, standing high in the city for wealth and station, and bound together by this intimate tie, came by almost unconscious tendency to mingle political ambition with religious and scientific pursuits.

"The devoted attachment of Pythagoreans towards each other, is not less emphatically set forth than their contempt for every one else. In fact, these two attributes of the order seem the best ascertained, as well as the most permanent of all. Moreover, we may be sure that the peculiar observances of the order passed for exemplary virtues in the eyes of its members, and exalted ambition into a duty, by making them sincerely believe that they were the only persons fit to govern.

"But this influence of Pythagoras was not bounded even by the populous city of Croton; much of Italy and Sicily were to experience the moral and political regeneration. Sybaris, Rhegium, Metapontum, Himera, and Catana, felt the edifying power of his doctrines. In Croton, the reverence of the multitude towards Pythagoras was unbounded; while a select body of the wealthy and aristocratic, to the number of three hundred, bound themselves in a mutual vow, and in an oath of obedience to their founder. This powerful brotherhood adopted a distinct diet and ritual, the token of their unity, which at length became so intricate, as to produce political results of a high order, though its initiatory course had been religious and scientific only. The characteristics of the Pythagoreans, however, embraced not only the elements of union, but of disruption also; for the haughty exclusiveness of its members, and their contempt for every other individual beyond their own religious and political pale, excited the bitter enmity of many of the wealthier citizens, whom Pythagoras did not consider it expedient to admit into his society. Notwithstanding, the order continued to acquire amazing ascendancy in the government of Croton, and, as its ramifications extended to other cities, it gradually influenced public affairs throughout nearly the whole of Magna Græcia. The political principles of the association were decidedly aristocratic, and diametrically opposed to the control of the people; in which respect, indeed, they coincided with the previous institutes of the city of Croton; and to this, probably, may be ascribed much of the rapid rise of the influence of Pythagoras.

"It seems more probable," continues Grote, "that the political Pythagoreans were those who were most qualified for action, and least for speculation; and we may reasonably suppose, in the general of the order, that skill in turning to account the aptitudes of individuals, which, two centuries ago, was so conspicuous in the Jesuits, to whom, in various ways, the Pythagoreans bear considerable resemblance. All that we can be said to know about their political principles is, that they were exclusive and aristocratical, adverse to the control and interference of the people—a circumstance no way disadvantageous to them, since they coincided in this respect with the existing government of the city; had not their own conduct brought additional odium on the old aristocracy, and raised up an aggravated democratical opposition carried to the most deplorable lengths of violence.

"Extreme strictness of observances," observes Grote, "combined with the art of touching skilfully the springs of religious terror in others, would indeed do much both to fortify and to exalt him. But when it was discovered that science, philosophy, and even the mystic revelations of religion, whatever they were, remained confined to the private talk and practice of the disciples, and were thus thrown into the back ground, while all that was seen and felt without, was the political predominance of an ambitious fraternity, we need not wonder that Pythagorism in all its parts became odious to a large portion of the community. Moreover, we find the order represented not merely as constituting a devoted and exclusive political party, but also as manifesting an ostentatious self-conceit throughout their personal demeanour, refusing the hand of fellowship to all except the brethren, and disgusting especially their own familiar friends and kinsmen."[1]

The reader is now rapidly approaching that juncture of decisive evidence that will prove the direct reception of the Bud'histic doctrines taught by Pythagoras, from the last Bud'ha of India, the far-famed Sakhya-Muni. It will demonstrate the sagacity of that profound scholar and philosopher, the late James Colebrook, Esq., and fully justify the suggestion of an author, who has taken at once a succinct and comprehensive view of Bud'hism in its present and past stages.[2] After speaking of the Stupas or Mounds of solid masonry erected over the ashes of the saints of the Bud'hist faith, and the relics contained within these shrines so sacred to Bud'hists, he observes, "we have no desire and no right to anticipate the pub-

[1] Grote's Hist. of Greece, vol. iv. p. 551.

[2] H. Prinsep, Esq., "Thibet, Tartary, and Mongolia." W. H. Allen and Co.

lication of the very interesting results which have attended the search of these Stupas. Suffice it that they are quite irreconcileable with any construction of the accounts received of the Bood'hist faith, that does not carry back the founder to the sixth century before our era. These, indeed, may not be the real tombs of the saints and disciples of Sakhya Muni, whose names are found in the vases and cerements, but the more probable inference is that they are so; still, whether admitted to be so or not, the appearance of the buildings, and the character of the inscriptions, indicates a date for their construction at least three or four hundred years before Christ; and the erection of these Stupas at that date over even fictitious relics, shows the sacred books recording the laws of these saints and disciples to be then the received faith of a large and wealthy population; and this is all we seek to establish. If Boodhism, however, existed with these books at so early a date, we are met by the difficulty of accounting for the silence of Greek authors of antiquity in respect to them. The very name of Boodh is met with nowhere in Greek literature before the time of Clemens Alexandrinus, and he mentions only incidentally one Terebinthus, who, coming from India, set up for a Booth (*Βουζα*,) and imposed on many. We certainly have difficulty in accounting for this silence, but it is not inconsistent with Greek habit so to treat barbarian literature of all kinds.

"How little do we find in Greek books of the history or literature of the Persians and Parthians, with whom they were in close relation, politically and commercially, for many ages. And it is to be observed, the Boodhist sacred books were the special property of the priesthood, and were mostly preserved and transmitted orally amongst them: probation, by long discipline, and by shaving the head, and assuming the yellow garb of a priest, was a condition antecedent to the acquisition of any knowledge of them; and the same is even now the case with rigid Bood'hists. Have not even the learned of Europe, with the advantage of a press, and a reading public eager for knowledge, been for many centuries acquainted with the existence of Boodhists with peculiar doctrines, without, until, very recently, obtaining any accurate knowledge of these sacred books? That the doctrines of Sakhya Muni spread widely over the western world, as well as over the east, is sufficiently known and established. Pythagoras brought the doctrine of transmigration into Greece at a period so close to that of the decease of Sakhya Muni, as to make it probable that he received it even from himself; but we have no direct evidence that the philosopher went further east than Babylon. The fact, however, that he derived his doctrines from an Indian source is very generally admitted; and it has other points of resemblance with Bood'hism, besides the belief in metempsychosis, or transmigration of souls. The discipline he established, and the life of silence and meditation he enjoined, with the degrees of initiation introduced, which was a kind of successive ordination, correspond exactly with the precepts of the Pitakattayan, and the practices reported in the Atthakatha. The Pythagorean institutions also are described as very monastic in their character, resembling thus closely in that respect also, the Viharas of the Boodhists of India. The doctrines of Pythagoras were widely spread over Greece, over Italy, and Asia Minor, for centuries after his decease, and under the name of Mythraic, the faith of Boodh had also a wide extension."[1] In support of this clear-sighted view of the Bud'hism of Pythagoras, and his reception of that doctrine directly from Sakhya Muni,

[1] Prinsep's Mongolia and Tartary, p. 159.

I shall shortly adduce the eminent authority of that profound scholar, the late H. T. Colebrooke, Esq., which though it be of an inferential nature only, will be amply demonstrated to be perfectly correct, by the thoroughly practical evidence with which I shall close this work. Meanwhile I would adduce the opinion of a most accomplished Orientalist, on the connection of the Platonic with the Hindu philosophy, leading as this opinion does, directly to the same inference with that of the celebrated writer just quoted.

"The transition of the Divine Mind," says Dr. Mill, "into the separate individual intelligences; the propagation of various orders of beings, from the highest down to the grossest, and most material; and the destruction of the world, by the absorption of the higher and lower existences, are points in which the Hindoo scheme wonderfully coincides with Platonism."[1] Again:—"It may here be remarked, by the way," writes the learned Colebrooke, "that the Pythagoreans and Ocellus, in particular, distinguish as parts of the world, the heaven, the earth, and the interval between them, which they term lofty and aërial.[2] Here we have precisely the swar, bhŭ, and antarícksha—heaven, earth, and transpicuous intermediate region of the heavens. Pythagoras, as after him Ocellus, peoples the middle or aërial region with demons, as heaven with gods above, men beneath, and spiritual creatures flitting unseen in the intermediate region. The Vedas throughout teem with prayers and incantations, to arrest and repel the molestation of aërial spirits; mischievous imps, who crowd about the sacrifices, and

[1] W. H. Mill, D.D., Principal of Bishops' College. Read before the Asiatic Society, Aug. 5th, 1835.

[2] "Λέγω δὲ μέρη, οὐρανὸν, γῆν, τὸ μεταξὺ τούτων. ὃ κὲ μετάρσιον καὶ ἀέριον ὀνομάζεται."—*Ocell.* c. iii., in *Opusc. Myth.*, p. 520.

impede the religious rites. Nobody needs be reminded that Pythagoras and his successors held the doctrine of metempsychosis, as the Hindoos universally do the same tenet, of the transmigration of souls. They agree, likewise, in distinguishing the sensitive material organ[1] from the rational and conscious living soul,[2] the Thumos and Phrēn of Pythagoras,—one existing with the body, the other immortal. Like the Hindoo, Pythagoras, with the Greek philosophers, assigned a subtle aërial clothing to the soul, apart from the corporeal part, and a grosser clothing to it when united to the body; the sucshina (or linga), sáríra and st'hula; sárírа of the Sanc'hyas. They concur, even, in the limit assigned to mutation and change, defining all which is sublunary, mutable; and that which is above the moon, subject to no change in itself. Accordingly, the manes doomed to a succession of births, rise no higher than the moon; while those only pass that barrier who are never to return. But I am anticipating upon the Vedantas, and will therefore terminate this treatise, purposing to pursue the subject in a future essay, in which I expect to show, that a *greater degree of similarity exists between the Indian doctrine, and that of the earlier than the later Greeks*. And as it is scarcely probable that the connection should have taken place, and the knowledge have been imparted at the precise interval of time which intervened between the earlier and later schools of Greek Philosophy, and especially between the Pythagoreans and Platonists, *I should be disposed to conclude that the Indians were in this instance* TEACHERS, *rather than* LEARNERS." [3]

The illustrious Orientalist who penned these acute remarks, had announced his intention of writing a series of articles on the extraordinary similarity, not to say the absolute identity, of the Pythagorean and Bud'histic

[1] Manas. [2] Jívatán. [3] Colebrooke, Roy. Asiat. Trans., vol. i.

systems of philosophy. This series of articles, as being profoundly instructive and as connected inferentially with Hellenic history, had been looked forward to by the literary world with the most lively interest. The lamented decease of the great scholar whose writings had adorned the pages of the most learned Journal of Europe, disappointed these ardent anticipations.

Supported by authorities drawn from a source hitherto overlooked, but of the most faithful nature, I rejoice in the honour of confirming the profound sagacity of so great a name as that of Colebrooke.

He who taught this philosophy, was that great missionary, whose name indicates his office and position—

Sanscrit	BUD'HA-GOOROOS,	BUD'HAS SPIRITUAL TEACHER.
Greek	PUTHA- GORAS,	
English	PYTHA- GORAS,	

APPENDIX.

APPENDIX.

No. I.

ON THE SACRED BOOKS OF BOODHISM.

FROM PRINSEP'S "MONGOLIA."

Of the sacred books of Bood'hism we have now three complete versions, in the Sanscrit, Tibetan, and Pali languages; and all have been carefully examined and reported upon by thorough proficients in each of these languages respectively. We have a Sanscrit version that was obtained in Nipal by Mr. Hodgson, the British resident at Katimandoo, and after being studied and partially abstracted by himself, was by him transmitted to the Royal Library of Paris, about fifteen years ago, and has there been closely examined by Messrs. Remusat and Bournouf, whose works on the subject are before the world. We have also a Tibetan version obtained through the same channel, and subjected by the government of India to the examination of M. Csoma da Koros. The result of his labours has appeared in several translations and abstracts, which were published in the Asiatic Researches of Bengal, and in the monthly Journal of the Asiatic Society, between the years 1835 and 1840. The Pali version was traced out by Mr. William Turnour, a high civil functionary of Ceylon. This gentleman first published in a separate volume the text, with a close translation of the Maha-wanso, an ancient poem on the origin and spread of the Bood'hist religion, compiled in the fifth century of our era from the Cingalese version of the Attha-katha, a work of much higher antiquity. He next published in the pages of the Journal of the Asiatic Society of Bengal, a series of valuable essays, with the heading of "Pali Bud'histical Annals;" and in these we find a complete analysis of the sacred books themselves, and a critical examination of the grounds for assuming them to be genuine, and for assigning to them a date and period very nearly corresponding with that claimed for them by the professors of the religion. We have no means of determining the precise date when the Sanscrit version of these Bood'hist Scriptures was prepared. It professes to have been made from an original in the language of Moghada, that is of Bahar, in which province both Pataliputra (the ancient Palibothra, now Patna), and Rajagriha, where Sakhya Muni was born, and which was the more ancient capital of that province, were situated. The Tibetan version was translated from the Sanscrit, and took the shape of the Kahgyur, in which it now exists, in one hundred leaf volumes, between the seventh and ninth centuries of our era. Tibet does not pretend to conversion to Bood'hism, till many centuries after the death of Sakhya Muni;[1] we cannot therefore, look in this quarter for evidence of the *date of the first appearance* of this religion in the world; but when we find that the version of its scripture now current there, and the Sanscrit version also, through which it was derived, correspond in all essentials with the Pali version of the same Scripture found in Ceylon, Siam, and Burma (for all these are identical), it is an undeniable collateral evidence of the genuine character of the whole; for there could be no collusion between the priests of all these distant regions. Still, in order to establish the antiquity of the original scriptures, we must seek other proofs than this conformity. The Pali books examined and abstracted by Mr. Turnour, consist of the Pitakattayan, the Attha-katha, and the Mahawanso. The first is *quasi* the gospel of the Bood'hists, containing the life, discourses, and precepts of Sakhya Muni himself, as derived from his own mouth, and put together by his disciples immediately after his decease. The Attha-katha is *quasi* the acts of the apostles, and contains the account of the settlement of the Pitakattayan, and of the succession of Theros, or chief disciples and preachers of the religion after Sakhya Muni; also of the schisms which took place in the first few centuries after the *Nirwan*, or decease, of the great saint and founder; and especially of the convocations held, as well to settle the gospel itself in the first instance, as to determine the points of difference, and to suppress the schisms as they arose.

[1] Mr. Prinsep was not of course aware of the striking authorities to the contrary, now first developed.—Ed.

No. II.

BUDHA OF THIBET.

FROM COLEMAN'S "MYTHOLOGY OF THE HINDOOS."

THE deity is supposed never to die; or rather, as soon as he is dead, to be again regenerated in the form of an infant. It need scarcely be stated that this regeneration is an act of priestly arrangement; it is, however, conscientiously believed by the millions of worshippers of the Teshoo Lama. In 1783, Mr. Turner, the author of the Embassy to Thibet, was sent by the British Government of India, to congratulate the infant Lama after the death of the old Lama, upon his resuscitation. The account of this interview, in which the holy young gentleman of eighteen months old, behaved with becoming dignity and decorum, is both interesting and singular. Mr. Turner says he did not speak, which he ingenuously confesses saved him, the ambassador, many words in the way of rejoinders, &c. However, he contrived to make the young Pontiff understand the inconsolable grief that the Governor-General, and the good people in India (those inhabiting the city of Palaces[1] especially,) were plunged into when he died, which was only surpassed by their unbounded joy and happiness when they found he had come to life again, to exercise his holy vocation for the benefit of his numerous worshippers. This gratifying compliment, or a string of handsome pearls which the Ambassador had presented to him, caused the infant Lama to regard him and his suite with looks of singular complacency, and to present them with sugar-plums, (not of the kind usually given by foreign potentates to plenipotentiaries, but of real confectionary,) from a golden cup which stood near him. The Ambassador continued to express the Governor-General's hope that the Lama might long continue to illume the world with his presence, and that the friendship which had hitherto subsisted between them might be yet more strongly cemented, for the benefit and advantage of the intelligent votaries of the Lama, and the disinterested worthy

[1] Calcutta.

inhabitants of Great Britain ; all which made the little creature look steadfastly at the speaker, and graciously bow and nod—and bow and nod—and bow and nod again, as if he understood and approved of, says Mr. Turner, every word that was uttered. Indeed, the Embassy had every reason in the world to be satisfied with the extraordinary politeness and attention of the young Lama ; for, on understanding that the English gentlemen had arrived, he was so impatient to see them, that he rose long before his usual hour ; and although he could not, during the audience, converse with, he kept his eyes constantly fixed upon them, and "when their cups were empty of tea, he appeared uneasy, and throwing back his head, and contracting the skin of his brow, continued making a noise till they were filled again." He was particularly struck with the movements of the hands of a small clock ; but his admiration was that of a philosopher, perfectly grave and sedate, as was indeed the whole of his behaviour ; but at the same time apparently natural and unconstrained. In short, the Holy Pontiff of Rome could not have conducted himself more appropriately than did, on that occasion, with all due allowances for circumstances, the infant pontiff of Thibet.

No. III.

THE JAINA SECT.

FROM DR. BUCHANAN'S JOURNAL, *As. Res.* vol. ix. p. 279.

HAVING invited Pandita Acharya Swámi, the Guru of the Jains, to visit me, he came, attended by his most intelligent disciples, and gave me the following account of his sect :—

The proper name of the sect is Arháta : and they acknowledge that they are one of the twenty-one sects, considered as heretical, by Sancara Achárya. Like other Hindoos, they are divided into Brahman, Kshetrya, Vaisya, and Sudra.

The Arhátas reject the Vedas, and eighteen Puranas of the other Brahmins, as heretical. They say that these books were composed by a Rishi, named Vyása, whom the other Brahmins considered an incarnation of the deity. The chief book, the doctrine of which is followed by the Arhátas, is named Yoga.

They admit that all Brahmins are by birth of equal rank.

The gods of the Arhátas are the spirits of perfect men; who, owing to their great virtue, have become exempt from all change and misfortune; and are all of equal rank and power. They are called collectively by various titles, such as Jineswara, Arhat, and SIDD'H but each is called by a particular name, or names, for many of them have a thousand appellations.

These Siddhas reside in a heaven, called Mocksha; and it is by their worship only that future happiness can be obtained.

The first person, who by his virtue arrived at this elevated station, was Adiparaméswara; and by worshipping him, the favour of all the Siddhas may be procured.

The servants of the Siddhas are Dévatás, or the spirits of good and great men, who, although not so perfect as to obtain exemption from all future charge, yet live in an inferior heaven, called Swerga, where, for a certain length of time, they enjoy great power and happiness, according to the merit of the good works which they performed, when living as men.

Swerga is situated higher in the regions of the air than the summit of Mount Méru, and its inhabitants ought to be worshipped by men, as they possess the power of bestowing temporal blessings. . . . . Below Mahá Méru and the earth is situated Bhuvana, or Hell, the residence of wicked men. These are called Asuras, and are miserable, although endowed with great power. Bhuvana is divided into ten places of punishment, which are severe in proportion to the crimes of their respective inhabitants.

The Arhátás allow that to kill an animal of the cow-kind is equally sinful with the murder of one of the human species. The death of any other animal although a crime, is not of so atrocious a nature. . . . The Arhâtas are frequently confounded by the Brahmins who follow the Vedas, with the Saugatas, or followers of Bud'ha; but this arises from the pride of ignorance. So far are the Arhâtas from acknowledging Bud'ha, as their teacher, that they do not think he is even a Dévatá . . The Jain Brahmins are all Vaidya, and dress like the others, who follow the doctrine of the Vedas. They have Gurus, who are all Sanyasis, that is to say, have relinquished the world, and all carnal pleasures.

The Sanyasis never shave, but pull out their hair by the roots. . . The Jains are spread all over India, but at present are not numerous anywhere, except in Tulava. They allege that they formerly extended over the whole of Ayra, or Bharatacanda; and that all those who had any just pretensions to be of Kshetriya descent, were of their sect. There are two kinds of temples amongst Jains; one covered with a roof, called Bash, and the other an open area, surrounded by a wall, and called Bettu, which signifies a hill. The Jainas deny the creation of man, as well as of the world. They allow that Brahma was the son of a king, and that he is a Dévatá; but they altogether deny his creative power. . . . In fact, this remarkable tenet, from which the Jainas and Buddhas derive their most conspicuous peculiarity, is not entirely unknown to the orthodox Hindus. The followers of the Vedas, according to the theology which is explained in the Vedanta, considering the human soul as a portion of the divine and universal Mind, believe that it is capable of perfect union with the divine essence; and the writers on the Vedánta not only affirm that this union and identity are attainable by a knowledge of God, as by them taught, but have hinted that by such means the particular soul becomes God, even to the actual attainment of supremacy. . . . Their belief in the extent of matter, and perpetuity of the world, is common to the Sánc'hya philosophy, from whom it was, perhaps, immediately taken. . . . Their precaution to avoid injuring any being, is a practice inculcated in the orthodox religion, but which has been carried by them to a ludicrous extreme.[1] The Jainas conceive the soul (Jiva), to have been eternally united to a very subtle material body, or, rather, to two such bodies, one of which is invariable, and consists (if I rightly apprehend their metaphysical notions) of the powers of the mind; the other is variable, and composed of its passions and affections. . . The soul so embodied, becomes in its successive transmigrations, united with a grosser body, denominated Andérica, which retains a definite form, as man and other mundane beings; or it is joined with a purer essence, varying in its appearance, at pleasure, as the gods and genii. This last is termed Vaicarica. They distinguish a fifth sort of body, under the name of Ahárica, which they explain as a minute form, issuing from the head of a meditative sage, in order to consult an omniscient saint, and returning with the desired information to the person whence that form issued, or rather, from which it was elongated; for they suppose the communication not to have been interrupted.

In Hindustan the Jainas are usually called Sauryas, but distinguish themselves into Srawcas, and Yatis. The laity (termed Srawcas), includes persons of various tribes, as indeed is the case with Hindus of other sects.

[1] Jaiña priests usually bear a broom to sweep insects out of their way; lest they should tread on the minutest being.

No. IV.

ON THE JAINAS.

From the Kalpa Sutra, by the Rev. J. Stephenson, D.D.

They maintain, like the Brahmins, that there is a number of heavens and hells, for temporary rewards and punishments. The gods, whom they allow to possess several of these heavens, are but beings who were once men or animals, enjoying the reward of inferior kinds of merit, and who must descend again to the earth, and be born anew, and continue ever in the whirl of transmigration, unless they become sages. The chief of these gods is named Sakra, or in Mághadhi, Sakke, the Sakko of the Bud'hists, and the Indra of the Brahmins. . . . . . The sage, who by meditation frees his mind from all worldly attachments, obtains at death, Nirvána, a state of perfect bliss, perfect knowledge, and freedom from all pain and irritation, and ascends to the highest heaven, called Siddha Selá (the Rock of the Perfect); he is exalted far above the gods, and becomes a special object of admiration to gods and men. . . . . . The Jain community consists of two great sections, somewhat analogous to our clergy and laity, each section embracing both males and females. The clerical names are Sádhis, *i. e.*, Sages. All profess celibacy, live in monasteries or houses, in communities of four or five to a hundred, in subjection to an abbot, and perform all the priestly acts of the Jain religion. The Sedhwinis, or Nuns, live also in separate communities, but are now very few in number. The Jain laity are called Srávakas, *i. e.*, Hearers; the females being properly termed Srávakis. They have among them a modified form of Caste; and what wonder, since in Southern India Mahomedans and Christians have the same. . . . . The practical part of the Jain religion consists in the performance of five duties, and the avoidance of five sins. The duties are:—1. Mercy to all animals. 2. Almsgiving. 3. Venerating the sages while living, and worshipping their images when deceased. 4. Confession of faults. 5. Religious fasting. The sins are:—1. Killing.

2. Lying. 3. Stealing. 4. Adultery. 5. Worldly-mindedness. A striking picture of the Jain religion is the keeping of the season of religious meditation, reading, and fasting, called the Paryúshana, or, popularly, Pajjúsana. It corresponds with the Bud'hist Wasso, and is divided into two parts, the fifty days that precede and the seventy that succeed the fifth of Bhadra, Sukla Paksha. The Svetámbaras fast, during the former period, and the Digámbaras during the latter. The last thing I shall advert to, *is the existence among the Jainas of the Confessional, and the necessity that exists of confessing at least once a year to a priest, and of obtaining from him ghostly absolution. Burdened consciences confess at all times, and have various kinds of fasts imposed on them as penances.* It is, however, only at the commencement of the holy season that it is considered imperative upon every good Jain to confess to a priest. I must own that I was at first a little startled at this article in the Jain creed, and I thought I must have made some mistake in interpreting the word Padikaman (*Sansc.*) Pratikramana, by which term the duty is technically expressed; but abundant oral and written explanations, as well as the context of several passages, where the word occurs, have removed every doubt.

No. V.

THE JAINAS.

FROM COLEMAN'S HINDU MYTHOLOGY.

THE Jainas, or Svarakas, or Swarkas, have been considered as a division of the sect of Budd'ha; but the principal tenet of their faith is in direct opposition to the belief of that sect. The latter deny the existence of a Supreme Being; the former admit of one, but deny his interference in the regulation of the universe. Like the Budd'has, they believe that there is a plurality of heavens and hells; that our rewards and punishments depend on our merits and demerits; and that the future births of men are regulated by their goodness or wickedness in every state of animal life. On these points the reader need only refer to the article "Budd'ha," to find a full description, which it would be unnecessary to recapitulate. Thus, like the Brahmins, the Jainas acknowledge a Supreme Being, but pay their devotion to divine objects of their own creation, with this difference, that the Brahmins represent their deities to be of heavenly descent; whereas the Jaina objects of worship, like, but at the same time distinct from, those of the Budd'has, are mortals of alleged transcendent virtue, raised to beatitude by their piety, benevolence, and goodness. Equally with the Budd'has they deny the divine authority of the Vedas, yet they admit the images of the gods of the Vedantic religion into their temples, and, it is said, to a certain extent worship them, but consider them to be inferior to their own Tir'thankaras. They, therefore, appear to blend, in practice, portions of the two faiths, advocating doctrines scarcely less irrational than those of atheists, and no less wild than the heretogeneous polytheism of the Brahmins.

The founder of the Jaina sect was Rishabedeva, who was incarnate thirteen times. After him twenty-three other sages, or holy men, became the Tir-'thankaras, or Gurus of the sect, who were incarnate twenty-seven times. Gautama, the present Budd'ha, was his disciple. The Budd'has state, that twenty-two Budd'has appeared on earth before Gautama. The Jainas describe twenty-four of their Tir-'thankaras. The Jainas derive their name from the word Jine (Ji, to conquer). A Jaina must overcome the eight great crimes, viz., eating at night, or eating of the fruit of trees that give milk; slaying an animal; tasting honey or flesh; taking the wealth of others, or taking by force a married woman; eating flour, butter, or cheese; and worshipping the gods of other religions.

The Jainas extend the doctrine of benevolence towards sentient animals to a greater degree than the Budd'has, with whom they agree in their belief of transmigration. A Jaina, Yati, or priest, carries with him a broom, made of cotton threads, to sweep the ground before him as he passes along, or as he sits down, lest he should tread or sit upon and injure anything that has life. A strict Yati will not, consequently, go out on a rainy day; nor, for the same reason, speak without first covering his mouth. He will neither drink water which has not been boiled; wash his clothes; bathe or cleanse any part of his body, from the apprehension that he should, by so doing, inadvertently destroy any living animal.[1]

[1] A strong instance of their strict adherence to this article of religion is related in Major Seeley's work, the "Wonders of Elrora." "An ascetic at Benares was, like the rest of the sect, extremely apprehensive of causing the death of an animal. Some mischievous European gave him a microscope to look at the water he drank. On seeing the animalculæ, he threw down and broke the instrument, and vowed he would not drink water again. He kept his promise and died."

No. VI.

HUC'S MONGOLIA.

CATHEDRALS OF THE MIDDLE AGES.

Ces monuments grandioses et somptueux, qu' on rencontre si souvent dans le désert, sont dus au zèle libre et spontané des Mongols. Si simples et si économes dans leur habillement et dans leur vivre, ces peuples sont d'une générosité, on peut même dire d'une prodigalité étonnante, dès qu' il s'agit de culte et de dépenses religieuses. Quand on a résolu de construire quelque part d'un temple bouddhique entouré de sa lamaserie, les Lamas quêteurs se mettent aussitôt en route, munis de passeports qui attestent la légitimité de leur mission. Ils se distribuent les royaumes de Tartarie, et vont de tente en tente demander des aumônes au nom du *vieux Bouddha.* Aussitôt qu' ils sont arrivés dans une famille, et qu' ils ont annoncé le but de leur voyage, en montrant le bassin bénit où on dépose les offrandes, ils sont accueillis avec joie et enthousiasme. Dans ces circumstances, il n'est personne qui se dispense de donner; les riches déposent dans le *badir*[1] des lingots d'or ou d'argent; ceux qui ne possèdent pas de métaux précieux, comme ils disent, offrent des bœufs, des chevaux ou des chameaux; les pauvres même contribuent selon la modicité de leurs ressources; ils donnent des pains, de beurre, des pelleteries, des cordages tressés avec des poils de chameau ou des crins de cheval. Au bout de quelque temps on a recueilli ainsi des sommes immenses; alors, dans ces déserts en apparence si pauvre, on voit s'élever comme par enchantement, des édifices dont la grandeur et les richesses défieraient les ressources des potentats les plus opulents. C'est sans doute de cette manière, et par le concours empressé de tous les fidèles, qu' on vit autrefois surgir en Europe ces magnifiques cathédrales dont les travaux gigantesques ne cessent d'accuser l'égoïsme et l'indifférence des temps modernes. . . .

1 C'est le nom du bassin dont se servent les Lamas pour demander l'aumône.

No. VII.

LAMAIC INFLUENCE OF TARTARY AND ROME.

FROM HUC'S MONGOLIA.

Aussitot que le Guison-Tamba se mit en marche, toutes les tribus de la Tartarie s'ébranlèrent, et on vit accourir de toute part sur son passage des foules innombrables. Chaque tribu arrivait avec ses offrandes : des troupeaux de chevaux, de bœufs, et de moutons, des lingots d'or et d'argent, et des pierres précieuses. On avait creusé des puits de distance en distance, dans tout la traversée du grand désert de Gobi ; et les rois des divers pays par où le cortège devait passer, avaient disposé long-temps d'avance des provisions, dans tous les endroits fixés pour les campements. Le Lama-Roi était dans un palanquin jaune, porté par quatre chevaux que conduisaient quatre grands dignitaires de la lamaserie. Les trois mille Lamas du cortége précédaient ou suivaient le palanquin, montés sur des chevaux ou sur des chameaux, courant sans ordre dans tous les sens, et s'abandonnant à leur enthousiasme. Les deux côtés du passage étaient bordés de spectateurs, on plutôt d'adorateurs, qui attendaient avec impatience l'arrivée du saint. Quand le palanquin paraissait, *tous tombaient à genoux*, puis s'étendaient tout de leur long, *le front touchant la terre*, et les mains jointes par dessus la tête. *On eût dit le passage d'une divinité qui daigne traverser la terre pour verser ses bénédictions sur les peuples.* Le Guison-Tamba continua ainsi sa marche pompeuse et triomphale jusqu'à la grande muraille ; là il cessa d'être Dieu, pour n'être plus que le prince de quelques tribus nomades, méprisées des chinois, objet de leurs sarcasmes et de leurs moqueries, mais redoutées par la cour de Péking, à cause de la terrible influence qu'elles pouraient exercer sur les destinées de l'empire. Il ne fut permis qu'à une moitié de la suite de passer la frontière ; tout le reste fut forcé de camper au nord de la grande muraille, dans les plaines du *Tchakar*. . . . . Les souvenirs de l'ancienne puissance des Mongols le préoccupent sans cesse ; il sait qu'autrefois ils ont été maîtres de l'empire ; et dans la crainte d'une nouvelle invasion, il s'applique à les affaiblir par tous les moyens possibles. Cependant, quoique la Mongolie soit très peu peuplée, eu égard à son immense étendue de terrain, il peut en sortir au premier jour une armée formidable. Un grand Lama, le Guison-Tamba, par exemple, *n'aurait qu'à faire un geste*, et tous les Mongols, depuis les frontières de la Sibérie jusqu' aux extremités du Thibet, *se levant comme un seul homme, iraient, se précipiter avec la véhémence d'un torrent partout où la voix de leur Saint les appellerait.*

No. VIII.

BUD'HISM OF ROME.

FROM DR. NEWMAN'S "LECTURES;" MORE PROPERLY "THE BIRMINGHAM MYTHOLOGY."

"CERTAINLY the Catholic Church, from east to west, from north to south, is, according to our conceptions, hung with miracles. The store of relics is inexhaustible; they are multiplied through all lands, and each particle of each has in it at least a dormant, perhaps an energetic virtue, of supernatural operation. At Rome there is the True Cross, the Crib of Bethlehem, and the Chair of St. Peter; portions of the Crown of Thorns are kept at Paris; the Holy Coat is shown at Trèves; the winding-sheet at Turin; at Monza, the iron crown is formed out of a Nail of the Cross; and another Nail is claimed for the Duomo of Milan; and pieces of our Lady's habit are to be seen in the Escurial. The Agnus Dei, blest medals, the scapular, the cord of St. Francis, all are the medium of Divine manifestations and graces. Crucifixes have bowed the head to the suppliant, and Madonnas have bent their eyes upon assembled crowds. St. Januarius's blood liquefies periodically at Naples; and St. Winifred's well is the scene of wonders, even in an unbelieving country. Women are marked with the sacred stigmata; blood has flowed on Fridays from their five wounds, and their heads are crowned with a circle of lacerations. Relics are ever touching the sick, the deceased, the wounded, sometimes with no result at all, at other times with marked and undeniable efficacy. Who has not heard of the abundant favours gained by the intercession of the Blessed Virgin, and of the marvellous consequences which have attended the invocation of St. Anthony of Padua? These phenomena are sometimes reported of Saints in their life-time, as well as after death, especially if they were evangelists or martyrs. The wild beasts crouched before their victims in the Roman amphitheatre; the axe-man was unable to sever St. Cecilia's head from her body, and St. Peter elicited a spring of water for his jailor's baptism in the Mamertine. St. Francis Xavier turned salt water into fresh for five hundred travellers; St. Raymond was transported over the sea on his cloak; St. Andrew shone brightly in the dark; St. Scholastica gained by her prayers a pouring rain; St. Paul was fed by ravens; and St. Frances saw her guardian angel."

See the account of the rival True Church of Bud'ha in this work.

No. IX.

ON PRODUCTIVE MACHINERY.

By Dr. Newman (See his "Lectures," or "Birmingham Mythology," page 293—4.)

"Were a miracle reported to me as wrought by a member of Parliament, or a Bishop of the Establishment, or a Wesleyan preacher, I should repudiate the notion; were it referred to a Saint, or the relic of a Saint, or the intercession of a Saint, I should not be startled at it, though I might not at once believe it. And I certainly should be right in this conduct, supposing my First Principle be true. Miracles to the Catholic are historical facts, and nothing short of this; and they are to be regarded and dealt with as other facts; and as natural facts, under circumstances, do not startle Protestants, so supernatural under circumstances do not startle the Catholic. They may, or may not, have taken place in particular cases: he may be unable to determine which; he may have no distinct evidence; he may suspend his judgment, but he will say 'it is very possible;' he never will say, 'I cannot believe it.'"

See this doctrine applied equally in favour of the Bud'hists in page 326-330 of this work.

No. X.

TARTARIAN LAMAISM.

From the Works of Mr. Alexander Csoma Cöröso, Siculo-Hungarian of Transylvania.

The great compilation of the Thibetan Sacred Books is in 100 volumes, called the Ká-gyur. They contain the doctrines of Shakya (Sakya), a Budha, who is supposed to have lived B.C. 1000.

SOME OUTLINES OF THESE WORKS.

Shakya declares that his privations and austerities during six years were of no effect; refreshes himself with substantial food; recovers his vigour—gives himself to meditation and arrives at perfection, or becomes a Boodha; he goes to Varanasi; teaches his doctrine first to five men, who had formerly been his attendants; afterwards disciplining fifty young persons of high descent, ordains and consecrates them; goes to Raja Griha (Palipootra); the king of Magad'ha, Kimbasara offers him a residence in a grove; brings over to his doctrine two young Brahmins; refuses to admit any one without the consent of his parents, issues orders prohibiting the seduction of nuns or priestesses, by monks or priests; Shakya, together with five hundred Arhatas or Saints, visits, in a miraculous manner, the great lake Ma-dros (Manassaroovára) in the North; relative temperance of Gautama's (Budha's) system and the Brahminical; use of flesh, with what restriction permitted to his disciples; how a priest *may give his blessing to any quantity of physic for seven days;* wonderful effects of almsgiving to a holy man; Sagama married to the son of a chief officer at Shravasti, in Cosala; her modesty, prudence, and accomplishments; a Vihara is founded in her name; she is delivered of thirty-two eggs, from which thirty-two young boys come forth; Sagama's offering at Shravasti; presents some pieces of cotton cloth for the monks and nuns to make bathing clothes of, since she had been informed that such garments had not hitherto been used; how to divide the effects of deceased religious persons; on the leaving off the feast of the confession; on disputes and quarrels of the monks; circumstances that induced Shakya to take the religious character; his reflections; sees the wretched condition of the agriculturists; gives himself to meditation; resolves to use food; is presented with a refined milk-soup by two maids; gives himself up to meditation; overcomes the devil; becomes a Bud'ha; celebration of the confession at every new and full moon; exhortation to the priests to examine themselves and to confess their sins aloud, *if they have any.* Besides rules for the confession of faults, numerous instructions regarding diet, behaviour, dress, attitude, and position of body; manner of eating and drinking, and when giving religious instruction to others; effects of despairing discourses on the miseries of life; several women of respectable families, at Shrávasti, visit the Viharas, in a garden near that city, conducted by Ch'har-Ka, a priest, who tells them whose Viharas they are. His modest behaviour. The priests of Shakya are said to have so many clothes, that for each business they make use of a different suit, and that through dressing and undressing themselves they have little leisure to read and study. Several rules respecting superfluous clothes of the priests. The seventh volume of the Dulva contains a list of the faults of the priests, divided into Greater faults and Venial Faults ; the chapels where the hair and nails of Bud'ha are deposited and reserved as sacred things ; priests prohibited from wearing rings ; they may keep vessels of copper, brass, bell-metal, iron, or horn. The veracity of Bud'ha thus expressed :—

"The moon, together with the host of stars, may fall down ; the earth, together with the forests, may lift itself up into the void space above ; the vast ocean may be dried up, but it is impossible that the Great Hermit (Maha-Saramana) should tell a falsehood." Prohibition of learning dancing or singing. Umbrellas allowed. Catyayana, with five hundred other priests, sent by Sakya, to convert to his doctrine the King of Hp'hags-rgâl, together with his consorts, sons, and officers. The Bodhiswatas descent to be in central India. Family not decided on by the gods. The Shakya himself decides on being incarnated in the house of Shudhodana. Being indisposed, the devil advises him to die. He is defied by the Nagas. Scene of Shakya's labours in Central India, or in the country of Mathura. Shakya's victory over the devil. The devil vanishes, much dejected on account of his ill-success. His final victory over the devil under the holy fig-tree in the neighbourhood of Gaya. Thus victorious, passes through several degrees of deep meditations and ecstasies, and at last, about day-break, arrives at the supreme wisdom in the thirty-sixth year of his age. Hymns and prayers of Tathágatá (Shakya). Is attended by the gods of several heavens. Successively converses with the gods of the highest heaven, down to the gods that dwell on the surface of the earth. The gods cause a shower of divine sandal powder to descend, and they thus sing his praises :—

"Gautama is without sin. He stands on high ground. The prince of physic is come to cure them of all their diseases ; none of those who come to see him shall go to hell for a thousand years. Free from all further incarnations, they enjoy the greatest happiness. These are the persons on whom alms may be bestowed. These alms shall *contribute to their final deliverance from pains.* Dispute about Shakya's relics. Its reconciliation effected by a Brahmin. Division of the relics, and building of Chaityas, or Shrines, for them."

Such is a very slight outline of the contents of the great Thibetian collection of the Ká-Ghyuar. Very valuable additional information on the Catholic doctrines of Tartary, may be seen in the 20th volume of The Asiatic Researches, written by the Thibetan traveller and scholar, De Cörös.

No. XI.

COLONEL MURE ON DEIFICATION.

"The most subtle casuistry can point out no general distinction, between the apotheosis of kings, or great men, in the historical ages of Greece or Rome, and that of popular heroes, in fabulous antiquity. It is further remarkable, that in the dark as well as the historical ages of classical Paganism, it is exemplified chiefly in Monarchical, and rarely, if ever, in Republican states."

"The critic," observes Colonel Mure, "who desires to avail himself of the light of history, in elucidating the obscurities of early fable, will reason as follows:—During the whole period of Classical Antiquity, on which that light clearly shines, there exists proof of the prevalence of this custom, under the same forms described in mythical tradition. By reference to historical analogy, it were as unreasonable to deny, on the mere ground of supernatural attributes, the real personality of Achilles, as that of Vespasian. . . . Perhaps, however, the most pointed illustration of the Greek system of apotheosis, *and generally of the basis of fact, in classical fables*, is that derived from the Saint-worship of the Roman Catholic Church. The arguments by which it has been proposed to set aside the human personality of Agamemnon or Achilles, would equally disprove that of St. Benedict, or St. Francis. Many of the Roman Catholic saints are gifted in the legends, which supply the chief, or only record of their existence, with attributes still more supernatural than those ascribed by Homer to the warriors of Troy. They have been promoted to celestial honours, and worshipped in all essential respects, as were the Greek demi-gods, or deified heroes. Yet, no one denies, that a large portion of them were real characters, connected with historical events. Nor is it easy to see, how an opposite inference can fairly be drawn, relative to the Greek heroes."

No. XII.

FROM THE PREFACE TO THE MAHAWANSO.

It became a point of interesting inquiry to ascertain whether the Bud'hists of Ceylon had ventured to interpolate this injunction, as well as "the five resolves silently willed by G'otamo," mentioned in the seventeenth chapter, into the Pitakattaya, for the purpose of deluding the inhabitants of this island; as that imposition might, perhaps, have been detected by comparing those passages with the Pitakattaya of the Burmese empire, and the Sanscrit edition presented to the Bengal Asiatic Society, by Mr. Hodgson. On referring, accordingly, to the Parinibb'ananasuttan in the D'ighanikáyo, *no trace whatever was to be found there of these passages.* But the "five resolves" alone are contained in the Atthakathá to that Suttan: but even there the command to Sukko, predictive of Wijayo's landing in Ceylon, is not noticed.

I took the opportunity of an official interview with the two high priests of the Malwatte and Asgiri establishments and their fraternity, to discuss this, apparently fatal, discrepancy, with them. They did not appear to be aware that the "five resolves" were only contained in the Atthakathá, not did they attach any kind of importance to their absence from the text. They observed that the Pitakattaya only embodied the essential portions of the discourses, revelations, and prophecies of Buddha. That his disciples for some centuries after his nibbánan, were endowed with inspiration; and that *their* supplements to the Pitakattaya were as sacred in their estimation as the text itself. On a slight hint being thrown out, whether this particular supplement might not have been "a pious fraud" on the priests of Mahindo, with the view of accelerating the conversion of the ancient inhabitants of Ceylon; the priests adroitly replied, if *that* had been his object, he would have accomplished it more effectually by altering the Pitakattaya itself. Nothing can exceed the good taste, the unreserved communicativeness, and even the tact, evinced by the heads of the Budd'histical church in Ceylon, in their intercourse with Europeans, as long as they are treated with the courtesy that is due to them.

The fabulous tone of the narrative in which the account of Wijayo's landing in Lanká is conveyed in the seventh chapter bears, even in its details, so close a resemblance to the landing of Ulysses at the island of Circé, that it would have been difficult to defend Mahanámo from the imputation of plagiarism, had he lived in a country in which the works of Homer could, by possibility, be accessible to him. The seizure and imprisonment of Ulysses' men, and his own rencontre with Circé, are almost identical with the fate of Wijayo and his men, on their landing in Lanká, within the dominions of Kuwéni.

> " We went, Ulysses! (such was thy command!)
> Through the lone thicket and the desert land,
> A palace in a woody vale we found,
> Brown with dark forests, and with shades around.
> A voice celestial echo'd from the dome,
> Or nymph or goddess, chanting to the loom.
> Access we sought, nor was access denied;
> Radiant she came; the portals open'd wide:
> The goddess mild, invites the guest to stay:
> They blindly follow where she leads the way.
> I only wait behind of all the train;
> I waited long, and eyed the doors in vain:
> The rest are vanish'd, none repassed the gate;
> And not a man appears to tell their fate."

> " Then sudden whirling, like a waving flame,
> My beamy falchion, I assault the dame.
> Struck with unusual fear, she trembling cries;
> She faints—she fails; she lifts her weeping eyes.
> 'What art thou? say! from whence, from whom you came?
> O, more than human! tell thy race, thy name.
> Amazing strength, these poisons to sustain!
> Not mortal thou, nor mortal is thy brain.
> Or art thou he? the man to come (foretold
> By Hermes, powerful with the wand of gold),
> The man from Troy, who wander'd ocean round;
> The man for wisdom's various arts renown'd,
> Ulysses? Oh! thy threatening fury cease,
> Sheath thy bright sword, and join our hands in peace!
> Let mutual joys our mutual trust combine,
> And love, and love-born confidence be thine.'
> 'And how, dread Circé! (furious, I rejoin)
> Can love and love-born confidence be mine!
> Beneath thy charms, when my companions groan,
> Transform'd to beasts, with accents not their own?
> O thou of fraudful heart, shall I be led
> To share thy feast-rites, or ascend thy bed;
> That, all unarm'd, that vengeance may have vent,
> And magic bind me, cold and impotent?
> Celestial as thou art, yet stand denied;
> Or swear that oath by which the gods are tied.
> Swear, in thy soul no latent frauds remain,
> Swear by the vow which never can be vain.'
> The goddess swore: then seized my hand, and led
> To the sweet transports of the genial bed."

It would appear that the prevailing religion in Lanká, at that period, was the demon or yakkha-worship. Budd'hists have thence thought proper to represent that the inhabitants were yakkhos or demons themselves, and possessed of supernatural powers. Divested of the false colouring which is imparted to the whole of the early portion of the history of Lanká in the Maháwanso, by this fiction, the facts embodied in the narrative are perfectly consistent, and sustained by external evidence, as well as by surviving remnants of antiquity. No train of events can possibly bear a greater semblance of probability than that Wijayo, at his landing, should have connected himself with the daughter of some provincial chieftain or prince, by whose means he succeeded in overcoming the ruling powers of the island, and that he should have repudiated her, and allied himself with the sovereigns of Southern India, after his power was fully established in the island.

The narrative is too full and distinct in all requisite details, in the ensuing three chapters, to make any further remarks necessary from me.

The eleventh chapter possesses more extended interest, from the account it contains of the embassy sent to Asóko by Dewánanpiyatisso and of the one deputed to Lanká in return.

The twelfth chapter contains the account of the dispersion of the Budd'hist missionaries, at the close of the third convocation in B. C. 307, to foreign countries, for the purpose of propagating their faith.

No. XIII.

SIVA, MAHADEO, OR RUDRA.

FROM COLEMAN'S HINDOO MYTHOLOGY.

THE Destroyer is represented under various forms. He is usually painted of a white or silver colour, with a third eye, and the crescent (which he obtained at the churning of the ocean,) in the middle of his forehead. Sometimes he is described with one head, and at others with five; sometimes armed with various instruments of destruction; and at others riding on the bull, Nandi, with Parvati on his knee; and again, at others, as a mendicant, with inflamed eyes and besotted countenance, soliciting alms from Anna Purna, a form of Purvati. He is also represented under the appearance of Kal, or Time, the destroyer of all things. . . Of the emblems of Siva, Mr. Patterson has conjectured that he has three eyes, to denote the three divisions of time,—the past, the present, and the future. That the crescent in his forehead refers to the measure of time by the phases of the moon, as the serpent denotes it by years; and the necklace of skulls, the lapse and revolution of ages, and the extinction and succession of the generations of mankind. He holds the trident in one hand, to show that the great attributes of creating, preserving, and destroying, are in him united, and that he is the Iswara, or supreme Lord, above Bramah and Vishnu; and that the emblem called *damara*, shaped like an hour-glass, with which he is sometimes seen, was actually intended to be such, to pourtray the progress of time by the current of sand in the glass. On the celebrated colossal sculpture of the *Trimurti*, or three-formed god (Brahma, Vishnu, and Siva,) in the caves of Elephanta, he has marked on his cap a human skull, to show his two-fold power of destruction and reproduction; and on another figure, in the same cave, he is represented in the attributes of his vindictive character, with eight arms, two of which are partly broken off. In one of the remaining six he brandishes a sword, and in another holds a human figure; in the third he has a basin of blood, and in the fourth a sacrificial bell, which he appears to have been ringing over it. With the other two he is in the act of drawing a veil, which obscures the sun, and involves all nature in universal destruction.

The bull Nandi, the *vahan* of Siva, is held in great reverence by the Hindus. This animal is one of the most sacred emblems of Siva, as the Egyptian Apis was of the soul of Osiris. The Egyptians believed that, when he ate out of the hands of those who went to consult him, it was a favourable answer. The Hindus, says Bartolomeo, place rice and other articles before their doors, as the animal passes along in their processions; and if he stop to taste them, consider it as a fortunate event. This, at least, he is very prone to do, to the serious injury of the Hindu shopkeepers, as he wanders, not in his most sacred capacity, through the streets of Calcutta, and other towns.

In the analogies of learned writers of ancient mythologies, Siva, in his character of the creative power, has been compared to the Jupiter Triophthalmos, or the triple-eyed god, the Zeus, or giver of life, of the Greeks; the Osiris of the Egyptians; and the Axieros of the Cabiri of the Phœnicians. Each of these is the personification of the solar fire, and the spirit of all created things.

In his destructive character he is Saturn, or the destroyer, Time. He is also worshipped as Shankạra, or the beneficent deity, as his followers attribute to him the benefits they enjoy from the mighty stream of the Ganges, which is fabled to have sprung from his plaited locks. This, however, the Vishnaivas deny, urging that it first flowed from the foot of Vishnu in Vaicontha (the heaven of Vishnu), when Brahma poured water over it as it was extended to compass the heavens, as related in the *Nara Singha avatar*, from whence it ran on the head of Siva, and descended from thence to fertilise the earth.

The Vishnaivas claim for their deity Vishnu, the title of Iswara, or the supreme lord: the Saivas contest his claim to this pre-eminence, and have bestowed on Siva that of Bhuvan Iswara, or the lord of the universe. The title of Iswara was first enjoyed by Brahma, until the sect of Siva overpowered the worshippers of that God; when Bhairava, the son of Siva, cut off one of his heads. After this, the Saivas, for a time, possessed the supreme power; but it is alleged that the Vishnaivas have since contested the palm of supremacy, and that sanguinary conflicts, attended with alternate victory and defeat, in consequence, ensued between the two sects, which continue even at the present day among their mendicant worshippers, who assemble at stated periods in immense numbers, at the fair of Hurdwar. The subject of their animosity, on these occasions, I have just related, being no other than the very important, but highly apocryphal point, whether the sacred Gunga issued from the foot of Vishnu or the head of Siva.

* * * * *

The Saivas have many sectarial marks: among which are—first, the *trisula*, or trident, to denote the dominion of Siva over heaven, earth, and the infernal regions. This weapon is supposed to be in continual motion over the face of the earth, and instant death would attend opposition to its points. He is from it called the Trident-bearer. Second, *Shúla*, representing the same symbol. Both of these are formed of white earth on the forehead and breast. Third, *Ciakshu*, or *tkkanna*, the sacred eye (or that in the middle of the forehead) of Siva. He is on this occasion called Trilocena, or the triple-eyed god. Fourth, *Agni*, or Ti, or fire; symbolical of the sun. Fifth, *Tirumana*, or the holy earth: the lateral strokes of this sectarial mark are white or yellow, that in the middle red. Sixth, The *tripundara*, or ornament of the three stripes, which also represents Bhavan with her three sons, Brahma, Vishnu, and Siva. It is made with sandal-wood and ashes. Seventh, The *linga*, painted on the neck, arms, and forehead. Eighth, the *crescent*, painted on the forehead yellow. Ninth, the same, with the *puttu*, or spot, of either red, white, or black.

No. XIV.

BHAVANI.

The contradictions which pervade all the parts of the Hindoo mythology are so strongly opposed to every thing in the shape of a consistent relation, that the farther we proceed, the more perplexed we become to reconcile every fresh legend with the fables already related. In the account of the creation, I have mentioned that the goddess Bhavani (or Nature), divided herself into three females, for the purpose of marrying her three sons, Brahma, Vishnu, and Siva; to the last of whom she united herself under the name of Parvati. Other accounts make Parvati the daughter of Brahma, in his earthly form (or *avatar*) of Daksha, named Suti. After her marriage, a dispute arose between that god and Daksha; who not only refused to invite his son-in-law to a feast given in honour of the immortals, but reviled him in terms which roused the indignation of Siva, and pierced the tender and affectionate bosom of Suti, who first resented, and then sank under the contumely; for, on hearing Daksha term him a wandering mendicant, a bearer of skulls, a delighter in cemeteries, a contemner of divine ceremonies, and unfit for the society of the gods, she took the part of her husband; and true to the Hindu creed, that when a virgin marries she leaves for ever her father's house, gave Daksha a memorable lecture in return, which would be too long to insert here, and might, moreover, prove a dangerous specimen of eloquence to some new-married ladies; who, in their zeal, might not always wait for proper occasions to exercise themselves in the recitation of it. I must, therefore, content myself with noticing the incident. Having defended her lord against parental slander and malignity, the sorrowful Suti retired to the banks of the sacred waters of the Ganges, and yielded up her life on the altar of domestic affection. Siva was inconsolable for the loss of his lovely and affectionate wife. On beholding her lifeless form, his senses forsook him: frequent fainting fits ensued; he clasped her to his bosom, pressed his lips to hers, called on her in the bitterness of his anguish to reappear to him; doubted the reality of her death, till again, too fatally convinced of his inevitable loss, he became overwhelmed with grief and despair, and finally sank down overcome by anguish and fatigue. In this state he was found by Vishnu, Brahma, and the other gods, who were not a little astonished at such an exhibition of *godlike* and intolerable woe. The immortal Vishnu shed tears, and attempted to console him, by telling him that nothing was real in this world, but that every thing was altogether *maya*, or illusion. Siva, rejecting this consolatory admonition, joined his tears to those of Vishnu; and thus united, they formed a lake which became a celebrated place of pilgrimage.

At length the beauteous form of Suti re-appeared before them, and with a heavenly smile exhorted the now delighted Siva to be comforted, as she had been again born as the daughter of Himavan, the ruler of the mountains, and Mena, and would never more be separated from him. The transitions from the bitterness of insupportable grief to unexpected happiness are at first tumultuous; but exhausted nature soon seeks that soft and halcyon repose, whose charm is throned in the heart, far beyond the sacrilegious reach of either the tongue or the hand of man. I must therefore content myself with saying, that after some due preparations, Siva and Suti, as Parvati, were reunited, and appear to have lived as happily together as married folks usually do: that is, sometimes in a state of inexpressible bliss, sometimes in ineffable indifference, and sometimes involved in a matrimonial thunder-cloud, the veil of which we ought not, if we could, attempt to penetrate.

" Above the stretch of mortal ken,
On bless'd Kailasas top, where every stem
Glowed with a vegetable gem,
Mahesa sate, the dread and joy of men.
While Parvati, to gain a boon,
Fix'd on his locks a beamy moon,
And hid his frontal eye, in jocund play,
With reluctant sweet delay:
All nature straight was lock'd in dim eclipse,
Till Brahmans pure, with hallowed lips
And warbled prayers, restored the day;
When Gunga from his brow, by heavenly fingers prest,
Sprang radiant, and, descending, graced the caverns of the West."

Sir William Jones's Hymn to Gunga.

Had Siva been content to have remained, like the exemplary benedicts of this thrice felicitous and favoured isle, becomingly at home, and not have wandered abroad at unseasonable hours, things would have gone on between them as they should have done, and the portentous cloud to which I have alluded (which often alarmed even the gods) would not, in all probability, have appeared.

But such matters are considered by the rulers of the universe of very slight importance, and both the reader and myself must be satisfied to take them as we actually find them, without adopting the Quixotic undertaking of attempting to make them better.

Before going farther into the life of Parvati, I must observe, on the authority of Mr. Patterson, that when Vishnu beheld Siva dancing about frantically with the deceased form of Suti in his arms, he cut it into fifty-one pieces, which Siva, who still continued in his frenzy, scattered in different parts of the earth. These spots he afterwards ordained to be the places of worship, to his own and his Energy's peculiar emblems. Daksha, who had been slain by Vira Badra, in consequence of the death of Suti, was restored to life, but with the head of a goat, on condition of his adopting the doctrines of Siva.

Mr. Patterson imagines that these circumstances arose from an attempt, on the part of Daksha, to abolish the worship of the emblem of Siva, in which he was unsuccessful.

Parvati had, as the consort of Siva, maternal claims upon Kartikeya, the leader of the celestial armies, and Ganesha, or Ganaputty, the god of wisdom.

They were both produced in a very extraordinary manner, as will be seen in the descriptions of them. Parvati is the goddess of a thousand names; and both her forms and powers are more various and extensive than those of any of the other Hindu deities. She acts sometimes dependent on, at others wholly independent of her husband, Siva.

As Bhavani, she is the goddess of nature and fecundity, and is invoked by women in labour. As Maha Devi, she is "the goddess," the *sacti* of the lord of the universe, Mahadeo. As Parvati, she is his constant companion. As Durga, or Katyayini, she is the Amazonian champion and potent protectress of the gods, endowed by them severally with their attributes, and wielding in her numerous hands their various instruments of destruction, with which, for their protection, they had armed her. In this character she has been compared to the Olympian Juno, and the Pallas, or armed Minerva, of the Greeks; but clearly thus blending in herself the power and divinity of all the gods, of incomparably greater importance than either. As Kali; she is their Diana Taurica, and personifying that black abyss, eternity, by which Kal (or Time itself) shall be destroyed (pictured by her trampling upon Siva in that character,) she is arrayed in attributes supreme over those of her husband.

Parvati has been described under numerous forms; but as they are only variations of the more important ones, Bhavani, Devi, Durga, and Kali, I shall content myself with noticing those under which she is most generally known.

As Parvati, she is described of a white; as Kali, of a dark blue or black ; and as the majestic and tremendous Durga (of whom I shall now treat), of a yellow colour.

In this character she is represented with ten arms. In one hand she holds a spear, with which she is piercing the giant Muhisha ; in another a sword ; in a third, the hair of the giant, and the tail of a serpent twined round him ; and in others the trident, the discus, the axe, the club, the arrow, and the shield. One of her knees presses on the body of the giant, and her right foot rests on the back of a lion, which is lacerating his arm. On her head she has a crown richly ornamented, and her dress is magnificently adorned with jewels.

No. XV.

CASHMIR.[1]

It appears very evident that Cashmir has been a regular kingdom for a period that transcends the limits of legitimate history ; and even if we feel disposed to contest the accounts of our author, and to dispute his series of Dynasties and Princes, we must still rest satisfied with the proof of its existence either under the names of *Caspatyrus* or *Abisarus*, as early as the days of Herodotus and Alexander. There can be no doubt, however, of the regular organisation of this state at a period much antecedent ; and it is probable that, in remote times, it exercised a more decided interference in the concerns of India than it has done for many centuries past ; it seems highly probable, also, that it was the original dominion of the Pándava princes, and that it furnished in them Sovereigns to the plains of Hindustan.

The religion of Cashmir has, in like manner, been Hindu from a very remote date. Originally, no doubt, it was the Ophite, or snake worship, but this is a part of the Hindu ritual, and the *Nagas* are included in the orthodox pantheon. The adoration of Siva was soon engrafted upon this, even if the two rites were not originally identified.

It appears that the Buddha schism was known in Cashmir at a very early period, and possibly preceded the introduction of a fully organised Brahminical priesthood ; it probably, in short, preceded the introduction of the Brahminical *caste*. Asoca, although a worshipper of Siva, is said to have countenanced this new faith. His son, Jaloca, commenced his reign with serious efforts to repress it, and it was possibly partly with this view that he introduced the colony of Brahmans from Canouj.

[1] From Professor Wilson's "Raja Tarangini," As. Res., vol. xv.

No. XVI.

ON THE STATE AND FUTURE PROSPECTS OF SANSCRIT LITERATURE.

Read by W. C. Taylor, Esq., Dec. 1834.—Journal of the Royal Asiatic Society, vol. II.

Sanscrit literature is perfectly anomalous; connected with everything, and identified with nothing; both in form and substance bearing a close resemblance to the extinct relics of ancient Europe, nothing but a common origin can account for the similarity. It was an astounding discovery, that Hindoostan, a land over which so many conquerors had passed in wrath, and left their foot-prints as they went, possessed, spite of the changes of realm, and chances of time, a language of unrivalled richness and variety; a language the parent of all those dialects that Europe has fondly called classical—the source alike of Greek flexibility and Roman strength. A philosophy, compared with which, in point of age, the lessons of Pythagoras are but of yesterday; and in point of daring speculation, Plato's boldest efforts were tame and common-place. A poetry more purely intellectual than any of those of which we had before any conception; and systems of science whose antiquity baffled all powers of astronomical calculation. This literature, with all its colossal proportions, which can scarcely be described without the semblance of bombast and exaggeration, claimed of course a place for itself—"it stood alone, and it was able to stand alone."

To acquire the mastery of this language is almost the labour of a life; its literature seems exhaustless. The utmost stretch of imagination can scarce comprehend its boundless mythology. Its philosophy has touched upon every metaphysical difficulty; its legislation is as varied as the castes for which it was designed.

No. XVII.

GREEK ALPHABET.

ON THE DYNASTY OF THE SAH KINGS OF SURASHTRA.

By Edward Thomas, Esq., Bengal Civil Service.[1]

After observing on Major Rawlinson's remarks on the Seleucidian æra, Mr. T. remarks: "In addition to this, were any faith to be placed in similarity of characters, many of the numerical symbols might be identified as possibly of Greek derivation; for instance, the ⊖ is the exact form of the Greek Θ, of the Sigæan (500 and odd B.C.), and Apollonian (a few years B.C.), alphabets.[2] But so also is the Indian cipher, recognisable as a Greek Θ, as indeed the Pali ⊙ th itself, is absolutely identical with the Θ of the Nemean and Athenian forms of the same letter. The Indian ш approaches closely to the outline of the Greek Ξ of Cadmus, and of the Sigæan characters. The coin figure of ꙍ is likewise a perfect rendering of the Attic Ω. B.C. 400.[3]

Amid all this, on the other hand, it is amply manifest, that whatever of enlarged ideas of arrangement and distribution of numerals the Indians may perchance have owed to the Greeks, they did not generally adopt their letters, or even their literal equivalent system, as modified to suit their own alphabet; and, judging from the strictly Indian forms retained by some of the *litoral* figures, now seen to have been in use under the Sáhs of Guzerát, it is almost necessary to infer that the *original outlines* of the figures themselves were either drawn from an anterior Sanscrit, or else from a more purely Pali alphabet than that concurrently employed in ordinary writing; *the admission of which fact in itself, goes far to demand a consequent concession, that the Indians were not indebted to the Greeks for any assistance in the matter.*

[1] Journ. Royal Asiat. Society, vol. xii. p. 42.

[2] *Vide* Edinburgh Review, or Quarterly, on Rawlinson's Discovery, in Journ. Royal Asiat. Society, 1847.

[3] See Fry's Pantographia.

No. XVIII.

CSOMA DE CÖRÖS ON THE HUNGARIAN AND SANSCRIT.

As a proof of early influence, early possession, language, and settlement, of the Indian nations, I would quote part of the Csoma de Körös' preface to his Tibetan Dictionary. Speaking of the Sanscrit, that learned Hungarian observes, "To his own nation he feels a pride in announcing that the study of the Sanscrit will be more satisfactory than to any other people of Europe. The Hungarians will find a fund of information from its study, respecting their origin, manners, customs, and language, since the structure of Sanscrit, (as also of other Indian dialects,) is most analogous to the Hungarian, while it greatly differs from the languages of occidental Europe. As an example of this close analogy, in the Hungarian language, instead of prepositions, postpositions are invariably used, except with the personal pronouns. Again, from a verbal root, without the aid of any auxiliary verb, and by a simple syllabic addition, the several kinds of verbs, distinguished as active, passive, casual, desiderative, frequentative, reciprocal, &c., are formed in the Hungarian, in the same manner as the Sanscrit."

No. XIX.

ON MASKS.

EXTRACT FROM A LETTER OF ED. UPHAM, ESQ., TO THE REV. J. CALLAWAY.

THE exquisitely satirical comedy of the "Birds" of Aristophanes, illustrates the machinery of masks, with a humour that is as inimitable, as its fidelity to ancient mythology and oriental doctrine is most striking. The comparison of this drama with the Indian doctrine of the heavens, the region of Jagandare, its inhabitants, the king of the gigantic birds, the Roc of the Himäleh, and its enchanted caves, gives a richness to his imagery, that renders its perusal a delightful treat. It is impossible to peruse this drama, and compare it with the Bud'hist doctrine of a hemisphere or region, covering, as a celestial cope, the earth tenanted by gigantic birds, gooroolas, &c., and their position in the mid-air, the very region of the Greek Satirist, *and suppose him to be ignorant of the great pivot of* oriental doctrine, or the intention of the exquisite machinery of his drama. How truly do the following elegant and spirited lines open the doctrine of the metempsychosis, whose judiciary inflictions are placed exclusively in this very region by Gaudamas Bana :—

> "Oh come ye men, ye brittle things, *mere images of clay,*
> *Ye flitting leaves, ye shadowy shapes,* ye creatures of a day;
> Poor wingless wretched mortals ye, like nothing but a dream,
> Give heed to us, and list for once to an immortal theme."

These few imperfect hints, show how closely the masks of the theatric spectacles resembled the exhibitions of oriental doctrine. It cannot, therefore, be doubted, that very important desiderata to the true origin of masks are opened to inquiry by your valuable translation of the Kōlan Natannawá. It exhibits the masks of the demons, and of the Jagandri, so as to show them *to be the true prototypes of the Birds of Aristophanes*, of the giants of Pollux, and the frightful forms of Lucian.

No. XX.

RULES ON THE FORMATIVE PROCESS OF THE GREEK.

The long sound of a is expressed indifferently by a, or by ā, just as either may approximate to the forms in which we have been accustomed to see words written in which these vowels appear.

The short vowel sound of u, in but, hut, rut, will appear indifferently as short a, e, o, u—all which symbols, though apparently differing, have identically the same powers ; for though the English articulation may produce a vast difference in the sound and sense of nat, net, not, nut, yet the Sanscrit brief vocalisation is constant in rendering all these forms by nut. Thus the short terminative o, Greek, becomes the short u of the Latin.

As the members of each class of consonants in Sanscrit are perpetually interchanging, so in the formative process of the Greek language these consonants assume a great latitude of appearance—Kh, k, g, gh, commuting their respective powers. In all these cases the eye is a keener instrument in detecting variations than the ear.

Rule 1.—Ecthlipsis of the short oo, or u, or a, as gokola, gok'la.

Rule 2.—Ă, ĕ, ŏ, ŭ, will be considered to have the same power; as pă, pĕ, pŏ, pŭ, a chief where the short sound is expressed by the u, in but, or the o in Dumbarton.

Rule 3.—The visargah of the Sanscrit is often supplied by the Greek or Latin S, as pa, a chief, or pas.

Rule 4.—The double o is indifferently written as u, or oo, just as it may approximate to the Greek way of writing any term specially noticed.

Rule 5.—C and K are used as identical when required by the Greek form, as Goc'las, or Gok'las; Lacedæmon, or Lakedæmon, both expressed by the hard sound of the k in kindle.

Rule 6.—The double o Sanscrit, when preserved in the Greek, often assumes the form of a, indicating the broad sound of that vowel by the Greeks; thus Poor-Salus, becomes Phar-salus ; and Soo-Lamas, Sa-Lamis; on the other hand, the long a, Sanscrit, becomes the o, Greek or Latin, as Trajya becomes Troja.

Rule 7.—The ancient sound of v, Sanscrit, is very frequently lost in Greek; as Aineanes for Vaineanes; Aijayan for Vaijayan, in Latin Ægæan. (For p. 129, see Rule 6.)

Rule 8.—The Sanscrit su is the Greek u *passim*, as Subœa becomes Eubœa.

Rule 9.—OI Greek is the Œ Latin and English, as Euboia, Eubœa. (For p. 55, see Rule 8.)

Rule 10.—The hard sound of b Sanscrit is often represented by the Greek ph, as Budhya-des for Phthiotis. It is thus evident that ph, Greek, could not have been pronounced as "f" in fine, but as ph in uphill. (For p. 104, see Rule 11.)

Rule 11.—The Greek "X" is the representative of the Sanscrit ks or ksh, as Oxus, Ooksha.

Rule 12.—B, P, V are commutable.

Rule 13.—The Greek υ is expressed by the Latin or English y.

Rule 14.—The Sanscrit S is often expressed by T, and Th of the Greeks; as Srawkes, Thrakes; Srooc'lo, Troglo; Someros, Tomaros. Soo-raksh, Tho-raks (Thorax).

Rule 15.—The j Sanscrit, is often eclipsed by y, as Bahoo-ja, Bahooya; Rajan, Rayan, and sometimes totally lost, as Ran, for Rajan.

Rule 16.—The Sanscrit v is often resolved by the Greek ω or ο.

As M'avusi beomes M'aoosi, or Mausi; El-vusium becomes El-usium; Sarawanica, Saronica; Helavas, Helous; Argwala, Argolis; Okshwali, Ozoli.

Rule 17.—Bhi, Sanscrit is represented in Greek by Phi, as Bhilipos, Philippos.

Dh, Sanscrit, is the Greek Th, as Athēnē, Adheenee; while the Sanscrit termination des, land, or country, is expressed by tus, dus, des, thus, tus, tas, tis tes.

Rule 18.—The Greek often prefixes an euphonic syllable to Sanscrit words beginning with a consonant, as—A'carna, for Carna, Apollo, for 'Bala, A-thaman, for Daman. (For p. 79, see Rule 19.)

Rule 19.—A, Sanscrit, very frequently becomes i, in Greek,—as Bolani, Bullini. (For p. 112, see Rule 6.)

Rule 20.—The Sanscrit y is the Greek i; as Antyoko, for Antiochos; this is of very constant occurrence. The oo is often converted to i, as Cichyrus, for Coocoorus

Rule 21.—Idem.

Rule 22.—The terminations, tus, thus, dus, des, tis, tes are the Sanscrit des, a land or country.

Rule 23.—The converse of Rule 14, Thraces and Thor, become Sracas and Soor; Tooran is Sooran, and Tho-rax is Soo-Raksh ("*the* defence," *par ëminence.*)

Rule 24.—H, in Maha is generally lost, together with its vowel as Maha, Ma; Mahi, Mai.

Rule 25.—The Sanscrit J, and Ch, expressed by the Greek Z; as Jinos, Zeenos; Chakras, Zagreus.

Rule 26.—The Sanscrit j, is often the Greek s, as Apollonos Balanoj, Thēseus Dhēseuj. Naucraros, Naugrarāj.

No. XXI.

VARIATIONS OF THE NAME BUD'HA.

Bud'ha, Buddha, Budda, Budh, Boodha, Booddha, Boutta, Pout, Pote, Pto, Bdho, Wode, Woden, Pat, Pet, Pt, Pta, Pte, Phthi, Phthe, Phtha, Phut, Phoot, Phot, Pht, Bot, Botti, Bout, Boutti, Bhatti, Bhutti, Pod, Bd.

GEOGRAPHICAL INDEX OF N. WESTERN INDIA.

	LAT. D.	LAT. M.	LONG. D.	LONG. M.
Abanti	23	10	76	0
Ace-sines *rises*, . . .	32	30	77	40
Acho	35	20	71	30
Acrobat	34	50	67	40
Adrius (Himalaya Range)				
Agra (Agræi) . . .	27	8	68	2
Akkehu	36	50	66	7
Amoo or Jihoon River .				
Arac	34	40	68	5
Arghasan	30	31	65	30
Astor	35	16	74	44
Attock	33	54	72	18
Balkh	37	0	68	10
Balti (*see* Bulti), *lies between*	34	40	74	40
	35	30	76	20
Bamian	34	50	67	38
Barata	34	15	72	10
Bashan	35	20	72	10
Beebee Nanee . . .	29	39	67	28
Behut	34	21	75	33
Benares	25	20	83	5
Bhini Badam . . .	34	18	68	37
Birgoo	32	5	78	30
Boodh-Rotas (Rotas) .	33	2	73	29
Bopal	23	17	77	30
Bulti, *between* . .	34	40	74	40
	35	30	76	20
Cabool	34	21	68	20
Cahun	29	20	69	15
Cama River . . .	34	24	70	35
Cashmir *or* Kironaya, *between* . . .	33	15	73	40
	34	36	75	30
Daman	30	33	70	71
Dan	28	20	66	10
Doda	33	2	75	18
Dola	31	0	73	16
Dor	34	12	72	39
Dulhuk	2	4	63	48
Duras, Dras, Draus .	34	22	75	30

	LAT. D.	LAT. M.	LONG. D.	LONG. M.
Erectheus, Erec, Arac .	34	40	68	5
Gad	32	40	67	34
Gaza	29	24	66	35
Ghorband	35	4	68	47
Gilghit	35	35	74	15
Goolkuts	31	58	69	22
Gurdan (Dewar) . .	34	25	68	8
Hamoon	30	42	61	8
Hazara	33	50	72	45
Hellopes (Hela Chiefs) .	67°	68°	21	0
Herat	34	22	62	9
Hesht Nuggur . .	34	15	71	40
Himalaya				
Hindoo Koosh, *between*	34	30	68	
	34	37	78	
Huzara	33	50	72	45
Hydaspes (Jailum) . .	34	21	75	33
Indus	31	20	81	15
Jailum	34	21	75	33
Kailas	31	0	79	0
Kandahar	31	37	65	28
Kerketcha (Kurkutcha) .	34	25	69	30
Kerku	35	8	76	[illegible]
Khyber Pass . . .	35	58	71	30
Kishen (Kishen Gunga) .	34	11	75	25
Kishtawar . . .	33	15	75	46
Koondooz River, *see* Oxus River				
Ladahk, *between* .	32-35°		75	30
			79	30
Le	34	11	72	14
Lahore	31	36	74	24
Lespos (Les *or* Lus), *between*	24	50	65	28
	26	15	67	18
Logurh	34	32	69	8
Lughman	34	16	70	51

	LAT. D.	LAT. M.	LONG. D.	LONG. M.
MAGAR TALAO	25	2	67	5
Mali Baia (Multan)	30	8	71	28
Malwa	24	48	76	12
Manasa	34	13	74	35
Mekran	25	28	58	66
Mer or Meru	34	0	76	0
Moultan	30	8	71	28
NILAB and Nile	33	46	72	17
Nubra	34	38	77	10
OIN	33	40	73	50
Ooch	29	13	71	6
Oude (Oita)	26	48	82	4
Ougein (Abanti)	23	11	75	35
Oxus (Ookshas) River.				
PAEN-I-OOKSH (Peneios), or Peneus. *Vide* Oxus.				
Pak	30	20	73	13
Pambur	33	38	75	40
Pamisus. *See* Bamian.				
Paropamisus (Huzareh) *between*	31	50	62	68
	37	0		
Peer Buksh	29	21	70	35
Pelasa	34	40	71	20
Phaliah-(n)	32	0	73	26

	LAT. D.	LAT. M.	LONG. D.	LONG. M.
Pisheen, *between*	30	20	66	30
	30	50	67	20
QUETTA *or* Shawl	30	8	66	56
ROTAS	33	2	73	29
SAIDON (Po-Saidon)	32	56	67	50
Sál *or* Shawl	30	2	66	55
	30	14	67	0
Sarawan	28	47	64	50
Scardus Mons (Iskadoh)	35	10	75	27
Shakur	34	10	71	4
Soo Meroo. *See* Meru	34	0	76	0
TAL and Talantus	35	40	72	10
Tatarus Pass	34	10	71	20
Tattaikas and Tatta	24	44	68	0
Teebhee	30	7	72	51
Tissa	35	33	75	20
Tatara Pass	34	10	71	20
Tomarus (Mér *and* Ser)	34	0	76	0
VIGI-PARA	33	47	75	4
XYNIA (Cashmir)	33	23	74	47
YELUM River	34	21	75	33

ON THE USE OF THE MAPS.

As the maps, both of Northern Greece and the Punjab, may be considered in the light of historical documents, the reader has in the majority of cases been furnished with a duplicate of geographical names; the one containing the Sanscrit in Greek disguise, the other its translation. In the map of the Punjab, names occurring in Palestine and Greece are often placed in the localities whence the emigrants of Palestine or Greece set out; as Phainica, Corubantes, Ashtoreth Carnaim, Phenician Dor,—Attac, Attica; Riv. Behoot, Behooti. A few of the names mentioned in this work, such as the Taulantii and Bullini, could not be inserted without very materially enlarging the bulk of the map. These, however, can be easily seen in the ordinary Classical Atlas. The following is a summary of the

GEOGRAPHICAL NOMENCLATURE OF NORTHERN GREECE.

	Lat. D.	Lat. M.	Lon. D.	Lon. M.		
Abae	38	35	22	56	Abooi . . .	People of Aboo or Ara Boodh.
Abantes (Eubæa) . .					Abanti . . .	People of Oujein.
Acarnania, Prov. .					'Carnān . . .	Land of the Carnas.
ACHELOUS . . .	38	50	21	20	AC HELAWAS . .	HELASWATER or INDUS.
Ægina	37	44	23	35	Vaiyj'ina . . .	Vaijaya chiefs.
Ænianes . . .					Vaineanes . . .	Brahmins.
Ætolia, Prov. . .					Ait-alyans . .	Oude dwellers.
Agræi	38	50	21	30	Agra	People of Agra.
Amphilochia, Prov. .					Am-Bhiloochs .	Bhiloochs of Am.
Apidanus, R. . .	39	20	22	15	Ap-i-Danus . .	Danaswater.
Araothus, R. . .	30	20	21	5	Arac des . . .	R. of Arac Land.
Aracanthus . . .	38	30	21	25	Ara-cand . . .	Mountain Country.
Argolis	37	40	23	0	Argwalas . .	People of the Arghasan.
Athamania . . .	39	25	21	20	Damania . . .	Land of the Daman.
Atintanes . . .	40	15	20	10	A Sindanos . .	Non Sindians.
ATTICA	38	0	23	50	ATTAC . .	PEOPLE OF THE ATTAC, and TATTA, TATTAIKAS, or TETTIGES.
Bo don .	39	44	20	57	Bodhan . . .	The Boodhas.
BŒOTIA . . .	38	20	23	20	BAIHOOTI . . .	PEOPLE OF THE R. BEHOOT.
Bomienses . . .	38	45	21	45	Bami-vensa . .	Bamian Tribes.
Cadmei	38	25	28	30	Gandamas . . .	People of Budha.
Callienses . . .	38	40	21	45	Cali Vensa . .	War Tribes.
M. Callidromus . .	38	44	22	30	Cul-Ait-Ramas . .	Tribe of Oude Ramas.
Callithera . . .	39	22	22	0	Cul-i-Thero . .	Tribe of Priests.
Cambunii Montes .	39	55	21	45	Cam-Bumi . .	Land of the Cama.
Canalovii Montes .	40	21	30	0	Gana Lava Mounts	Tribe of Lova.
Cassopæi . . .	39	20	20	45	Cassoopas . .	Cashmirians.

	Lat. D. M.	Lon. D. M.		
Centaurs	39 30	22 45	Candahaurs	Candahar people.
Cephallenia	38 15	20 35	Gopal-inia	Kingdom of Cabul.
Charadrus R.	39 20	20 50	Kira Dras	R. Dras of Cashmir.
Chæronæa	38 30	22 50	Kaironaya	Kingdom of Cashmir.
Chaones	40 0	37 11	Cahun-es	Cahun chiefs.
Cithæron	38 11	23 20	Cathiran	Catti chiefs, or Cathirs.
Copais Lake	38 27	23 7	Gopa-is	The Gopa Lord, or Crishna.
Corax Mount	38 28	20 37	Ghoraka	Ghoorka Hills.
Corinthus	37 54	22 54	Cor' Indus	People of the Cori and Indus.
Crissa	38 29	22 28	Crishna	Crishna town.
Crissæus Sinus	38 20	22 30	Crishnæus Sinus	Crishna Bay.
Ctimene	39 7	22 2	Catti-menavi	Catti-men.
Curetes	38 30	21 30	Coree-des	Land of the Coree.
DELPHI	38 28	22 31	DELBHAI	CLANS OF DELBHI OR ARJUNA.
Dodon	39 44	20 57	Dodān	The Dodas.
Dolopes	39 8	22 10	Dola-pes	Chiefs of the Dola or Dhola. Range.
Dryopes	39 10 38 50	21 0 22 20	Drawapes	Chiefs of the Dras R.
Elymiotis	40 10	21 40	Yelumyŏ-des	Land of the R. Yelum.
Enipeus	39 20	22 15	Anu-pŏ-ooksh	Chiefs of the Lower Oxus.
Ephyra, or Ephura	39 12	20 30	Hi-pur	Hya town.
Erikinium	39 48	21 45	Erak-inyum	Erac Chiefs' town.
Eubœa	38 30	24 0	Su-Bahooya	Great War Caste.
Evenus	38 25	21 40	Hi-Vena	Hya Brahmins.
Glykys			Gulcuts	Goolcuts.
Gomphoi			Gang-Bhai	War Clans.
Haliacmon	40 20	22 20	Ho-Lacmon	The Lughman.
Hekatompedon	39 55	21 5	Ekatān-Budhan	Meditative Budhists.
Helicon	38 18	23 0	Hela-gana	Hela tribes.
Heracleum	40 0	22 38	Heri-culyum	Town of Budhas Tribe.
Hestiæotis	39 45	21 35 22 10	Heshtyu-des	Land of the Eight (cities).
Hipairus (Epeirus) Prov.			Hi-pa-ira	Hya Chiefs Land.
Homolium	39 45	22 45	Om-alyum	Brahm-town or Brampton.
Hyantes	38 30	21 50	Hyan-des	Hyas Land.
IONIANS			HYĀNIANS	THE HYAS OR HORSE TRIBES
Kheraunii Montes	40 15	19 20	Kheran	Mountains of Kharan.
Kerketius Mons	39 30	21 35	Kurkutcha	Kurkutcha Mountains.
Lacmon	39 45	21 25	Lughman	Lughman.
Lamienses	39 0	22 35	Lama Vensa	Lama tribes.
Lapithæ	39 30 40 22	30 0	L'hopati	L'hopatos or Bhutias.
Larissa	39 27	22 30	Lawaris	Lahore kingdom.
Ledon	38 27	23 45	Leh-tan	Leh-land or Ladakh.
Lingos Mons	39 55	21 20	Lancas M.	Lanca' Hills.
Locri-Ozolæ	38 23	22 20	Logurhi Ookshwal	Logurh settlers on the Oxus.
Lycorea (Lucorea M)	38 32	22 45	Logurhea	Logurh town.
Magnetes	39 30	23 0	Mag' gane-des	Land of the Maghas.
Makedonia, Prov.			Magadhanya	Magadha Land.
Molossi	39 40	20 50	Mool-wusi	Moola Pass people.
Olympus	40 7	22 20	Oolam'pus	High Lama Chiefs.
Onochonus R.	39 20	22 10	Oona-gana	Tribe of Oona, near Kondooz River.
Ossa Mount	39 47	22 42	Ooksha and Oocha	Oxus and Ooch.
OTHRYS	39 0	22 40	ADRIS OR ŎDRĪS	THE HIMALAYAN MOUNTAINS.

	Lat. D. M.	Lon. D. M.		
Pagasæ	39 24	22 55	Pak-wasi	Pak-town or Pakton.
Pambotis	39 50	20 55	Pambor-des	Pamboor Land.
Pamisus R.	39 27	22 0	Bamisus	Bamian Chiefs' River.
Pandosia	39 18	20 35	Pand'wusi	Pandoo town.
Parnassus Mount.	38 32	22 30	Parnasa	Hermit's Mt.
Parnes Mount.	38 11	23 43	Attac Benares	Benares Mt.
Parorae	39 45	21 10	Parwa Rae	Parwa Chiefs.
Passaron	39 40	21 5	Pashwaran	Peshawer people.
PENEIOS, R. OXUS	39 35	22 5	PAENI-OOKSH	CHIEFS OF THE OXUS.
Perhœbi	39 45	22 0 / 22 30	Perhaipi	Peacock Chiefs.
Phæstus	39 26	22 30	Phais-des	The Hyas Land.
Phaloria	39 45	21 40	Phal-war	Sivas town.
Pharcadon	39 30	22 10	Parkutan	People of Parkuta, near Cashmir.
Pharsalus	39 17	22 22	Pur-Salus	City of Shal.
Pheræ	39 25	22 44	Peer Rae	Chiefs of Peer.
Phocis, Prov.			Bhojas	North-Indian tribes.
Phthiotis	39 0	22 30 / 22 45	Bhudyo-des	Bhutias, or Budha's Land.
Phrugia pura	38 45	22 20	Birgoo-pur	Birgoo town.
Pieria	47 0	22 20	Biharia	Land of Viharas.
Puthium	42 0	22 25	Budhyum	Budha town.
Salamis	37 55	23 30	Su Lamas	The High Lama chiefs.
Salmon	40 0	22 10	Su Laman	The High Lamas.
Saronicus Sinus			Sarawanicus, S.	Gulf of Sarawan.
Scotussa	39 26	22 35	Su Catti-wusa	Great Catti town.
SPERCHIUS	38 55	22 5	SBERGIUS	THE GANGES, R.
Stymphœa	39 50	21 15	Sthan-p-Haya	Land of the Hayas.
Talares	39 30	21 20	Tullar-es	Tullar chiefs.
Taphos	38 38	20 50	Tou-phous	Thibetians.
Tempe	39 53	22 45	Dembhe	The Cleft.
Thesprotia	39 25	20 25	Des Bharatia	Land of the Bharatas.
Thraces	45 0	22 35	Srawcas	Jainas.
Titarus Mons	39 55	21 50	Tatara	Tatara Pass.
Tomaros	39 50	20 45	Soo-Meroo	The Great Meroo Mount.

INDEX.

BRADBURY AND EVANS, PRINTERS, WHITEFRIARS.